FOR DUMMIES

BESTSELLING
BOOK SERIES

Archaeology For Dummies

Cheat Sheet

W9-BWY-141

A Brief Timeline of Prehistoric Humans Revealed by Archaeology

4+ million years ago: Earliest human ancestors appear in Africa, as seen in the fossil bones.

2.5 million years ago: Earliest artifacts appear in Africa — chipped stone tools.

Around 2 million years ago: Artifact finds and bones indicate early human forms in Asia and Europe.

Around 250,000 years ago: Beginning of the Middle Paleolithic era; chipped stone tools found in Africa, Asia, and Europe.

Around 100,000 years ago: Earliest modern human skeletal remains; still many Neanderthal remains as well.

Around 30,000 years ago: Beginning of the Upper Paleolithic era; Neanderthals gone; standardized tools of stone, bone, antler, ivory; portable art, cave art; humans reside in to Australia and a bit later in North and South America.

Around 10,000 years ago: Ice Age ends; beginning of the Mesolithic era (called the Archaic era in New World).

Around 8000 – 9000 years ago: Earliest food production in the Middle East and probably Asia and elsewhere.

Around 3500 B.C.: Earliest true civilizations begin to emerge in Mesopotamia, Egypt, Indus Valley, and China

Around 1500 B.C.: Earliest true civilizations begin to emerge in Mesoamerica and South America

Archaeology For Dummies®

Cheat Sheet

Digging and Recording Supplies

Here are typical excavation tools in an archaeological fieldworker's pack:

- **Pointed 4-inch Marshalltown trowel** (and maybe a square one too)
- **3-meter measuring tape** (harder to find than inches-and-feet increments) or other small tape
- **Butter knife, grapefruit or regular spoon, and pocketknife**
- **Artist's spatula and dental pick** (ask your dentist for old or broken ones)
- **Sharpened wooden chopstick or length of bamboo** for softer digging
- **Small, clean (but cheap) paintbrush** for brushing away dirt
- **Roll of plastic flagging** in a bright color
- **Water-resistant field notebook** (check dig requirements)
- **Compass** (cheap or expensive)
- **Pencils, waterproof markers, waterproof pens, and/or space pen**
- **Line level** for measuring depths from a level string
- **Zipper-lock plastic bags** of all sizes for finds

Safety and Health Items

Here's a list of items relating to health and safety that you may want to have on hand at an archaeological dig:

- **Refillable canteen or water bottle**
- **Bandages and a small bottle of iodine or tube of antibiotic cream**
- **Prescription medicines, clearly labeled**
- **Aspirin, anti-diarrheal medicine, and sore muscle liniment**
- **Sunblock lotion**
- **Insect repellent and something to relieve any bites/stings**
- **Toilet paper**
- **Antibacterial hand cleaner**
- **Emergency food** (like a granola bar and a small bag of peanuts)
- **Tweezers for removing slivers and stings**
- **Small flashlight**
- **Work gloves**
- **Waterproof matches**

For Dummies: Bestselling Book Series for Beginners

Archaeology FOR DUMMIES®

by Nancy Marie White

WILEY

Wiley Publishing, Inc.

Archaeology For Dummies®

Published by
Wiley Publishing, Inc.
111 River St.
Hoboken, NJ 07030-5774
www.wiley.com

Copyright © 2008 by Wiley Publishing, Inc., Indianapolis, Indiana

Published by Wiley Publishing, Inc., Indianapolis, Indiana

Published simultaneously in Canada

For general information on our other products and services, please contact our Customer Care Department within the U.S. at 800-762-2974, outside the U.S. at 317-572-3993, or fax 317-572-4002.

For technical support, please visit www.wiley.com/techsupport.

Wiley also publishes its books in a variety of electronic formats. Some content that appears in print may not be available in electronic books.

Library of Congress Control Number: 2008935270

ISBN: 978-0-470-33732-5

Manufactured in the United States of America

10 9 8 7 6 5 4 3 2 1

WILEY

About the Author

Being an archaeologist was something **Nancy Marie White** wanted to do from the time she learned how to spell the word as a kid. She was interested in Native American cultures, outdoor adventure, and the romance of finding ancient things and lost knowledge. After earning a BA in history, she went to live in Mexico, where she saw that studying archaeology and the rest of anthropology would lead to a fascinating life. She earned a PhD from Case Western Reserve University in Cleveland (home of rock and roll), and is now professor of anthropology at the University of South Florida, Tampa, and a long-time member of the Register of Professional Archaeologists.

White's research includes finding and sometimes excavating sites of all time periods. She's currently studying how late prehistoric agricultural societies in the U.S. Southeast became complex and why they had no beer. She also investigates campsites, villages, and mounds of earlier Native American hunter-gatherers, fishers, and gardeners, and lost towns and forts inhabited by historic Indians, European-Americans, and African-Americans. Her one kid, Tony, spent an entire childhood camping in the woods and digging, and now studies engineering. White tries to travel often in order to go somewhere different to visit archaeology. She really believes in public archaeology and the potential of the distant past to show us a lot that might be useful in the modern world.

Author's Acknowledgments

Thanks are due to many people who helped with this book in different ways. Archaeologists Lee Hutchinson and Jeff Du Vernay read the manuscript and offered great comments. Malaysian social scientist Cheng Sim Hew asked good questions about archaeology's value to society. Help with figures, text, ideas, and details came from Robbie Baer, Bill Bingham, Susan Harp, Ned Jenkins, Roy Larick, Erin Kimmerle, Rochelle Marrinan, Erin Murtha-Celii, John O'Hear, Rob Tykot, and Rich Weinstein. Wiley editors Michael Lewis, Megan Knoll, and Tim Gallan are superb. Offspring Anthony Orlando White and parent Adela Dodero White read and commented upon everything and provided constant encouragement and laughs.

Thanks also to all archaeologists and other scientists whose work I've described here; I apologize for not being able to cite you by name. I realize I've taken on a huge responsibility in representing the entirety of the archaeological profession and the specific work of thousands of colleagues around the world in a single (and, I'm hoping, user-friendly) volume. Perhaps readers will let me know about any errors. After all, archaeology is a continual process of finding out new information about old things!

Publisher's Acknowledgments

We're proud of this book; please send us your comments through our Dummies online registration form located at www.dummies.com/register/.

Some of the people who helped bring this book to market include the following:

Acquisitions, Editorial, and Media Development

Senior Project Editor: Tim Gallan

Acquisitions Editor: Michael Lewis

Copy Editor: Megan Knoll

Assistant Editor: Erin Calligan Mooney

Art Coordinator: Alicia B. South

Technical Editor: Lee Hutchinson

Editorial Manager: Michelle Hacker

Editorial Assistants: Joe Niesen, Jennette ElNaggar, David Lutton

Cartoons: Rich Tennant (www.the5thwave.com)

Composition Services

Project Coordinator: Patrick Redmond

Layout and Graphics: Reuben W. Davis, Melissa K. Jester, Christin Swinford, Christine Williams

Proofreaders: Laura Albert, Caitie Kelly, Penny Stuart

Indexer: WordCo Indexing Services

Publishing and Editorial for Consumer Dummies

Diane Graves Steele, Vice President and Publisher, Consumer Dummies

Joyce Pepple, Acquisitions Director, Consumer Dummies

Kristin Ferguson-Wagstaffe, Product Development Director, Consumer Dummies

Ensley Eikenburg, Associate Publisher, Travel

Kelly Regan, Editorial Director, Travel

Publishing for Technology Dummies

Andy Cummings, Vice President and Publisher, Dummies Technology/General User

Composition Services

Gerry Fahey, Vice President of Production Services

Debbie Stailey, Director of Composition Services

Contents at a Glance

Table of Contents

Part III: After the Dig: You've Only Just Begun........... 133

Chapter 9: Processing Excavated Materials in the Laboratory.....135

Chapter 10: Studying and Analyzing What You've Excavated 151

Chapter 20: More Than Ten Archaeological Sites to Visit Outside the United States 335

Chapter 21: Ten Fun Archaeological Experiences.................343

Introduction

· ·

*A*rchaeology is exciting adventure and discovery. It's also sometimes horribly misunderstood and wrongly stereotyped. Many well-educated people still think that archaeology is bones, dinosaurs, or fossils, but it's *none* of these. Archaeological remains are things *humans* left — artifacts or garbage stains in the soil or ruins of huts or palaces. Others think archaeology must mean only Egyptian temples or Roman ruins, but archaeology is *everywhere* that humans have been, including your own back yard and even the moon.

Today archaeology is a big part of popular culture, in movies, computer games and the news. Authors write about everything from archaeology's role in science fiction to its practical use in the modern world. More professional archaeologists, more History Channel specials on the ancient past, and more opportunities to see and participate in archaeology now exist than ever before.

This book aims to explore the science, describe the thrills, and show you what archaeology is all about, whether you want to get involved via the armchair or in digging.

About This Book

I've tried to pack a lot into this book to give you at least a little taste of many things in the smorgasbord of archaeological topics, including ways that archaeology affects your own life that you may not have thought of before.

Here's what you'll see in these pages:

- ✔ What archaeology really is (and misunderstandings about what it isn't).
- ✔ The many different kinds of archaeology out there, each of which investigates different things.
- ✔ How archaeologists think and how they use scientific method to reconstruct the past from the material record.
- ✔ How to do archaeological fieldwork — survey *and* excavation.
- ✔ The huge amount of work you need to do *after* fieldwork for processing and analysis of the stuff you dig up.

✔ The story of the whole human career — from the first humans through modern times — known only or mostly from archaeology.

✔ Guides to help you understand, visit, and do archaeology.

I aim in this book to demystify archaeology, to tell you what it is, how it's done, where you can do it, and what you can learn from it about humanity. You should be able to open to any chapter and see the topic of choice, and you can also find everything on the topic by looking in the index.

Conventions Used in This Book

Here are a few little things to keep in mind as you read this book, to avoid confusion over some details.

Archaeology versus archeology

Both spellings of the word are fine. Usually you see the *-aeo* version because most people, including my editors and publisher, think it's classier! But the U.S. federal government (which, in official documents, always calls itself "Federal"), and other entities, have spelling rules insisting on the *-eo* version. Once, when reporting a dig on federal land, I spelled the title "Archaeology." Officials told me that (among other revisions) I had to take the *a* out, so I redid the title as "Rchaeology." For some reason, they weren't amused.

Dates

Reading about past times, you see dates given in various ways. In this book, I use the terms *B.C.* ("before Christ" — about 2,000 years ago and earlier) and *A.D.* (Latin words *anno domini*, translating to "year of our Lord" and actually meaning after the birth of Christ — so there is no A.D. 0). A.D. is always written before the number to make sense in Latin. These are still the most commonly used ways of writing dates in English. Some writers use *B.C.E* ("before the common era" or "before the Christian era") and *C.E.* ("common era") to mean the same things but without religious overtones. Another notation is *B.P.,* meaning "before the present"; to change B.C. dates to B.P. dates, just add 2,000 years.

Measurements

Nearly all modern archaeology uses the metric system because that system is internationally understood and the world standard for science. Exceptions to this rule may pop up when you're mapping and digging historic sites where objects may have originally been deliberately constructed in feet and inches, so measuring them in the same units makes more sense.

You may not be used to metric measurements, so in this book I sometimes give them in feet and inches. But just remember that an inch is about 2½ *centimeters* (cm), a *meter* (m) is a little over a yard, and about 30 centimeters is a foot. If you do end up switching to the metric system for archaeology, you may never go back!

Anthropology

Most of the archaeology done today is part of *anthropology,* the social science that studies humans in all their biological and cultural aspects. Some archaeology falls under the heading of classics or some other field (as I describe in Chapter 3). In this book, I try to give you a little of all kinds of archaeology while emphasizing that archaeological findings aren't just cool artifacts or ancient treasures but rather clues to exploring human behavior.

What you're not to read

You don't have to read the sidebars (the text in gray boxes) — that material is interesting but tangential. You don't have to read text that's flagged by the Technical Stuff icon either. After all, technical stuff isn't for everybody.

My Assumptions

In writing this book, I assume that you the reader

- ✔ Have always loved to read about archaeology or watch it on film.
- ✔ Like seeing archaeological sites and museums.
- ✔ Want to join a dig or at least visit one.
- ✔ Are studying or considering studying archaeology at a college or university.

✔ Love old stuff and the excitement of discovery, puzzles, and figuring things out.

✔ Enjoy imagining the human past.

If any of these statements is true about you, this book should help you explore archaeology's many and exciting dimensions.

How This Book Is Organized

This book is divided into six parts: Part I defines archaeology and its varieties and thought processes. Part II describes the fieldwork — finding things. In Part III, you find out what to do with everything after you find it and how complicated it is to piece together the puzzle of the human past. In Part IV, I relate what archaeology has revealed about that past — all 2 million years of it! Part V gives you an idea of why archaeology is relevant to your life and how you can go do some yourself. Part VI lists places to visit archaeology.

Part I: Archaeology: Seeing Past People Today

This part introduces you to archaeology, how archaeological sites are formed, and the nature of the evidence. I give you a little of the glorious history and adventure of archaeology and also try to counteract the stereotypes and mistakes common in the public media. I list the many different kinds of archaeology and discuss how archaeologists think about and try to solve the mysteries they investigate, including an example from my own work.

Part II: Archaeological Fieldwork: The Adventure Begins!

In this part, I describe the adventure of fieldwork, how you can prepare, what to bring along, and what you can expect. Then I answer the common question, "How do you know where to dig?" You discover how archaeological survey locates sites, and then the actual excavation and all it entails, from equipment to technique. Finally, I go over the ethical issues involved in archaeological investigation, from dangerous field conditions to respecting local communities and descendants of the people whose stuff you're digging up.

Part III: After the Dig: You've Only Just Begun

The work *after* the dig is the largest part of archaeology. Part III explains how you process and analyze the materials and data from the dig and then how you piece the past together. I describe laboratory work and artifact analyses and then show you how archaeology tells the story of past human behavior based on those material remains. To show the wide array of viewpoints in archaeological interpretation, I give you some of the major theoretical perspectives used to understand past societies.

Part IV: Archaeology Reconstructs the Whole Human Past

In this part, I run briefly through the great drama of what archaeology has found out about our ancestors and their lives, from the time of the earliest humans through the emergence of ancient civilizations. Only archaeology brings this past alive! Even in historic times, archaeology shows much more than history can ever tell you, especially about people whose history was never written (or was written poorly). Finally, I show you how the method of archaeology — using material culture to interpret human behavior — is useful to study the modern world in ways no other science can.

Part V: Archaeology Is for Everyone

This part is about public archaeology (which is really all archaeology today). Here I show you the many different kinds of interests in archaeology: political, financial, practical, recreational, professional. I give you some case studies of recent hot controversies in archaeology. You explore how archaeological findings affect many aspects of life in ways you may not expect. I also give you tips on how to get involved in archaeology yourself.

Part VI: The Part of Tens

In this part, I list (about) ten neat places to visit archaeology in the U.S. and outside the U.S. I also include ten fun archaeological experiences. You may soon add your own entries to these lists!

Icons Used in the Book

Throughout this book, you'll see these icons, which I use to highlight important information or direct you to interesting tidbits.

Archaeology is all about discovery! Though I discuss exciting excavations and findings throughout much of the book, this icon tells you about specific fun details of particular finds.

Archaeology is a scientific pursuit, often with some complicated processes, operations, and even equipment. This icon signals examples of areas where you need much more expertise than I can provide in this book. But at least you see the technical terms (and you can use them to impress friends).

I use this icon to remind you about the most crucial concepts in archaeology and to point out corrections or true versions of some mistakes.

Archaeology brings us face-to-face with our human heritage, whether wonderful or disgusting. I use this icon to mark aspects of human nature worth thinking about as you discover archaeology's potential.

Whenever I provide specific advice that will aid in actual archaeological work or your study of archaeology, I use this Tip icon.

I use this icon to point out important safety-related information, misconceptions, and other dangers that may threaten your archaeological work or experience.

Where to Go from Here

Jump around and read whatever chapter or section catches your interest. Or read the book from front to back. The choice is up to you. Archaeology provides wonderful stories of the past and often high adventure in the present. It's also very relevant to modern life. This guide tells you what basics you need to know to understand and do it. But you don't need a pith helmet and safari clothes — old jeans, a bandanna, bug spray, sunscreen, and an open mind should suffice! After seeing how to do archaeology, you yourself can move, as the old *Firesign Theater* folks said, "forward into the past!"

Part I

Archaeology: Seeing Past People Today

The 5th Wave   By Rich Tennant

"And believe it or not children, some of your ancestors could be related to this fellow right here."

In this part . . .

Archaeology is exciting and romantic — the thrill of discovery, the recreation of the glories of the human past! But it's complicated too, and much confusion exists about what it is and how it works. In this part, I define archaeology and explain how it developed and branched into specialties. Chapter 1 shows you how archaeology is unique in its method of investigation. I explain what archaeological evidence consists of and how archaeological sites are formed; you also get some of the background and history of how archaeology was developed by those early adventurers and explorers. Chapter 2 makes it clear that archaeology isn't dinosaurs or treasure hunting or looting artifacts for sale. All the many kinds of archaeology can be confusing, so Chapter 3 helps you sort them out. To understand how an archaeologist thinks and investigates, read through Chapter 4.

Chapter 1

What Archaeology Is

Archaeology is exciting adventure and romantic intrigue as well as amazing scientific investigation. That's how you see it in movies and the news, and even if the excavation is downtown under the sidewalk or in the middle of some farmer's field, that adventure is still there because you're trying to make the unknown known. The dig unearths not only neat artifacts from ancient times but also the often-dramatic stories of how past humans got along in the world — maybe with some lessons for the present day.

Because confusion and misconceptions about the nature of archaeology are everywhere, in this chapter I define archaeology and show you how it really is detective work on a big scale. Here you discover how archaeological sites are formed, how modern archaeology developed, and even how you yourself probably do archaeology all the time without realizing it!

So What Is Archaeology Anyway?

A simple definition: *Archaeology* is finding out about past human behavior by studying the material evidence left behind.

Archaeology doesn't necessarily look at the people themselves, but always examines their stuff. Archaeology is very distinctive among all the *social sciences* (studies of humans and their behavior) for its unique method: studying people not by watching or reading about or talking to them but by analyzing what material things they left behind. *Material things* means people's possessions, residues, and anything else visible or tangible — from the tiniest seed bead or corn kernel to the tallest pyramid, from the most nondescript kitchen garbage to the most beautiful gold craftwork. Today it also means people's hair and DNA as well as dark stains and other features in the soil left from burying, building, and so on.

The method: It's detective work

Archaeology is exactly like detective work — in fact, it *is* detective work! Most police or private detectives use all the methods archaeologists use:

- Carefully measuring, recording, and photographing the evidence at the (crime) scene.
- Using painstakingly accurate techniques to recover, process, and analyze the evidence.
- Getting background information on all the people, places, and times involved.
- Interviewing knowledgeable people about what happened and what other evidence they may have or know about.
- Using techniques from other sciences like physics and chemistry to learn more about the evidence.
- Stopping for coffee and doughnuts (or a cold beer) at a little place close by to see what else you can find out.
- Compiling all the information to describe what happened.
- Stating your case and arguing it, sometimes involving other experts, politicians, journalists, and the public.
- Continuing to investigate if you can't tie up all the loose ends.

Everyone does archaeology sometimes

Archaeological knowledge is about us. You can do the archaeology of the far distant past or the very recent past. Everyone does some archaeology, probably nearly every day. For example, you may know by the car in the driveway who is home, or by the things thrown around the living room what the roommate or kids have been doing in there. Parents, especially, do a lot of archaeology ("Did you brush your teeth before bed?" "Sure, Mom. Always, Mom." "Then why is the toothbrush still dry?").

The goal: Understand people

When you do archaeology, you don't dig just to get some cool artifact (that's treasure hunting or looting). You don't really want the finds for yourself, anyway — they go into collections or museum exhibits for all to enjoy and study further, if desired. No, you want to understand past people through what they left on and in the ground (or elsewhere). You examine the once-lost traces of the past for several good reasons. The goals of archaeology are to

- ✔ Study the human past across space and time.
- ✔ Reconstruct past human behavior and ways of life.
- ✔ Understand past cultural systems (social, economic, political, religious) and how they changed through time.
- ✔ Help conserve the fragile material record of past peoples and interpret this heritage for people today.
- ✔ Bring the story of the human past to the public for enjoyment, education, and even practical use.

The Nature of Archaeological Evidence

Anything made by humans is an artifact, including a thought, a song, or a smile. In archaeology, artifacts are human-made material objects — you have to be able to see or measure them and retrieve information from them.

Your *materials* are all the physical items you dig up or otherwise obtain from the archaeological sites, and your *data* are all the bits of information you retrieve from the dig, the sites, and all the physical remains. So you may wash, sort, and identify your archaeological materials in the laboratory. Then when you list each type of artifact and ecofact (more on these in the following sections) on a table, you create data. The same is true for all the information you record as you excavate a feature or make a map — these are more data, as are all your notes, files, photos, and other information. The following sections describe some categories of these material remains.

Artifacts

Any object made by humans is an *artifact*. Usually you think of ancient ceramic pots or arrowheads, and indeed these items are everywhere at archaeological sites. But a temple or palace is an artifact too — one made up of individual artifacts such as bricks or stone blocks. A stone used to hammer and chip other stone to make the arrowhead is also an artifact; even though it's not deliberately shaped, it's covered with grinding and chipping marks and thus modified by human activity. Finally, the flakes of stone chipped while making stone tools are also artifacts, though they may or may not have been discarded. Most often, artifacts are portable objects excavated and brought back to a laboratory for study.

Ecofacts

Ecofact is a term archaeologists invented to classify natural objects used by humans without modification. Animal bones left from dinner or pollen from gathered plants are ecofacts. But if a bone has been modified to become a harpoon point, that modification makes it an artifact. Even phosphates or other chemicals in the soil are ecofacts showing that people threw their organic waste on the ground.

Features

Anything that's made by humans but is too big to bring back (intact) to the laboratory is a *feature*. Features can be garbage pits, hearths, *post holes* or *postmolds* (where poles were once in the ground), graves, roads, drip lines from roofs of old buildings, building foundations, storage pits, clusters of artifacts, and even footprints. Technically you can cut out a block of soil around a feature such as a footprint and bring it back to study under better conditions in the lab, but most features have to be excavated (or studied and then preserved) where they're first uncovered.

Sites

Archaeological sites are places where human habitation or other activity took place and where artifacts, features, and ecofacts are all found. You can have sites of different sizes, shapes, and time periods, from a small stone quarry where bits of chipped rock are lying around to the ruins of a big palace where bits of the quarried stone blocks are left lying around. Depending upon what's preserved, a site can be small or large, shallow or deep.

Components and boundaries

When people of one time period use a place that people of an earlier time already used, they add another *component* to a site. A multicomponent site at a prime location such as a shoreline can have cultural deposits going back thousands of years, one component overlying the next. The ideal site has a nice, culturally sterile layer between each component so you can tell them apart. In reality it seldom works out like this. Later people come in and dig into the site and mix the older stuff with their stuff and never even think of how the archaeologist of the future is going to figure it all out!

Not all sites are visible. Sometimes you do archaeological survey to locate sites, including using special techniques if remains are buried or underwater. (See Chapter 6 for more on survey.) Finding the boundaries of sites is also sometimes tricky and may be impossible without digging.

Regions and isolated finds

You can investigate archaeological sites within a whole natural region, such as a river valley or island. Or you may do archaeological survey within an arbitrary project area, such as someone's property lines; in this case, you do your best to see where the actual past archaeological site extends, but you may never know exactly.

Individual artifact finds of just one or two items are also sometimes called sites if they may indicate a specific activity there. But one arrowhead isn't enough — it may have fallen from a deer who galloped away after being shot. Criteria for what qualifies as a site can vary according to the archaeologist doing the work and the project guidelines. Many professionals now record specific *isolated finds* (IFs) or *artifact occurrences* (AOs) to indicate something was going on in the past, even if they don't have enough evidence to make it a site.

How Archaeological Sites Form

Archaeological sites can develop over great or small amounts of time and space, and through large or small actions of humans and of nature. What archaeologists call *site formation processes* can be divided into two categories: cultural and natural processes.

Cultural processes

The cultural activities that contribute to the formation of archaeological sites are simply everything that humans do that results in material evidence. The following list gives you some examples:

✔ **Finding raw materials and making artifacts:** Making everything from chipped stone tools to pyramids (and the waste these processes leave behind).

✔ **Leaving evidence of activity:** Using material items and physical spaces, moving objects around, leaving residues, repairing and remaking things — basically, leaving any marks or debris in an area where you performed some activity.

✔ **Discarding things (deliberately or by accident):** Making garbage dumps, dropping things, or storing items and forgetting about them.

✔ **Reusing past things:** Taking old pyramids apart to get blocks or bricks for new construction.

✔ **Digging into or disturbing ground containing past things:** Plowing up old sites and/or bulldozing them to construct new ones.

Natural processes

Mother Nature also contributes to the formation of archaeological sites. Here are some of the ways:

✔ **Physical processes** such as wind, gravity, rain, storms, drought, volcanoes, and other climate and local weather conditions.

✔ **Biological processes** such as animals burrowing into the site and bacteria and other organisms causing decay.

✔ **Chemical processes** such as weathering stone, rusting iron, and decomposing dead plants and animals in acidic soils.

All these processes affect the way the archaeological site is composed and looks. They can be large scale (volcanic ash covering the whole city of Pompeii) or very small scale (an iron artifact rusting beyond recognition). They can be destructive (wooden buildings decaying completely and leaving only dark stains where posts were in the ground), or they can actually preserve the site (the Pompeii ash). Sometimes they both preserve and destroy at the same time: Where I work in the southeastern U.S., I often see the effects of river floods washing away parts of prehistoric riverbank villages, but covering up other parts with several feet of new sand, and thus preserving them better (and making me have to dig deeper to find them).

You have to be sure to distinguish the effects of all these processes as you're doing archaeology. It helps to know something about the physical sciences and be a good anthropologist who understands human behavior too. In fact, to be an archaeologist you often need to be a jill- or jack-of-all-trades! If you're not already, a few seasons of fieldwork will help you see what soils indicate human use, what a decayed wooden post looks like in the ground, or how a big orange heavy thing may just be a rusted iron artifact.

How Archaeology Became a Modern Science

Archaeology has had so many colorful figures and astounding discoveries that you really don't need Hollywood to invent fictitious ones! Here I briefly review the history of archaeology, its finds and adventurers, and how the field developed into the sophisticated modern science it is today. Many famous, flamboyant, and fascinating personalities were pioneers in the development of archaeology (and models for characters like Indiana Jones). I've included some of my favorites. Most of them have biographies if you're interested in reading more — you don't need made-up Indiana Jones stuff to get armchair adventure!

Early diggers

Historical records say that a sixth-century B.C. Babylonian king and princess were the first to dig up remains of their own society's glorious past, restore a by-then ancient Sumerian temple-pyramid, and display artifact finds in the palace. Later historians told tales and legends of the ancients, and people have probably always dug things up, especially to sell as souvenirs and treasures of the glorious past of someone somewhere.

But real archaeology is only traceable (so far) back to the Renaissance (14th through 17th centuries), when a passion for learning about the classical past developed. Wealthy folks traveled to ancient lands like Egypt and Mesopotamia and collected *antiquities* (old items, usually sculptures) dug out of ruins. Also, European antiquarians explored monuments (Roman buildings, Stonehenge, and so on) on their own lands. Antiquarian societies and collectors accumulated loads of items and began to establish museums to display them by the 18th century. Pompeii was accidentally discovered in the late 1500s, and digging was conducted in earnest as early as 1738.

Most of the knowledge of the past that people had until modern times came from historical writings or myth and legend until real science began to emerge in the Western world. The Bible told people what had happened in the past, and folktales supplied the rest. As early as the 1500s, northern Europeans who found Stone Age arrow points were calling them elf-shot or elf-arrows!

Nineteenth-century archaeology

By the early 1800s, naturalists and early scientists had accumulated a good body of artifacts and archaeological knowledge and were using it to interpret humanity's past in an orderly fashion. With historical models, they charted the progress of human society through time.

Early classification

Two important Danish guys played a major role in early classification efforts. Christian Thomsen organized the finds at the national museum and wanted to exhibit stages of human achievement (and also apparently figure out how to divide the stuff up into display cases). He picked a three-age sequence: stone, bronze, and iron. Jens Worsaae excavated sites and found that stone tools were indeed deepest and therefore oldest; bronze tools were on top of them, and iron artifacts on top of the bronze. Later, the Stone Age was subdivided into Old (Paleolithic) and New Stone Age (Neolithic); the deepest-oldest idea became known as the *law of superposition*.

These cultural classifications became popular all over Europe, and the terms are still used today — with the following big differences, however:

- A single age can fall under different calendar years in different places.

- Human "progress" and "stages of development" are misnomers because a single universal path of cultural development doesn't exist; different cultures change to become more or less complex through time in their own ways.

- Archaeologists recognize that these cultural classifications are biased and based purely on technology, as if that's the only important aspect of human development (ignoring art, literature, architecture, math, religion, and so on). On the other hand, technology *is* easier to see in the archaeological record!

Explorers, adventurers, and looters

Many fascinating early archaeologists sought adventure and intrigue in searching out the remains and exquisite artifacts of the ancient past. They didn't really "discover" various sites because local people always led them there. But the good archaeologists published the information and drawings and brought back antiquities for display. The more crass among them grabbed ancient treasures to sell for profit or display on their own estates. You've probably heard of some of these colorful people and their exploits:

- With Napoleon's 1798 invasion of Egypt came scientists and artists to document the remnants of ancient civilization. One find was the Rosetta Stone, with a second-century B.C. text in Greek and two Egyptian languages. French scholar Champollion used it to decipher ancient Egyptian writing systems.

- ✔ Giovanni Belzoni was a strong man in the circus before he became famous for his Egyptian tomb-robbing exploits from about 1817 to 1820. He blasted, dragged, and levered away monuments to capture giant statues, mummies, and other relics to display and garner fame.

- ✔ Travel writer John Lloyd Stephens and artist Frederick Catherwood studied and produced works on the wonderful pyramids and other monuments of the Maya civilization in Mexico and Central America in 1841 and 1843.

- ✔ Ephraim G. Squier and Edwin H. Davis surveyed burial mounds, earthworks, and temple platforms of the Mississippi and Ohio valleys (1848) and published their detailed descriptions for all to see.

- ✔ U.S. president Thomas Jefferson excavated a prehistoric Native American burial mound on his estate at Monticello, Virginia, with the intellectual goal of finding out scientific details (1788).

- ✔ Wealthy businessman Heinrich Schliemann thought Homer's classical story of the Trojan War was really true and went to find and excavate Troy in northwestern Turkey (1871). Then he dug another site from Homer's legends: Mycenae in southern Greece, which was possibly the citadel of King Agamemnon.

Late 19th and early 20th-century improvements

The goals of archaeological pursuits became more sophisticated and scientific by the late 19th century as investigators realized they needed systematic study to make sense of the wealth of finds. Here are some notable figures of this time in archaeology's history when more careful digging developed:

- ✔ **General Pitt Rivers** excavated on his country estate in southern England in the 1880s, opening Bronze-Age burial mounds, an Iron-Age fort, and a Roman military camp. He meticulously measured, drew, and even photographed his work and finds, laying the foundations for the modern archaeological method.

- ✔ **Sir Flinders Petrie** accurately surveyed Egyptian pyramids and excavated tombs, mummies, and cemeteries with precision. He devised a method to discern cultural chronologies by examining changes in artifact styles through time.

- ✔ **Sir Arthur Evans** excavated (and partially restored) the palace ruins at Knossos, on the Greek island of Crete, beginning in 1900. His discoveries brought to light the Minoan civilization (3000 to 1200 B.C.) that predated the Mycenaean state made famous by Heinrich Schliemann (discussed in the preceding section).

- ✔ **Cyrus Thomas,** head of the Smithsonian Institution's Division of Mound Exploration, collected information on thousands of mounds then being looted like crazy, especially in the U.S. Mississippi Valley. He had thought the mounds were built by a vanished people, but his findings changed his mind, and he reported in 1894 that the mounds were indeed made by ancestors of diverse Native American groups.

The early 20th century: Fabulous finds and academic advances

Sensational finds and colorful figures continued to make amazing discoveries in the early 20th century. Archaeologists did more orderly excavation, and synthesis of the results became more commonplace during that period.

Famous early figures

As you've probably realized, archaeology was a leisure-time pursuit for the wealthy, those with time to travel, and many British colonial-type holdovers investigating the pasts of various intriguing destinations during the early 1900s. Here are a few of these characters:

- **Howard Carter,** who had worked with Flinders Petrie in Egypt (see the preceding section), was funded by the Earl of Carnarvon to explore the Valley of the Kings. He discovered the spectacular tomb of King Tut, a relatively unimportant pharaoh whose burial place is notable because it *wasn't* looted like all the others, so it was full of glorious wealth.

- **Sir Leonard Woolley** dug in Syria in 1912, assisted by T.E. Lawrence (Lawrence of Arabia), with whom he also engaged in spy activities for the British government. After World War I, he excavated the famous Mesopotamian city of Ur in Iraq (see Chapter 14) and took 50 years to write a ten-volume report on all the everyday mud-brick houses and the royal graves full of gold, silver, and other riches.

- **Gertrude Bell,** an Arabic-speaking British travel writer and fascinating political figure in the Middle East, investigated Mesopotamian ruins and was also involved in British intelligence. She organized the Iraqi Department of Antiquities and Museum and was instrumental in the emergence of the modern country of Iraq.

- **Gertrude Caton-Thompson** worked in Egypt and then excavated at Great Zimbabwe in southern Africa in 1929. She said those ruins originated with indigenous African people, a view that the colonial government later outlawed until investigators eventually proved it to be true.

- **Sir Mortimer Wheeler** was a major British archaeologist by the 1920s. He followed and improved the exacting techniques pioneered by Pitt Rivers and dug sites of many kinds, from Roman towns to the famous Iron-Age hill fort Maiden Castle in southern England. Then he went to India and brought to light the ancient cities of the lost Indus Valley civilization in Pakistan. (See Chapter 14 for a discussion of these civilizations.) He was a dashing public figure and early television personality as well; many think he was one of the real-life models for Indiana Jones.

Archaeology gets more academic

Scholars realized that their major goal should now be to organize some of the vast amounts of information that digs were providing. V. Gordon Childe, an Australian who delved into archaeology across Europe, produced the first major syntheses of prehistory. He talked about the processes of change in the deep human past that led to the Agricultural Revolution and the Urban Revolution — in other words, food production and later the emergence of early states. His many works include *The Danube in Prehistory* (1929), *New Light on the Most Ancient East* (1934), and one of my very favorite archaeological titles, *Man Makes Himself* (1939).

In the early 20th century lots of fossil finds that show that early humans first appeared in Africa came to light. Most of this study wasn't archaeological but the subject of human paleontology or paleoanthropology. But the famous Louis Leakey did go to Olduvai Gorge in Tanzania to look for the earliest human evidence because he had seen crude-looking chipped stones there that he thought were early tools (and they were — see Chapter 12 for more).

During the Great Depression of the 1930s, U.S. president Franklin Roosevelt began programs to bring jobs to the country, including a great deal of archaeological work, especially in the poor region of the South. Hundreds of mounds and other sites were dug and thousands of bags of artifacts retrieved and piles of data accumulated. By then, academic institutions were beginning to train archaeologists who could supervise workers and then synthesize the findings for major regions. They used conveniently-named archaeological cultures (usually based on a pottery type or other characteristic artifact) and time periods (ditto) to organize the information and tell the story of the past, one time period after the next. This descriptive approach is called *culture history* (even when it concerns prehistory or the time before writing). Archaeologists still use this approach today, of course, but with much more than just simple description. I discuss it more in Chapter 11.

Early developments in explaining the past

Many 19th-century antiquarians studying relics of the past saw finds of stone tools with bones of extinct forms of animals, demonstrating the great antiquity of humans. They noticed that Native Americans were still making stone arrow points, easily comparable to chipped stone tools elsewhere in the world to see the work of the human hand. Geologist Sir Charles Lyell demonstrated the great age of the Earth and how its past processes were the same as the ones acting today (the principle of *uniformitarianism*). Charles Darwin used that knowledge to develop a systematic scientific theory of evolution, accounting for the development of all life forms (in his *On the Origins of Species* in 1859), later extending it to human development too.

New archaeology of the mid-20th century

After World War II, several intellectual currents came together to influence a mini-revolution in archaeology. The technologies developed in wartime combined with the growing desire to be more scientific. Some archaeologists were dissatisfied with simply describing what was found and where (producing culture history). They wanted to understand how past cultures functioned and answer questions about how human systems were organized. The movement they originated was called the New Archaeology. Here are some of its influences:

- New technologies like aerial photography and computers.
- Other scientific breakthroughs like radiocarbon dating.
- Growing concerns about civil rights, human rights, and the natural environment.
- Growing concerns about historic preservation and loss of archaeological sites to growth and development or new farming practices.

Late 20th-century archaeology

After New Archaeology had been around for a couple of decades, archaeologists decided they couldn't call it new anymore and started using the term *processual archaeology* because the method explores cultural processes. Most archaeology done today is processual archaeology, as I discuss at greater length in Chapter 11.

Of course, every action has a reaction, and the response to scientific archaeology in the 1980s was that it was too ethnocentric or biased in favor of the dominant culture (which it is) and ignored the human story and meaning of the past. This response was a more humanistic archaeological approach (clumsily) called *postprocessual archaeology;* I describe it more in Chapter 11. Postprocessual archaeology contributes a lot to modern practice and is valuable for making you understand how you know what you know about the archaeological record.

Modern 21st-century archaeology

Today you combine the description of culture history with the scientific approach and an awareness of biases you may have in your research. You must be acutely aware of the issues of heritage (whose ancestors are you digging up?), political uses of archaeology (to forward someone's land claims, for example), and conservation of the resource (or *historic preservation* — saving sites and monuments from destruction).

Many laws enacted in the late 20th century now protect archaeological remains all over the world's lands and seas. They also generate more archaeological investigation in the path of construction and development. Many new techniques and precise methods may mean you spend more time filling out forms and other paperwork (or computer work) than digging. But it's all worth it because you also have the glory of the discovery!

In the rest of Part I, you see how contemporary archaeology has become enormously professional, what it really studies, and all the many specialties that have blossomed. I also show you how archaeologists use scientific method to come to logical conclusions about the materials and data they discover.

Archaeology in the field

Fieldwork has always been the special tradition of archaeology, no matter what type you're doing. You go out there and find the lost traces of past peoples (archaeological survey) and dig them up (excavation), and, yes, possibly encounter adventure along the way. But you're also aware of far more ethical and safety considerations these days than were some of the historic figures I described earlier in this section, who barged into another country and hired local natives to dig huge trenches that sometimes collapsed on them!

Because you have so much more to think about and plan in doing modern archaeology, in Part II I describe all the steps in accomplishing fieldwork, from the research design and list of supplies and equipment to bring to the strategies for deciding where to dig and careful procedures for excavating in very small increments. I show you how to record everything you do and find so that you offset the destruction you cause by digging with the value of your new information about human behavior in the past.

Archaeology in the lab

The largest part of archaeological work is what you do after you excavate: process, analyze, and care for your finds and for all the information you've gleaned about the past. To get a handle on what is for some an overwhelming amount of labor and responsibility, Part III gives you a rundown of all the steps in laboratory work, from the time you bring in your bags of dirty artifacts to the preparation of your final report. I describe what a good archaeology lab should be and list many of the fancy ways you can analyze artifacts and draw out of them fascinating bits of information about their makers and users. You also see how to put all the bits together and use different theoretical orientations to tell the story of the past in different ways.

Archaeology's human story

Combining the accumulated knowledge of centuries of investigation, archaeology gives you the story of the entire human past on this planet. In Part IV, I relate this story for you, showing how the material finds and exciting sites indicate what people have been doing over the last couple of million years (and sometimes why!). New digs and new scientific methods incorporated into archaeology have brought alive astounding details about our prehistoric ancestors who moved around the landscape hunting Ice-Age big game, settled down after the Ice Age to grow crops, and invented true civilization in many places a few thousand years ago. These big steps in the human career changed society enormously and had serious consequences for us today. Even in historic times, when you have written records of what people were doing and thinking, archaeology — the material remains — shows a lot of what you didn't know before about your ancestors and yourself.

Archaeology in the public sphere

The greatest shift moving into the 21st century has been the awareness that all archaeology is public archaeology. The work is usually paid for by the public, and the findings are part of the whole human heritage. Archaeology has gone from being a fun hobby or rich man's pursuit to being a scientific method for understanding human nature over the long term.

You can walk in the footsteps of the renowned and sometimes infamous characters who pioneered excavation methods and unearthed sensational finds. But today you also realize that archaeological findings really matter. Not only are they important in the (smaller) world of professional archaeology and interpretation of human systems and activities, but they also have meaning in the wider world of humanity at large.

In order to show you archaeology's importance to the general public and why you care about it, Part V explains all the political and social connections of archaeology today, including relating past people to living descendants and preserving archaeological sites and antiquities from looting so that they're there for everyone. I note some of the latest controversies in the field and how you can have competing interpretations but also practical uses of the past. I also list many ways you yourself can participate in archaeology and get you ready for the experience. This book has thick layers rich with information, so dig in!

Chapter 2

What Archaeology Isn't and Why That's Important

In This Chapter

▶ Realizing that archaeology doesn't deal with dinosaurs

▶ Debunking popular stereotypes of archaeologists and early people

▶ Understanding the threat of looting

*W*hat's the difference between what archaeology really is and how the popular media portray it? Thanks to Hollywood, the stereotype of the archaeologist has been either a bearded old absent-minded professor or a dashing younger guy with a whip and gun. Okay, now they've added a sexy gal with a weapon — I'm not sure that's progress. No other science or social science is so misunderstood!

I devote this chapter to explaining some misconceptions about archaeology for several reasons. One is that I want you to understand clearly the difference between what's archaeology and what's often something much more disreputable. Another reason is that some of the misconceptions are harmful and can lead to destruction of the archaeological record that represents much of our human heritage.

Dinosaurs, Fossils, and Rocks: Not What Archaeology Is About

You may think anything you dig up or anything that's really old is the subject of archaeology. Not so. *Archaeology is about people!* Yes, that sounds like an old line from a bad movie, but if it helps you remember, all the better. Archaeology studies *human behavior* from the material evidence *people* have left behind. So the subject of archaeological study can only be a few million years old.

Some fossils but no dinos

Paleontology is the study of dinosaurs and any other fossils left from earlier life forms on the planet. Fossilized bone usually turns to stone or is otherwise preserved. You can have other fossils besides bones, such as *coprolites* (preserved feces), eggs, animal footprints, and so on.

But archaeologists never study fossils that aren't associated with human activity. A couple of examples include

- ✔ Bones of animals that may have been species hunted or scavenged by really ancient humans (or at least living at the same time as those early humans).

- ✔ Fossil bones that were lying around and found by humans living long after the animal was gone, even extinct. Humans even made artifacts from fossils, such as petrified wood and coral chipped into nice stone tools.

Dinosaurs all died out some 65 million years ago. They were absolutely not around when the earliest humans appeared some 4 million years ago, Fred Flintstone notwithstanding!

Understanding how rock studies aid archaeology

Archaeology has ties to other scientific fields that involve the earth itself:

- ✔ *Geology* is the study of the earth and its materials and processes, including rocks, soil, and all other *inorganic* (non-living) components. Archaeologists may sometimes learn or make use of geological knowledge for many reasons. For example, many types of *siliceous* rocks (containing silica) have properties that allow them to be chipped and flaked into sharp points and edges. This characteristic was enormously useful to humanity for over 2 million years, until people learned how to make other sharp cutting tools of metal. So archaeologists study different rocks used for making stone tools, building monuments, and all kinds of other human uses.

- ✔ *Geography* is the study of the earth's natural and human features, and includes making lots of maps. So archaeologists need to know lots of geography to understand past human systems working within natural systems.

- ✔ *Geomorphology* is the study of landforms and how they originate and are shaped and changed through time; it's an area of geology and geography that archaeologists find extremely useful. Mountains rising, earth segments moving, rivers flooding and changing paths, and coastlines eroding or building up all affect human settlement and activity.

Hollywood Stereotypes: Time for a Dose of Reality

Popular portrayals of archaeology are fun. They include romance and adventure, gold, pyramids, lost arks, crystal skulls, and other (supposedly) valuable artifacts. But seldom do they show how archaeologists use the material remains to find out what past human societies did and why they flourished or died out. In addition, media creations of prehistoric human life seldom draw on archaeological research to portray things accurately. So you have to be careful what you believe!

The real archaeologists versus the movie heroes

Indiana Jones faces intrigue and international spies, but you never see him excavating slowly and carefully. Lara Croft wears short-shorts and a gun, both highly impractical during fieldwork. (Why is she never bitten by a mosquito or spider on those bare legs?) And *none* of these glamorous characters sits in the lab for months after the excavation painstakingly sorting the pieces of artifacts and annotating the site map to put together the picture of the past people whose remains were just excavated.

The activities of tomb raiding and treasure hunting — desecrating graves that may be someone's sacred ancestors or grabbing gold from underground or underwater to get rich — are *not* what modern archaeologists do. Nor do they wear funny hats (well, not that often), carry whips or pistols, or fight off Nazis or international smugglers (except in very rare cases!) The notion that all archaeology is adventurous is a little off-base when you consider how much paperwork (or computer work) and tedious laboratory processing it involves. But yes, you do get the lure of the unknown; you never know what the excavation will uncover, even if it's a 1950 cola bottle.

Some archaeologists study how popular culture portrays the profession. Books and Web sites point out the mistakes amid all the fun in the movies and even archaeology-related toys. Lost prophesies, extraterrestrials, and even more mundane things like artifacts inappropriate for the time period are common; many are featured on a "bad archaeology" Web site (`www.badarchaeology.net`). In 2008, an *Archaeology* magazine article described real scientific research on the several actual crystal skulls known — they're all demonstrated to be fakes from Mexico.

The stereotyped archaeologist is a charismatic, eccentric scholar (sometimes true) with esoteric knowledge about unusual topics like prehistoric stone hide-scrapers or marble jars (always true) and little awareness of the real world (seldom true, I hope). Movie archaeology always occurs in exotic places, even though many real-life archaeologists do archaeology in their hometowns or backyards!

Real past people versus movie savages with dinosaurs

Past peoples, especially in prehistoric cultures known *only* through archaeology, are often shown inaccurately in popular media. The worst offenders are shows like *The Flintstones* and movies such as *One Million Years B.C.* that show people with dinosaurs.

Possibly even more unfortunate are portrayals of prehistoric people as stupid, savage, or stupid savages. A good archaeologist never uses the term *primitive* to describe a culture or society. This description is *ethnocentric* — judging another culture based on the standards of your own. Perhaps early people used less complex technologies like stone tools or had simpler social organization (no kings or presidents — or maybe no real leaders at all), but that doesn't mean they were dumb. People may have been even smarter in the time before writing — they had to keep all their accumulated knowledge in their heads and pass it down to succeeding generations carefully.

Similarly, depictions of ancient civilizations are rife with mistaken imagery that often makes the people in them act just like modern businessmen or frustrated housewives, except that they're in Egypt building pyramids or in Rome being gladiators. And they're always so clean, which is interesting because indoor plumbing is really a pretty new development in civilization.

Treasure Hunting and Looting: Not the Goals of Archaeology

Another inaccurate view of archaeology is that it's all about finding artifacts. In reality, you find out about past people *through* artifacts, which is very different. An artifact with no information on its original archaeological context, even displayed as an art object, is scientifically worthless.

People digging only for artifacts are called *looters*. Ethical collectors, who obtain artifacts for fun and keep good records on them, may be helpful to archaeologists. But looters, unethical collectors (sometimes called *pothunters*), destroy the integrity and scientific value of archaeological sites in their quest for personal profit. Some unprofessional individuals claim they sell artifacts to finance the dig. Real archaeologists consider it unethical to buy and sell irreplaceable artifacts unearthed from archaeological sites. Instead, they only study and conserve them for the public good. Unfortunately, looting has happened since the beginning of human culture — some call it the world's second- or third-oldest profession.

Archaeology is *not* grave-robbing or tomb-raiding, which are either illegal or unethical (and sometimes both). Archaeologists excavate a grave only with the permission of the state and the descendants of the dead (if they can be found) or to investigate whose grave it is, especially for modern crime scenes.

Early archaeology and looting: The Elgin marbles

In 1801, Lord Elgin, the British ambassador to the Ottoman Empire (which controlled Greece at the time) got permission to remove the 2,500-year-old marble sculptures from the famous Parthenon in Athens. The gorgeous statues and friezes from this famous temple showed scenes from classical myths and stories; Elgin shipped them to England, which eventually bought them to display in the British Museum where they still are today (see Figure 2-1).

Even in his own time, Elgin was criticized for stealing the heritage of the Greek people. But Elgin was very interested in archaeology and the past, and this action was how he showed it; in fact, his actions are typical of the view of archaeology at the time. (See my brief history of the field in Chapter 1.) The idea was to claim for the Western, scientific, supposedly superior world the great monuments of the past from places now fallen from ancient glory.

Today the debate rages over whether England should keep the Elgin marbles or give them back to Greece, their rightful owner. The argument centers on who can take care of them better, given rough treatment over the decades by the British but decay and neglect of monuments in Greece. Nationalism and issues of deep heritage and tradition, as well as modern politics, all come into play. This kind of debate is part of the history of archaeology. Many individuals grabbed treasures from ancient Egypt or Mesopotamia or Peru or elsewhere, claiming to want to study them and care for them. Now archaeologists know better and respect the heritage of the peoples whose ancestors they're digging up!

Figure 2-1:
Some of
the famous
Elgin
marbles in
the British
Museum,
London.

Give a hoot: Don't loot (or trade in antiquities)

Many laws protect ancient monuments in all countries today (and see my discussion in Chapter 16). But people still steal *antiquities* (artifacts from ancient civilizations or prehistoric cultures) and sell them to arts dealers or auction houses, or directly to wealthy collectors. Business writers advise investing in antiquities, even though it's often illegal and always unethical.

Smuggling antiquities never commands the police or customs attention that drug smuggling or other illegal international activity does, which is too bad; dangerous drugs can hurt and kill many people, but stealing the past of a nation damages the heritage of everyone! Extremist groups in Iraq are even financing their terrorist tactics by smuggling ancient Mesopotamian artifacts out of the country and destroying their own rich archaeological past.

Education is of course the solution; people need to realize that what they're doing is damaging someone's ancestry. But it's hard to get across to many people how taking arrowheads from a public park is a crime (even though it is). You can point out that if everybody did it, all the arrowheads would be gone and unavailable for scientific study. Worse than taking the artifacts themselves are the damage and destruction that looting causes to the rest of the site. Tunneling into the mound, pyramid, or shipwreck to get the gold or whole pots to sell damages all the other evidence.

Another way to look at it is to imagine that you're at a flea market and you see pages of an ancient diary being sold off, one by one, to different customers who think they're cute and quaint. You suddenly realize the diary was written by your grandparent and must have been stolen from your attic. Each page is going somewhere different, so you'll never be able to put the whole thing back together again.

Or think of another situation in which some country sends astronauts to the other side of the moon. They study everything but don't share their findings with anyone else. To make things worse, they blow up the whole place they studied and make it impossible for anyone else to investigate it.

After reading this book, I hope you understand why looting of artifacts and sites is unethical, destructive, and just plain wrong. Instead, I hope you want to work hard to save the past for the future.

Archaeologists Aren't Always Digging

The same reasons that archaeologists discourage looting propel their interest in *not* digging. They've already excavated enough still-unstudied material to fuel archaeological investigation into the next century. Plus, archaeologists have an ethical obligation to report on what's been dug prior to digging any more. Furthermore, they're developing so many new scientific techniques that today's excavation and analysis standards may seem crude and ignorant compared to what may be possible in the future. (Yes, I'm waiting for that *Star Trek* tricorder that I can point at the site to tell me what's underground, and at the artifact to tell me its composition, date, and the name of the person who made it!)

So you may not want to dig but to study what's been stuck on a dusty lab shelf since someone dug it up. You may prefer to discourage digging because, after all, you destroy when you dig.

Lab work doesn't mean you don't have exciting moments. You can make discoveries that are just as thrilling as fieldwork when you open a bag that's spent decades in storage and see what materials it contains. I've had this experience, crawling up on high shelves in federal storage facilities to open paper bags containing finds from digs in the 1950s, so trust me, it happens.

Archaeology Isn't Necessarily Exotic; It's Real Work

The romantic, exotic locales often portrayed for archaeology are usually quite rare. Most archaeology occurs in mundane settings: in the woods, on the prairie, downtown amid sidewalks and buildings, or in some farmer's field. You still make exciting discoveries, of course, and you never know what you may uncover. But it's usually not gold or treasure!

You may think archaeology is pretty easy — just get a shovel and maybe a metal detector and start digging. But it's really a difficult and precise science. Doing it incorrectly may mess up exactly what you're trying to find. You can't assume that anyone who can hold a shovel or trowel can excavate properly. That's like thinking anyone with a scalpel and some sutures can remove your appendix. Archaeology is very picky, enormously tedious work that requires expert technique to prevent damaging the evidence. Archaeology is the only science that destroys its subject matter while it investigates it. For this reason, it requires a great deal of skill, enormous amounts of record-keeping, and endless patience.

So you need skills, courage, wisdom, and thorough scientific training to do archaeology, not just the enthusiasm for adventure, discovery, and learning of past people. Hidden dangers in archaeology can be physically real — such as that snake that slithered into your excavation trench — or intellectually insidious — such as thinking native peoples were too stupid to know how to build pyramids and therefore ancient astronauts from another planet must have arrived to show them how!

Archaeology is about people

You can do archaeology anywhere that people have been or have left their stuff. A lot of today's archaeology concerns the recent historic past — sites that may at first glance look rather dull, such as early 20th-century houses or stores, railroad lines, or factories. People live in all kinds of locales, which usually aren't flashy swamps or deserts. These less-exotic sites are often poorly documented in the historic record because they were used or lived in by people whose everyday lives were never written about — working class folks, minorities, women, and children. With archaeology, you can give some history to those who have little.

Any archaeological study is going to tell you about human nature and what people went through in the past to get along. Excavating prehistoric foraging peoples' camps or early farming sites can bring alive the struggles as well as the successes (and failures) of past human adaptations. You may even identify with the same problems they faced: getting food, shelter — all the things you also need. After all, archaeology is about people, and you're people, too.

A case study: Archaeology of modern garbage

A famous and much-lauded archaeological project demonstrated how much you can discover about modern society from using archaeological methods to study garbage. It started as an assignment by University of Arizona Professor Bill Rathje to his class to study the material remains — trash — from contemporary urban neighborhoods.

Students combined careful examination of all the contents of this waste with questionnaires filled out (anonymously) by the people living in neighborhoods of the city of Tucson. The findings were astounding; they demonstrated that people

- ✔ Threw out a huge amount of usable food — 10 percent to 15 percent of all the garbage was food. Middle-income households wasted more than poor or rich ones.
- ✔ Said they drank 40 to 60 percent less alcohol than they really did.
- ✔ Drank more expensive liquor in the richest and poorest neighborhoods (with middle-class folks drinking the cheapest booze).

After this pioneering work in the 1970s, the Garbage Project, also known as Le Projet du Garbage or garbology studies, expanded to include excavations in landfills. I was privileged to help Rathje conduct one of the landfill excavations, in which a giant machine bored a hole into the huge pile of garbage and picked up chunks of it in ten-foot intervals. We bagged and labeled the chunks and took them back to the archaeology lab to sort by raw material (paper, plastic, metal, and so on) in proper archaeological fashion. The only differences from a traditional excavation were that the artifacts were a bit more modern, and they (and thus my crew and I) smelled really bad!

Tabulating and analyzing the materials from landfills has produced extremely valuable data on consumer choice, waste management, and recycling. Unexpected findings from landfill excavations included the following:

- Most of the stuff doesn't biodegrade; thousands of newspapers from as long ago as the 1950s were excavated and found to be perfectly readable (albeit smelly).

- Though you'd think plastics make up the largest component of landfills, they don't. That distinction goes to paper, which makes up between 40 and 50 percent of the landfill junk.

- Construction debris accounts for 20 to 30 percent of the material in landfills.

- Landfills often have nice annual layers marked by yellow lines — caused by annual discard of telephone books!

The garbage studies are one of the best examples of how archaeology can have real-life practical value for modern society and give you information you just can't get from history, economics, or any other investigation. This study also shows you what archaeologists really do — not go after treasure in the conventional sense, but seek out the priceless knowledge of human behavior.

Chapter 3

So You Want to Do Archaeology? What Kind?

My office phone often rings with a caller asking something like "I found a fossil bone — can you tell me if it's from a dinosaur?" I have to explain that archaeology studies things left by people, so fossils of extinct animals can be identified by paleontologists in the biology department.

As I'm constantly informing my callers, *archaeology* is the anthropology of past people. You can specialize in a geographic region, a particular kind of research question, or even a technical method in archaeology. You can even specialize in a type of philosophical perspective and write a lot but maybe not even dig any more. You probably never realized that archaeologists do so many different kinds of things, so in this chapter I give you an overview of the many varieties of archaeology you can pursue.

Archaeology as Anthropology

In the Americas and many other places, archaeology is part of anthropology (like pediatrics is a specialty within medicine). *Anthropology* studies humanity from both biological and cultural perspectives. Its four fields are these:

> ✔ **Cultural and social anthropology** studies living cultures, whether like Margaret Mead in the far-off exotic Pacific islands or in the different ethnic neighborhoods of a modern city.

- ✔ **Biological (or physical) anthropology** studies how humans evolved over millions of years and the genetic and other physical variations among humans today.

- ✔ **Linguistic anthropology** studies how languages evolve and interact with culture.

- ✔ **Archaeology** is the cultural anthropology of the past. It's the only branch of anthropology where you don't need the actual people — just the stuff they left behind. And the method is different: You use the material remains to figure out past behavior, not the living people's actions.

- ✔ **Applied anthropology** is sometimes called a fifth specialization. It means taking the methods and findings of anthropology to be of some use in the modern world. Because most archaeology these days is in some way public (discussed more in Chapter 16), archaeology is applied anthropology.

In some other countries archaeology resides in classics or natural science divisions of universities (sometimes in departments of art history or Oriental or Middle East studies), or in separate archaeology departments apart from other social sciences. But modern archaeologists everywhere are asking social and cultural questions (not just digging up pretty objects for museums), so perhaps this separation is a little extreme.

The Scientific and the Humanistic in Archaeology

Science is one method of knowing things, based on testing hypotheses and acquiring knowledge systematically. Archaeology is a social science *and* a special *method* of studying about people from their material remains. It can be part of the humanities too.

Most archaeologists use scientific method, coming up with hypothetical explanations based on what they find and then testing those ideas with the next dig, using *empirical* (observable) evidence. Humanistic study emphasizes more how humans feel, think, and value things in life — what artifacts meant to them.

You can study architectural ideals, artistic values, or spiritual beliefs of past people scientifically. You can also speculate about them in a humanistic way, relating to past people as a fellow human. (What did they believe that led them to make such glorious tombs or sacrifice so many servants at the ruler's funeral? What did those servants think at the time?) Humanistic models of past human societies aren't usually scientifically testable, but they use imagination and expand your ways of viewing the past. They work best with historic archaeology (discussed later in this chapter), when you already have some idea of what those past people thought because it was written down somewhere!

Most archaeologists today combine scientific and humanistic approaches, depending upon their theoretical and philosophical views (and often on the sizes of their budgets and who funded the dig).

Different Fields for a Plethora of Purposes and Places

You may fall in love with the archaeology of a particular place and all its unsolved mysteries. Or maybe a specific time period or one kind of artifact fascinates you. Whatever the case, the following sections give you an idea of the many different archaeological paths you can take.

Regional specialties: Digging in one place

Many archaeologists begin work in one area of the world and stay there year after year uncovering more ancient secrets. You may fall under the spell of Egypt or Mesoamerica (Mexico and Central America) and all their pyramids. But you can get involved in the archaeology of Arkansas and find it equally compelling. Egyptian archaeology is so famous that it has its own specific word (Egyptology), but we don't yet have a term like Arkansasology.

Much of my own work is tied to a geographical region, one Florida valley where I've been digging for years. As I get deeper (pun intended!) into its past, I target specific gaps in information and try to fill them (the earliest people here? Earliest agriculture? Reasons for building mounds? Results of the 16th-century European intrusion? A vanished 19th-century town? The real story of African-American turpentine workers in the backwoods?)

Every place humans have ever been has archaeology that someone can specialize in (even the moon!).

What's special about anthropology?

Just as every pediatrician or heart surgeon is a practitioner of medicine, archaeologists generally do anthropology. Unlike other social sciences, anthropology emphasizes these things:

- **Culture:** Shared human knowledge, beliefs, symbols, behaviors, customs, social organization — all the things that depend upon learning and transmitting knowledge (as opposed to relying on animal instinct).

- **Cultures:** Ethnic groups or other individual populations recognized by some shared ways of life. For example, *Western* culture is the Euro-American world with its Judeo-Christian, capitalist foundations. Now Western culture is spreading widely over the globe as tribal peoples or countries become Westernized. Anthropologists often study original or indigenous cultures before, while, and/or after they become Westernized.

- **Archaeological cultures:** The material record of specific past cultures. Most often, an archaeological culture consists of assemblages of particular artifacts and other material patterns because you can't always determine ethnicity from the artifacts. (For example, right now you're probably wearing clothes, a watch, or a cellphone made in another country.)

- **Cultural relativism:** Judging all cultures by their own standards, as opposed to *ethnocentrism,* or judging other cultures by your own values (like Romans calling all those other folks barbarians).

- **A holistic perspective:** Seeing humans as both *biological* and *cultural* beings at the same time.

- **Cross-cultural comparison:** Seeing how the same things are or aren't done in different cultures through space and time.

- **Fieldwork:** Going out to make your own observations, not just sending out a questionnaire, using census data, or reading what someone else said.

- **Understanding "the Other":** Learning about whatever group isn't yours, based on ethnicity, gender, or any other criteria established for the particular study being done. Some anthropologists are of course part of the group they study, but they want to be able to interpret that group to everyone. If you're a middle-class citizen, learning how homeless, impoverished people think is understanding "the Other."

Temporal specialties: Digging within one time period

You may prefer the archaeology of one time period and become expert in recognizing the typical artifacts and filling in the picture of how people lived right then.

For example, Paleolithic archaeologists really need to know about stone tools — how they were made, broken, and used and how the stone was obtained — because stone is mostly what they have to work with. From such a remote time in the human past (up to 1 or 2 million years ago), usually stone is all that's preserved. Many Paleolithic archaeologists learn how to chip stone tools themselves. They may look at the Paleolithic artifacts, house patterns, or other aspects at many different places in the world.

If you do Pre-Columbian archaeology, you specialize in North and South America (the New World) before Columbus arrived and Old World invaders and colonists changed everything.

You may specialize in 19th-century archaeology, and all its particular kinds of artifacts. You'd know china patterns, metal items such as gun parts, brick types, architectural designs — everything identified with that century.

Expertise in specific artifacts or site types

You may have a fascination for something specific in the archaeological record. Here are some examples of artifact expertise:

- Many *lithic* (Greek for "stone") experts live and breathe stone tools. You can study the tools all over the world and through time, and even learn to manufacture them (through *flintknapping*, or flaking stone).

- Some archaeologists love pottery, with all its great variation. Here you can make your own pots to compare with the prehistoric ceramics, measure dimensions of vessels, or study all the designs and the *temper* (crushed rock or other material) mixed with the clay. For 20 years, one expert has studied the beautiful, enigmatic patterns stamped onto pots in the U.S. Southeast 1,500 years ago. Another specialist developed a method to show a rollout of the painted pictures going around Maya vases as one continuous rectangular photograph.

- Perishable remains are rarely preserved, but you can still study them. An archaeologist digging a dry rock shelter in Pennsylvania found fragments of plaited baskets up to 9,000 years old. He became an expert on this ancient technology and studied it worldwide, from preserved fragments to basketry imprints on fired clay pots.

- Experts in *cordage* (string or yarn) and weaving study not only preserved fiber fragments but also the imprints of cords or fabrics on clay.

- Any other technology you can imagine — from historic industrial bridge or watercraft design to prehistoric beadmaking — has its archaeological specialists.

You may become fascinated by a particular type of site to specialize in. Some examples include the following:

- ✔ A *Paleo-Indian* (ancient Native American) bison kill site on the American Plains requires expertise in 7,000- to 12,000-year-old stone tools, bison and other animal skeletons, digging in a particular kind of soil, and so on. For a Paleo-Indian site in Florida you need the same knowledge, and also you need to know how to dive because the best sites are underwater.

- ✔ Quarry sites where past people went to get stone are favorites for lithic specialists. Here you can find chipped pieces, from chunks to discarded broken tools, but not necessarily the garbage from people having lived there. Historic quarries for building stone are also fun to study; you can see how those people actually carved out huge blocks and transported them.

- ✔ Cave and *rock shelter* (shallow cave) sites require not only expertise in typical types of cultural and natural deposits but also a decided lack of claustrophobia! They may be uncomfortable if you have to squat on planks (see Figure 3-1) to dig so as not to walk on the floor and mess it up while you brush rocks and artifacts and do paperwork.

- ✔ Rock art sites have painted and/or engraved designs and pictures; they're found worldwide and may be tens of thousands of years old. To study them you need expertise in pigments and rock types and sometimes even climbing cliffs!

Figure 3-1: Digging in a French Paleolithic rock shelter.

✔ Spectacular architecture — mounds, pyramids, planned cities, and monuments — has lured archaeologists for centuries. To study these features, you need knowledge of construction engineering, architecture, and maybe even astronomy if your buildings are aligned with the sun at the summer solstice.

✔ Various kinds of industrial sites, like mills, waterworks, and irrigation systems also draw plenty of archaeological attention. Whether in prehistoric or historic times, you want to know how the people built these structures and why, how they succeeded or failed, and even what the lives of the workers there were like.

Archaeological Specialties by Setting, Goals, and Techniques

The varieties of archaeology depend upon what you're looking for, why you're looking, and what you're finding. Many of these varieties overlap; with archaeology, you're always doing several different things at once!

Prehistoric and historic archaeology

You find quite a big difference between researching the *prehistoric* human past, where everything known is from archaeological discovery, and the *historic* past, where someone wrote down information you can also use to interpret the finds.

Prehistoric archaeology

Everything that happened before writing was invented is called *prehistory*. That's hundreds of millions of years of life on earth (including dinosaurs). But *human prehistory* goes back only a couple million years (NOT including dinosaurs). This period is what archaeologists study (described more in Chapters 12 through 14).

Almost everything people have ever done has been during prehistoric time. Inventing artifacts, inventing culture in the first place, organizing societies, developing belief systems — anything you can think of about how people live, think, and behave, was already done for 2 million years before the invention of writing. Only in recent time did people start writing down descriptions of how they did it.

As a prehistorian, you reconstruct that deep human past based on what you find, with only loose comparisons to known cultures. You need knowledge of historic cultures that are descended from or close to your prehistoric people. (See Chapter 11 for a discussion of how archaeologists use analogy with known cultures). Folk tales and native traditional stories usually go back centuries or more. They reflect common knowledge passed on through generations. (Now you don't sit around the fire with the grandparents and learn everything any more; you read books — like this one! — or look it up on the Internet.)

Historic archaeology

The earliest writing is only about 3,000 to 5,000 years old, and you can't always read or even recognize it. (See discussions in Chapter 14). Writing usually came along with other complex systems of the first ancient states. Historic archaeologists can specialize in any literate culture: early Chinese, Greek, or Roman civilization, medieval or colonial peoples, even early 20th-century towns.

After you have written records, you have more information about what you're digging up. But historic archaeology has its peculiarities and problems too. Here are some of them:

- History began in different times at different places. So North America (north of Mexico) had no written record until Europeans "discovered" the place and started writing about the people they saw there in the 1500s.

- Only a very few people of a certain kind write history: those who can write (and get published). So written records reflect any biases and ethnocentrism they may have.

- Different cultures invented writing for different reasons. In ancient Mesopotamia, it was for keeping economic records. Indus valley civilization (in Pakistan) and Etruscan (ancient Tuscany, Italy) writing haven't really been deciphered yet but seem to record religious things. Mayan glyphs (Yucatan, Mexico) recorded sacred, political, and military history — in other words, who conquered whom.

- Usually, history is written by the winners. This means conquerors wrote little about the people they conquered, and what they did write was probably from a biased point of view. Indigenous cultures known from a few descriptions by outsiders are often called "people without history."

So an archaeologist can be hindered as well as helped by history. You may find documents from the earliest explorers who met the native people whose village you're excavating. But those explorers didn't describe all the natives' artifacts or how the people disposed of garbage or built houses — the evidence you're finding in the ground.

In later times too, historical records seldom record everyday behavior (how people slept, bathed, even went to the bathroom). Yet all this behavior can be in the archaeological record.

Underwater archaeology: Difficult and expensive

Archaeology is hard work — even harder in a place where you can't stand up normally or breathe. Digging underwater is perhaps 100 times more expensive than digging on land, and it takes longer, too — you can only breathe with your gear for so long down there. Plus, you have to contend with water pressure, sharks, tides and currents, lousy visibility, and many other hazards.

Also, it's usually a logistical nightmare — you have to get the boats, breathing apparatus, and all the equipment for regular diving. Then you also need a whole different set of digging and recording technology (discussed more in Chapter 7).

You may see more divers visiting (and looting!) archaeological sites than archaeologists who know how to dive. So archaeology will always welcome professional, ethical underwater archaeologists who aren't after treasure they can sell.

Here are some examples of the great variety of underwater sites and specialties:

- **Nautical archaeology** studies ship-building and watercraft in particular. Shipwrecks are everywhere — in mid-ocean, in ports, in rivers, and in lake bottoms. They're capsules of particular kinds of human behavior (often within larger economic and mercantile systems) at a specific time. They can be merely sunken, or storm-tossed across a wide area. In some port areas wrecks lie on top of other wrecks!

- **Maritime (or marine) archaeology** includes shipwrecks and everything around ports and particular seafaring cultures (including some terrestrial archaeology, too).

- **Prehistoric** or **historic underwater archaeology** investigates sites often now submerged because of rising sea levels since the end of the Pleistocene (Ice Age). Sea level is hundreds of feet higher than it was 10,000 years ago, so many settlements are waiting to be discovered! You can find ancient Paleolithic campsites near drowned freshwater springs, or whole villages abandoned when the water rose. Other changes in landscapes — storms, tidal waves, and other forces — can drown parts of port cities or other coastal sites.

Heinrich Schliemann and the Classics

The Trojan War (between Troy and Greece) took place in about the 12th century B.C., and its story was already centuries old when ancient Greek historian Homer wrote it down in his epic poem *The Iliad* in about the seventh century B.C. Wealthy German businessman Heinrich Schliemann thought the story must be more than just legend and went to search for Troy. He found and excavated the site in northwest Turkey in 1870. It had so many occupation layers that scholars still argue which one was the original Troy of the legend. Schliemann didn't find the famous Trojan horse, but he did blaze a trail for classical archaeology, comparing historic documentation with the archaeological record.

Classical archaeology: All those statues!

Ancient *classical* civilizations — Greece, Rome, and related areas — are the foundations of Western culture. Classical archaeologists study the art, architecture, and written documents of these societies passed down through the ages. So classical archaeology is a type of historical archaeology.

The classics are still so important in our consciousness that this archaeology is sometimes considered a separate discipline. For example, Florence, Italy, has an archaeology museum with all the classical materials and a few Bronze Age predecessors (pottery and other artifacts). A separate prehistory museum across town has everything from the earliest tools of the Paleolithic through the Bronze Age.

Some classical archaeologists work more in the tradition of art history or languages, exploring styles of vase painting, sculpture, or ancient texts. Some university classics departments are separate from anthropological archaeology. But many classicists are tending lately toward anthropological explanations — what did those ancient artworks show about the societies that made them?

One thing you can know for sure: All those classical statues that seem so pure in their white marble appearance were really painted bright, even garish colors (some even have traces of paint remaining). So our classical ideals may be more manufactured than real.

Forensic archaeology

The popularity of crime-scene shows has brought forensic studies to the public consciousness. *Forensic* means relating to the legal system and to public debate in court — in other words, evidence! *Forensic archaeology* is the use of archaeological survey techniques to locate hidden crime scenes (like buried bodies) and excavation techniques for precisely recording finds.

Crime scene investigations

Forensic sciences identify material items and human remains involved in law enforcement cases. Forensic biological anthropology deals with skeletons or human tissue. The archaeological techniques involved in this sort of investigation provide accurate, clear evidence in legal cases. It's far better than having the cops quickly shovel out the corpse and disturb all the evidence around it!

In reality, all detective work is archaeology because you're using the material evidence to interpret past human behavior of some kind. You may map out where the body lies and the things around it. You interview people and check the written records. Whether it's a burned-down house, a car-crash pileup, or a murder scene in the woods, you're carefully recording and collecting finds. Even that blood-spatter expert on the detective team reconstructing the crime is studying the material evidence and so doing archaeology.

War crimes and disaster investigations

Archaeology also assists international investigations of genocide and mass murders. Working for the United Nations or other humanitarian organizations, archaeologists excavate graves of "disappeared" people — victims of political regimes that may now be on trial. They dig up detailed evidence of these horrible crimes and locate and identify remains for relatives of victims. Sometimes the skeletons aren't identifiable; artifacts like clothing are all that are left to provide identification.

Natural disasters like tsunamis, mudslides, explosions, fires, and earthquakes also claim victims whose remains and identities are archaeologically excavated. This is true for human-made disasters too. Archaeologists helped recovery efforts after the 9-11 World Trade Center attacks, the Oklahoma City bombing, and other tragedies, as well as after Hurricane Katrina.

Crash victims

Any plane crash site is of course investigated with archaeological techniques. A team of archaeologists is still looking for Amelia Earhart, the famous pilot who disappeared in the Pacific while she was trying to fly around the world in 1937. Using typical survey and excavation techniques, they're recovering suggestive artifacts, including a possible piece of her shoe.

Even military victims of wartime have been subjects of archaeological investigations. Pilots shot down in Vietnam in the 1960s are now being excavated from remains of crashed aircraft. Personal artifacts — even dog tags found while screening the shoveled soil — aid identification.

Forensic archaeology takes a special kind of dedicated investigator. The processes may be slow and difficult if you're dealing with thousands of victims. Emotional involvement with the events and victims' loved ones is often unavoidable and much more than the typical archaeological dig usually requires. Plus you have to be ready to respond at the last minute to calls from law enforcement officers. Finally, you have to be willing to testify in court, should that be required. It may mean you have to reveal personal details about your own life.

Historic preservation, heritage, and community archaeology

You may think historic preservation means saving famous buildings like George Washington's (or Elvis's) home. But it also means saving archaeological sites, even ones that don't look like anything because they're all in the ground. You can investigate the heritage of a whole nation or a small community with archaeology.

Historic preservation

All governments have some laws requiring location and protection of historic and archaeological sites, at least on public lands. Historic preservation specialists may work in private foundations or government agencies, or even as lobbyists working with legislators to improve laws or raise funds to protect sites or investigate them further; in fact, sometimes they spend more time raising money and public awareness than digging. But you can't dig the sites if they aren't preserved!

George Washington's famous 18th-century estate Mount Vernon, on the Potomac River in Virginia, included much more than just his plantation mansion. Archaeological excavations give clues about other buildings and aspects of his life that are long gone. Uncovering the foundations of the original blacksmith shop and forge allows an accurate reconstruction of this building.

Fascinating results came from excavating Washington's original distillery (see Color Figure 5). Archaeologists compared evidence in the ground with his writings about the industrial technology and constructions. Now the plan is to reconstruct the distillery as well, right on its original foundations, next to the restored gristmill. Visitors will one day be able to see how the first U.S. president was one of the greatest whiskey producers of his time. (But will they serve samples to show how it probably tasted?)

The heritage of communities and ethnic groups

Archaeologists often work with specific communities to preserve and investigate both the standing buildings and the archaeological (in the ground) evidence of their past. This process can include digging, documenting oral histories of elderly residents, even proving descent of modern folks from past cultures whose remains lie buried.

You may research the past of a particular ethnic or indigenous (native to the land) group. They may want to learn when their ancestors first arrived or how they lived. Several Native American groups have tribal archaeologists who survey, dig, run museums, and educate the public about their ancient ways. Archaeological study can validate land claims or help raise money for the local people through archaeo-tourism. It can bring people knowledge of their heritage that may be lost to history or never known at all. Pride in your cultural heritage is much enhanced with the hard data of archaeology!

Cultural resources management (CRM) and contract archaeology

A huge part of the archaeology done today is devoted to finding and saving remains of the human past so that they can be investigated. This may be required by law or part of a public or private effort. Locating archaeological sites, evaluating them, and excavating or preserving them are the main tasks of cultural resources management, which includes contracting out for such expertise.

Cultural resources management

Important historic buildings, objects, or archaeological sites are *cultural resources*. Managing them means deciding how to protect, use, and study them. But cultural resources management (CRM) means first you have to *find* the sites — yes, the foundations of historic buildings, but especially the prehistoric sites that may have no visible trace on the landscape. You also have to know your laws really well. Then you have to figure out how to interpret the sites to the public (or not), and whether you can even destroy them to build something else.

Officials who manage cultural (and natural) resources and lands can be government archaeologists. More often they hire *contract archaeologists,* who survey and find sites and then evaluate their significance. Archaeologists at the U.S. National Park Service (NPS) under the Secretary of the Interior, as well as other federal agencies, manage sites at parks, military bases, national forests, and other public lands. Every U.S. state has a State Historic Preservation Office (SHPO — those government agencies love acronyms) that does or reviews archaeology. Most countries have official plans for safeguarding their archaeological heritages and specialists who carry these plans out (including issuing permits for visiting archaeologists' digs).

Other government archaeologists specialize in antiquities laws, to conserve their national heritage from looting, and in public interpretation of sites and archaeo-tourism to bring the past alive to visitors.

Contract archaeology

Private companies, non-profit agencies, and university anthropology departments doing contract archaeology now do more archaeology than anyone else. Contract archaeology is often for profit, but should always be done at the same high research standards as any other kind of archaeology. This is sometimes difficult if the contracting agency or client needs the work done fast or doesn't want to pay much.

Usually contract archaeology means you start with survey and work through three phases, in the CRM lingo:

- ✔ **Phase I: Survey:** You inspect the records of a planned building project to see if any known sites fall in the project area and then do the field-work to find any other sites that may be there. (See Chapter 6 for more on archaeological survey.) A *reconnaissance survey* is less in-depth than a complete Phase I, and may not involve actual fieldwork, only checking existing records. Or it may be just a quick walk-over of the project area, not involving any detailed field inspection or shovel tests (very small excavations) to see what's buried. Depending on what you find, you may get the proposed construction altered to avoid archaeological sites — moving a proposed highway a hundred feet northward, for example. Or you may see that nothing significant is in the way that requires any more archaeology.

- ✔ **Phase II: Test excavation:** You may need limited excavation to evaluate the importance of promising sites. For example, if you find artifacts on the ground surface, you may dig test excavations (maybe a meter square) to see if you uncover intact *cultural deposits* (undisturbed layers containing artifacts, food garbage, or other indicators of past human behavior). Or you may find nothing at all of significance because these cultural deposits have all been plowed up or otherwise disturbed and lost their scientific information.

- ✔ **Phase III: Excavation:** Really significant sites may have to be destroyed anyway in the name of progress (or whatever is being built). So then you do *salvage archaeology* (now called *data recovery*), where you get to dig much bigger areas to recover and study as much as you can before it's all gone. Check out Chapter 7 for more on how to do excavation.

The shovel bum life

As a fieldworker in contract archaeology, you may be called a "shovel bum." The peculiar (but often celebrated) lifestyle means going from project to project and region to region digging small shovel tests all day. You get to be outdoors and do physical work, but you often spend weeks not finding anything. This keeps the clients happy (because they don't have to pay for more work at significant sites) but isn't so exciting. Plus you may not have benefits of regular employment.

I know some shovel bums who've gone back to school for advanced degrees and better jobs. I also know some who love the lifestyle and have been doing it for decades. You do get to be the first to uncover something exciting in the field while the PI (*principal investigator,* or head of the project) may be back in the office writing the last report! You may even be sent back to the office yourself to help write the report on your fieldwork and finds.

You generally need to write reports describing the work and results of all phases of investigation. Usually you have to do them by strict deadlines. Builders may tell you, "My bulldozers are waiting!"

Any archaeology involves many ethical considerations, which I discuss in Chapter 8. But contract archaeology has additional issues because you're serving clients, usually for profit. I've had clients offer me more money *not* to find anything (no, thanks!). They wanted to get going on their projects without delays to meet government regulation. This is like telling your doctor you'll pay more to be told the scan shows no cancer in your body. There still may be something important in there needing attention.

The CRM industry

Some think that CRM and contract archaeology differ from academic (university or museum) or research archaeology, but they're wrong — all archaeology should be done to the same standards. Many academics do contracts, and many CRM and contract archaeologists do long-term research. Ideally, they differ only in the amount and speed of work done. Academics do train students, and private firms do earn profits, but often they all work on the same projects.

Archaeology by CRM agencies and firms may not be published in regular archaeology books and journals. They often just don't have time before the next project to write more than the official reports filed away in government agencies. These reports are often called *gray literature* because they're less available; however, they're increasingly becoming easier to find as electronic documents.

Museum archaeology and collections management

In a museum you can do lots of exciting archaeology, and (possibly) not get as dirty. You certainly won't get as many bug bites!

Research on museum collections can bring amazing results. Now that archaeologists have chemical techniques to analyze them, residues on pots that have sat on a shelf since they were dug up a century ago may reveal what past people were eating. Piecing together new finds from your site with those excavated earlier and stored on the shelf may give you a whole new picture of past life. Other museum specialists may help you identify a rock, plant, or animal that's the key to some past event.

Museum work

Museum work involves everything from leading tours to fund-raising to setting up exhibits. You have to know archaeological theory to make sure you reconstruct past people's lives without ethnocentric biases of modern times (showing all those cave guys dragging cave gals around by the hair is out these days). You have to know ethics and antiquities laws so you don't acquire looted artifacts or contribute toward the loss of someone's heritage.

Curation and collections management

Curation means caring for things, often for the indefinite future. First you have to clean your finds and number and analyze them in the laboratory after the dig. (I describe processing and analyzing finds in Chapters 9 and 10.) But then artifacts and archaeological data must be stored so that they

- ✔ Won't decay or be damaged
- ✔ Are all completely listed in comprehensive catalogs
- ✔ Never lose the information of their original *provenience* (location)
- ✔ Can be easily located for further research
- ✔ Can be available for public appreciation in exhibits and then put carefully away while others are pulled out for new exhibits
- ✔ Are in a good system of information management, as well as management of objects

Archaeological collections management is expensive and labor-intensive. Many professionals ignore it because it's more fun to dig; remember that last scene when Indiana Jones's lost ark is put in a box on the shelf with the rest of the collections?

Listing every item in every bag is tedious — endless hours making computer databases isn't most people's idea of fun. Treatment of fragile items may require smelly chemicals. Storage of materials in sturdy, non-degradable containers means you become an expert in acid-free paper and curation cabinets. Conservation means you repair, photograph, and scan original maps and notes, or piece together statue fragments. As a curator, you're an expert in climate-controlled, secure artifact and records storage away from humid air, termites, rats, and burglars.

Most people don't realize this stuff is all a part of archaeology too! Plus you have to argue continually for more space for collections. Sometimes you can discard some artifacts (*de-accession* in museum lingo), but this is tricky because you really want to keep everything — it may be useful for future research. Archaeologists of the 1930s threw out animal bones and charcoal, thinking it was just garbage. Well, it was — then. Now it can be used for radiocarbon dating and reconstructing diet and environment!

Avocational and educational archaeology

Amateur or *avocational* archaeologists do it as a hobby, not as a profession. This doesn't mean you don't do it well, however! The word *amateur* comes from the Latin for "love" — you do it because you love it, not because you're getting paid! Many avocationals are ethical collectors and volunteers who work with professionals or on their own. They may even publish articles about their finds or record them with government archaeology offices.

Public education in archaeology often includes programs for volunteers or amateurs. You may hear of an archaeology day or month with various activities like digs and artifact replication. Education specialists often help teachers with lesson plans or take traveling exhibits to schools to expand the curriculum. Unfortunately, archaeology isn't taught in most elementary and high schools, so kids end up thinking it means dinosaurs. Archaeology education programs also take place in museums and parks and with kids' groups like scout troops and camps.

Other kinds of archaeology

You can emphasize a particular part of the past that holds your interest in your archaeological study. Here are some of the many specialty terms you may see:

- **Landscape archaeology** considers the whole integrated environment in which people lived. For this specialty, you need to know geology, landforms, biology, and ecosystems to see resources available and how people would have used, even shaped their surroundings. *Environmental archaeology* is another term for this.

- **Geoarchaeology** combines geology, geography, and archaeology in various ways, whether studying soils, rock formations, and landforms or remote sensing, imaging, and mapping techniques (using fancy instruments such as radar and magnetometers to get images below the ground or map with 3-D laser technology).

- **Mortuary archaeology** involves specialists who excavate human graves, often to relocate them out of the path of some new construction. Or they may study different kinds of burials to learn about social organization and religion.

- **Bioarchaeology** refers to the study of human skeletons and their contexts, and requires training in biological anthropology.

- **Field archaeology** (going out and digging) can be contrasted with *laboratory archaeology* (processing and analyzing materials and data that come in from the dig), but most professionals and amateurs do both.

- **Theoretical archaeology** means figuring out what happened in the past by using particular models and assumptions about how humans behave at a general level. (Writing archaeological theory is often a way to avoid the hard physical labor of digging, however.) Sometimes it's the first step in the process, and sometimes it's the last. Different types of theories (explored in Chapter 11) include *cognitive* archaeology (humanistic, dealing with how people thought in the past), *processual* archaeology (scientific), and *culture history* (descriptive). Some may call all this "armchair" archaeology, but thinking is hard work too!

- **Ethnoarchaeology** (studying living cultures and their material stuff) and *experimental archaeology* (replicating past artifacts yourself) are two techniques used to help interpret what you're digging up. (I tell you more about these in Chapter 11).

- **Biblical archaeology** looks for evidence in the ground to support the historic record of the Bible, both Old (ancient Hebrews) and New (time of Jesus) Testaments. So it's a particular form of historical archaeology. It used to aim to prove biblical truth (and sometimes still does) but more often lately is grounded in real science (making it far more exciting).

- **Archaeoastronomy** studies how past peoples related with the sky, including aligning monuments with the sun, moon, or planets and using astronomical knowledge for religious or other purposes.

- **Garbology** is a wonderful term for the archaeology of our very modern trash, as collected weekly from our homes or deposited in landfills. It can tell us things about ourselves (consumer behavior, waste, biodegradability — described more in Chapter 2) that we can't get anywhere else. (And yes, this includes digging through movie stars' trash to find out what they're up to as well.) It's still archaeology!

Special Studies Related to Archaeology

Certain specialists in other sciences relate their work to the archaeological record. To do these specialties you need training in a whole additional area *besides* archaeology.

Zooarchaeology: Animal remains

Zooarchaeologists identify animal remains at archaeological sites. They're biologists specializing in zoology, and often in certain categories of animals (shellfish, fish, or mammals, for example). Some of the things zooarchaeology can show you about the excavated remains:

- ✔ What animal species are present at the site, as compared with what was available in the general environment
- ✔ What animals people were eating or using for some other resource (like making bone tools)
- ✔ What the environment was like based on what critters are present
- ✔ Whether the animals were domesticated and were being raised by the people or whether they were hunted or captured wild

Paleoethnobotany: Plant remains

Paleoethnobotanists can identify plant remains preserved at an archaeological site and tell some of the same things about past diets, environments, and domestication. They can see what resources people were using for other purposes (medicinal plants and drugs, industrial plants such as cotton or gourds for containers). To do this, you have to be a good botanist in the first place. Then you also have to recognize tiny plant fragments all charred, beaten up, and aged perhaps many centuries!

Archaeometry: Archaeological sciences

Archaeometry means various techniques in the physical and natural sciences (chemistry, physics, biology) used for archaeological goals. They include everything from complicated dating methods to figuring out the component elements in the artifact raw material in order to trace where it came from. You can specialize in any one or several of these.

Archaeometric techniques usually involve the use of big complex instruments in scientific laboratories and acronyms or abbreviations only understandable by the initiated. Some examples of techniques for materials analysis:

- **A scanning electron microscope (SEM)** can see details of materials at extremely high magnification — even tiny cut marks or cell walls.

- **X-rays** can show the insides of artifacts (or mummies!), as can CAT scans and other medical techniques.

- **X-ray fluorescence (XRF)** shows component elements within metals and ceramics to see the source of the material.

- **Instrumental neutron activation analysis (NAA)** also shows trace elements to tie raw materials to sources.

- **Light stable isotope analysis** (of carbon, nitrogen, oxygen, sulfur), can show mineral components of bone to see what the person or animal ate.

- **Thermal ionization mass spectrometry** (of lead, strontium) also shows bone minerals.

- **DNA analysis** gives information on plant and animal species and relatedness of human remains to different populations

I describe in Chapter 10 some further examples of archaeometric techniques used in dating archaeological finds.

What Kind of Archaeology Do You Want to Do?

You may start out with one kind of archaeology, then switch to or add another. Or you may do many at once. Certainly in most kinds of archaeology you work with specialists in other fields, sharing knowledge and maybe making new discoveries together.

Most projects combine many of the specialties described in this chapter. A good archaeologist should at least know where to send finds for finer analyses.

The particulars of the archaeology you do depend upon where you go to do it or how you get involved. If you're excavating Paleolithic hunter–gatherers foraging around the landscape for mammoth meat and edible roots, you won't need to know the trace elements in copper and silver artifacts. If you specialize in marble architecture, you probably won't need to send out any bones to the zooarchaeologist. But if you happen to excavate a 17th-century sword in your backyard while planting flowers, you may be inspired to become a historic weapons expert, as well as a conservation specialist (to learn how to keep the thing from rusting any more).

Chapter 4

How Archaeologists Think and Work

A rchaeology is detective work. You determine what you're looking for, and then gather the evidence — material clues and otherwise — and piece it together. This may involve adventure and even changing plans in mid-project, but it will certainly require some really tedious work! Then you use what you find to explain what happened in the past. Sometimes you get different or conflicting answers, so you may need to go get more evidence of different kinds.

In this chapter, I show you the steps that often take place in an archaeological project. As you may expect, a lot of planning is involved before you take part in any fieldwork. I also tell the story of a typical archaeological investigation I conducted researching a mystery mound. It led through false starts and confusing clues, but in the end, the mystery was solved — unlike many archaeological puzzles, which remain for generations of investigators to examine.

How an Archaeological Investigation Begins

The first thing to do when you begin an archaeological investigation is determine what you're looking for and why, and then how to go about finding it. After you determine this, you can decide what tools you need, what kind of schedule, how many workers, what kinds of techniques and special studies, and how long (and how much funding) it will take. Modern archaeology stresses conservation — *not* digging. You destroy the record forever as you dig, so if you're going to disturb it, you have to be asking real research questions or saving what you can in the face of some impending destruction.

For example, if you have information and artifacts from an earlier dig at an archaeological site but no idea how old it is, you can dig only a small portion to get some charcoal for radiocarbon dating. Or if you can preserve most of a site by suggesting a planned construction be moved away from it, you can excavate only the small portion that's in the way of some construction that can't be moved. In that case, you know you only need a few weeks and a few workers to dig up that part.

Determining your research goals

You may have any number of reasons to do archaeological research, such as

- ✔ You want to know about a specific issue in the past. (How old are these mounds? Why were they built? When did farming start in this region?)

- ✔ Little is known about the archaeology of a particular place, so you want to find out just what's there to be able to tell its story, perhaps for the possible descendants of the past people who made the site.

- ✔ An archaeological site has been uncovered by some disturbance (bulldozing for construction, looting), and you want to know what it is and whether it's worth saving.

- ✔ Some proposed disturbance (construction, land-clearing) may threaten archaeological sites, so you want to find out whether any are there and whether they're important and worth saving.

Keep these goals in mind as you plan your research design.

Coming up with a research design

Before you do an archaeological project, whether *survey* (looking for sites) or excavation, you need to have a *research design*. This is usually a document detailing what you're looking for in any scientific study and what your plan is to find it. It guides your work and, for archaeology, justifies why you're doing it in the first place (because you destroy your subject matter as you dig). Here's what should be in a research design:

- ✔ **The goals of the research:** What exactly do you hope to find? You typically state these goals as scientific hypotheses you want to test: "If this is true, I should find that."

- ✔ **Your methodology:** What are the sets of methods you need to reach the goals? What are your basic assumptions and *theoretical perspectives* (discussed more in Chapter 11) — in other words, ways of explaining how people behaved in the past (whether purely descriptive, scientific and analytical, or humanistic).

- ✔ **Your strategies, methods, and specific techniques:** How do they all work?

- ✔ **The logistical details:** What's the project schedule? How many people are participating?

A research design may sound difficult to compose, but it's not. Say you're looking for a lost wallet. It's not the lost ark, but it's more important right now. Your goal is to find it. Your methodology combines physically looking with talking to people. You assume it's not stolen. Your methods are to go to where you last had it and to every place you've been since. Your techniques are to rummage around (excavate, if you will) in all those places and also to ask everyone in all those places whether they've seen it. One theoretical perspective is your view that people are basically nice — if someone found the wallet, you can probably recover it at the lost-and-found center. If you don't find it, you may need to change your initial assumptions and conclude it's been stolen!

Planning the archaeological project

In Chapters 6 and 7, I tell you more about planning archaeological survey and excavation projects, respectively. Here I describe a few examples of archaeological research designs and how they fit into the entire project plan.

Archaeology, like any other science, begins in several different ways, from the well-organized, ideal long-term project to the last-minute salvage of something important to investigate before it's gone. You often change directions as you conduct the investigation.

The ideal project

The ideal archaeological investigation lists well-thought-out questions you hope to answer. You then include the "where" and "how" that you need to get the answers to those first questions, and you can't forget the "how much will it take" — not only in money but also in time, labor, and paperwork.

For example, say you're a federal archaeologist who wants to research the ruins of the old homestead in the woods over in the north section of the park. Your goals may be to get enough information to see whether it's even a significant site. If it is, you want to be able to explain it better to the visitors and protect it in the park. Your plan may include the following:

- Investigate land records in the courthouse and park archives, see who owned the site before the park bought it, and find out whether any drawings or photos of it exist.
- Look in the library or courthouse for old maps that may have the homestead on them.
- Talk to old-timers in the area who may know of the family that lived there back in the day.
- Excavate a few test squares in the yard around brick foundations of the house and barn.
- Have park volunteers help dig, screen, and process finds in the lab, and then see what you can reconstruct of the homesteaders' lives and how long ago they were there.

You estimate how long this plan will take, given the number of workers and days you have. Do the background work first (or on rainy days) so you know where the best places to dig may be. The park funds the project for as many weeks as it takes and gives you the labor and the supplies and the time in your office to write the report and management plan for the site.

The more typical project

Circumstance usually intervenes to change the ideal project. Budgets and workers get cut, volunteers may not show up, equipment breaks, weather is unseasonably awful, or the shelter you wanted to use for a lab is damaged.

In trying to track down old documents on the homestead, you find that all the archives were destroyed in the courthouse fire. However, one old map you discover in the dusty back drawer of the little local library shows several buildings on the site, not just the house and barn that appeared on the land survey when the park bought the site.

So now you have to dig in a few more areas near where those old buildings may have been to see whether you can find their "footprint" in the soil, and figure out what they were. There you find artifacts — crockery, metal tools—100 or more years older than what you expected. You get community publicity by giving a local talk and showing that this homestead actually dates to the first founding of the county. More volunteers and funding support appear! One old-timer who shows up for your talk tells you that when he was a kid he heard the place used to be a mill operation before it was just a homestead. Now you must take on historic industrial archaeology too.

Salvage archaeology

Salvage or rescue archaeology gives you little time for advance planning. Say you get a call reporting artifacts and bones eroding out of the lake shore. You have to go see what they are before you can even determine what research you need to do. Human bones are covered by strict laws, and you may even need to bring in the medical examiner. If the artifacts and bones are all washed around, you may not even be able to tell whether they're together!

It's very much like detective work: You know a murder has occurred, but you have to go examine the body and all the stuff around it and talk with the witnesses and bystanders before you know what questions to ask next. As soon as you know the murder weapon was the brother-in-law's gun (based on that material evidence, the scientific match between the gun and the fatal bullet), you begin to narrow down your investigation!

Limiting the work

Sometimes you have to compromise and give up one research possibility to get a better one accomplished. You may need to focus on what's less known.

For example, as part of a huge project in the southeastern U.S., I excavated many sites in a valley where people had lived continuously for thousands of years. We had limited time and funds; because we knew more about the later prehistoric people and really wanted information on the earliest inhabitants, we had to bulldoze away (and abandon) the later cultural deposits to excavate the deeper, older material more quickly. We had no choice because the government was building a big canal and needed us out of there fast.

Changing in the middle of the work

The nature of archaeology means that investigations *are constantly changing* in schedule, focus, and goals. You may have bad weather or equipment breakdowns. Most interesting is when you find something different from what you expected and alter your research questions, sometimes even within a single project. Changes keep archaeology exciting!

How Archaeologists Use Science

Archaeological interpretations are supported by the scientific investigation of many different kinds of evidence.

Using the scientific method and testing hypotheses

The *scientific method* works like this:

1. **You ask a question about something you observe and collect background information on what's already known about it.**

2. **You come up with possible explanations — your *hypotheses*.** These statements must be *testable* — for example, you have to be able to say, "If we find this, then we should also find that."

3. **You test your hypotheses by experimenting or otherwise collecting data that will support or refute them.** Your tests usually require new or different data from what you used to make the hypotheses.

   If the test refutes a hypothesis, you need a new explanation that's also testable. If the test upholds the hypothesis, you may want to test it again anyway with more data or different methods to keep refining your explanation.

4. **If many of your hypotheses are supported, you can use them to make a whole model of how something works.**

5. **If your model can be applied in many situations, you can develop a theory or law.**

Here's an example of how these steps may work in archaeology:

1. Archaeologists observe prehistoric burial mounds and earthworks in the eastern United States, and ask what kind of societies made them.

2. They hypothesize that these structures were built by settled societies supported by intensive maize (corn) agriculture who had the labor to create such constructions. This hypothesis is based on the background information that many cultures in the world began to build large structures and monuments after settling down and beginning to farm.

3. They excavate many of these sites containing mounds and earthworks over the years to test this idea by looking for evidence of agriculture (domestic plant fragments, cultivated fields).

DISCOVERY

Hypothesis testing at San Luis Mission

A good example of testing hypotheses came at the 16th-century Spanish mission site of San Luis in Tallahassee, Florida (which I describe in Chapter 19). It's a huge site, and funds were limited, so the archaeologist had to have a good research plan. He did small test excavations at different areas of the site. The Spanish documents said the site had a church and other European buildings, and also a big Apalachee Indian council house.

He knew Spaniards would have had rectangular buildings and Apalachee had round ones. The test dig uncovered a few large dark circles in the reddish soil. He thought these features were evidence of big timbers holding up a structure, so he cross-sectioned them to make sure they were shaped like posts. They were arranged in a wide arc, so he calculated the circumference of a round building they may have held up. He drew this circle on the ground and hypothesized that it may be a large structure. To test this idea, he excavated just a few other spots along the circle to see whether he found any more large postmolds. And he did. The pattern of the structure was huge (140 feet in diameter), so he knew it was most likely not just a Native American house but the actual council house location.

However, the hypothesis isn't supported. They find hardly any maize remains. They do find fragments of weedy local plants from small gardens, but not evidence of intensive farming. Furthermore, they find lots of bits of wild plants, showing people were still moving around collecting non-domesticated species.

With the original hypothesis seemingly refuted, the archaeologists come up with this explanation: Even if people weren't producing their own food on a large scale, or even settling in one place, they could still build massive public architecture.

Another, independent test of the hypothesis has been to examine the bone chemistry of the human skeletons. A maize diet leaves a specific signature in bone, but these skeletons show the people ate mostly wild foods.

4. The archaeologists propose a model that suggests a culture doesn't need settled farmers to build large structures or radically shape its landscape.

5. This model has been confirmed elsewhere in the world, a reminder that humans don't behave the same everywhere!

In archaeology, as in other fields, scientific methods never prove things but rather only support or reject hypotheses. The good part is that science is self-correcting — scientists perform new tests of old hypotheses all the time (although rejecting a mistaken idea can take a while).

Making assumptions about the past

You have to be careful in archaeological interpretation because you can't expect people in the past to have done things the way they're done in your society. You may find cases of hypotheses that seem to hold up under initial testing but that aren't supported by later work with newer methods. The invention of the telescope changed the way early astronomers viewed the solar system. (You mean everything doesn't revolve around the Earth?) In the same way, tools like radiocarbon dating or high-tech remote sensing methods have changed some views of the past.

For example, fancy remote sensing developed by the military made it possible for archaeologists to see things through the jungle. Areas where they thought the prehistoric Maya did only low-level agriculture showed up on the radar and sonar images with fancy raised, ridged fields and other constructions for intensive crop management. They weren't even visible on the ground because, well, it's a jungle in there!

The basic assumptions you begin with may be wrong. For example, early archaeologists in the Amazon used a theoretical perspective called *environmental determinism* — meaning the environment determines what people do. They thought that prehistoric people there were simple hunter–gatherers who were later transformed into modest farmers by influences moving eastward from the great civilizations that built pyramids in Peru. The assumption was that it was too hot and humid in the jungle to be very ambitious, so obviously people there were mostly lying around in the hammock all the time.

This thinking was of course very *ethnocentric* (judging other cultures by your own standards). It was an assumption made by scientists from temperate climates who found it difficult to get around in the rainforest. Later archaeologists found evidence of plenty of complex prehistoric Amazonian societies. They documented large mounds full of beautiful pottery, huge cultivated areas, immense earthworks, roads, and canals through the jungle. Aerial photos and satellite images helped them find patterns that they couldn't even see on the ground (because of the forest and the trees).

Case Study: The Mystery Mounds in the Florida Jungle

Here's a story from my own work to illustrate how archaeologists think, how they test hypotheses, how you can be really wrong, and how you can begin again with new assumptions and methods. It all happened over a period of many years in the large river valley where I work in northwest Florida. I'm interested in all prehistoric and historic time periods in this rural, remote area. The local people love archaeology and have been gracious over the years in sharing their knowledge and artifact collections with me and other professionals.

This valley has dozens of prehistoric mounds that date anywhere from A.D. 100 to 1500. Many of them have been common knowledge for a century or two, because people are always interested in them. But in the thick forest many still remain to be discovered as well. For me, the best way to find new ones has been to ask the people who hunt, fish, and otherwise tromp through the woods and see things. All these earthen constructions are on the riverbanks or smaller streams, so one day when some local folks told me about a mound deep in the swamp, I asked whether they could take me there.

Discovering a new mound

We went down the river in a couple of boats and then trekked a mile through the Florida summer jungle carpeted and draped in poison ivy. We finally got to a nice earthen mound sticking up out of the low floodplain. It was sitting on the bank of a tiny creek that had a couple inches of water. A prehistoric Native American mound should have contained typical artifacts. But we didn't find the tiniest potsherd or stone tool or chipped stone flake. Because most of the surface was covered in vegetation, I assumed these objects were beneath the surface waiting to be found.

Eliminating impossible interpretations

I checked the official state archaeological site file to see whether this mound was already recorded. One state archaeologist thought he'd seen it years earlier, and agreed to come with me to see whether it was the same one. We went down the river many miles; he wanted to go in the winter when it was more of a freezing swamp. The little creek was dry, so we walked along it and got to the mound, but it looked different, even bigger.

We dug a couple of shovel-test excavations this time. One into the flat ground on the creek bank, where the village that went with the mound should have been, had nothing but yellow-brown sand. The other hole, into the bottom slope of the mound, uncovered two tiny prehistoric pottery sherds in the top few inches. But far deeper was a rusty piece of iron. This discovery didn't make sense; iron would have been from later historic times and therefore should have been on top.

Things got more complicated when the state archaeologist returned to his office, got out his files with the sketch map of the mound he thought he'd visited, and found it was a different one. We conferred and realized we had *two* mounds on different bends of the same tiny creek.

We went back to map the mounds and dig more small tests, this time on the mound summits. The soil there was an interesting coarse reddish sand. But we found only a couple of more pieces of iron and a blue and white historic crockery sherd. We knew lots of hunters had been around here over the decades, but would they have brought nice plates in for their lunches?

The biggest realization was that this just couldn't be a prehistoric mound site. A prehistoric mound is a ceremonial place that people live around; their artifacts should have been everywhere, and they weren't.

Researching remaining possibilities

To paraphrase Sherlock Holmes, when you have eliminated the impossible, whatever is left — however improbable — must be the answer. If the mounds weren't prehistoric, they could only be either natural or historic in origin. We had only two other possibilities.

The mounds may have been built by the natural river flooding and dumping sands in a pile that just didn't erode away somehow. To determine this, I asked a geologist and a geographer specializing in soils to come to the site, and we dug another deep hole. The soils specialist determined the coarse reddish sand wasn't typical of low-lying swampland, and the geologist said the mounds didn't look natural at all.

So humans had made the mounds in historic times, but when and why? The first thing I did was talk with a timber company expert. I asked for any reason people would have built a mound during logging operations. He got out an old movie showing how they cut timber in the 19th century and hauled it out with mules or floated it out in canals. But they didn't pile up earth for anything. In fact, he said, that swampland probably wasn't even logged because it was so low and wet that wagons would have gotten bogged down.

In hopes of finding a clue, I decided to see whether anyone else had owned the land in the past. I went to the county courthouse to look up the land records. There I realized that the mound location was so remote, it hadn't even been surveyed into official government Sections. When I asked how I could look up something that didn't even have a section number, the lady said she didn't know, but I should ask old George.

This elderly gentleman was sitting among the deed books doing historical research. He had been the clerk of county court for 50 years, and really knew the local land. He said, sure he knew the mounds; they were Civil War forts!

Finding historical answers

George said he'd played on the mounds when he was a kid, and adults had told him they were Confederate forts, big gun batteries. But when I asked what they were doing a mile deep in the swamp, he had no answer. I knew the South had lost the war, but their generals weren't stupid. Why would they build fortifications so far from the river?

I knew I could find lots of historical documentation for the Civil War. Generals, engineers, and strategists wrote down everything they did. So I consulted a good historian who knew where to look up old documents. He found official war maps and records detailing the planning, construction, and abandonment of the two forts. These records answered the question of why the forts were so far away from the river. Turns out, they weren't.

The two forts were indeed built right on the riverbank. The tiny creek had then been the big river channel. The forts were built to defend against the invading Union navy. Slaves brought coarse red soil from upriver to make the mounds, which then became the platforms for big cannons. Whatever soil they got had those couple of prehistoric Native American potsherds in it! Then, in the river right below the forts, they placed obstructions — sunken boats, logs, and chains. The idea was that the bad guys would come up the river and be stopped, and then the Confederates could shoot them.

But the Union boats never came, and the two forts were soon abandoned. The obstructions made the river shift its channel eastward. The original channel filled in and mostly dried up, becoming the tiny jungle creek that disappeared in the dry season (see Figure 4-1). The forts became overgrown, shrouded in green foliage, and forgotten.

After learning all this, I changed tactics and went back to both forts with metal detectors. My crew unearthed more metal, nails, and even a possible cannon part. We never found the soldiers' camp, but we did march through the jungle, using the old Civil War map to locate the obstructions in the former river bed — big metal slats sticking up from the forest floor!

The investigation of the two mystery mounds is typical of an archaeological project in that the research questions and conditions often change. You find yourself looking for something different from when you started. But it's also *not* a typical project because I got final answers. Most archaeology, especially with prehistoric sites, never permits complete reconstruction of what happened in the past. At least when you have historical records you can get some idea. For more ancient times, many puzzles must remain (at least until better tools come along).

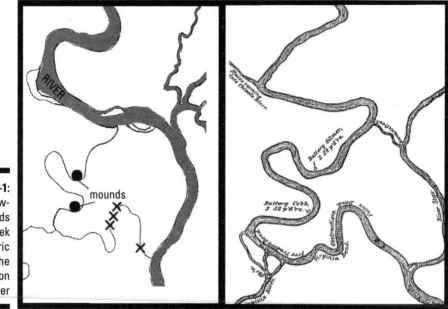

Figure 4-1:
Map show-
ing mounds
on the creek
and historic
map of the
two forts on
the river

Using the discoveries for modern applications

The information about the forts has been helpful in modern times. Scientists and engineers have been trying to explain why this river dumps so much sand just at this place, blocking navigation. I've been able to show them that the river's just trying to get back to its old natural channel, not the new one it was forced into by military tactics in times of war. Human manipulation of the natural environment is nothing new, and archaeologists can contribute a lot by showing its effects.

Part II
Archaeological Fieldwork: The Adventure Begins!

In this part . . .

The heart and soul of archaeology is fieldwork. In Chapter 5, I get you ready by spelling out the equipment and knowledge you need. Chapter 6 describes how to find sites and know where to dig. In Chapter 7, I ask and answer questions about why you're digging in the first place before delving into the logistics and daily labor of excavation. Finally, Chapter 8 explores archaeological ethics in the field.

Chapter 5

Supplies and Equipment You Need

*M*any (often unusual) kinds of supplies and equipment are necessary for a proper excavation, and this chapter covers them all. You may have small tools, big earth-moving machines, or cases of toilet paper for the outhouse! Each fieldworker brings some items personally, and the director brings some as part of the larger inventory of excavation and recording equipment. Different projects have different requirements, depending on where you are in the world, who's in charge, and what the field conditions are. The most important thing to bring is a mellow attitude. The dig will be much more rewarding if you take everything that happens (no matter how awful) as just part of the adventure!

What to Pack for Fieldwork

The field or project director usually gives you a list of what to bring. Most projects expect you to have a field pack for your own belongings, hand tools, and notebook.

All the stuff you bring on a dig stands a good chance of getting damaged or destroyed, so start with a good, sturdy — but perhaps not new — pack. Used military packs of heavy cotton canvas are great, though I always buy a ballistic-nylon bag in a bright color so I can see where I set it in the woods.

Digging and recording supplies

Ask what hand tools are supplied or whether you need to buy some for yourself. Here are typical excavation tools in an archaeological fieldworker's pack:

- **Pointed 4-inch Marshalltown trowel** (and maybe a square one too)
- **3-meter measuring tape** (harder to find than inches-and-feet increments) or other small tape
- **Butter knife, grapefruit or regular spoon, pocketknife, artist's spatula and dental pick** (ask your dentist for old or broken ones)
- **Sharpened wooden chopstick or length of bamboo** for softer digging
- **Small, cheap paintbrush**
- **Roll of plastic flagging** in a bright color
- **Water-resistant field notebook** (check dig requirements)
- **Compass** (cheap or expensive)
- **Pencils, waterproof markers, waterproof pens, and/or space pen**
- **Line level** for measuring depths from a level string
- **Zipper-lock plastic bags** of all sizes for finds

Color Figure 4 shows many of these items, including the yellow waterproof (surveyor's) notebook. If you buy them, put your name on them in waterproof marker. I often paint my tools (like trowel handles) a bright color so I can find them if they get dropped. Most U.S. archaeologists use the well-made Marshalltown brand of trowel, originally intended for bricklaying.

Other hand tools for fine excavation are sculptors' paint and clay spatulas (like mini-trowels). Old butter knives and grapefruit spoons, sharpened chopsticks, and dental picks are all handy for close work. Many such tools are available from specialty archaeology supply companies, or forestry-, scientific-, or surveying-equipment companies.

For recording, you usually want waterproof writing implements. The space pen (invented for astronauts) uses pressurized ink and writes on wet paper and upside down. It's now widely available in cheap (and expensive) varieties.

Safety and health items

All fieldwork should have safety rules, a field first-aid kit, and persons skilled in medical assistance. But bring basic supplies like aspirin or bandages. I've never heard of any archaeological project that didn't have one or more of the following: sharp metal tools, bugs, excessive sun, poison ivy, stinging nettles, occasional bad weather, heavy physical work, and lots of dirt.

Here's a list of items relating to health and safety that you may want to have on hand; you can see some of them in Color Figure 4:

- ✔ **Refillable canteen or water bottle**
- ✔ **Bandages and a small bottle of iodine or tube of antibiotic cream**
- ✔ **Prescription medicines,** clearly labeled
- ✔ **Sunblock lotion, insect repellent and something for bites/stings**
- ✔ **Aspirin, anti-diarrheal medicine, and sore muscle liniment**
- ✔ **Toilet paper and antibacterial hand cleaner**
- ✔ **Emergency food** (like a granola bar and a small bag of peanuts)
- ✔ **Tweezers** for removing slivers and stings (and unruly eyebrows)
- ✔ **Small flashlight, waterproof matches, work gloves**

Your dig leader will probably advise getting a tetanus shot (or other immunizations) before you go. Timing is important; the tetanus shot lasts ten years, but it makes your arm sore for days, so do it early.

Water

Water may be provided, but you usually want your own canteen or bottle as well. Using a refillable container is better for the planet, and you may want to buy an unbreakable, insulated wide-mouth bottle with a carry strap (write your name on it!) so you can have *cold* water and even ice cubes for an emergency such as a swelling bruise or a sting. On some digs water is scarce and so kept for drinking only, not washing.

Bug repellents and remedies

Insect repellent never repels all the bugs, but you can find many remedies for stings and bites. Besides commercial ones, you can use tobacco or meat tenderizer, which has an enzyme (papain, from the papaya plant) that dissolves protein the insect left in you. But don't get it in your eyes — it'll dissolve your cornea, too. Rub either of these treatments in with water (or spit) for a little relief.

Bathroom needs

Sanitary conditions differ from project to project. You may have a modern bathroom or an outhouse. Or you may just be out in the woods and expected to go behind the nearest bush. If this is the case, remember to bring your shovel and bury your waste (seriously). A good book (whose title my editors have censored), *How to Sh** in the Woods,* gives additional pointers on this topic.

Your field pack should have toilet paper, just in case. Flatten a partial roll and shove it into a sealed plastic bag— much better than using those nice green leaves that may be poison ivy!

Living conditions

Your living conditions depend upon the project. You may need to bring bedding for the bunkhouse, a lantern for the campground, or towels and soap. Avoid scented soap because it attracts bugs. Forget nice clothing (except for after hours) because it'll get wrecked. Leave at home personal items that can get lost or damaged. On the other hand, used paperbacks or even a guitar or other such entertainment are often welcome at the field house.

If you're physically disabled, you're not necessarily excluded from archaeological work. I've had fieldworkers who were hard-of-hearing, visually impaired, and even a guy with no hands! Some of the labor is writing, measuring, and fine digging. Children who can't do precise work can screen soils for finds or help take soil samples. They can even backfill at the end when you're just throwing the dirt back into the hole. Some field projects have included mentally disabled youth groups and the elderly. You can work out accommodation in advance. A small fold-up camp stool is useful if you can't sit on the ground, or a kneeling pad may help you dig more comfortably.

Personal needs

Your needs and habits dictate what else you should bring. Include gum, mints, lip balm, safety pins, wallet and ID, sunglasses, hand lotion (unscented), facial tissue or handkerchiefs, or whatever's usually in your pocket or purse. Women can look good in the field, so makeup is usually okay (but mascara should be waterproof!). Women should also remember menstrual supplies; keep them clean in a sealed plastic bag. When the field season begins, I put most of my purse contents into my field pack.

If you use an MP3 player or other personal listening device, be sure to ask whether it's acceptable; you may miss important directions as you dig. Also, expect that it will get covered with dirt. If you smoke, ask about the dig's smoking rules; expect to put out cigarettes on the bottom of your boot and then pocket the butts to throw away later.

Have something to read (yes, sealed in a plastic bag) in case you have to sit around waiting (for the rain to stop or the director to show up). You can also use that time to catch up on field notes or to socialize with the crew.

Dress requirements

Your project will usually recommend what to wear. Work gloves (not the garden kind — they don't last) are good, and a hat. (I use a bandanna to protect my hair from spider webs and branches.) I always require long pants and sturdy boots with steel insteps for shoveling. Some digs forbid heavy boot soles that leave a deep imprint in the soil. For other digs in soft sand and open air, shorts and thinner shoes are acceptable. A summer dig in the forested eastern U.S. often means wall-to-wall poison ivy, so long-sleeved shirts and gloves are a must.

Don't forget rain gear, even a 99-cent plastic rain poncho. (The day you forget it, rain will come!) You may want your own camera and personal journal/notebook (also labeled with your name and in waterproof containers).

If you buy new boots for a dig, break them in first by wearing them around the house or on short walks. Otherwise, your feet will hurt, which is the last thing you need during a dig.

Here's a list of items you usually should *not* bring:

- ✓ **Firearms, other weapons, or illegal drugs**
- ✓ **Valuables** such as fancy jewelry
- ✓ **Perfumes or scented soaps or lotions** — they attract even more bugs.
- ✓ **Nylon, polyester, or other synthetic clothing** if you're in a hot area

Equipment for the Survey or Dig

Field equipment depends on the project: whether it's *survey* (looking for sites) or excavation at one site, where you are in the world, and other conditions. Chapters 6 and 7 give more details on survey and excavation, respectively; here I summarize the tools you generally have provided on a project.

Supplies for recording everything you find

You want paper records even if field-rugged laptop computers and other electronic devices are available. (Batteries never die on a pencil and paper!) You'll probably have an official field notebook to write down how much you dig, what you find, and other information. You may draw finds on graph paper, perhaps using a protractor and ruler to get distance and angle you've measured with tape and compass.

Then you need to fill out many forms. A form for each *level* (arbitrary vertical amount you dig — say 10 centimeters) or *stratum* (visible natural or cultural soil layer you dig) is standard. You may also need to fill out a form to describe the *stratigraphy* (soil layering); another for features such as soil stains, house patterns, graves, or architectural fragments; and another for project photos. You list artifacts and other finds daily in a field log. Write the *provenience*, the information about where each find comes from, in the log and on the bag you put it in (using — big surprise — waterproof marker).

You'll probably also use measuring devices such as a *transit,* or electronic *total station* and a *global positioning system* (GPS) device (fancy instruments described in Chapter 7) for mapping your site. Many instruments feed data into a computer right in the field. Cameras are also important for recording.

Supplies for digging

You often lay out excavation units with string and stakes. Shovels and trowels have been standard digging tools for centuries. Even if someone invented a power shovel, it would still need hands to guide it. Finer tools are for uncovering delicate items. For a quick sample of what the deep soil may contain, you can use a soil probe, coring tool, or bucket auger (discussed more in Chapter 6).

Ideally you expose and record each item in the ground before removing it. Many projects begin with shoveling up levels of soil and throwing them into a screen for sifting. Quarter-inch mesh is the standard screen size, with smaller mesh for waterscreens. With a waterscreen, you hose away the soil — which feels great on a hot day — and leave the artifacts. You may use a *flotation machine,* (described in Chapter 7) for finer screening of soil samples.

Larger equipment

For some projects, archaeologists need larger equipment to dig. You may even use a heavy earth-moving machine such as a backhoe or a front-end loader to remove upper soils quickly, especially if you're trying to get down to a deeper stratum below the topsoil. Of course, you need a careful operator who can take off a couple of centimeters at a time and stop before hitting that whole ancient pot.

To find archaeological sites or find what's buried at a site without digging, you can use *remote sensing* methods like aerial photography, ground-penetrating radar, or metal detectors. Even if specialists with technical equipment complete these tasks, you may have to help move the instruments around. Often these tools give you a picture of some subsurface anomaly, but you still have to dig to find out what it actually is. I discuss remote sensing more in Chapter 6.

Knowledge and Skills You Need

You want to know a few things about your archaeological project before you go. What are the research goals of the fieldwork? What are the local conditions and the geography of the region like? More than anything, you want to bring along a positive attitude.

Helpful knowledge and educational background

A basic college-level archaeology course is good to have before you do fieldwork; it helps you understand the general goals of looking for sites and digging. You also want to check out the conditions (like plants, animals, rocks, and weather) you can expect in the region where the project is located. You want to know about the local people too, and what they think of the archaeology. Most of all, be familiar with the aims of the field project: What will you be looking for? What will it look like when you find it? Ask whether you can read anything about previous similar field projects and the archaeology that's already known in the area.

Geometry and mapmaking skills are helpful, as are outdoors experience and knowing how to find your way in the woods or desert or city (not to mention knowing how to read a map and use a compass).

Psychological requirements for archaeology

You may think that working outdoors, doing manual labor, remembering so many things to write down, and living with so much dirt may not be so bad — until you get that first insect bite or sore muscle.

Archaeology isn't an adult version of summer camp.

When I take students to the forests of the eastern U.S. for summer fieldwork, I promise them they'll itch, hurt, or both the whole time. I also point out that they'll be with the same crew every day (and maybe evenings too), have little time to themselves, have to dig all day and do field logs or maps all evening, and even wait in line for the shower. My students also have to take turns cooking and cleaning the camp, and we often stay in tents (so it's very intense.)

To appreciate an archaeological dig fully, you should be the kind of person who's tolerant of physical discomfort and the foibles of others when it's all for a good cause. Because the first exciting find — perhaps your first stone tool or piece of pottery — is usually enough to make it all worthwhile.

Bringing the best attitude for adventure

The very best thing you can bring to participate in archaeological work in the field, laboratory, or classroom is the eagerness and enthusiasm to carry you through any discomfort or annoyance. I always announce to my field crew that they all *will* get along no matter what, and nobody is allowed to whine. If someone has a problem, all should help (here — try my new antihistamine cream on that sting). When someone makes a wonderful discovery, all should share in it — stop their own work to exclaim over it and photograph it, laugh with the person who found it, and hope the team makes more such finds.

Don't carelessly ignore safety rules and get hurt or endanger the scientific research of the dig. You also don't want to act in such a way as to offend the local people (your hosts). Respect for the cultural resources, the finds and scientific techniques of the project, and the directors and crew chiefs is always required. If you're not sure what to do, or think you've made a mistake, always ask for help so you don't compromise the project records and finds.

Take the attitude that you're fine regardless of what happens, and that everything is part of the adventure. You never know what you may find or what may happen next, but you'll certainly end up having fun!

Chapter 6

Archaeological Survey: Finding Where to Dig

*I*n this chapter you get the answer to the perennial question asked of archaeologists: How do you know where to dig? *Archaeological survey* (discovering archaeological sites) is usually the first step in fieldwork. You first find sites and gather information and artifacts from them using little or no excavation before seeing what's important in a whole region.

What Is a Survey?

Often, your goal is to find out where sites are located in an area that no one has examined. But you can't just stick your shovel in the ground anywhere and expect to find artifacts. Though humans have probably walked over every square inch of land on Earth, they've chosen only particular places to live and conduct other activities. These choices are based on certain characteristics — like landforms, water, and other resource availability — that you need to know in order to do a better job in archaeological survey.

Survey is the searching for archaeological sites within a specific project area. You usually use multiple methods of background work combined with on-the-ground fieldwork.

Archaeological survey expeditions may target particular sites known (or suspected) from historic sources, or they may aim to test hypotheses about the kinds of places past people preferred to live, such as high ground near water. Here are some examples of typical kinds of surveys:

- You may be doing contract archaeology in a 30,000-acre proposed reservoir area or a 100-acre planned housing development. You work within specific boundaries and a tight schedule so your client (the government, a development company) can fulfill the legal regulations before construction begins.

- You may have a general research program to explore prehistoric settlement in a geographic region that has caught your interest. Here you can work at your own pace more freely across the landscape.

- Maybe you're searching for a particular site, say, a lost 19th-century town, so you search around the area shown on old maps.

Most archaeology done today is survey — locating sites in the path of some proposed construction or other land disturbance. Many laws require that cultural resources (archaeological and historic sites) be examined before earth-moving takes place. Usually, survey is necessary just to find out what's there. Then you need to see whether what's there is significant and worth saving. Before the highway, housing development, or reservoir is built, the cultural resources must be found, inventoried, and evaluated. In the U.S., even projects on private land may require this step if the proposed project is big enough (as defined by applicable laws) to affect the whole community.

Doing Background Work for Archaeological Survey

Before you begin an archaeological survey, you need to know both the reasons for and the rules of the survey. You also need to know the goals and requirements, which generally depend either on who's paying for the project or your own research aims. Before you do the fieldwork, you need to see what's already known about your project area.

Documentary sources

Written materials describing archaeological and historic sites on your project area land may be located in many places:

- Government offices can be gold mines with official site records, reports of earlier regional surveys and archaeological investigations, old maps, soil surveys, and land records. These documents may show settlements, mounds, or ruins no longer visible.

- If you're headed to the library (university or city), see if you can get your hands on a *Sanborn map,* which can help you relocate historic buildings in urban areas. The Sanborn Company provided fire insurance since the mid-19th century in the U.S., so it had maps of every building for many successive years. You can see how newer buildings covered "footprints" of older buildings. The town hall may also have these maps, and similar maps are sometimes available outside the U.S.

Be sure to check out even the small local library and/or historical society. They may have historic accounts by the first residents or travelers that can provide clues to both prehistoric sites (mounds, pueblos, or other ruins) and historic places.

↙ You can also find a great deal of historic information from Internet maps and images.

Oral history and local informants

Anthropologists call people who help them learn the local culture their *informants*. Archaeologists' informants are usually residents who know the region and can help find sites (and have already found sites). Sometimes they're from *descendant communities* whose ancestors' sites you're trying to find (and with whom you *always* communicate to do proper, ethical survey).

Here are some places you can find good archaeological informants and resource people for your survey area:

↙ Local archaeology societies and artifact collectors always know where sites are. They may share their data and allow you to photograph their finds; you may have to assure them you're interested only in learning.

↙ Historical associations at local museums or libraries collect a great deal of information not only on historic sites but also prehistoric ones. They can also tell you which local experts to call.

Archaeological survey: Expect the unexpected!

Archaeologists are known for their can-do attitude and ingenuity in dealing with unexpected situations. This image is often true on survey, where you never know what you'll find. For example, you always need permission to be on people's land looking for artifacts or talking with them about where sites may be. But be sure you know whose responsibility getting that permission is. Once I surveyed the corridor of a proposed state highway that local residents didn't want crossing their lands. I thought the state (New York) had gotten permissions in advance — but no. I had to persuade unhappy landowners to let my crew walk their cornfields looking for stone tools and ancient pottery sherds. One farmer met me at the door with a shotgun! I finally persuaded him we were on his side, and that finding something important may help move the highway away from his land (although in the long run, we didn't find any sites on his 100 acres).

✔ Foresters, loggers, land managers, surveyors, farmers, ranchers — anyone who works outdoors — all know the landscape and may be artifact collectors themselves.

✔ Elderly residents of an area are often fountains of knowledge about both historic and prehistoric sites. By interviewing them (collecting *oral histories*), you can also find out things not obvious from the archaeological record, like how more recent historic sites were used. (See how interviewing an old-timer helped my quest for a lost mound in Chapter 4.) Such people are often happy to discuss the past and how their lives used to be with someone who is really interested in documenting it.

✔ Flea markets and other local hangouts for people interested in old things are great places to ask for names of collectors. In one small town in the U.S. Southeast, my student crew and I got names from the ladies working at the ice cream shop where everyone sat around and shared local gossip.

Once I was surveying an old ranch that was to become an office park. As my crew and I twisted and pushed a hand-corer into the top of a hill that looked like a prehistoric Indian mound, the old ranch foreman drove by and stopped to say hi. He told us he'd pushed that dirt up into that mound himself while clearing to build the road and barn nearly 50 years ago! That certainly saved us some heavy labor, but if we'd found and talked to him first, we could have saved a lot more work.

Remote sensing and geographic information systems (GIS)

Remote sensing means you look for objects from afar with sophisticated technology. It's a lot like using the sensors on *Star Trek* to find out what's out there before you actually go out and see! A *geographic information system* (GIS) is a fancy computer database with layers of all your spatial information. It shows where sites may be and what kinds of places people chose to live.

Remote sensing methods

Instruments used in remote sensing can detect hidden buildings in the jungle, patterns of buried structures (like canals, roads, and walls), or even ancient living areas and *middens* (old garbage piles). Human waste may make crops or other vegetation cover grow better (or worse). With remote sensing, you can "see" what's under the ground without having to do the work of walking and digging (though the technical devices may be more expensive).

First, of course, you look at your maps — old and new, however many kinds you can find. The elevations or availability of water or other characteristics may make you suspect the presence of an archaeological site in certain spots on the map. Then you can check these spots on remote sensing images.

Here's a list of some remote sensing methods:

- ✔ **Aerial photography** has been used since World War I, when low-altitude flyers noticed interesting stuff on the landscape below. You can buy photos, get them free on different databases, or hire a plane (or hot-air balloon) and take them yourself. Even famous aviator Charles Lindbergh did aerial archaeological survey in the southwestern U.S. in 1929 and Central America in the 1930s. His wife, author Anne Morrow Lindbergh, leaned out of the plane and took pictures of ruins. (Well, they landed to take pictures too).

- ✔ **Infrared aerial photography** uses non-visible parts of the light spectrum. It can show patterns invisible to normal photography.

- ✔ **Radar systems** used from space can penetrate clouds, jungle, or sand to give images far different from photographs. The driest place on earth, the Sahara desert, is just monotone sand in photographs. But in radar imagery, it's crisscrossed with branched forms — old channels cut by running water in the wetter, remote past.

- ✔ **Proton magnetometers** depend on slight differences in magnetism to locate anomalies, especially metal objects. They're most used for underwater survey and spotting shipwrecks or other submerged features.

- ✔ **Satellite imagery** (whether purchased or free from a Web site) is *multispectral* — it sees what your eyes can't. So you can see anomalies that may be buried cultural features.

Although geophysical survey methods done for remote sensing may be difficult to learn, they're useful, powerful tools. However, you still have to go out and *see* what's actually out there! That zigzag anomaly on your screen or printout may be a lost wreck of a historic steamboat, but it also may be someone's old refrigerator or Grandma's discarded Model-T!

Remote sensing is a rapidly growing area of archaeological research (and see Chapter 7 for additional techniques used right on the archaeological site). Most of the technology was pioneered by the military to see what the enemy had on the ground, but it's now widely available to scientists or anyone for more-peaceful uses. Even GPS receivers are now more accurate since the U.S. military unscrambled the satellite signals, and the images from space keep improving. The U.S. National Aeronautics and Space Administration (NASA) now even has its own archaeology division!

Geographic information systems

A geographic information system (GIS) is a computerized set of different "layers" of data. For example, you may have a GIS with separate layers for your site's water sources, elevations, vegetation types, bedrock, and archaeological sites you've already found out about. All the layers are then *georeferenced,* or tied into the map with exact coordinates.

When you overlay these different layers onto the map, you see interesting patterns to guide your survey. For example, all the earliest prehistoric sites may cluster along one stream or over one type of bedrock. You then go to those areas to see whether you can find any more such sites. You can even overlay the modern road system layer to get directions on how to get there.

GIS applications include lots of complicated computer modeling and hypothesis testing. In the previous example, you may hypothesize that the archaeological sites were quarries where people got raw material for stone tools from surface outcrops of that bedrock. They lived along and used the stream because it was easier to carry that heavy rock in a boat!

GIS techniques may take a while to master, but they get faster every year with new software and hardware. And using computers is much faster than manually coloring in squares on sheets of sheer graph paper overlaid on top of your maps to get different GIS layers (and yes, some archaeologists actually used to do this)!

Be careful you don't get so tied up in the technology that you forget you're looking for clues on human behavior in the past! A danger with using remote sensing and GIS is that the end goal may become mastering the equipment and expertise or producing awesome maps rather than answering archaeological questions. Remote sensing, other instrumentation, and GIS are just the beginning, never the end product. They're archaeological tools, just like a shovel.

How do you know where you are?

This is always a great question on archaeological survey (as in life). Reading maps that haven't been updated in years can get an archaeologist quite lost! You can start at a known place on the map and pace or measure with a long tape an exact distance, taking the direction with your compass. Or you can aim to walk to other landmarks on the map — but then they may be ambiguous, or gone. Or you can use a *global positioning system* (GPS) device that bounces signals off satellites to pinpoint your location. Accuracy depends on how much you pay for the GPS unit; a hand-held device costing $100 should get you within 100 feet or better. A multi-thousand-dollar unit with other fancy features will have accuracy to within a couple of inches.

You can put a dot on your map to show your (or your site's) location. You probably also want numerical coordinates from your map or GPS receiver. You can measure these coordinates in degrees, minutes, and seconds of latitude and longitude, but most archaeologists use UTM (Universal Transverse Mercator) coordinates. Sixteenth-century Flemish geographer Gerardus Mercator first thought up this system of measuring a round globe (like the Earth) on a flat surface. UTM coordinates are measured in meters and given in northing and easting numbers within zones on a grid covering the earth.

As you do field survey, you can plug your GPS unit into the computer and get the site locations you've recorded put onto a GIS layer. But even with fancy electronic devices, you still need a map. The batteries never die on a map!

Preparing for Archaeological Fieldwork

After your background work is finished (or at least well underway), you can begin to plan the field survey. Besides getting a good crew and equipment, you want to plan for any specific conditions you may encounter.

Assembling a crew and assessing field conditions

A good field crew makes all the difference. Because archaeology is hard work, the crew must have good knowledge and attitudes. (For more on proper field knowledge and mindset, head to Chapter 5.)

The perfect crew

You want to have people whose skills complement one another and who've already helped plan the work. If you're a perfect crew member, you know car engine mechanics, computers, mapmaking, emergency medicine, writing and precision note-taking, photography and videotaping, historical methods, outdoor basics, social graces, and ethnographic methods (to interview local people and get information on landscapes and sites). And you have a charming and mellow personality and love physical labor in the hot sun or biting cold (or biting flies — all part of the adventure).

Field conditions

You have to try to anticipate field conditions, from weather to the kinds of finds you may discover. If it's the rainy season, bring your plastic rain poncho. (Actually, bring several cheap ones because they'll get torn up by the tree branches or shovels.) If you're near wetlands and expect to find waterlogged artifacts, you need closed containers to keep them wet until they can be stabilized. If you're going to be far from town, get enough food and water for the day and know how far the nearest hospital is. Always bring enough toilet paper for woods, outhouses, and even gas station restrooms!

Field safety is crucial: Every project needs a first-aid kit, directions to the nearest emergency room, and a safety plan with rules and procedures!

Wherever you are, find the nearest coffee shop, ice cream parlor, local bar, or other hangout. It'll be a great source of both relief and knowledge. Not only can the crew get refreshment at the end of a rough day, but you also attract the attention of the local people. When they see you're so dirty and your truck says "archaeology," they often start telling you about their artifacts and sites they've found themselves!

Gathering survey equipment

In Chapter 5, I describe equipment and supplies you need in your individual field pack. The survey team will need even more stuff for general use. Some projects have a toolbox or a whole truck neatly packed for each crew (because different crews may cover different areas). Other teams have shovels and other tools loose and rattling around the vehicle every time it hits a bump.

Much of your equipment depends on the type of survey and geographical location. Here's a list of some typical survey crew equipment:

- Shovels, trowels, coring tools, augers, finer digging equipment, and screens (usually quarter-inch mesh) for digging and sifting.

- Colorful flagging tape, pin flags, or other tags for marking the locations of finds so you can easily return to them after lunch.

- Machetes for clearing forest paths and root cutters for the obstructing branches or vines.

- Multiple copies of maps and directions for finding your way around; have one set laminated or waterproofed just in case.

- Measuring tapes, rulers, compasses, graph paper, and clipboards for sketching maps, drawing finds, and recording locations on maps. You also may want GPS units and laptop computers (with extra batteries) to record coordinates of finds and enter data as soon as possible; another option is waterproof notebooks and pens (which never need batteries).

- A *Munsell color book* helps you record soil colors by matching them to very precise, numbered color chips (but this job is probably best left to someone who's not colorblind).

- Waterproof markers, plastic bags, and magnifying glasses for marking, inspecting, and storing finds. Sturdier containers such as plastic vials or old film canisters are good for fragile items.

- Special forms for recording various operations like individual cores or shovel tests or daily worker hours. Each project may have different types of forms.

- First-aid kit, insect repellent (and remedies for after they bite you anyway), sunblock, rain gear, extra work gloves and sun hats, long-sleeved shirts, or mosquito head-nets for protecting the crew from the elements.

- Water and food for keeping the crew from keeling over. A big cooler keeps water cold and allows refilling of individual canteens.

- Copies of all paperwork, official identification, and permissions for assuring landowners (and the local sheriff) that you've been okayed to walk on the land and dig.

✔ Reliable vehicles for transporting the crew to and around the project area. These may include sturdy cars, trucks, 4-wheel-drive vehicles, a boat and trailer, all-terrain vehicles, or whatever else is called for by the situation.

✔ Basic tools for carpentry, mechanics, and equipment repair. These supplies can include anything from a toolbox for helping in vehicle breakdowns to files for keeping shovels and trowels sharp to duct tape and lubricating oil (which always come in handy for various purposes).

Using what's already known to plan field survey

Your survey goals help you plan each day's work. You want to complete inspection of the project area in the allotted time, so you may aim to cover so many acres or target zones per day. If sites are already recorded on your map, you want to field-check them to see whether they're still there, or to get an idea of what typical artifacts and site locations look like. If you have different types of terrain, you may do the difficult places (thick forests, high plateaus to climb) first. Or you may do the easy stuff first if you're out of shape from sitting around the office or lab and need to get in condition for fieldwork!

Maps are the best planning devices. During background work, you should have which areas on the map showed good potential for having archaeological sites. Maps also show where disturbed ground surfaces may have exposed artifacts, or a historic building foundation may be present. You can see where you may be able to drive in and where the only access is on foot. (Or by helicopter — at least one archaeologist searching for Mayan sites in the jungle has done survey by chopper.) Land conditions (and budget) dictate whether you can drive in easily or need 4-wheel-drive (or a mule).

If you haven't finished background work, days of inclement weather can be spent visiting the local town hall records, interviewing people, or staying back at the camp or field house washing artifacts (or doing laundry or cooking, if those services aren't provided for you).

Doing the Field Survey

After all this planning and background work, you're ready to go out into the field and make discoveries! You may be simply walking over open ground, inspecting the surface for artifacts. Or you may be crashing through the forest and digging small shovel tests to see what's hidden below ground.

The most crucial point to keep in mind is that you *have to* take the time to write down your site discoveries and artifact finds on the bags, in the notes, on the map and forms, in the computer, and other places, too. Otherwise, you're just looting!

Doing a surface investigation

Much archaeological survey consists of driving around looking for standing ruins or open ground where the surface is visible and you can find artifacts. This *surface inspection* is still the easiest, most common way of finding sites.

Open deserts or other exposed places are easier to survey if human activity left ruins still visible on the ground that you can see even from your vehicle. Sometimes called *windshield survey* this kind of quick reconnaissance can give you an idea of what's there. But you really need to get out and walk around the sites to get more information and samples of artifacts and *ecofacts* (animal or plant remains used by people, like food garbage).

Where vegetation covers the ground, look for exposed places, like plowed fields or dirt roads. The turning of the soil unearths artifacts, and if they've been rained on they may be washed clean and sitting on little pedestals of dirt, waiting for you to find. But be careful of damaging crops as you walk! Ask farmers if they've already picked up certain types of artifacts, so your results aren't biased by the absence of these types among your finds.

Even in pastures and forests, you can surface-collect in churned-up areas from cattle hooves, wild-hog rooting, or burrowing animals' diggings. Any disturbed, open ground can expose artifacts or soil blackened by human use.

Doing subsurface survey

When vegetation cover (forest, jungle, or even pasture grass) prevents you from seeing anything on the ground surface, you've got to dig. Even in open places with surface artifacts, you want to know what else may be buried. Here are some of the most common subsurface survey methods.

Shovel testing

Shovel testing is the most standard method of subsurface survey. You dig a hole 50 centimeters (about two shovel-widths) square and up to a meter deep (depending on your strength, your soils, and your project requirements). Some crews cut corners and dig round holes — though this method is faster, I don't recommend it because you can't see the soil layers as well.

Shovel tests are big enough to uncover a good sample of artifacts. You screen soils as you dig, so a two-person team — one to dig, one to screen — is good. A three-person team can have someone record locations, soils, and finds while the others dig, and the jobs can rotate. (A four-person team can have someone to go out for coffee or stand around and tell jokes.)

Shovel tests are sometimes called *test pits,* but this terminology is confusing because *pit* is also a term for an archaeological feature (such as an ancient fire pit or garbage pit). Shovel tests are also differentiated from *test excavation units* (or test units), which are for formal, more controlled (and slower) excavation. (See Chapter 7 for more on test excavation units.)

Coring or soil probing

Other, faster methods of digging a tiny bit use various kinds of tools available from forestry, engineering, or geology supply companies. Here are some of them:

- ✔ **Hand augers or coring tools** can go deeper than you can in shovel tests. I often core into the bottom of shovel tests just to make sure nothing is down there. You can buy 3- or 4-inch bucket augers or even use a bulb planter. You turn and push these tools into the soil and pull up a solid sample of soil (and maybe artifacts). Sometimes this process takes a lot of strength if you're in clayey soils.

- ✔ **Posthole diggers** are cheap, easy to find in hardware stores, and easy to use. They don't go deep but do require a lot of strength.

- ✔ **Soil probes** are usually small-diameter tubes you push into the ground to pull up a sample that you can see in the cut-away side of the tube. On the downside, they may not be able to go very deep, and depending on your soil, you may get them stuck in the ground and have to call someone stronger to pull them out.

- ✔ **Power augers** are large drills, usually gasoline-powered, with handles. They go down fast but are heavy, noisy, and expensive (and can be dangerous if you're not hanging on). They also churn up the soil into bits and may break artifacts.

For any of these smaller subsurface exploration methods, you have to be careful that soil from up above isn't falling into the bottom of the hole you've dug. You don't want the confusion of finds from a later time period falling down to depths that may contain earlier, deeper materials. Often you can tell by color whether your soils have mixed.

For all subsurface sampling you do, you always need to backfill the hole! It's not only the professional thing to do, but it's also better for the safety of everyone (including whatever animals may come walking along). You may want to put the soil you dig out on top of a tarp, so that it's easier to slide and dump back into the hole.

Sampling in archaeological survey

You can't inspect and shovel-test everywhere, so you need to sample. How you determine where, how, and how much to take in your sample depends on survey conditions and goals. In some cases, whoever is requiring the survey may specify the kind and amount of sampling they want you to do.

Your *sampling unit* may be a square mile, an acre, a square on a grid that you establish, or even a *transect* (line across your project area) that you pick to inspect. Your *sample size* (how many units to examine) may depend on fancy mathematical calculations. But most often you determine it by how much time and money you have and how much space you have to cover.

Non-probabilistic or judgmental sampling

Non-probabilistic or *judgmental sampling* is a fancy way of saying that you look for archaeological sites where you think they may be, based on your knowledge of the area. Or it may mean looking every place that's easily accessible within your time frame.

The advantages of judgmental sampling are

- ✔ You find a lot of sites fast.
- ✔ You find out about the area's archaeology.
- ✔ You collect baseline data that you can build on.

The disadvantages of judgmental sampling are

- ✔ You won't find any sites in unexpected areas.
- ✔ Your sample is biased, not necessarily representative of the whole area.
- ✔ Your scientific, quantitative (statistical) study may not be as accurate.

Probabilistic sampling

Probabilistic sampling means you use mathematical methods that give you a less biased, more representative sample. (This is how opinion polls work — asking only a few thousand people and projecting to the whole country.) Probabilistic sampling comes in three forms:

- ✔ **Random:** Every sample unit has an equal chance of being chosen. This kind of sampling is unbiased and easy to do: You assign numbers to sample units and then pick numbers randomly by computer or random number tables (but not by pulling numbers out of a hat — your hand introduces bias). Disadvantages are that the units picked may cluster in only one part of the project area, and that you're not putting your existing knowledge of the archaeology here to good use.

✔ **Systematic:** You choose sampling units at a fixed interval (such as every third unit). This method is great to get good coverage of a whole area, but it may miss archaeological sites that happen to be aligned according to the same system or to a smaller system. So you may systematically dig a shovel test every 100 meters across your area, but if typical sites are usually only 40 meters wide, you may miss them. Even if you dig every 50 meters, you may just happen to end up in the space between the sites.

✔ **Stratified:** You divide up the project area into meaningful parts (or *strata*) and then sample within each one. Three typical strata may be the areas around the house, next to the river, and on top of the hill. You can then sample within those three strata by random, systematic, or judgmental means.

Most archaeologists use some combination of these sampling strategies. For example, you may do shovel testing at 30-meter intervals in the area next to the river, which has a high probability for site location, and at 100-meter intervals in the areas farther from water, which have a lower probability for past human settlement. This would be a stratified systematic sample. You may throw in a couple of judgmentally placed shovel tests too, just to cover some gaps on your survey map and leave no large zones uninspected.

You need to know how to pace 30 meters or 100 meters and dig the next shovel test — just measure your paces and calculate how many you need. As you dig your tests or inspect the surface, you also put the information on the map, maybe by color-coding shovel tests according to whether you found anything in them and cross-hatching all surface-collected areas.

Record everything during archaeological survey!

You may think some information is irrelevant during survey, and you don't have time to write everything. But you never know what may become important.

On one survey, I found an early 19th-century Creek Indian village in what was now a park. During surface collection, the crew got a few pieces of Native American pottery, chipped stone, and sherds of British china and black glass. We then dug shovel tests to look for undisturbed cultural deposits and to see whether the site had been bulldozed away during the construction of the park. When one test uncovered a feature with artifacts in it, I jumped in my truck to drive over to the other shovel-testing team with the news. The tailgate window was open, and when I hit a bump too fast, it crashed down and shattered. Good thing I recorded this mishap. Much later in the lab we found tiny squares of clear glass in two bags. I knew it didn't look like 19th-century stuff, and the notes confirmed that these bags were open in the back of the truck the day the window broke, and bits of modern safety glass had flown into them.

Recording where stuff comes from: Provenience

Provenience is a crucial concept in archaeology. You may be familiar with the idea of the *provenance* of an artwork; next to the art in the museum, you see a little card showing the artist's name, the materials used, what year it was created, and a catalog number. In archaeology, the *provenience* (the more common way of spelling it) is all that and more. It's all the information about a find that may possibly be useful. Without it all your finds are scientifically useless, and all the work you've done planning and surveying is for naught. Keep provenience in mind in every kind of archaeology you do. That shouldn't be too hard because you'll be writing it on all your forms, notes, and bags of finds.

Provenience data may include

- The project name and institution.
- The name of the person recording the information and the others on the crew.
- The date, day of the week, and even the time of day (because the position of the sun and shadows may have influenced your finding something).
- A verbal description of the location ("on the surface of the southern end of the field, in the darker soil right next to a cow patty, 5 meters south of Smith Road and 100 meters east of its intersection with Brown Road" or "in Shovel Test 2, depth of 40 centimeters, in the darker soil").
- Exact location coordinates from the map or GPS.
- The name and number of the archaeological site containing the find; you can make up names and provisional numbers as you go along, and then get official site numbers later — check out "Site numbering and naming" in the next section for more on this process.
- Any other information that seems important ("donated by Farmer Brown, who says he found it in the darker soil on the south end of his field five years ago when he was plowing," "found in the screen," or "found in the shovel test before the dirt was shoveled out and into the screen").

Recording, photographing, and interviewing

In archaeology, you lose what you don't record. Your notes and records are probably even more important than the finds themselves; even if you lose an artifact, you can still study and find out about past human behavior from it if you have its photo and know its provenience.

As you locate new sites or relocate old ones, you need to write everything down in your own field notes, record sites on the map by number and name, and list your finds, sites, and other data on various forms. You also want to record in other media like photography and videotaping — not only the crew, the sites, and the finds but also the information, the sources, and the local people pertaining to your project.

Site numbering and naming

You may have your own numbering system for new sites that you find, but in most places you get official site numbers. In the U.S., the system begun by the U.S. National Museum (Smithsonian) and now used in every state has the following codes:

- ✔ The number of the state in alphabetical order (by the contiguous 48 states — Alaska, Hawaii, and Washington, D.C., are 49, 50, and 51, respectively). So Alabama is 1, Georgia is 9, Mississippi is 22, and Ohio is 33.

- ✔ The official county abbreviation, usually the first two letters of its name. So Ross County, Ohio, is 33Ro, while Itawamba County, Mississippi, is 22It. But Hocking County, Ohio, is 33Ho and Houston County, Alabama, is 1Ho.

- ✔ A number corresponding to the order in which sites are found or recorded in a given county. So 22It606 was recorded before 22It622.

Site names are assigned by whoever records them. You can use the name of the landowner or local informant, of a nearby geographical feature such as a lake or canyon, the original historic name, or something particular about the site. I've recorded the Yellow Flower site and the Stuck Truck site after memorable experiences at those places.

So 8Ja2777 may be the 2,777th recorded in Jackson County, Florida, and named the Smith-Brown site after both its owner and its discoverer. 8Ja2, the Mound near Kemp's Landing, was found and recorded a century ago and only later given an official number. In the U.S., inventories of recorded sites are kept in State Historic Preservation Offices (SHPO), which also house those old maps. These offices also officially issue the site numbers for the sites you've discovered.

Site forms

The SHPO will also have the official *site forms* for you to record sites. Some states' forms are complicated and require many pages of information and instructions. Many forms and directions are now online. Some states have simpler forms for amateur archaeologists; they'd rather amateurs file the easier forms than not file at all. Many states want you to complete the form before they will give you an official site number.

Here's the basic information needed for an archaeological site form to record new sites or update the data on previously known sites:

- Site name, number, date of recording, and name of recorder
- Location, exact coordinates, description of how to get there, and attached map (such as a U.S. Geological Survey quadrangle map) showing where the site is
- Type and age of site, or of various components of the site
- Geographical setting — landform, nearest water, elevation, vegetation cover, soil types, and so on
- Sketch map or drafted map and photos of the site
- Names of landowners and people with collections and information from the site
- Artifacts and other finds from this site, including which ones indicate particular time periods or activities, and where these materials are now stored
- Significance of the site, especially in terms of the criteria specified in the National Register of Historic Places (the U.S. list of really important sites), and why you judge the site to be significant or not
- How you found the site and what work you did there
- How disturbed the site is — whether it has intact cultural deposits below the surface (or whether you can even tell this at all)
- What the site's being used for today (and whether that can threaten the archaeological deposits) and what you think it was used for in the past
- Name of the person doing the form (if different from the one recording it), institutional affiliation, address, phone number, and e-mail address
- Titles of any reports or publications on the site (including the survey report on your project that you should start writing)

Really unexpected conditions during an archaeological survey

Here's a story of how I experienced *really* unexpected conditions during archaeological survey in the southeastern U.S. The job called for inspection of the banks along a big river to find prehistoric and historic sites that may be endangered by erosion. The river had a huge dam, and I was warned that sometimes they opened or closed its floodgates to generate electrical power. This event could of course affect navigation conditions, but a big warning horn would sound before it happened.

One cold January day, my partner and I tied up our little survey boat to a small branch and climbed up the steep bank. We proceeded to find lots of artifacts on the surface of a plowed field. It was a huge prehistoric site, and our packs were laden with heavy stone tools and potsherds. We began to climb down to get lunch and cameras out of the boat when we discovered that the floodgates had apparently been closed, preventing water from flowing out of the dam. We hadn't heard the horn because we were over a mile downstream. The water level in the river had dropped some 15 feet, and

our little boat was hanging vertically, dangling over the rock of the lower bank. Our lunch, life jackets, and camera had fallen out and were floating downstream!

My heroic partner jumped into the river to save the camera. Just then the little branch broke and the boat plunged down into the water so fast that it sank (we'd forgotten to plug the flotation holes under the seats!). I threw him a rope and pulled him out. Then, as he sat drying in the cold winter sun, I hiked up the bank again, through the fields and into town (because this was before cellphones). I got the government rescue vessel to pull up our boat and tow it back to the ramp. It was so heavy from taking on water that, when we finally winched it up out of the river and onto the trailer, it broke the axle! So we had quite an equipment repair bill. The camera was saved, even though its waterproof case hadn't been closed. The film was wrecked, but the photo log was intact except for three entries that we had written in non-waterproof ink.

Other recording tasks during survey

Some projects require you to fill out forms for each shovel test. Others just ask for detailed notes describing everything. Most surveys need photographs of every site found, and of the general landforms (forests or lake shores). Photos can help justify your survey strategy — "We couldn't shovel test there because that low area was underwater at that time of year." Videotaping is also useful as a way to remember everything (but you probably won't get an award-winning film of your muddy crew, or their dialog when they're tired or bug-bitten).

Cataloguing and caring for your finds

During survey, you keep exact records of the locations of your sites and finds. You also list all the materials you recover (and their proveniences) in a *field catalog* (inventory), with entries for each bag of materials from each site.

Even in the field, treat finds carefully. Artifacts take on new (and misleading) scratches and other characteristics if they're rolling around in a bag together — they may even break! Cushion fragile items and store them in boxes. If you didn't bring plastic bubble wrap, beat-up field shirts are great! Liquor stores have sturdy boxes (in case you ever visit those places during survey). You may want to wash some finds to see what they are. But never use the crew drinking water — you may run out and have to quit early.

Most important, be sure you don't lose provenience information that goes with the materials. Taking a couple specimens out of different bags to compare them is dangerous — you need to remember which bags they came from. Better to write a catalog number right on the artifacts first!

Planning for adverse field situations

Field conditions and findings are predictable only so far. Different circumstances may require you to change techniques, adjust (or accept) problems, and/or get outside help. You may be denied permission to look on some land, find it takes longer than you thought to cover an area, or encounter various safety hazards (anything from dumped toxic waste to an angry bull in a pasture). Or you may find that much of the land is already bulldozed away and that sites that may have been there are destroyed. So you can quit early and stop at that coffee shop or bar to find out what may once have been there.

You have to be ready for any disaster or expedition mishap. Batteries die, equipment breaks down, and sometimes your GPS (and emergency cellphone) won't work because satellite signals aren't picked up in thick forest. Serious injuries can happen, too, so have a safety plan before you go! Remember, the sites, artifacts, and evidence of the human past are valuable, but they're not worth getting hurt or seriously injured for. (But tired and sore are okay.)

Deciding when to get outside help

Certain finds require additional expertise. Standing historic structures or ruins may be best interpreted by an architectural historian. Conservation specialists can stabilize fragile artifacts. Those local people may be helpful enough to show you where things were or rescue you when your vehicle breaks down! If they're descendants, they may even interpret your historic artifacts because they know what their great-grandparents used them for.

Specialized surveys require particular additional work (and jargon). For example, surveying the small squares of land where cellphone towers are to be built means surface inspection and possibly shovel testing. But you also have to evaluate the *viewshed*. This urban-planning term means how the proposed tower will affect what you can see — whether its construction will interrupt the scenic or historical value of the landscape.

Writing Up Your Survey Findings

So you've walked plowed fields and roads, driven all over the place, and come back from the field with many boxes of great finds and piles of paper-work and computer data. Now it's time to put it all together and see what you have and how it answers the original questions guiding your survey.

Before you even write up your results, remember that laboratory work and processing and interpreting finds and data always require *much more time* than it took to find everything. I discuss lab work more in Part III.

Writing what you've found

Your survey may or may not have a specific deadline and report guidelines, but it always covers everything you've done and found. Here's a list of what's usually in your report or other written product:

- ✔ The survey goals, requirements, and why you did the work

- ✔ The environmental background (current and past environments, if possible) of your project area, including maps and maybe a GIS data-base (which I discuss in the section "Remote sensing and geographic information systems (GIS)" earlier in this chapter)

- ✔ The archaeological and historical background of your project area, including sites that were already recorded before you began the survey

- ✔ Your survey strategy, methods, and techniques, including why you chose them and how you made decisions

- ✔ The sites you discovered (or previously known sites you went back to), everything you found at and found out about them, whether they're culturally significant, how disturbed they already are, and whether they may be useful for further research

- ✔ A summary of what all your information means about human behavior in the past in this survey area

✔ What you recommend be done about all these prehistoric archaeological sites, historic sites and structures, and any other cultural resources (such as an old cannon you unearthed or a waterfall you discovered was sacred to the native people). Discovering whether cultural resources need more research before proposed construction or whether construction plans should be changed to avoid and preserve them may be the main reason for survey

✔ What additional research can be done here or in similar areas to enhance the knowledge you've obtained or to test hypotheses further

✔ How your findings may be interpreted to the public — local residents, descendant communities, and the wider audience (tourists, landmark commissions, schoolkids, prospective buyers of homes in the proposed housing development — the possibilities are endless)

Making a contribution to archaeological knowledge

No matter what the size of the archaeological survey or how long it takes, you're ethically obliged to produce something describing your work. Mostly your survey report describes the *settlement patterns* — how archaeological sites you found occur over space and time. You can answer bigger questions too, like how far people had to go to get things they wanted. Did you find carved prehistoric seashells 500 miles inland? That's a pretty good sign that trade and exchange systems extended over huge distances. You may even relate your findings to modern issues like whether prehistoric people abandoned the area or rebuilt after a hurricane or earthquake. Then you see whether you can relate your findings to any living people — for example, if you found the original homesteads of the modern residents' ancestors.

Culture change is another aspect you can document, especially if you have sites and materials from different time periods. Did prehistoric farmers settle closer to rivers than earlier folks so that they could grow crops better there? Did people move away from rivers when railroads made transport faster? Discovering these kinds of culture changes helps you understand past human behavior in many different ways.

Finally, you want to write the results of testing your ideas about the human past and new hypotheses for future surveys to investigate.

Your report will be the *only* record of many of the archaeological sites you write about before they're destroyed, so write up well what you do find!

Chapter 7

The Archaeological Dig

. . . .

. . . .

In Chapter 6, I showed you how to know where to dig — how to find archaeological sites. In Chapter 5 you saw a list of everything you need to bring along and how to prepare for fieldwork. Now it's time to dig!

You can't just start throwing dirt around, however; you need detailed procedures and techniques. This chapter describes how you plan and carry out an archaeological excavation.

Questions to Ask Before You Dig

Before you dig, you have to make sure you're doing it for the right reasons, in the right places, and for the right kinds of results.

Does your reason for digging justify destroying the site?

The first important issue is your reason for digging. Archaeological excavation, by its very nature, obliterates the cultural remains you want to study — *digging means destroying!* It's very much like taking a medical biopsy from your body. If you're going to slice off a piece of flesh to examine, you'd better be able to justify such a barbaric and invasive practice.

If your site is going to be bulldozed in the path of some construction anyway, you want to get all the information you can for the amount of time, money, and labor you have available. But if your site is protected — for example, in a public park — you need a good explanation for why you want to disturb it.

So why are you digging?

You have many kinds of goals for your dig. Some are similar to what you're looking for when you do archaeological survey (detailed in Chapter 6), but some specific to one site only. Then you also have the lofty theoretical goals of social science (as I detail more in Chapter 11). A few examples of these types of excavation goals, moving from specific to general, include

- Recovering certain kinds of remains or exposing one area of the site to understand it
- Reconstructing what happened at your site in the past and when
- Figuring out the functions of the site and its parts
- Interpreting the significance of the material things you're finding to the original people who made and used them
- Understanding the processes of change or stability at your particular site and in the general region

Have you organized your research?

For any excavation, you want to know in advance what you're looking for. Of course, you'll probably find other things you weren't looking for — that's part of the adventure of archaeology! So anticipate the unexpected as well.

When you plan a dig, it's different from planning, say, construction. For a building, you can estimate how many board-feet of lumber you need, how many boxes of nails, roof shingles, doors, and so forth. Even then, you run into unexpected circumstances like weather and wastage. But you have a drawing of the building and know what the finished product is supposed to be. Archaeological digs are even harder to plan because you never know what you'll find, and the circumstances may change in mid-project when you unearth far more complex remains or far deeper layers than you expected.

Research design

Before you dig, you need to write a *research design* or plan for your work. It should include the following:

- The research questions and goals of the investigation (what kinds of things you hope to discover about the human past)
- Verification that you got the required permits from governments or permission from landowners to do the dig
- What procedures you'll use
- How much you'll dig and with what methods, crew size, and equipment

✔ What results you expect, and what you'll do if you encounter anything unexpected

✔ How you'll treat the finds and information you recover

✔ What will happen to the site after the dig

✔ What analyses you'll do of the whole project and materials

✔ What kind of reports you'll write and for whom

✔ Where and how the materials you excavate and notes and records will be stored for any future researchers or other interested people

Research questions

Your research questions can be numerous and are often based on what you already know. Here are some examples:

✔ You may be looking for basics to identify the site — how old it is, what kinds of remains it may have, and whether any of it is still undisturbed.

✔ If you know about a part of the site already, you may want to find other parts. For example, you've got the pyramid or palace, so now you want to find where and how the common people lived.

✔ You may be seeking a specific detail — like charcoal for dating or animal and plant remains for reconstructing environment and subsistence.

✔ You may need particular materials or data to test your hypothesis. For example, you may target finding many different types of stone artifacts to analyze their raw materials. Then you can see whether they were made in the same place or came from different places. Your research goal is to trace trade and interaction between different societies across the landscape.

✔ At historic sites, you may be looking for findings that support or refute your historic hypothesis that, say, a foundation represents the home of a known person or that people's lives were different from written descriptions.

Are you doing test excavation or larger-scale data recovery?

Test digs use smaller excavation units (maybe 1-x-1-meter squares or a single trench) just to see whether the site contains interesting and undisturbed cultural deposits. Here I'll use the terminology of cultural resources management archaeology (CRM) because it's the most common today; see discussions of CRM in Chapter 3. In the CRM lingo, *test excavation* is Phase II, a limited amount of digging. After doing survey (Phase I) to locate sites, you may test a few that look promising to see whether they're significant enough to merit further work, especially if they're scheduled to be destroyed.

Outside the CRM world, you may test a few different sites to get an idea of the archaeology in a previously unstudied region or to compare them in relation to specific characteristics.

Phase III is *data recovery* because you dig as much as you can before the unavoidable destruction of a site. (However, this is kind of a misnomer because you recover data in all stages.) You may also hear it called *adverse impact mitigation* or *salvage excavation*. Outside CRM, many sites are excavated on a larger scale just to continue pursuing old research issues and investigate new ones. Large excavations like this are sometimes called *block* or *area* excavations.

Have you considered remote sensing?

In Chapter 6, you see the benefits of using remote sensing (fancy instruments and techniques that "see" below ground without digging) to find archaeological sites during survey. Remote sensing is useful to investigate individual sites you're going to dig as well. Techniques include examination of aerial photographs and satellite images to see patterns on the ground from afar, as well as machinery and procedures you bring to your site and use on the ground surface. One of the latter methods is chemically testing soils to see which parts of the site show greater or lesser amounts of human activity — people always leave garbage and residues.

Other on-site remote sensing methods fall into the category of *geophysical prospecting*. They are techniques involving complicated instruments you move across your site, sometimes along a grid or multiple *transects* (straight lines) to get a picture of what's actually there before you dig. Here are some of these techniques:

- **Ground-penetrating radar (GPR)** sends radar pulses into the ground to locate anomalies such as canals and structures; it works best in dry sand.

- **Proton magnetometry and fluxgate gradiometry** sense deviation from the earth's magnetic field caused by buried items; they work well to find burned surfaces and iron objects.

- **Metal detectors** sense iron and other (but not all) metals; they're far less useful at prehistoric sites where metals weren't used yet.

- **Electrical resistivity** sends electrical currents through the soil to monitor different conductivity levels, which indicate buried objects; it works well to find rock walls, boulders, and empty spaces like canals.

DISCOVERY

Geochemistry shows possible Maya market

Scientists investigating the Maya site of Chunchucmil, in Yucatan, Mexico, wondered how this large, bustling prehistoric center arose in a climate that was dry and unfavorable for agriculture. Testing soil chemistry revealed linear patterns with phosphate concentrations 40 times higher than elsewhere across the site. Organic wastes (especially foods) produced by humans decay quickly in the tropics, leaving phosphorus in the ground. So archaeologists thought these results meant that farm crops were brought in from elsewhere and traded at a marketplace. The parallel rows of rocks at the site are additional evidence, indications of small temporary structures that may have been market stalls. To test their hypothesis, the researchers found a modern market in Guatemala that still had a dirt floor and examined its soils, which had similar concentrations of phosphates along the vegetable dealers' stalls.

One model of the Classic Maya (A.D. 300 to 900) economy has been that farmers paid taxes or tribute to the ruler, who then redistributed the funds to everyone. This new research suggests food was traded for local resources in real markets, possibly by a class of merchants. So the study provides information on both ancient human economic systems and social/political organization.

Because these technologies are non-invasive, you're not destroying part of your site to learn something about it. The anomalies you see in the instrument's readout may be patterns of structures such as walls or buildings or features (visible evidence of some specific human behavior) such as rock-lined fire pits or burials. But for all the fancy machinery and computer processing, you sometimes still only see a blob or a spike in the graph that you can only identify by digging down to it.

The best approach is to try several remote sensing methods to see whether you get the same results. Then you can better determine where to dig (or where not to).

Are you reconstructing or restoring?

Some archaeological excavation has goals of not only finding out about the past but also physically duplicating it in one of two ways: restoration or reconstruction. *Restoring* what the site would have been like may mean picking up all the fallen bricks and columns and putting them back together to rebuild the temple or palace. *Reconstruction* may mean building a new structure right on top of the outline of the old one, perhaps using the same materials past people would've had available. Or maybe you dig down into a mound and then put it all back to show how the monument originally looked.

Choosing reconstruction or restoration affects the way you dig. You may have to number bricks or building blocks to be able to put them together properly. Or maybe you leave features like garbage pits or burials unexcavated so people can see them in displays. Other times you don't want to restore items to their original appearances and functions. Piles of crumbling ruins may be just as attractive to the public (and much cheaper to maintain).

Museums and governments who fund digs often desire reconstruction. They want people to see past glories and the historical heritage of the community. But reconstruction and restoration can have problems. You may have little idea of how those columns and bricks once went together or what color they were painted, so you have to be careful not to impose your own notions of what ancient structures were like (as some famous archaeologists have been criticized for doing). When you try to use original types of materials, you may end up violating modern building codes. Restoring buildings exactly as they were can also exclude tourists in wheelchairs or otherwise disabled.

Planning the Archaeological Excavation

Your preliminary planning gives you some guidelines, but you still need to develop your excavation schedule and needs. Don't forget to include a few extra days for the project, in case you're slowed by bad weather or equipment breakdowns. Because digging can be very hard labor, be sure to include lots of break time and days off so workers can recuperate, relax, and also visit other sites (and sights) in the area.

In Chapter 6, I describe the ideal type of archaeological fieldworker for doing survey (looking for sites). An excavator needs similar qualities — the willingness to work very hard and still have a mellow attitude no matter what difficulties arise. To dig properly, you need to be enormously painstaking and picky with details. You must finish all the paperwork and recording for one piece of the excavation before you begin the next. It can get tedious because you want so badly to move all that dirt and see what's there! But patience is all part of the deal.

Field conditions for excavation are similar to those described for survey work in Chapter 6. You need to take into account health and safety hazards and all other dangerous and tricky aspects of the field situation. (In Chapter 8, I describe the archaeological, ethical, and safety standards in more detail.)

It takes a special person to put up with the day-to-day work of digging. You don't necessarily need to be big and strong to shovel, but you do need a constant eye for detail and patience to do long series of repetitive small tasks.

Deciding how many excavations and how deep

Some archaeologists say you should write your research questions and then figure how much you think you need to dig to find your answers. But this amount is very hard to predict. You usually first determine how much time and labor you have, and that helps you figure out how much you can do!

How much to dig

The best strategy is to start with your given limitations and priorities and work from there. You may only have a month of summer vacation to dig, or only a week before the bulldozers come! Or you may be able to go back to the same site every season for many years. With rougher soils and more remote sites, or with a topnotch crew and some heavy equipment, your project can be slower or faster.

In my experience, an average crew of three or four people can dig a 1-x-2-meter excavation unit 1 meter deep, in 10-centimeter increments, in soft soil, in about two weeks (including all recording and backfilling). Of course, finding lots of features and artifacts, losing days to weather, or taking two-hour lunches down the road at that coffeehouse or bar can mess up this schedule.

Where to put excavation units

You place excavations based on what you already know or want to know. So if your remote sensing located anomalies that may be cultural features, you want to dig down to check them. Or if you have surface artifacts and want to find how widely the site extends, you work out horizontally from that center in many directions. If you have standing ruins, you may want to dig next to them to see what they were.

For a shallow site (or one where you want to see a wide horizontal layout), you can open large block units measuring many meters on a side. If your deposits are deeply buried, you dig deeper, but you still need wide units just for safety, in case your walls fall in. (You don't want to be buried yourself along with the ancient remains!)

Placement of excavation units simply wherever you think they'll turn up the best results is usually called a *judgmental sample*. All your digging is sampling because you never dig the whole site. The sampling strategies I describe for finding sites in Chapter 6 apply to placing excavation units at one site, too. So you can also put units randomly or systematically (according to a pattern you devise, like every 50 meters). You may *stratify* your sample (divide the site into meaningful chunks like domestic area, ceremonial area, garbage dump) and use random or systematic sampling within those areas.

Sample excavation plans

Here are some sample research plans I've used in the eastern U.S.:

✔ At a prehistoric mound site, I had three weeks and a crew of ten. I wanted to know when the mound was built and the archaeological cultures that had used it, so I dug one unit at the base of the mound slope to get below its construction layers to the original land surface (we got charcoal for dating and layers of piled-up soil from mound-building). Another unit I put east of the mound in what I hoped was the village area. We got one kind of pottery deeper than another, indicating two different time periods, and also a feature (a pit) full of household garbage.

✔ To get as much as possible out of a site that was to be destroyed for reservoir construction over a four-week project I first assigned teams to pick up all surface artifacts in the plowed field. Then we dug a couple units randomly placed to see whether undisturbed prehistoric materials existed below the disturbed plow zone. When we found intact material, I used heavy equipment (a front-end loader) to scrape off the plow zone over a wide area. This process exposed features (garbage pits, postmold patterns from poles in the ground indicating structures, and even human burials), which we then dug out.

✔ At a historic site I knew was a 19th-century mill, I used heavy equipment to explore a long depression that I thought was once the old mill race channel. The small bulldozer cut across the channel and exposed its square, human-dug cross section. It also cut into the edge of a stone building foundation. So I stopped the machine then and excavated the mill building foundations by hand; I even found an old millstone thrown to one side.

✔ At a Native American campsite consisting of piles of *shell midden* (seafood debris), I picked one big circular pile and excavated a 1-x-5-meter trench through the center of it to get a good sample. Each 1-meter-long segment of the trench was dug separately for better control, to contrast what was in the center with what was at the edges. To see what activity was outside these garbage piles, I also dug a 1-x-2-meter unit in the sand between the shell piles. Finally, I trenched across another pile and found it to be of a different age than the first.

Knowing when to stop

Usually you dig until you reach *culturally sterile* soils, meaning they have no more evidence of human activity. But you want to be sure you don't have anything buried deeper than that. Pyramids can be constructed over other (smaller and smaller) pyramids. Campgrounds can be inhabited on top of earlier people's camps, or even on top of buried pyramids (or vice versa). You want to dig to the bottom of the cultural deposits — the natural surface that the first people there walked on.

You may have to stop if you don't have the tools to investigate something special, or if you expose graves of people whose descendants don't want them disturbed (among other reasons). Even if you don't get done everything in your research plan, you can leave some things to investigate next season (if there is one).

You usually don't dig a whole site. Even if you have all the time and money in the world (which you never do), you want to save something. In the future, new excavation technologies unheard of today may produce new kinds of information. If the site is completely gone, further investigation is impossible. For example, U.S. diggers in the 1930s threw out animal bones and charcoal — after all, they were just ancient garbage! Now they can be used for dating; revealing environments, diets and health; and many other things.

Considering safety

Every dig should have a safety plan, safety rules, and, if necessary, a designated safety officer. All the crew should know the location of the first-aid kits and the nearest emergency medical service. Locate modern things that may already be underground — phone and electrical lines and water and sewer pipes. Hitting these can have awful consequences! I discuss more details of safety and ethics in Chapter 8, where I give you examples of what can go wrong at a dig.

Using Old Archaeological Technology and the Newest Equipment Too

Chapter 5 gives you lists of what to pack for your individual fieldwork needs, illustrated in Color Figure 4. Each project also has general equipment and supplies for digging and recording, depending upon what work you're doing.

Basic digging tools

Some archaeological digging methods (like shoveling) haven't changed in decades or even centuries. An endless variety of tools can be useful, depending on the kind of project and finds and soils. Here's a list of things besides personal tools needed for a typical excavation:

✔ Shovels. Get enough shovels for each digger because everyone will need one when you backfill. Make sure they're long-handled — forget the short-handled spades unless you really want a backache! I prefer square-bladed shovels with wooden handles for better grip, cleaner square walls, and chopping roots in the way. They're also good at cutting sod in square slices in case you have to put the grass back on the site when you're done. Round and pointed shovels are good for backfilling quickly but not for skimming flat floors or walls.

✔ Hand tools like trowels (pointed and square — Marshalltown brand is best), spatulas, spoons, knives, dental picks, ice picks, tweezers, paint brushes, sharpened cane or chopsticks, or bamboo skewers for finer digging.

✔ Picks (small and large) and *mattocks* (wide-bladed picks) for digging especially rough stuff, rocks, or compacted shell middens.

✔ Dustpans, buckets, large scoops, or even plastic gallon jugs cut into scoopers for removing soils you've just loosened.

✔ Wheelbarrows for removing large amounts of soil you've just dug up.

✔ Screens, preferably of different mesh sizes depending upon soils, expected finds, and whether you're doing dry or waterscreening.

✔ Large heavy-duty plastic bags (trash compactor bags) or feed bags for soil samples.

✔ Water pump (if you're waterscreening) with a connector system that can divide off pipes and hoses to go to separate screens. (Of course, you need a local source of water to use for this item too.) I always bring extra spark plugs for the water pump, which amazingly doesn't seem to work if it gets a lot of water on it!

✔ Resealable plastic bags and waterproof markers for bagging and labeling finds; tags for finds you can't easily contain in a bag; and tinfoil and plastic or glass vials for charcoal samples and small or fragile items.

✔ Clipboards, waterproof pens, pencils, paper, rulers, graph paper, and field notebooks with waterproof paper for recording all notes, lists of finds, details of excavations, photo logs, and so forth.

✔ Field forms for recording specific information like levels excavated, features, layering of soil strata in unit walls, burials, and house patterns. You also need your field catalog forms for listing bags of finds.

✔ Compass, large measuring tapes (30 to 50 meters long) and small ones (3 meters long), and protractors for mapping and drawing finds in place.

✔ Line levels and plumb bobs for measuring locations accurately in place in the unit (fishing line sinkers make great, cheap plumb bobs).

✔ String, rope, and stakes or other sturdy poles (like cut pieces of iron re-bar) to lay out your square or rectangular excavation units.

- ✔ Colored flagging tape, pin flags, or other markers to indicate finds and help you protect and record them.

- ✔ Basic tools like screwdrivers and wrenches for fixing equipment and files for sharpening metal edges.

- ✔ Chain saw, machetes, weed whips, axes and hatchets, big branch cutters, and/or little root clippers depending upon how much vegetation you expect to move out of the way.

- ✔ Gas and oil for the power tools and rags to clean up spills.

- ✔ Extra gloves, bug spray, and other personal supplies for the crew.

- ✔ Cameras (and even videocamera) and photo log sheets, with waterproof cases.

- ✔ First-aid kit, including directions, distance, and phone number to nearest emergency room and maybe even medical insurance cards of the crew members and their medications and allergy information.

- ✔ Two-way hand-held radios and hand-held or fancier GPS units.

- ✔ Plastic sheeting to protect equipment and excavations from rain and dust.

- ✔ Locks and chains to secure equipment to trees for security.

- ✔ Lots of water (with ice, for emergencies) and food.

- ✔ Duct tape and lubricating oil (always)!

Much of the more specialized archaeological equipment is sold by forestry or engineering supply companies, and you can find archaeological supply companies, too. Many archaeologists make their own screens using lumber, bolts, nuts, and hardware cloth. You can always find other useful stuff just by looking around. For example, metal and bamboo skewers for shish kabobs are useful in many excavation tasks.

Some equipment (even — and especially — an ax) requires training, coordination, and common sense to use. So if you've never used it before, ask for help! Otherwise, you can chop off your foot or poke your eye out.

Mapping equipment

You can choose from many different devices (in varying levels of complexity) to map your site. For a simple sketch map, use a compass and tape measure and draw it to scale on graph paper. A Brunton compass or pocket transit can sit on a small tripod and be leveled to give you more accurate readings.

Most digs use more sophisticated mapping equipment, like the kind you may have seen surveyors use for measuring the road corridor or laying out property boundaries. The following list gives you some examples:

✔ A *transit* is a mapping device consisting essentially of a telescope, a big compass, and a tripod to keep it all level and precise. You set it up over your site's *datum point,* a point from which you'll measure everything. Then you look through the scope at a *stadia* (measuring) rod, and write down the numbers you see and your *compass* (horizontal) and *scope* (vertical) angles. Simple calculations give you the distance, direction, and elevation of all your points. You map points around the whole site — features, excavation units, elevations, roads, streams, and other things. Then you put all the points on paper and connect the right ones to make your two-dimensional map.

✔ The *plane table, alidade,* and *theodolite* are similar mechanical instruments that work along the same principles. A plane table gives you a map right there in the field instead of your having to take measurements back to the lab to calculate and put on paper.

✔ *Total stations* and other electronic versions of transits or theodolites are now common in archaeology. They measure the distance, direction, and elevation with a laser beam from an *electronic distance measuring device* (EDM). This beam is picked up by a prism target (rather than a stadia rod) held at the point you're mapping. Electronic instruments are fast and accurate and don't need you to clear a huge swath through the forest to see the rod (because the laser beam is thinner). More important, you can connect the data-logger to your computer and have it draw the map for you. The disadvantage is that these devices are heavy, sometimes complicated to use, and very expensive.

✔ *Photogrammetry, 3-D laser scanning,* and other fancy spatial technologies are often used for more-specialized mapping, especially of standing buildings and monuments, rock walls, or other ruins. The equipment takes photos from different angles or scans zillions of points by laser on solid surfaces. With these data, you can create fine three-dimensional images that show things not easily visible to the eye (such as shallow carvings on the rocks at Stonehenge). Instruments and expertise are very expensive here too.

Two-way hand-held radios are helpful in the mapping process. They allow the person behind the instrument to talk to the person holding the rod or laser target, though they may be far apart. You also want a plastic cover for the instrument because it's severely affected by rain! Most instruments come with hard plastic covers, but you can drape plastic sheeting over them for protection and quick reuse after a brief shower.

Bigger equipment

For some projects, you need additional larger-scale equipment, such as the following:

✔ A dining canopy, huge umbrella, or other cover over the excavation to shield it from sun and rain. You can find shelters of varying quality on the market — keep in mind that cheaper ones may blow over. Sometimes you can fabricate shelters with arcs of PVC pipe, large plastic sheeting, and some kind of webbing or rope to hold it all down.

✔ A lockable field cupboard to store your equipment and tools in at the site so you don't have to lug them home each night.

✔ Hydraulic coring machines for deep samples of your site. These monsters usually come on trailers and need to be driven into your site by truck or all-terrain vehicle.

✔ Lumber and other supplies for shoring up your trenches if you're digging deeply. This precaution is certainly required for safety and may also be the law!

✔ Lumber and supplies for fabricating items you may need, like tables or even an outhouse building to provide a reasonable toilet in the field.

✔ Flotation apparatus (see "Recovering remains with flotation" later in this chapter) to process soil samples. (This can be done back in the lab too.)

Heavy earth-moving equipment

You may think that taking a backhoe to your site is like using a hatchet to remove your appendix, but big machinery saves lots of time and effort when used carefully. Many sites have an upper layer of modern or disturbed soils that you're not interested in, so stripping this dirt quickly helps you get down to the good stuff. Yes, you can accidentally damage some precious remains, but you can do that with your shovel too.

A good equipment operator can take off very thin layers at a time and respond well to your hand directions as you walk beside the machine and look at what it's uncovering. Earth-movers aren't cheap to rent, and some archaeologists buy and learn to operate their own. The following are good machines to use:

✔ **Front-end loader:** Has an open, wide bucket to scrape off soils and pick them up or push them off to the side.

✔ **Backhoe:** Has a narrow bucket to dig quickly very deeply and give you an idea of how deep your site's cultural deposits extend. It often comes on the same machine as the front-end loader.

✔ **Scraper pan:** Cuts off the soil in thin slices and removes it cleanly to somewhere else. The self-loading kind is the best.

✔ **Hydraulic excavator:** Has a telescoping arm that allows it to sit off to the side and dig without disturbing the cultural deposits. It's a good choice for small-area stripping.

- **Dragline:** Has a huge arm and can take away lots of dirt while sitting off to the side. It has treads that tear up soils, though, so it isn't great for large sites.

- **Very small loader with backhoe bucket:** Quickly tests sites you identify on survey to see whether they're even worth further excavation.

These machines aren't so good to use:

- Bulldozers with treads (rather than wheels) that gouge out the soil and with so much power that they lack the control to push off thin slices of soil

- Road graders with long vertical blades that only level and make smooth surfaces (whether by cutting off soil or pushing soil into depressions)

Whatever machinery you use, be sure to explain to the operator *exactly* what you want. (They're used to moving lots of dirt at a time, not little bits.) And be sure to remove or cover the teeth on the end of the bucket or blade.

Finally! Doing the Archaeological Excavation

Now that you've got your equipment and supplies, your paperwork in order including permits, and your research design laid out, it's time to dig in! Okay, maybe not quite — you have to do a bit of prep work on your site before you get to the real digging. But you're almost there, I promise.

Setting up a dig and mapping it

Because you have to know the precise location of everything you find, your first step is to map your site and lay out your excavation units.

Making a site map

Establish where you want your site's datum point, from which you map everything, and then set up your mapping instrument over this point. The datum can be in the middle of the site or at the edge; a standard practice is to put it outside the southwest corner of the site. That way, everything you map can be in terms of distances north and east of the datum (and you won't have to move it if you realize something important may be under it). You also need to map your site datum in relation to an official marker whose exact location, including elevation above sea level, is known. This point can be a spot on a published map, or a real government survey marker on the ground.

Next you can set up a grid over the whole site with stakes and string, on paper, or electronically. With this system, you name excavation units in terms of the grid lines, choosing a corner of your unit to be the unit datum. If your site datum is in the southwest corner of the site, and your unit datum is its southwest corner, you use measurements going north and east from these points. So Test Unit 55E60 (named after its southwest corner) is north 55 meters and east 60 meters from the site datum. As you dig, you measure locations of all finds in relation to the grid points in a similar fashion. So an artifact you uncover in Test Unit 55E60 may be at 55.42E60.13 if it's 42 centimeters north and 13 centimeters east of the test unit's southwest corner.

You can also just name units A, B, C, or 1, 2, 3 and map them directly from the site datum, without even using a grid. As long as you keep track of precisely where everything comes from, you're doing okay!

Laying out units

After you decide where to dig and how big of an area to open, you lay out excavation units. Most archaeologists use string or flagging tape and stakes or other kinds of markers.

The top section of Figure 7-1 shows a 1-x-2-meter excavation or test unit (affectionately abbreviated "TU") at a typical site. It's laid out in cardinal directions (the trowel points north) with wooden stakes and string. The three small dark circles are prehistoric features that were measured precisely from the unit corners, which are drawn on the overall site map. Color Figure 1 also shows a unit (2 x 2 meters) with a feature.

Digging strata and levels

When you dig, you excavate in small increments, very slowly so as not to miss anything and to maintain good control. As you dig, you pay attention to the layering of soil, removing one layer at a time and numbering them sequentially.

A *soil stratum* is a layer already there in the ground. Excavation *levels* are artificially determined layers you designate. Here are some examples of these different layers to dig within your excavation units:

- ✔ **Natural strata:** Each different layer of soil you can see (based on color, texture, and contents) that formed naturally can be taken out separately. In the upper part of Figure 7-1 you can see the toposoil stratum and lighter subsoil underneath it.

- ✔ **Cultural strata:** Each layer of soil you see that contains different cultural contents mixed into the natural stratum, such as black soil with artifacts, black midden filled with shell or rock, and lighter soil with no artifacts between midden strata.

Figure 7-1:
A 2-meter
square test
unit with
features and
excavating
a cross
section.

   ✔ **Arbitrary levels:** You use these levels when you can't see soil layers well enough to determine where they begin and end. Make sure they're a uniform thickness, such as 10 centimeters, and keep in mind that you have to correlate them to the natural and cultural strata after you can see those layers exposed later in your unit walls.

   ✔ **Some combination of the above:** One method may not be sufficient for your site. For example, at a site that had materials of different time periods all mixed together, I dug out the 1-meter thick cultural stratum in 5-centimeter levels, hoping to get some control over what was earlier (deeper) and later (shallower).

Standard excavation techniques require you to stop at the end of each stratum or level to describe and map the unit *floor,* including any features or artifacts in place and the soil colors. In the top section of Figure 7-1, which was dug in 10-centimeter levels, you see Floor 3 at the bottom of Level 3, 30 centimeters deep. Color Figure 1 also shows a unit floor, in a light-colored natural stratum underneath the cultural stratum packed with white shells and black greasy soil from human use.

Don't mix materials and data from different levels or strata! You want to maintain control of not only the depth of finds but also the associated soil, so you can interpret them later.

Shoveling and troweling

Often, you start excavating with a shovel and then switch to smaller tools to be less destructive when you start finding things. You also begin to trowel when you're getting to the bottom of your stratum or level, to make a cleaner unit floor than you can get with a shovel. You can shovel dirt directly into a screen, buckets, or wheelbarrows or trowel it into dustpans or pails.

After you expose things like artifacts or features, you use finer tools and brushes. Metal tools can gouge bones or other soft objects, so I recommend sharpened pieces of cane, chopsticks, or bamboo skewers. For harder objects, scrape out the dirt around them, and then brush them off so you can identify them. (Only brush artifacts, not soils around them.)

Be sure to expose items *in situ* (Latin for "in place"). That way you can measure, draw, photograph, and record everything exactly as it lies before you disturb it and lose its context forever when you take it out of the ground. Most sites contain so many finds that doing this for everything would take forever, so smaller finds often come out of the screen. That's why you dig in the small increments of strata or arbitrary levels — to keep at least some control over where things came from.

Recording archaeological features

One reason you want clean, nicely troweled unit floors is to be able to measure precisely. Another reason is to see features, the visible evidence of specific human behaviors. Some typical features include

- Dark circular or oblong stains in the soil marking the remains of pits that were for storage or garbage.

- Other, wider dark stains or soil discolorations that can show house floors or other human-made structures.

- *Postmolds,* or small, dark, usually circular stains left from posts stuck in the ground. Either they decayed in place, or they were pulled out and the hole filled in with vegetation that decayed and turned dark. Square postmolds mean more recent structures with sawn poles.

- Fire pits, basins, or hearths with signs of burning.

- Charred timbers or reddened, hard soil areas that may be from burned buildings.

- Clusters of artifacts or bones.

- Graves, stone or brick walls, or other obvious marks left by people.

Always treat features very carefully. You can dig small ones out and bag up their contents. Or you can leave them on a pedestal of dirt as you remove the rest of the stratum or level around them. Then you dig them out or cross-section them, digging deep enough to make sure you can see what they are.

This procedure is what you see back in Figure 7-1, where one feature (upper right) was pedestaled in Floor 2 (20 centimeters deep) where it first appeared, and two others appeared in Floor 3 (30 centimeters or about one foot deep). Then the worker cross-sectioned the pedestaled feature and bagged all soil from the south half for later processing. At the bottom of the figure you see the cross section with two big potsherds in it. The feature was a garbage pit. It's clearly basin-shaped, though worm tracks make it less distinct. After photographing and drawing this cross section or profile of the feature, the worker removed the north half, putting it in a separate bag.

You see a similar procedure in Color Figure 1, where the fieldworker is cross-sectioning a small pit full of black soil and shell. This feature was the earliest cultural evidence from the site, where the prehistoric campers first came to bury their garbage from a clambake by digging this pit into the light-colored natural riverbank soil. Then they stayed a long time and left all the rest of the garbage (from many more clambakes) piled up in the thick black stratum you see already excavated in the photo.

Larger features you uncover, such as walls or structure patterns, are not completely or even partially removable, especially if they're rock or brick constructions. You may need to rethink where you place excavation units to expose more of these features so you know what they are.

Measuring

As you're digging, you shovel soil (and often artifacts and other objects) away. But specimens you can uncover in the ground before you dig them out can be recorded more precisely, in place, in three dimensions.

If your datum sits in the southwest corner of the site, you can measure distances north and east from there. (See "Setting up a dig and mapping it" earlier in this chapter for more on establishing a datum.) Or you can measure the angle and distance from that corner. You get depth measurements with a string tied at ground surface to the datum corner stake and held out level over the find, as shown by your tiny line level hanging on the string. Then measure the depth from the string. You use a *plumb bob* (pointed weight on a string) held over the find to get more precise measurement. On some digs, you use the transit or total station for this job, holding the stadia rod or target over each find to get its location. But for short distances, a tape measure is more accurate.

Screening

Most modern archaeology uses some kind of screen to sift the soil for artifacts and *ecofacts* (plant and animal remains used by people). Even if you trowel slowly, you can miss tons of miniscule finds if you don't screen. A standard screen size is quarter-inch mesh, but you can use finer mesh if your soil will go through it. You have a couple of different choices when it comes to screening: dry and water.

Dry screening

Dry screening is easier to set up than waterscreening, but it's still hard work because you shake the screen (be sure it has legs to hold it up), and you have to dump it between each session to get out the pebbles, roots, and other stuff you don't want. You can set it up next to the unit so that the soil that sifts through is right there ready to fill the excavation back in. But don't put it so close that the pile of soil under it starts falling back in by itself!

Waterscreening

You need a source of water to waterscreen (duh!); if you've got a natural stream or lake nearby, you can pump water from it. (You may need an official permit to pump, so check that out ahead of time.) You can also make a water source if you excavate (perhaps with heavy equipment and beyond your site boundary) deep enough to reach the water table. Then you set up your pump, hoses, and waterscreen station. You have to bring the dirt there in wheelbarrows or buckets.

It may be very worth the trouble to waterscreen, because it allows you to use a finer mesh and capture tiny objects that may change your interpretation of the site. For waterscreening I use eighth-inch mesh, with window screen inserts to catch tiny things. (One season we got tiny European glass seed beads — the first finds that showed the site wasn't prehistoric.)

Recovering remains with flotation

Soil flotation is an easy technology using water and fine screens to recover tiny and fragile remains. Some flotation devices are simple buckets with their bottoms replaced by screens. You pass soil through the bucket while standing in shallow water and holding the bottom of the bucket submerged. You also have a strainer handy to skim light stuff (charcoal, charred seeds, fish scales) that floats off the top.

Another type of flotation machine is a manufactured tub or barrel (or homemade 50-gallon drums) with a hose stuck into the bottom and a shower head on the end of it inside. You turn on the water to fill the barrel, and put inside a bucket with a screen or two graduated screens in the bottom and a spout on top. As you dump the soil into the bucket, larger and smaller items are caught in the bucket screens. Light, sometimes very tiny things float off the top and down the spout into an even finer screen.

The materials you recover are called the *heavy fractions* (what sank into the screens), and the *light fraction* (what floated out), or sometimes labeled the *A, B,* and *C fractions,* respectively). You put these materials together with their accompanying information somewhere where they can dry (I use squares of nylon tied closed and hung from a clothesline). Later you sort through them.

Excavation techniques seriously influence results! In a recent dig, I made the crew carry all the soils from a big prehistoric garbage pit feature back to the lab for flotation. They were heavy bags, hauled into the truck, out of the truck, down the stairs, out to the machine — and floating them took many weeks of muddy work. But the animal bones we recovered from this garbage dump gave a beautiful picture of life at the site. Not only did we get enough charcoal bits for a date (A.D. 1200), but the flotation technique also produced many tiny bone bits of birds, fish, and large and small mammals. Many of the fish vertebrae were very tiny. Without the fine screening of the flotation technique, we would have lost 68 percent of the fish species.

Taking soil samples

I take 9-liter soil samples (a chunk that's 30-x-30 centimeters by 10 centimeters thick) for flotation from each stratum or level excavated in each unit. Also, I process all soils from features by flotation. Those important tiny clues that can give you answers to big questions may show up in the flotation barrel. Any soil samples destined for flotation should be chunked out with a shovel or at least troweled out in big solid hunks, so as not to scrape and destroy as many of the tiny preserved seeds or other fragile remains.

Just be sure you don't make the bags of soils so heavy that they either break or are unmovable. Plus, if you're not doing flotation at the site but rather back at the lab, be sure you don't have so many heavy bags of soil that you can't fit them in your vehicle.

Many archaeologists also take additional soil samples just to save, in case future studies may be possible. I take a 1-liter sample of soil from each level or stratum in case I can do pollen analysis or other research. They end up being heavy boxes on the lab shelf, but they're worth it later!

Doing special digs: Mounds, buildings, caves, and more

Specialized kinds of sites call for specific techniques. Some have long histories of efficient use, but others you may need to develop as you work. Here are some examples:

- ✔ **Mounds or mounded earthen constructions** such as walls and enclosures may have *stratigraphy* (layering) that shows basket loads. (*Basket loads* are individual piles of construction soil, often of different colors, that spread out when they're dumped and become small lens-shaped deposits.) You can sometimes cross-section or trench earthen constructions like these to get details about how they were built.

- ✔ **Standing architecture or stones,** even in ruins, can be large obstacles requiring lots of planning. Whether you have stone-block pyramids, adobe walls, or giant *stelae* (tall, standing stones) and sculptures, you need to plan what you're going to do with all the pieces, how to map them in three dimensions, and how to dig the soil around them. For fallen structures, you can number and map pieces in place and then remove them to get to underlying pieces, leaving standing portions and working around them.

- ✔ **Caves and rock shelters** (shallow caves) may have layers of rock fallen from the roof and sediment washed in and out by water and wind. You may need to perch over the floors you're digging (as shown in Figure 3-1 in Chapter 3) so as not to step on them.

- ✔ **Shell midden** sites are usually dug the same as any other site, but the shells in the soil may make it difficult to dig with shovels or take out levels as thin as 10 centimeters. Using picks, 20-centimeters levels, and waterscreening (because you're usually near the source of the shellfish) are your best bets. In Color Figure 1, you see the shell midden stratum that has small river clams, a little easier to dig through than big oysters.

- ✔ **Dry sites** may have sand blowing all over — a safety hazard that can also obscure features. But the sand helps with preservation, so be ready for fragile organic materials. Be sure you have plastic vials or other sturdy containers to hold fragile items such as bone, wood, or seeds and protect them from harm after they're excavated.

- ✔ **Volcanic ash-covered** sites are rare, but they have amazing preservation even when organic remains are long decayed. The trick is to know that voids in the deposits show where something once was. Fill these hollows with plaster, and you get casts of plant crops in the field (at a Central American site) or even the bodies of victims (at Pompeii).

- ✔ **Wet sites** are submerged cultural deposits dug by pumping water out of the ground, usually with *well points* (like huge straws around your unit to suck it dry). De-watering requires lots more machinery, but you get organic (plants and animals) remains that otherwise wouldn't have been preserved, like wooden or bark artifacts or cloth. But they're fragile, so you need to keep them wet — maybe in sealed bags with water — so that they don't dry up and degrade.

- ✔ **Underwater archaeological sites,** from drowned occupational areas to shipwrecks, require a whole set of additional expensive techniques — and you have to know how to dive. See the "Methods in underwater archaeology" sidebar in this chapter for more on excavating underwater sites.

Ending the dig

How you end your dig depends upon whether you're coming back. You can cover excavation units and fence them off if you're returning next season. Otherwise, you want to backfill — always a professional (if backbreaking) obligation. If you've carted your dirt away to a distant screen, you have to cart it all back! For sites that are about to be destroyed for construction, you may get the machinery the builders will use, or their operators, to backfill. Or they may not care whether you backfill because they're coming the next day to push it all away anyway.

You may want to leave plastic sheeting or other indicators at the bottom of your units so that future workers will know where you already dug. You may pull up your stakes, pick up everything, and even put sod back depending upon what's required by the landowner.

Methods in underwater archaeology

It's way more difficult to excavate carefully underwater and expose your finds exactly as they lie. Here are some typical methods, which are very different from what you do on land:

✔ You may find sites the old-fashioned way through the historic record or a story of a find someone made while fishing, or you may need remote sensing devices such as magnetometers or sonar.

✔ Finding your exact position underwater is now easier with GPS (global positioning systems) devices.

✔ You may use a grid of PVC pipes to lay out your excavation units and waterproof plastic slates or laminated tablets to record things.

✔ You probably won't excavate with shovels; you may use a dredge or *airlift,* a hose that sucks up sediments and dumps them into a screen on a barge for others to sort through for artifacts.

✔ You may do your fine digging with a trowel, but you can also fan the sediments with your hands to make the moving water uncover objects.

✔ With everything moving around in the water, you need to be extra careful to record things quickly and well. Waterproof cameras help a lot!

✔ You need a conservation plan and equipment for preserving the waterlogged items you find; after they're exposed to air, they may start decaying or shriveling right away.

✔ You want to have a lot of knowledge of what different water conditions do to artifacts. Shipworms eat wood, iron rusts, and a pile of silver coins can transform into a large black mass that looks like a dumb old rock.

Recording Excavation Information and Finds

Without careful notes and recording, any archaeological dig is just looting! A good rule of thumb is "Whenever in doubt, write it down."

Okay, so you may also fill out so many forms and do so much paperwork that it seems you're working in the department of redundancy department. But the more places something is recorded, the less information is lost to mistakes.

Provenience

The concept of *provenience* is all-important in archaeological excavation. You write it on the bags, tags, forms, notes, and many other places. It's everything about where stuff comes from!

Chapter 6 lists some of the information you need to record provenience during archaeological survey. When you're excavating, you may need even more information:

- Project and institution name, your name, and probably the names of all other crew members who helped with this find.
- The day, the date, and perhaps the time of day.
- The precise three-dimensional location coordinates, if possible, and what datum they were recorded from.
- The excavation unit, level or stratum, and depth.
- Whether it was recovered by shoveling, troweling, or in the screen.
- Any other particular information, such as "within the red soil area," "northwest corner of unit," or "2 centimeters east of the stone ax."

Field forms and notes

Typical field forms describe each excavation level in detail. Other forms are for individual features, excavation unit wall stratigraphy, and other things your dig may uncover. You usually have a form to log in each photo in minute detail (camera settings, direction facing, subject, photographer, date).

On field inventory forms, you list bags of materials as they're recovered each day — this list is your field specimen catalog. You assign field catalog numbers to each bag and write them on the form and bags. A simple system is to use the site number and then sequential numbers after that. So the first bag of artifacts from Test Unit 1, Level 1 at the Walnut site 22It539 may be numbered 22It539-01. (If this site number looks like gibberish to you, head to Chapter 6 for more on the site-numbering process.)

Your official field notes include much more than what's on forms. You write down what you did all day, specific finds, units, levels or strata, features you worked on, who visited, how well the equipment worked, what the weather was like — anything that can affect how the materials and data are interpreted. If two people work on the same thing and one forgets to put the date on the bag, that information should be in the other person's notes so it can be recovered. Field notes also show why you made certain decisions.

Photography and computer data entry

You can have a site photographer or take photos yourself. The photo log is very important; many pictures of dirt all look alike. You must decide whether you want digital cameras or regular film. I often use both, as well as a video camera — not necessarily for making award-winning movies, but just to have another source of information to help figure things out.

Besides loading digital photos onto your laptop in the field, you can do the bag inventory and record other data electronically. You can put finds on your site map as they come out of the ground and see what patterns you may have. This map gives you a better idea of where to expand the digging.

Procedures for unusual finds

Your dig supervisor will usually be familiar with artifacts and other finds unearthed as you dig, but not always. You're the person directly in contact with the materials as they're being uncovered, so you may see some pattern others don't.

If you're not sure whether something is an artifact or other item worth saving, *save it anyway!* It may be something new nobody has yet discovered. It may look like a dumb old rock but be a real artifact. It may be a natural item that still gives indications of past peoples' environments. Things I've saved include *fulgurites* (natural creations of sand fused by lightning), mud-dauber wasp nests (which would have needed a straight wall to form on, meaning a prehistoric native house), and river pebbles (not sure what they mean yet). Even if what you've saved is worthless, better to be sure. You can always throw it out in the lab after you see what it really is.

For special finds, outside assistance may be required:

- ✔ Unexpected kinds of finds may call for specialists — a firearms or basketry expert, or a geologist for unusual soils.

- ✔ Fragile remains that are wet or partially decayed or broken in place can be saved by an *archaeological conservator* — your local museum may have one.

- ✔ *Human skeletal remains* require special treatment according to laws and also archaeological ethics. You may need a biological anthropologist to determine whether they're ancient or recent (though preserved clothing also helps here). You're also obliged to find any modern descendants and communicate with them about the next step — you may need to leave skeletons in the ground out of respect. I discuss finding human skeletons more in Chapter 8.

Chapter 8

Laws, Ethics, and Safety in Field Archaeology

. . . .

In This Chapter

▶ Getting permission to dig

▶ Preparing for dangerous conditions

▶ Working with communities and the media

▶ Being sensitive of indigenous peoples and descendants

. . . .

*I*n Chapter 6, I show you how to find archaeological sites and determine where to dig, and in Chapter 7, how to conduct excavation. You may think you're ready to go out and do fieldwork, but besides knowing what to do, you really have to know what *not* to do in the field.

This chapter describes ethical and safety standards in archaeological fieldwork. I explain how to interact with everyone interested in or affected by the dig and how to stay safe while wielding metal archaeological tools. I give you examples of what can go wrong and how to anticipate it. This chapter shows you how archaeology does indeed include the adventure of the unexpected but sometimes the undesired as well.

Gathering Information from Landowners, Residents, and Officials

As part of your preparation for archaeological survey or excavation, you always want to have permission to dig and knowledge of any laws pertaining to the land. You also want to find out about the land's past from owners, local residents, and *descendant communities* (people whose ancestors may have lived there) and see how your work will affect them (and vice versa).

All archaeology in the 21st century is in some way *public archaeology*. It's usually supported by public funding, and it often investigates the human heritage that belongs to everyone. So keep the public in mind as you dig.

Know the laws about digging

Different laws cover different kinds of land, and human graves come under another whole set of laws. The following sections give a general idea of the legalities (but be sure you get specifics for the particular area of your survey or excavation).

Private land

In the U.S., any artifacts unearthed on someone's private land, no matter how archaeologically valuable, belong to the landowner. In most other countries, the government takes charge of archaeological sites and artifacts to promote the heritage of the people. Although this practice sounds like better protection for sites, it can lead to looting or concealing finds.

You need permission to walk and look for artifacts (and certainly to dig) on any private land. Although it may be customary just to cut across someone's yard or field, you're trespassing if you do it without permission. If you pick up artifacts or dig a hole without permission while you're there, you're really asking for trouble.

Public land

You need a permit to do any archaeology on public lands in the U.S. depending on who owns them (states, local governments, or the federal government). A research permit application asks you to justify why you want to survey and pick up finds or dig on land that's protected. As I describe in Chapter 7, digging means destroying the evidence forever, so you'd better have a very good reason!

A famous law, Section 106 of the National Historic Preservation Act (NHPA), requires U.S. government agencies to take into account any archaeological sites before they build something or disturb the ground. Much of the archaeology done in the U.S. today results from this law, as well as other federal, state, and local laws covering *cultural resources* (archaeological and historic sites).

In most countries outside the U.S., a permit is necessary for any archaeological excavation, and the finds often have to stay in the country and be studied there. Many countries also have laws requiring survey or protecting archaeological sites in the path of construction.

Human graves

Even on private land, cemeteries are protected by law, so you can't just go dig there. Archaeologists sometimes help officials move graves out of the way of construction sites. Archaeologists' professional expertise means less disturbance to the remains of people's loved ones. In addition, they may study the old graves and skeletons to identify who's there or see what they can discover about the remains.

Unmarked human graves or bones are covered under different sets of laws. But nearly everywhere, you have to obtain permission to disturb them. So if you uncover unexpected human bones, you have to call authorities and first determine whether the bones are modern or ancient. You may need a *bioarchaeologist* (skeleton specialist) for this task. If they're modern remains, the medical examiner or other legal officer takes charge.

With ancient skeletons, you also need to comply with various laws depending upon where you are. Usually, you report them to a state archaeologist, and you're obliged to find out who the descendants may be. You may be allowed to excavate and study them under certain circumstances, but often you just rebury them.

Excavated skeletons

In the U.S., many laws cover human skeletons already excavated from archaeological sites. The Native American Graves Protection and Repatriation Act (NAGPRA) of 1993 required that human skeletal remains from federal land or dug with federal money be inventoried. Museums and other repositories had to give to any culturally affiliated peoples these inventories or lists of what remains they had. These peoples then had the opportunity to *repatriate* (take back) the bones and *funerary objects* (artifacts in graves). Sometimes Native American groups allowed study before repatriation, and sometimes they didn't. Many revered ancestors were reburied respectfully.

Problems arise when the remains are clearly indigenous Americans but can't be tied to any living group, which often happens if the skeleton is many thousands of years old or it's in an area where the native people's identity is unknown. Early European invaders wiped out hundreds of ethnic groups very quickly before these groups could be recorded. Many historic Native Americans who did survive could get less-brutal treatment if they hid their native heritage and passed for white or black. So tracing these connections is difficult.

I give you more to think about on these issues later in this chapter, and also in Chapter 16's discussion of who owns or controls the interpretation and materials of the past.

Other buried stuff

Utility lines (gas, electric, telephone, water) are everywhere underground. Before you dig, contact the companies and government agencies to get maps of where they run. Disturbing them may be not only illegal but also dangerous! In many places, you can call a toll-free number to have someone come out and flag the locations of all the utility lines in the area where you're planning to dig so you can avoid them.

Find out about buried toxic waste and other things that can be hazardous or confusing before you dig. Government agencies are supposed to know where these hazards are. Often, local folks can tell you this too. One farmer helped me understand the many dark features I'd exposed in his field. His dad made them in the 1920s when a flood killed sheep and pigs and he buried them! I did uncover a pig skeleton, complete with an iron ring in its nose!

Know the neighborhood where you're digging

Archaeologists must consider the various *stakeholders* or people interested in and affected by the past, the archaeological sites and finds. Each kind of stakeholder may have different reasons for this interest — often conflicting. And many of these reasons may conflict with your archaeological goals.

Local residents

Wherever you're digging or surveying, get to know the local people. That way they don't call the sheriff to see what you're doing. Also, they may be able to help you. They know the land and its history, including how natural places have changed over time. They may know about lots of archaeological sites and share artifact collections with you. They may even rescue you when your vehicle breaks down. Digging is easier and more ethically desirable if you have community support. You can also find the best places to stop after a day of digging for ice cream or a cold beer.

Other stakeholders

You won't believe the number of groups and people who may have an interest in the archaeology you're doing. Here's a list of some of them:

✔ Friends or family of the landowner, even people who manage the land for someone else who may have given you permission to be there.

✔ Anyone descended from or claiming to be descended from the people whose remains you're excavating (discussed more in the section "Respecting Native Americans and Other Descendant Communities" later in this chapter, and also in Chapter 16).

- ✔ Amateur (*avocational*) archaeologists who don't want you on their own special sites, or who do want to share with you what they've found at your site.

- ✔ Looters who don't want you on their special sites.

- ✔ People who are unclear on the law and think if you find a site on their land, the government will take it away.

- ✔ Other archaeologists who may have previously worked at the site or in the region and may or may not agree with your work and results.

- ✔ People who think archaeology is easy and want to come out and dig with you (or dig into your units after you leave for the day).

- ✔ People who don't care about archaeology but just don't want a bunch of college students, dirty people with shovels, hippies, and/or noisy folks next door or down the road.

- ✔ People who don't care about archaeology and absolutely don't want you on their land. (Maybe they're growing marijuana or doing something else they don't want you to see.)

- ✔ News reporters who want to get in on the dig and report it.

- ✔ Civic groups and historical societies interested in how your findings fit in with their community history.

- ✔ The general public who want to watch and maybe even learn from what you're doing.

- ✔ Specific groups such as school kids or teachers who want to observe and/or participate.

Field Ethics and Local Communities

I describe doing archaeology in, with, and for local communities in greater detail in Chapter 16. Here I discuss your ethical obligation to these important stakeholders to involve them in your work one way or another.

Positive community interaction

As an archaeologist, you have to be humble and realize you can find out a lot from so many others who know the land and the community.

Good ethics require that you share your archaeological investigation with the public. You benefit in ways you may not expect. You also share the concept of *stewardship,* preserving the heritage of the human past for the benefit of all.

Here are a few things you can do:

- ✓ Besides getting permissions and permits, let local law enforcement and neighbors near the dig know what's going on.

- ✓ Give a talk on your project for the local library, chamber of commerce, scout troop, or historical society.

- ✓ Hold an archaeology day where you can talk about your dig, show pictures, have people show you their artifacts, and teach them how to do old crafts such as pottery-making or *flintknapping* (stone tool chipping). I always have kids practice spear-throwing with sharpened cane poles and targets of mammoths drawn on big sheets of paper and stuck to bales of hay.

- ✓ Designate a day when the public can come help you dig and screen (under close supervision).

- ✓ Enlist neighbors to be stewards — to help guard your site from looters as they realize its importance to the community's human heritage.

- ✓ Assign a different crew person each day to greet visitors and explain clearly the archaeological project goals. Have a few of the nicest finds to show people (or if you're afraid of looters, some of the most boring finds so people don't want to go treasure hunting after you leave).

- ✓ Work with communities to see what they themselves want investigated about their cultural heritage.

Publicity

The local (or wider) press will often be very interested in the archaeology you're doing. Write a press release yourself (it helps avoid inaccuracies) to share details of the project with local newspapers, radio, and TV. In small towns, you may be the most interesting thing going on at the moment and get good coverage.

Invite media reporters to your dig and show them around. You can say you hope their stories don't encourage looting. You may ask them not to give directions to the site. They may offer to have you review what they write or say. Sometimes they also want to participate so they can write about the experience.

Publicity is usually helpful, especially if it brings volunteer workers or people with useful knowledge and artifacts.

Case study of a forgotten stakeholder

A story from my own work illustrates the concept of stakeholders in the archaeological process. My university was planning new buildings. Because a previous archaeologist had surveyed our campus, I knew of a significant prehistoric site right in the construction zone. University officials asked me to dig it to salvage as much as possible before the construction crew bulldozed it. I wanted publicity to see whether anyone had previously collected artifacts and even invite people to join in the dig. The university said no. The buildings were to be fraternity houses, and the project was controversial because they were being built with state money. So we just did the work quietly and submitted a report.

The next year the university planned to tear down the handball courts and build a new parking lot. Of course, the handball courts were on the only other significant prehistoric site on campus. To dig on state land — even at my own university — I needed to get a research permit from the state. So I did that advance paperwork and also an advance report to the university grounds and maintenance office. Another requirement was to contact the office that monitors all activities going on all over campus. Finally, I needed to report our planned work to the campus cops as well.

This time the school allowed me to have a public "archaeology day" when people could come watch or participate. I had news reporters, a Boy Scout troop, professors and students, and artists fascinated with the pink spear point I'd excavated. Several students were interested in how ancient hunters had lived near the small pond (now channeled into a drainage ditch) a thousand years ago on the same land where they now attended classes. My crew and I served the public and the archaeological resource. But I forgot one stakeholder — the parking office!

The archaeology students and I had all parked in a dormitory lot nearby. It was summer, and no students were in the dorm because budget cuts had meant no classes. Ours were the only vehicles in the lot, and we all had parking permits — but not for that lot. An hour before the public program (when many more cars would fill the lot), the parking official showed up to write tickets. I had to go to the parking director's office and plead for an exception. I had forgotten a stakeholder who wasn't even interested in the archaeology at all, just in keeping the rules.

Respecting Native Americans and Other Descendant Communities

I mentioned above the laws about digging human skeletons. But the ethical responsibilities you have as an archaeologist toward the past people and their present descendants are much more complicated than just staying within the law.

Respect for human remains

Some people love to have their own past and families investigated. You may say, sure, dig up my grandmother and do scientific study on her skeleton! But all cultures don't share this attitude. For many, including Native Americans and other indigenous peoples around the world, respect for the ancestors means not disturbing them at all. For others, it may mean limited study of skeletons or artifacts. Religious and traditional beliefs are important here.

When you can't avoid excavation of graves because of some construction, religious specialists and others may need to be present to conduct ceremonies and direct archaeological recovery and reburial of remains.

When you may need to stop digging

If you do uncover human skeletons, the most important step besides the legal actions is *consultation*. You want to explain the situation to the community and bring in all interested people to meet and discuss alternatives within the law.

Many archaeologists just don't excavate burials at all to avoid any problems. Others recognize that you can discover so much about past health, diet, disease, environment, and daily life from studying human bones (discussed more in Chapter 10). As an archaeologist, you're usually an anthropologist too. So you're acutely aware of the ethnocentrism in treating some people's remains as sacred and protected in cemeteries, and other people's remains as scientific specimens sitting on museum shelves.

Keep in mind human dignity as you dig. People walked and acted and lived where you're uncovering the remains they left behind. Always plan and consult with anyone who may be affected before you dig. Then be ready to uncover something in the ground that you must immediately cover back up.

Dealing with Dangerous Archaeological Field Conditions

Any outdoor activity involving metal tools, deep holes, and groups of happy, energetic people is bound to have many natural and human-made hazards. The following sections show you some specific areas to watch out for.

Tools and careless crew members

You always want to know how to use machines and hand tools carefully.

Even a trowel needs to be used precisely: You should hold it at a 45-degree angle to the ground, and you should be slicing off the soil, not scraping it. Otherwise, you'll obscure soil colors and features and scrape artifacts. If roots are in your way, cut them with your clippers. Pulling them up can damage your flat floor or wall.

Handling shovels, picks, machetes, and even well-sharpened trowels means using caution at all times. Government projects often have safety manuals and specific rules. Here are some general examples of proper procedures and injuries resulting from misuse of archaeological equipment:

- ✔ Picks and shovels can easily hit arms, legs, and especially feet — this is why you always wear long pants and sturdy boots. My own heavy leather boots have a nick in the toe where I accidentally hit them with the corner of a *mattock* (a wide-bladed pick).

- ✔ Even walking through the forest just carrying tools, you can get hit if you follow too closely and a vine grabs someone's shovel or machete and swings it back at you.

Research benefits from community interaction

When doing archaeology near small towns, I always check out local libraries. I love to meet librarians, learn from their knowledge, give them extra archaeology books I've accumulated, and see what old historic documents they may have, such as donated family papers. Librarians also love research and figuring stuff out.

Once a library stop had amazing results. For years I'd been searching for a prehistoric mound that an early explorer recorded in the bend of the river a century ago. This explorer had dug up beautiful native pottery and even some early Spanish glass and brass items (now in the Smithsonian Museum of the American Indian). But the mound's location was lost. I'd taken crew after crew, season after season, to comb the riverbank swamps looking for it, with no success. One day we walked in to see the town library's new building, which featured an exhibit of artifacts loaned by local people, including pottery from this mound and a map showing its exact location! A man had collected artifacts there when he was a kid some 40 years earlier. The librarian was just as excited as my archaeology crew. She called the man, and he came right over and offered to take us directly to the mound — or where it had been. Back then he'd gotten there on a trail bike through the woods (now there was a road). The mound had been eroding away on the riverbank edge. Now it was completely gone, but he was able to point to a tree on the bank that had been right next to it. I got an exact location and GPS coordinates. He graciously allowed us to study and photograph his collection and write an article about it.

- ✔ That old maxim about stepping on your shovel blade and having it bounce up and bash you in the face is very true, and not just for cartoon characters. Whenever you put a shovel on the ground, turn it face down.

- ✔ Anything sharp being thrown to someone else can hurt. I heard of someone getting a pointed iron pin through the eyeball.

- ✔ Heavy wheelbarrows of dirt (and even full buckets of soil) are guaranteed to give you a backache. Only fill them half full. If you try to push a wheelbarrow that's too heavy for you, it will inevitably tip over, spilling all your precious soil full of artifacts.

- ✔ Sticking trowels, ice picks, or other pointed tools in your pocket or pack can result in their poking through and impaling you.

- ✔ With heavy equipment, be absolutely clear on various safety procedures and issues from fire hazards to use of gas and oil containers. With any heavy machinery or deep excavations you need to wear a hard hat.

- ✔ Shore up any excavation that goes more than 4 feet deep so it doesn't cave in on the diggers, especially in soft sand. Have a ladder to get in and out. An alternative is to dig in stepped segments to get as deep as you need to.

- ✔ Objects you stand on to take site and whole-unit photos (ladders, buckets, or the truck roof) can be unstable and result in falls or dents.

Always check directions and get instruction before using heavy or power machinery. An archaeologist I worked for wasn't very safety-conscious. She handed a chain saw to a worker and ordered him to clear a few trees near the excavation unit. Afraid to say anything, the guy took the machine and tried to use it for the first time in his life. Within a couple minutes he had sawed into his own thigh! (Don't worry, I drove him to the emergency room.)

Get help to use machines!

On the crews I supervise, I always ask first whether people know how to use machinery. Once I didn't get the chance as we went out to a deserted island in the Gulf of Mexico to do archaeological survey. The ranger taking us in the boat had earlier left his ATV (all-terrain vehicle) on the island to fix. While the crew and I were swimming and waiting for him, he had fixed it and asked two students to run it along the beach a few miles back to the camp house. When we arrived at camp in the boat we found the two had never before driven an ATV, and had crashed and rolled it! The artifacts they had picked up were lost. One student had a cut face requiring stitches, so we had to get off the island quickly and to an emergency room.

Hazards of Mother Nature

You can check the particular natural hazards in the area where you're digging and take precautions against them. Here are some common ones:

✔ Insects bite and sting! Use repellent and have first aid (including ice for swelling) to use after they bite. Gloves, long sleeves, long pants, and headgear help here.

✔ If you're very allergic or get many stings at once, you can have a severe reaction. Then you need a quick shot of epinephrine — in the field or an emergency room — to prevent shock. If you know you're extremely allergic, carry an epinephrine injector in your pack (but get a prescription from your doctor).

✔ Ticks carry Lyme disease and other fevers. Non-disease ticks still burrow their heads into your skin and stay there (yech!), so know how to get them out properly with tweezers. Redbugs or chiggers also burrow (completely) into you and stay. One remedy is suffocating them by covering them with nail polish.

✔ Poison ivy and oak, stinging nettles, thorns on trees, and even branches that poke your eyeball can do severe damage. In my region of the southeastern U.S., poison ivy carpets the ground and makes lush canopies up into the trees. To go anywhere in the forest I need to be completely covered. Then I need to watch that my pack and the exterior of my clothes don't ever touch bare skin. Some commercial products specifically treat poison ivy, and others you can put on your skin in advance to prevent getting it.

✔ Snakes usually don't bite unless you pick them up, which should be strictly against project safety rules! They usually head away when they hear you coming. But know what snakes occur in your area and what to do if they bite anyway (go to the emergency room!). See the sidebar "Wildlife encounters in the field" for info on snakebite kits.

✔ Other animals you may not think of as vicious can bite you, so rabies and other effects are possibilities here. You can often fend them off with whatever tool you have in your hand.

✔ In some regions, disease organisms in the air and soil can get you. Read up about valley fever, trench lung or trench fever, Hantavirus, and others and whether they're risks associated with your site. Check for chemical hazards in the soil too, such as fertilizers on farm fields, septic or chemical waste areas, and even old cattle dip vats full of arsenic. (I've suffered through all these!)

Wildlife encounters in the field

Every summer field season, I get poison ivy blisters. The oil soaks through even the long sleeves and thick jeans. I'm used to it and have cortisone cream in my pack.

I use meat tenderizer on bee stings or ant bites (wet it and rub it in). It has an enzyme (papain, from papaya) that dissolves the protein the bug leaves in you. But don't use it near your face, because it'll dissolve your cornea too! I carry liquid antihistamine for insect stings. It's for kids in this form, but it gets into your system faster.

I've had various animals fall into open excavation units. Usually they're removable from afar with your shovel blade. Or you can leave a long board in the unit as a ramp for any animal that falls in to climb out on. I once removed an amazingly vicious possum by pushing it with the shovel into a bucket lowered on a rope and quickly hauling it up and out. Birds have nested in our screens and even once in a unit wall (destroying the stratigraphic layers we wanted to record!).

You have to expect that you'll not always look your best or act with your most refined behavior in the archaeological field situation. One season, I accidentally took out a wasp nest with my face while walking through the forest to set up an excavation. Not pleasant. Ice from the water cooler helped swelling, and I took a couple big swigs out of the antihistamine bottle in my pack. The stuff does make you dopey, so I sat on a log all day while my face swelled up till I resembled an elephant-woman. The field crew was sympathetic and dug more carefully than ever. They picked up all my fallen tools and put my pack back together. Next day, the swelling disappeared, but it left me with a sagging face.

On another project I used sturdy feed bags for soil samples. I grabbed a bunch of bags from the pile on the ground and headed toward an excavation unit, but the crew were pointing at me and yelling. A snake (a pretty, very deadly copperhead) had nestled into the bag pile for a nap, and now was in my arms! I quickly dropped everything and avoided tragedy. (By the way, snakebite kits aren't recommended these days because people misuse them. Yes, I carry one in my pack. For 20 years it's worked very well — as a magic charm preventing any bites.)

The next day when we were sitting around on overturned buckets eating lunch, I jumped up and yelled at the sight of another copperhead. Someone snapped a photo; it was a plastic snake, pulled along on clear fishing line by a mischievous crew member! They all had a laugh to see the photo with me spitting cheese and crackers and pointing at the ground with an agitated expression. They refused to give me the photo, probably planning to use it for future laughs.

Animals and plants live outdoors, and you usually don't. So you may want to read up on wildlife in your site area. Be prepared with guidebooks to identify the critters and emergency medicine guides to identify remedies.

Part III

After the Dig: You've Only Just Begun

The 5th Wave   By Rich Tennant

"And everything from my dig is brought here where it's identified, classified, interpreted, and then eaten."

In this part . . .

Most people don't realize that the work after the dig is the largest part of archaeology! It's often the reason that many digs never do get reported or described completely in print — finishing the job takes years!

In Chapter 9, I introduce the archaeological laboratory and show you what to do with all your information and finds to get them ready for study. Chapter 10 highlights different ways you can analyze your artifacts, and then Chapter 11 details the many ways (and fancy theoretical backgrounds) for telling the story of what you found and reconstructing human behavior in the past.

Chapter 9

Processing Excavated Materials in the Laboratory

*Y*ou may ask, "Why doesn't Hollywood show archaeologists sitting at laboratory tables all day?" After all, that's the biggest part of archaeology, and you can make thrilling discoveries right there in the lab too. Actually, you've seen this sort of work on crime-scene shows, where the lab tech cleans something up and finds out it's the big clue to the mystery.

So you need to know what to do with everything you bring back from the dig. In this chapter, I show you how an archaeological lab is set up. Then you see the first steps in processing all your materials, including how to clean, number, identify, and store finds and keep good records. Finally, I discuss *curation* — caring for everything so it can continue to be useful for research. Managing archaeological collections is complicated (and a specialty in itself)!

Setting Up an Archaeology Lab

Archaeology laboratories show up in universities, colleges, museums, archaeology company offices, and sometimes governmental agencies. You may even have a field lab to begin dealing with excavated materials right away.

You don't need a lot of equipment, space, and extensive training to start a lab. The fundamental operations, after all, are what you do all the time at home. You take care of material objects by

- ✓ Cleaning them
- ✓ Repairing them
- ✓ Putting them away in orderly fashion
- ✓ Storing them under good conditions

Of course, unlike with archaeological finds, you probably don't need to write numbers on all the socks in your drawer or pots and pans in your kitchen, or keep a list of exactly where you got each one.

Basic archaeology lab needs

In the lab, you do dirty, clean, wet, and dry work and store artifacts, other materials, and lots of paper. You need a typical scientific laboratory as well as items specific to archaeological collections (such as curation supplies).

Some things an archaeology lab needs to be:

- ✓ Spacious enough for both work and storage, and well lit
- ✓ As clean as possible (which can be tricky with all that dirty stuff like soil and unwashed artifacts around)
- ✓ Climate-controlled, because inhospitable temperature and humidity can cause further decomposition of many specimens
- ✓ Pollution-free, also to protect specimens
- ✓ Safety-conscious, with fire alarm and first-aid kit
- ✓ Secure, to prevent theft or loss; security needs are especially great (lockable cabinets, drawers, and doors) if you're doing forensic cases requiring careful chain-of-evidence documentation

Here's a list of some basic things an archaeology lab needs to have:

- ✓ Tables (long and wide), chairs, and good lighting (high-intensity lamps)
- ✓ Plenty of shelving, adjustable if possible
- ✓ A big sink with a sand trap (if possible) that deposits any soil into a container that you can then empty without clogging up your pipes

And finally, this list shows you the basic supplies needed in an archaeological laboratory:

- ✔ Regular office supplies, including waterproof markers and pens, rulers, compasses, protractors, wide clear tape for map repair, 3-ring binders, and storage supplies such as plastic photo holders or sheet protectors.

- ✔ Black and white India (indelible) ink and quill pens (nibs and handles) or very fine-point waterproof felt-tip pens.

- ✔ Plastic dishpans or other tubs for washing artifacts; brushes (including old toothbrushes).

- ✔ Kitchen strainers and geological screens of different mesh sizes for further sorting of soils.

- ✔ Resealable plastic bags of all sizes — the usual curation standards are 4 mils thick. (A *mil* equals 0.025 millimeters or 0.001 inch; even garbage bags are usually only 1 or 2 mils thick) — and acid-free paper bags.

- ✔ Plastic or glass vials or other sturdy containers for small finds; discarded plastic 35-millimeter film canisters from photo shops work well, as do contact-lens vials from optical shops — and they're free (though they've stopped making many of them, so get them fast).

- ✔ Acid-free paper, paper tags, cardboard boxes of different sizes, and foam padding for storing materials.

- ✔ Acryloid B-72 solution, polyvinyl acetate, acetone, clear nail polish, polish remover, Duco cement, and white glue.

- ✔ Clean sand in a small box or other container to hold drying artifacts you've glued back together.

- ✔ Scrap paper, newspaper, rags, towels, and paper towels.

- ✔ Cafeteria-style trays (or get cardboard beer-crate bottoms at the store).

- ✔ Mechanical hand tools like screwdrivers, as well as tweezers and a few hand tools from excavation, like dental picks and butter knives, to chip off hardened dirt from specimens.

- ✔ Physical lab items such as pipettes or eyedroppers, beakers, and magnifying glasses.

- ✔ Magnet (any size) to see if your decayed old artifact is made of metal.

Fancier equipment: Magnifiers, measurers, music

If you spend long hours in the lab, you want fine equipment to do the job well under pleasant conditions. Here are some examples of what to have:

✔ **Scale for weighing artifacts:** A food scale from the discount store is adequate, or you can spend thousands of dollars on scientific scales that go to hundredths of grams. Figure out what your requirements are before you commit to an expensive scale.

✔ **Calipers and other measuring devices:** These instruments can be mechanical (cheaper) or digital and battery-operated; again, use your personal requirements as a guide.

✔ **Magnifying lamps** to see tiny stuff.

✔ **Microscopes** to see even tinier stuff.

✔ **Books and other reference guides** for identifying materials such as shells, animal bones, seeds, and artifact types in your region.

✔ **An archaeology lab manual** for laying out proper procedures; you often update this as you figure what works and doesn't.

✔ **Small refrigerator** for fragile specimens, film, and your lunch.

✔ **Computer, printer, scanner, and software** for data storage and processing, making maps, scanning and processing images and photos, creating and manipulating databases, and word-processing.

✔ **Map cabinet** with big, wide drawers for site and area maps.

✔ **Footstool and ladder** to get to high shelves.

✔ **Radio or CD player** for some relaxing music while you work!

A lab crew with tons of patience

Lab work takes some of the same skills as fieldwork, but it requires a different set of skills as well. You have to sit for hours happily washing artifacts, making maps, or sorting tiny bits of animal, vegetable, and mineral matter under the microscope. As in the field, you have to worry about trivial details. Otherwise, mistakes creep in and the integrity of your finds is lost.

Many people find lab tasks relaxing. Others find the painstaking work tedious and frustrating; they just want to see what something is, not spend forever patiently scraping off the encrusted dirt in microscopically thin layers.

But wait! You must work slowly on one task at a time. If you lose the knowledge that came in with the artifact or if you forget which bag you took an unnumbered specimen from, your find is worthless! The *provenience* data (all the information about where something came from) is the most important information you process. See Chapters 6 and 7 for more on bagging and tagging artifacts during survey and excavation, respectively.

You want a lab crew of mellow folks who can help each other keep track of things. The ideal is to have the field crew become the lab crew — that way, crew members won't wonder about how or why something came in a certain way from the field. Until you actually process materials from your first dig, you can't imagine how much information is lost in bringing excavated materials and information from field to lab!

Processing Excavated Materials

You should clean, stabilize or repair (if needed), catalogue, identify and classify, measure, and photograph (if desired) archaeological materials before you store them. Doing these things all at once to avoid repeatedly taking artifacts in and out of bags reduces error and damage to the specimens, but most labs don't have the room or the labor to do this.

Cleaning artifacts and ecofacts

Don't wash finds in the sink, where mud will instantly clog up the drain (even if you have a sand trap)! Tubs of water and old toothbrushes work fine, and you can dump the dirty water outside when you're done. Here are some hints on cleaning:

- Gently brush stone and other hard materials underwater so you don't splash drops of muddy water everywhere.

- Prehistoric unglazed ceramics may be cleanable by just holding them underwater and rubbing them gently with fingers, though the broken edges may need brushing to see the *temper* mixed with the clay or to clean surfaces that can be glued to other pieces.

- Only brush shells and hard bone if necessary, and with a very soft brush.

- Try cleaning softer bone by dry-brushing or brief immersion; it may be too fragile to clean at all.

- Chip rusted iron with small metal tools to get the rust chunks off, but be careful because the artifacts may be quite fragile. Some pieces may be rusted through so that you have nothing left to clean!

- Either rinse or gently dry-brush perishables such as bone, wood, feathers, leather, cloth, and other organics; they may also need immediate conservation, soaking in preservative solutions, drying, or keeping wet, depending on the material.

Needless to say, you have to be careful no matter what you're cleaning, or you can end up losing information or ruining an artifact:

- ✔ Don't dump a whole bag of artifacts into the water. As it gets muddier, you won't see everything, and tiny items can be forgotten and mixed in with the next bag's stuff.

- ✔ Don't scrub a soft artifact and make new patterns on it with your brush.

- ✔ Don't wash something if it looks fragile.

- ✔ Don't clean an artifact if you see some deposits on it that may indicate what it was used for. DNA analysis of blood on a stone tool can determine what animal species it came from. Residues on pots can reveal what substances the containers held.

- ✔ Don't lose track of what you're doing. As you wash finds, lay them out separately by provenience to dry — with their bags and information — on newspaper in trays or in a *drying rack* (stack of wooden-sided box screens). Artifacts separated from their provenience data are worthless.

Conserving or restoring the materials

You want to prevent your finds from disintegrating; you may go further and restore them. The following sections give you an overview of how to conserve your artifacts and decide on the extra step of restoration.

Conservation

Stone, ceramics, and other hard materials are usually okay after cleaning, though you want to soak the salt out of anything excavated from salt water.

Preservative solutions help for crumbling potsherds or bone. Museum curators use Acryloid B-72 and polyvinyl acetate (PVA), two chemicals that can (supposedly) be removed, to stabilize delicate items. If you can't get these products, a thin solution of Duco cement and acetone (nail polish remover without the oils and scents) or white glue (make sure it has PVA) and water can work. I try not to use chemicals if possible; they can damage the potential for radiocarbon dating, bone mineral analysis, or other materials studies.

Rusty metal may rust more without quick treatment. If enough of the object remains intact, you can put it into an *electrolysis bath,* where electricity draws corrosion out; this process works for silver and other metals too. Waterlogged wooden artifacts can sit in a warm bath of polyethylene glycol (PEG) that eventually replaces the water in the wood and conserves the object.

Materials often have to sit for months in these baths, so they can take up space in your lab. The chemicals required may be hazardous, so get expert advice before you do such conservation! Be sure you follow a specific safety plan in handling, storing, and cleaning up after using chemicals.

Preservation versus restoration

I mention in Chapter 7 that archaeologists and heritage specialists argue about reconstructing a site versus restoring it or preserving it as is. This debate also applies to artifact conservation.

Different actions depend on different goals. Do you put the artifact back together and fill in the missing parts as well as you can with some modern material? Or do you just stabilize it as is and prevent future decay? Reconstructing an artifact to show how it may have looked for an exhibit may be great for interpreting the past. Preserving it with minimal treatment may allow it to be studied further by chemical and other analyses in the future.

I can tell you that gluing sherds of a pot back together is great for the photo but it makes fitting the pot back in the box or narrow drawer harder. Plus, if different sherds came from different proveniences, you have to make all those additional notes in the catalog to account for what happened to each sherd.

Examining the soil samples

You may have lugged back to the lab all those bags of soil you took as samples to undergo the flotation process, which I describe in Chapter 7. Putting these soils through water and fine screens, you can recover lots of very tiny stuff that gives you new ideas about your site.

Smaller soil samples for permanent storage or future study can just be boxed up and put on the shelf. Let them dry out first so that they're less likely to grow mold. Soil is heavy, so don't put too many soil samples in a box, or you won't be able to lift it! And make sure you don't put the heavy stuff on the highest shelf! Not only can it fall on you, but also it's also harder to retrieve.

Cataloguing and numbering

After everything's clean, you can catalog all your finds and number them so that provenience information is clear and won't be lost.

Cataloguing

Several tasks come under the heading of cataloguing:

- ✔ Updating your field catalog with any new information discovered in the lab. For example, you may find that what you thought was a stone chip is really a finished stone tool. (I describe this process in Chapter 7 and give you an example of the form in Figure 6-1 in Chapter 6.)

- ✔ Doing individual catalog sheets for each bag from each provenience — listing all the materials in each now that they're clean and you can see what they are. You may also list weights, measurements, other attributes.

- ✔ Assigning numbers to each item if needed. These can be put into a computer database as well if they're not in one already.

- ✔ Writing the provenience/catalog number on each item.

Numbering archaeological materials

Assigning numbers depends on what system you're working in. You may just keep whatever numbers you already used in the field, such as the site number first, then additional numbers in sequence.

Many museums and other institutions require that artifacts be labeled with long accession numbers that are then put into a huge catalog book or database with directions to understand what those numbers mean! Some catalog numbers include the year and a lot number assigned to a large body of artifacts. Some even include additional code numbers to indicate what kind of material it is (stone, bone, ceramic, and so on). Many collections are now on a computerized bar-code system.

Writing catalog numbers right on the materials is crucial — if you misplace the items, you always know the provenience. Here's how to do it:

- ✔ The standard is to write with indelible black (india) ink and quill pens with metal tips. Writing on stone and other hard materials wears out a pen quickly, so metal tips are important. Some labs use fine-point felt-tip waterproof pens, but they wear out almost instantly and are expensive.

- ✔ For dark materials that won't show black ink, use indelible white ink and a pen dedicated only to white writing so that your inks don't mix.

- ✔ Wipe and clean pens as you go along so they don't clog up.

- ✔ Some lab directors like to paint a swath of clear nail polish, white paint, or even white correction fluid on the artifact and write the number on this patch. I think this tactic looks sloppy, and it can sometimes chip off more easily than just an inked number.

- ✔ However, for porous materials such as some ceramics, you may need to make a solid surface to write on. In this case, clear nail polish is best — just paint a small area, let it dry completely, and then write the number.

✔ Write the number in an unobtrusive place on the artifact, like the back-side that probably won't be photographed, so that you don't cover up its important features. This guideline also holds if you're slapping on a bar code sticker.

✔ Always write numbers over newspaper or scrap paper, and have the acetone handy for spills. A tipped bottle of indelible ink can make a permanent mess! Be sure to let the ink dry before you put stuff away.

✔ For artifacts that just can't be written on (such as a rusty iron object), use a paper tag tied on with string or some other secure method for numbering.

✔ Many labs don't write numbers on their thousands of specimens until they get them out to study them because it takes so much time and labor (and the number is on the container anyway). But numbering every item so that you never lose proveniences is an important professional practice.

✔ Work with one bag of artifacts at a time. I can't stress enough how important it is to keep artifacts with their own provenience information.

Classifying artifacts by types

After you've cleaned and numbered your artifacts, lay out everything and see what you've got. You may be able to easily identify them by raw material or general artifact type.

After the general initial identification, you get into the classic archaeological practice of using *artifact typologies.* These are guides established in specific geographic areas that list each type of artifact associated with that area. A good typology has non-overlapping criteria so you can sort things into clear categories. But many typologies aren't well developed. (For example, type 1 may be painted black and type 2 painted red, but now you've excavated a piece with both red and black paint, for which no type name exists). You may need to establish a new type, or just describe your item by noting the closest known type it resembles. You see this dilemma in real life if you try to classify someone else's stuff — is this a serving plate or a wall decoration? An expensive brand-name watch or a cheap fake?

Here's how you can make preliminary identifications and then do the research to refine them based on different materials:

✔ Chipped stone tools can be *unifacial* (flaked on one side) or *bifacial* (flaked on both sides). Bifaces can be *projectile points* (often called arrowheads even though they're usually spear points) or knives or choppers or other types. You can usually find regional guides to chipped-stone tool types. The type names sometimes show the first sites where they were found (like Agate Basin points, from a Wyoming site), or combine that with some name based on appearance (my favorite here being the Susquehanna Broad, a wide projectile point named after a New York river valley).

✔ The flakes left from manufacturing these stone tools are the *lithic debitage*. They're also classified in many ways. *Primary flakes* have some of the outer stone still on them. *Secondary flakes* are the inner, presumably better material, and usually flatter. You can subdivide further from there too, based on size, color, and type of raw stone material. You also want to tell whether the stone has been thermally altered (heated) to make it easier to chip. Many guides to studying debitage can help you.

✔ *Ground-stone* artifacts, meaning they were smoothed rather than chipped, can be axes, mortars and pestles, bowls, beads, statues, and many other things. These finds are usually easier to classify based on published regional typologies.

✔ Prehistoric pottery typologies abound in archaeology! Dedicated workers pore over broken bits of everyday kitchen ware. Some potsherds are easy to classify into types established for the region. Their decoration, whether molded into the wet clay, painted on, or otherwise, will be easy to see. For plain sherds (or maybe all sherds), you want to describe what is called the *paste,* meaning the clay itself and the temper material it was mixed with. Ceramic type names often reflect their appearance and the place or site where they were first recorded, such as "Rockport Black" (Texas, painted with natural asphalt) or "McGraw Cordmarked" (Ohio, impressed with twisted cords before firing).

✔ Metal artifacts are first classified by raw material if possible. You'll know iron because of its magnetic properties and gold because it never tarnishes. After that, classification gets more complicated, so you'll want special expertise and guidebooks to what's usually found in your region. Look for detailed typologies for iron nails of all time periods, sizes, and shapes; for brass decorative items and jewelry in different parts of the world; and for parts of lamps, guns, swords, machines, and anything you can think of made of metal. If you're lucky, your metal artifact is a coin with its identification stamped right on it!

✔ Wood, bone, shell, and other materials may have decayed too much to identify, so you may have to list them as worked fragments (as opposed to ecofacts, which weren't shaped into artifacts). But you can identify a pointed bone pin, engraved piece, basket fragment, or shell bead.

✔ Historic crockery, such as earthenware (softer), stoneware (harder), china, and so on, is well described in many guides (even antiques manuals). Some tips for identifying it: Porcelain is translucent, and real Chinese porcelain is thinner and more finely decorated than English imitations. If you have the bottom of the vessel, you can even read manufacturers' marks.

✔ Historic materials of glass and other substances are classified in many guides. First you can sort them by color and then by shape into bottles, jars, bowls, and so forth as well as tell if they're machine-made (with regular mold marks) or hand-blown (less symmetrical and regular). For historic metal, glass, and many other items, old Sears catalogs are great to get identifications!

Look online for more typologies and guides for classifying artifacts. But also realize that (especially for prehistoric artifacts) archaeologists constantly argue about whether the typologies they use today reflect the ways that the past people who made the artifacts would have classified them. This controversy shouldn't concern you too much — at least you have a system to use to study these material bits of the past!

Classifying ecofacts and other materials

Biological and geological specimens you've brought back from the dig are often much easier to classify. You can tell shell from bone from pebble from soil. For more precise classification, get guides to various species' shells or skeletons, or call for help from specialists such as *zooarchaeologists* (who study animal remains from archaeological sites), *ethnobotanists* (who study archaeological plant remains), and geologists. I discuss these specialties more in Chapter 10.

Granulometric analysis means soils are classified by grain size — large, medium, and small are sand, silt, and clay, respectively. Mixtures of these grain sizes create different kinds of loam. Official soils manuals can help you determine what kinds of soil grains you have. You can also get a set of geological screens and sift your soil through them to see what proportions of what grain sizes you have.

Different kinds of soils are deposited in different ways, so you can find out about the site formation processes at your excavation. (I discuss site formation processes more in Chapter 2). Fast water deposits sand, and very fast, large volumes of water can dump loads of clean white sand — good evidence in your stratigraphy of a big storm or hurricane!

Coprolites are a cool kind of ecofact to study. They're dried up old pieces of excrement, or fossilized feces (say that ten times fast!) They're seldom preserved, but you'll know them when you see them. A good zooarchaeologist can tell whether a coprolite is human or animal, and sometimes what species of animal. Coprolites have tons of information about the individual from whom they came (diet, DNA), but they must be stored carefully.

Weighing, measuring, and other recording

For every artifact and ecofact, you may want to record the weight, color, length, and other measurements. Be sure to describe particular markings or other attributes — you may even sketch the item or put it on the scanner to have its picture taken and added to the catalog. You may be doing a hand-written catalog sheet or a computer database entry or both. Remember to copy information carefully — the more times you transfer numbers into various records, the more chances you have for error.

Other tests and little tricks are useful to collect information about archaeological materials. A historic archaeologist I know swears he can tell various types of crockery by licking them! To see whether the little white chunks in your potsherd are really crushed shell temper you can drop acid on them — put a drop of hydrochloric acid, and if the white stuff fizzles, it's shell or limestone. The list goes on, but you get the idea! Your lab director and standard archaeology laboratory texts will have all these hints.

Sorting flotation remains

After you've processed your soil samples through the flotation barrel (described in Chapter 7) and come up with little piles of stuff that finally dried, you're far from done. You need to sort the recovered remains into the same categories of artifacts and ecofacts and include them in the counts from each provenience. You may have large materials in the *heavy fraction* (the largest-mesh screen, probably the ¼-inch). The *light fraction* (from the finest screen) may have tiny charred seeds, fish or rodent bones, beads, and maybe bug cases and tiny modern roots. You need a microscope or at least a magnifying glass to see and sort everything. You may want to save any charcoal you pull out for radiocarbon dating.

Tweezers or wooden sticks are good tools for sorting dried flotation remains that you've poured out onto a tray. Sewing needles jammed (using pliers) into the tops of chopsticks are also useful here. You can pick up little charcoal bits with static cling by using very fine paintbrushes.

As you sort the fine remains, you separate each kind (seed, shell, stone, etc.) into different tiny bags or vials, possibly many for each provenience. Label each container with the provenience, and put it all together with the bigger stuff to get the whole picture.

Processing Information and Paperwork

Along with all the material things you need to take care of, your archaeological excavation data are very much in need of attention in the lab after the dig. You usually have both electronic data and piles of paper, and possibly information in other media such as film.

Maps

Regardless of whether you're using a paper or electronic map (or both). you still need a well-drafted map for publication, one that fits on a page in whatever report you're writing. You may want a huge map of the whole site, close-up maps of each unit and its features, or even three-dimensional images of the strata and materials in each unit. You may do GIS (geographic information systems) layers for materials and attributes of your site, to see what they look like when overlaid. (Did all the examples of one type of artifact come from the place of the highest elevation?)

Other records

Putting your catalog of all materials recovered from the site onto a computer database or spreadsheet includes putting in all the accompanying information. Then you can sort for various things you want to know (discussed more in Chapter 10), like a table of all the stone artifacts. You may scan or transcribe individual workers' field notes into a word-processing program for future use. You may have many other paper records to put into electronic format:

- Field forms and photo logs, unit floor and wall stratigraphy drawings, and feature drawings
- Notes from other participants or visitors
- Information from local collectors about their collections and photos of their artifacts
- Historic or environmental records of interest for your site
- Catalogs and data from previous people's investigations at your site
- Business cards and information on important places near your site, such as the hardware store, the best coffeehouse, and the bar

Don't forget to back up all computer work every day! Losing your data is like bulldozing your site!

Preliminary documentation

In Chapter 10 I show you how to analyze your finds and information, and in Chapter 11 you see how to put it all together to report on your dig. But right when you get back from the dig and into the lab, you may want to send out some preliminary news. Supporters, volunteers, donors, and workers on your project all like to know how it's going. A summary of your excavation work may even include photos of artifacts washed and glued back together.

Don't forget to write thank-you notes to supporters as well. This is also important for collectors who've shared their data (and if you want to publish their names or photos of their artifacts, be sure you write them again to ask permission).

You may want to create or update a Web site on the project to share information. You can even include a discussion board.

Curation and Collections Management

Proper storage and research facilities are necessary for archaeological specimens and records. Curation means not only storage of collections but also making them available for future investigations. So you need to have the space, the facilities, the staff, and the supplies.

Taking care of your collections: They're forever

Curation is a huge responsibility, but you take it on when you dig up the stuff in the first place. It's a lot like having kids — if you want them, you've got to care for them! Archaeological materials are non-renewable resources. If they're lost or destroyed, they're forever gone. You want to curate them, as the standards usually say, in perpetuity.

Standards and supplies

I recommend that you look at published curation guidelines, such as U.S. government standards ("Curation of Federally Owned and Administered Archaeological Collections" or 36 CFR 79) or individual states' standards, available online. You can also find companies that sell everything from archival-quality supplies (like acid-free paper) to giant rolling space-saver cabinets for collections storage and easy access. The whole point is to store the materials in ways that they won't degrade. This includes paper archives. Maps can be redone on *mylar* (a plastic that doesn't decay as fast).

You can put electronic versions of all your data on CDs, but always back them up, not only with paper copies but also some other medium, such as a flash drive. As quickly as technology changes, you may not even be able to use today's common format in the future! I still have lots of data on floppy disks (remember those ancient artifacts?), but few computers now read them.

Research protocols

Collections management also means facilitating future research with your materials and data. You should always keep a few tables empty in the lab to have space for boxes of specimens that someone wants to get out and study. Many museums have spaces dedicated to visiting researchers, with photographic stands and everything. Such visitors may want to compare your finds with theirs, take different kinds of measurements, or study them with new techniques or instruments. Fancier places keep piles of thin white cotton gloves to wear for handling artifacts that body oils can damage. Many museums and other artifact repositories have strict research protocols listing steps you need to complete in order to get permission to study their collections and procedures you must follow during the study.

Some archaeology labs have enough labor and expertise to begin putting all their collections in electronic format (with photos) and online for any researcher to use. This is a wonderful development and should result in much good future investigation. Having the photos online has also helped when thefts have happened — everyone can see what's been stolen and watch for it to show up with dealers or in artifact shows or auction Web sites!

The ethics of collections management

It's unethical to excavate and then not care for the materials and information recovered. On government projects, it's illegal too! Unfortunately, you *never* see archaeology adventure movies with characters who sit and number artifacts all day. It's just not considered the exciting part of archaeology even though it takes usually ten times as long as excavation! Another misfortune is that collections curation and management also receive far less grant funding and public support.

Future collections research

In archaeology, you often have the opportunity to do further research on older archaeological collections. If materials are well cared-for, you can continue to study them in the future, especially when a new technique or instrument comes along.

Good collections management is just as much part of archaeological research as excavation. For example, with the advent of AMS (accelerator mass spectrometry) radiocarbon dating, where you only need a tiny bit of charcoal to get a date, many old collections of plant remains were examined again. Tiny charred fragments of domesticated species could be directly dated, and they proved that domestication took place earlier than expected. Crusted-on deposits scraped off old ceramics weren't only dated but also examined for chemical composition to see what had been cooked or brewed in those pots!

So my final note about laboratory work is this: You just have to do it. Many have called it archaeology's "dirty little secret" that stuff gets excavated and then stuffed onto the shelf and ignored forever after, like Indiana Jones's lost ark. Doing the digging and then not processing, studying, and caring for the materials and data is no better than looting. And if you don't do the work sooner rather than later, you can lose a lot. I remember reading the autobiography of a famous 20th-century archaeologist who said she dug a site, put the materials in wooden boxes on the shelf, and was unable to get back to them for about ten years. By that time, termites had eaten all the boxes. So everything all fell together in one big pile. With all provenience information lost, her work was worthless!

Chapter 10

Studying and Analyzing What You've Excavated

*I*n Chapter 9, I cover how to wash your finds and then label, photograph, measure, weigh, and record them, and put them in curation-quality bags and boxes with proveniences written on them. That's a lot to do — you may think you've spent longer processing the materials and data than the time that all the stuff sat in the ground! At least now your work is finally finished, right? Wrong. The real science is just beginning. But the next steps ramp up the excitement because new discovery is equally possible in the laboratory.

This chapter gives you the steps for analyzing your materials. Then you can see their relationships in time, space, and activity. They have a lot to say to you (but don't hold the artifact up to your ear to listen; that never works).

Documenting How Finds Occur in Space and Time

If you've already been entering your information into a computer database as you collect it, this step may be easier and faster — until the computer crashes. Always make backups! By now, you have a list of what has come from each provenience. Next, you want to make new lists of different kinds of artifacts by provenience and of all the artifacts in each large (and then smaller) provenience — say all the pottery sherds in Excavation Unit 1, listed according to the depth, level, or stratum where you found them.

Remember, *provenience* is all the information on exactly where the item came from, in three-dimensional space, including the date of the find and name of the finder. It's one of the most important concepts in archaeology. If you lose it, your finds are scientifically useless! So take special care to keep track of proveniences in the lab as well as during the fieldwork.

Making charts of finds

Artifact tables take many forms, but they all show (in a logical fashion) what you've dug up. If you're an accountant, or even if you just balance your checkbook on your computer, you know making these kinds of tables with a spreadsheet or database program is pretty easy. With this system, sorting by row or column is fast and shows you the information you're trying to extract from the pile of data. In the old days, archaeologists spent hours creating these tables by hand. A few holdouts still do it this way; other old-fashioned scholars know they can just ask a typical computer-savvy student to do it.

Charting finds in horizontal space

To see what's different in separate *horizontal* areas of your site, you want a grand list for each artifact type, showing how many you found and where — the numbers and proveniences across the site. For example, Table 10-1 lists each pottery type in the first column; other columns show the number (N) of *sherds* (broken pieces) of each type, their weights (Wt) in grams for each provenience, and the totals. The columns (Units 1, 2, and 3 and Surface) are different horizontal spaces, and each row shows an artifact type. Variations among columns tell you that different activities may have taken place across your site, identifying *activity areas*. This kind of table doesn't yet show vertical space (the different depths of sherds in each unit). Because it shows numbers, however, the table gives you quantitative data to work with.

Right away, you can tell a few cool things from this table. The fancier pottery, with incised lines, stamped patterns, and red paint, is rare except in Unit 3. If this unit is, say, near the mound or temple, you may suggest that the decorated pottery (especially the red ware) is for ceremonial uses, and the plain stuff is for everyday use. You can also see by the weights compared with the numbers that the red sherds are bigger. Maybe they're less broken and stomped-around with the everyday garbage and so are more special.

If you tabulate the other artifacts, animal bones, and other *ecofacts* (natural objects used by people but not made into artifacts) in this fashion, you may find a bigger pattern. If animal bones from certain species are also only found in Unit 3 with the more special ceramics, this pattern may indicate special animal foods used only in that area — maybe ritual feasts using those fancier decorated pots. Think about your family holidays; when else does Grandma bust out the turkey, cranberry sauce, and fancy china? For everyday dinners at your house, you have more utilitarian dishes and foods.

Table 10-1	Ceramics from the Cold Creek Camp Site				
	Unit 1	Unit 2	Unit 3	Surface	Totals
Type	N/Wt (g)	N/Wt (g)	N/Wt (g)	N/Wt (g)	N/Wt (g)
Cold Creek Plain	50/200	39/165	10/127	100/432	199/924
Cold Creek Stamped	2/10	6/25	78/754	10/47	96/836
Cold Creek Incised	1/3	4/15	65/657	6/22	76/697
Cold Creek Red-Painted	0/0	1/11	93/920	2/25	96/956
Totals	53/213	50/216	246/2458	118/526	467/3413

Putting amounts and weights of each artifact type sometimes helps you see other trends, especially when you're dealing with broken items such as ceramics. Dividing the weights by the numbers of each type gives you the average weight per specimen, which is significantly greater for some types than for others. In Table 10-1, the weights of the red sherds average about 10 grams each, but weights of the other types average about 4 grams. However, even the plain stuff is large in Unit 3. This may indicate a more special area where all the pots were used more carefully rather than kicked around.

From your historical research you may know that pots and other artifacts were ritually broken into just a few pieces after a feast, so you can hypothesize that you found evidence of this custom in the prehistoric past too. Making additional tables showing the percentages (both by number and by weight) within the rows, the columns, or the entire table also helps you to see such patterns. For example, 97 percent of the red sherds at the whole site came from Unit 3, but within Unit 3, only 38 percent of the sherds were of the red type.

Charting finds in vertical space

After charting sideways in space, now you must go up and down. The way different artifacts are distributed in *vertical space* in each test unit can show how styles and activities change through time. For this kind of study, you need carefully controlled information, with all depths measured. You can't use artifacts that came from disturbed places like the ground surface. You may have excavated in arbitrary levels, like 10 centimeters at a time, or in the cultural or natural *strata* (layers) that were visible in the ground. (See Chapter 7 for more explanation of these). Now you can tabulate your finds according to these levels or strata.

Remember, you can assume artifacts buried deeper are older (unless you see signs of disturbance), so you can arrange your table something like Table 10-2, with the artifact type names on the left and the shallowest level or stratum as the first column. Then you continue toward the right of the table to get a visual representation of your artifact distribution going downward through those levels or strata and see what artifacts are earlier or later than others and what other types came from the same depths.

Table 10-2 Ceramics from the Cold Creek Camp Site, Test Unit 3

	Level 1: 0–20 cm	Level 2: 20–40 cm	Level 3: 40–60 cm	Totals
Type	N	N	N	N
Cold Creek Plain	0	3	7	10
Cold Creek Stamped	4	20	54	78
Cold Creek Incised	21	20	24	65
Cold Creek Red-Painted	54	30	9	93

In Table 10-2, you can see the real differences from the shallowest material to the deepest because you've carefully excavated in 20-centimeter (8-inch) levels. Level 3, the deepest and earliest, shows more plain pots and stamped pots were in use during that time. On the other hand, the red ceramics are pretty rare in Level 3 but grow in numbers through time to become the main find in Level 1 (the latest). From this information, you can hypothesize that painting pottery red was a later development, maybe associated with increased ceremonial feasts (if the animal bones follow a similar pattern).

Of course, you're making a lot of assumptions here. You're assuming that

✔ You have a representative sample of all the pottery at the site

✔ The sample wasn't disturbed or mixed by burrowing rodents

✔ Your lab workers have counted everything accurately instead of goofing off all day

But at least you have a nice hypothesis you can test with the next excavation.

Using bar charts

A good way to quickly show the information in your tables is with charts and graphs. Figure 10-1 shows what a bar chart of Table 10-2 may look like.

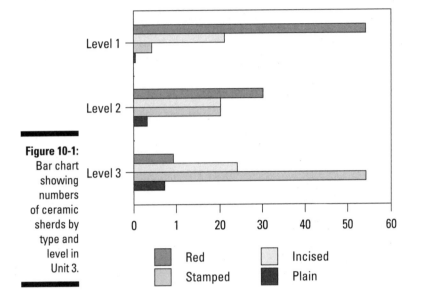

Figure 10-1:
Bar chart showing numbers of ceramic sherds by type and level in Unit 3.

Red   Incised

Stamped   Plain

If you put the deepest level at the bottom of the chart, you can instantly see the increase in red pottery through time.

Another bar-chart option consists of listing artifact types across the top and time on the side, and centering the bars under each type to give what are called *battleship-shaped curves* (because they supposedly look like the shape of a battleship from above). These charts more easily show changes in the popularity of different artifact types and styles.

Figure 10-2 shows this kind of chart with a much bigger ceramic assemblage. Starting at 1200 (your earliest date), you see that type 4 is already the most popular and that type 2 is just starting to be used. In fact, type 2 never gets much use, and the peak of its popularity (its widest bar) is right before 1250. By that time, type 4 is dwindling, and type 3 is coming into use. By 1275, type 1 is invented and soon takes over in even greater frequency: It peaks at 1350 but is still in widespread use by 1400 (the latest date you have for your site), a time when the other types have mostly disappeared. You can graph any artifact type this way — even artifact attributes such as skirt lengths or tail fins on car models — to show increasing and decreasing popularity.

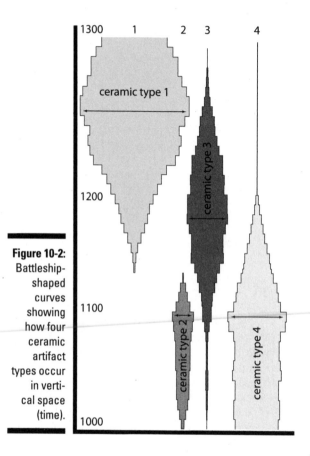

Figure 10-2:
Battleship-
shaped
curves
showing
how four
ceramic
artifact
types occur
in verti-
cal space
(time).

Making discoveries during the laboratory analysis

Your exciting findings in the lab can rival the thrill of uncovering a long-lost artifact in the field (and you won't be as dirty in the lab). By organizing your data in tables and graphs, you get a picture of the different activities in space and changes through time at your site.

Table 10-1 suggests that fancier ceramics indicate special behavior in the area of Unit 3. Further evidence for this idea may come when you see other unusual artifacts or animal bones in the same location. They all may show ritual activity not seen elsewhere at the site. Other patterns may jump out at you from the charts. For example, the deeper levels of Unit 3 don't have as much special stuff, but Table 10-2 shows that the shallower levels do. This pattern may mean that the ritual behavior began later in time.

Putting your finds onto your map

A good map is crucial for seeing how the artifacts and other data behave at an archaeological site. You already have the map you made during fieldwork showing geographic features (streams, hills) and your excavation units and surface collection areas. Now it's time to add on the new information you've extracted from the artifact and ecofact assemblages. Many simple computer graphics programs (or even the word-processing program you used to make the bar chart) can draw distribution maps, or you can do them by hand.

On a two-dimensional page it's hard to show the three-dimensional space of the archaeological site, but a series of maps can do this. Figure 10-3 is a typical site map with a north arrow, a scale, and contour lines showing how the land rises or falls — in this case, in half-meter (20-inch) increments or contour intervals; you can see the slope down to the river. It shows the mound and the excavation units, and I've put different symbols to show the distributions of four types of pottery across the site. This method is another quick way to show activity areas or other information. The red sherds cluster close to the temple mound, so they may be for ceremonial purposes.

Geographic Information Systems (GIS) is just a fancy way of piling on maps with layers of data to see the whole picture in vertical and horizontal space. Archaeologists used to draw it all on clear sheets they could lay on top of each other. Now they do it electronically and save time for other activities (like further analyses, or that coffee shop down the road).

An example of two GIS layers at your site or survey area may show both activity areas across the land and change through time vertically. Figure 10-3 demonstrates one of these layers, showing all pottery across the site. You can make separate maps for each level excavated and for all the other types of finds besides pottery. You can add more layers showing soil types or other natural features too, to reveal additional information

All kinds of computer programs — some written specifically for archaeological analysis — can map different characteristics of your data. Certain artifacts, feature types, or soil types may cluster more in one area or be associated with certain other artifacts. Plus, such maps also show gaps. If you should've dug in one place that was near the coolest stuff and you didn't, this fact will also jump out at you after you get a finished map.

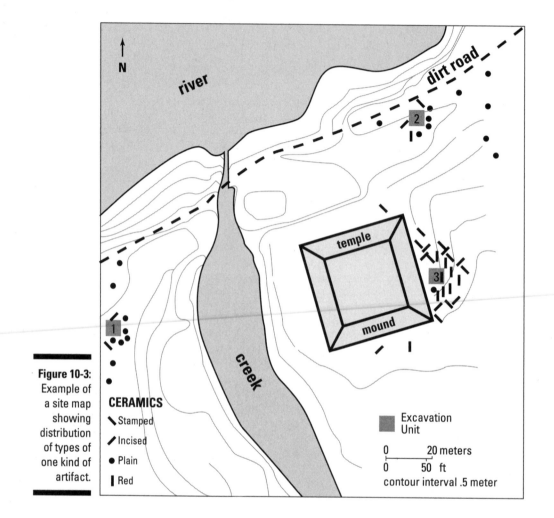

Figure 10-3:
Example of a site map showing distribution of types of one kind of artifact.

Analyzing Specific Materials: Stone, Ceramics, Bone, and Metal

After your artifact information and other data are mapped out in space and time, you're ready to see what new things you can add to all of it. You probably used classification systems already established for the artifacts in your area to sort the specimens in the lab. You can get even more out of them by looking at more specific attributes in their form, what they're made of, and other characteristics that may show how their original owners used them.

When you classified all your potsherds according to the established types in Table 10-1, you used the criteria of where you found them (in the Coldwater Creek region) and what their surface decoration was (none, stamped, incised, or painted).

The *typologies* (classification systems, discussed more in Chapter 9) for any given area were probably established by the first archaeologists to dig there and write a report. Archaeologists set up and refine artifact typologies all the time. They have to organize everything, so they make up these categories. Further work may help to improve these categories (or even to show that the original typology does not work well — the basis for many arguments).

Basic analyses

To see additional variability among your artifacts, you can pick other attributes of shape, style, or decoration that may be significant. You do this at home all the time when you put your stuff away in an orderly fashion (even if sometimes you can't remember where you put it). So when you can't find the big holiday serving platter with the other platters, you remember you put it in the bigger cupboard, with bigger items like the barbecue tongs and ice bucket, where it could fit. Size is the meaningful attribute here and not a common function of all the artifacts grouped together in the big cupboard.

For your excavated ceramic assemblage, you may look at vessel shapes and rim decorations. If the Coldwater Creek red-painted sherds, unlike the others, are mostly from big vessels that, by the angle of the rim, seem to be open platters, they're probably more likely to be serving plates, whereas the other ceramics are for cooking or storing. If serving food is more important at ritual feasts, more of the red plates may break in the feasting area as opposed to another part of the site. Again, doing such exercises means putting more data on tables, measuring rim angles, and so forth. So yes, you have to take finds out of their bags again, lay them all out on the table, and do something else with them. Good thing you have them all numbered by provenience so they don't get back into the wrong bags!

Use wear and residues on artifacts

Characteristics to look for on your artifacts are things that show how they were changed or damaged from use (called *use wear*). Look at your shoes; the soles are probably worn unevenly from walking in a particular way, and maybe the back of the heel of your right shoe is worn because you lay it on the floor while you're driving. This kind of evidence helps you see artifact function. You swear it's use wear!

Coming soon to a lab near you

You may remember that a crucial piece of evidence for nailing the Unabomber was his DNA left on a postage stamp on one of the bomb packages he mailed. Everything humans do (including stamp-licking) leaves residues, though some are larger than others. With fancy physics and chemistry, scientists can analyze baked-on food in pots, dried liquids in jars (even ancient wine), and chemicals used to embalm mummies. Some specialists are identifying bloodstains on stone tools by DNA analysis so they can tell what species of animal was hunted (or even whether human blood was involved).

These tests are all very specialized and costly, but they're becoming more common. When DNA testing becomes affordable enough, you may find it everywhere in archaeology (like you do in crime-scene TV). Physical and chemical testing to identify materials are also becoming less expensive, or at least more common in archaeology.

Use-wear studies are common with stone tools, where scraping or cutting dulls and scratches the sharp edges. Other materials can show use wear or even breakage patterns that may demonstrate what they were used for. From *experimental archaeology* (making new evidence to find out about past materials), archaeologists have discovered some different patterns under the microscope that indicate scraping versus cutting, and so forth. You can imagine an archaeologist hammering out a fresh flint blade and then using it to cut 500 pieces of rope, 500 bits of meat, or 500 globs of fat, and then observing and photographing the edges (and also cleaning up the mess)!

What artifacts are made of

Another attribute that differs among artifacts of the same type is the *raw material* they're made of. Sometimes this characteristic is easy to tell by sight. Here are a few examples:

- ✔ Local flint for chipped stone tools may be one color, and exotic stone may be other colors.

- ✔ Shell tools can be made from shells of different species gathered in different regions.

- ✔ You can sometimes classify bone tools such as hooks or pins according to the type of animal bone used, perhaps even to the species level. Sometimes even animal DNA can answer such questions.

- ✔ Pottery may be of different-colored clays, but a more distinguishing characteristic is the temper, which can be crushed stone or shell, sand, plant fibers, and even fired clay from other pots (smashed in a fit of temper). The temper mixed with the clay may show a specific tradition of craftwork from a local area or time period.

✔ Metal artifacts are sometimes easily identifiable by their raw materials. Iron is frequently so rusted that it becomes a heavy orange glob with little form left. (A 500-year-old Spanish iron spike I excavated looked like an orange turd until I broke it open and saw the square cross section of the spike.) Silver turns black, and copper (as well as brass and bronze, that are made with copper) becomes green. Gold, of course, never tarnishes — the reason for its great value. If that ring from your loved one is making your finger green, it's not pure gold. Sorry.

Organizing artifact tables to show raw materials can give you cool information about economics and interaction (how far folks were going to get what stuff). Items made of raw material that had to come from farther away were often more valuable; maybe these objects cluster in the ceremonial areas of the site. Small amounts of potsherds with uncommon tempers or shapes may indicate interaction with people outside the region; maybe the in-laws were bringing a covered dish for the holiday.

Plotting the distribution of artifact raw materials over large spaces can be fascinating. For example, drinking cups of big whelk shell occur all over the eastern U.S. in late prehistoric times. A big shell cup in a grave in Ohio clearly indicates a long-distance interaction. You can say it was probably trade, but other possibilities exist, such as gift-giving, theft, or maybe early midwestern spring-breakers going to the beach and bringing back shell souvenirs. Archaeologists do know from early historic times that Native Americans drank a ceremonial holly-leaf tea called black drink from shell cups. Finding these cups as far away as Ohio means you can trace this custom both deep into prehistoric times and widely across space from the Gulf of Mexico, where the shell and holly leaves originated.

Don't try these at home

Today, archaeology uses other sciences more than ever. So, beyond what you can *see* of different raw materials, you can actually use other methods of determining the origins of an artifact.

Fancy physics such as x-ray fluorescence and mass spectrometry can tell the *trace elements* in stone or metal. These are traces of various elements distinctive to the region where the artifact's raw material came from. The average archaeologist doesn't have the gizmos to do these studies in the lab. Just like for radiocarbon dating (or dry cleaning), we send out the specimens to a specialist service (and pay for it). The physicist or chemist can show the patterns, and then the archaeologist must interpret what they mean. This process is very much like your doctor sending you out for an x-ray, where the technician is an expert in applying the radiation and imaging to your body, but the doctor must interpret what the resulting picture means.

Stone tools across the Pacific

A neat example of trace element analysis is a recent study showing how prehistoric basalt *adzes* (ground-stone tools for cutting wood) made of stone originating in Hawaii were distributed as far as Tahiti and islands of French Polynesia. The trace elements in the basalt were characteristic of a particular Hawaiian stone quarry. Ancient sailors distributed stone from this quarry around 2,500 miles of remote Pacific islands. This reveals many things, including the sophistication of native navigators and their craft (all without GPS and radios). They may have preferred transporting small heavy stuff like stone rather than, say, bulky piles of fruit or wooden sculptures — it would make the boat more stable. Being able to travel by boat over such huge distances a thousand years ago or more shows how skilled prehistoric people of the Pacific really were.

Special Studies of Archaeological Finds

Though archaeologists don't do dinosaurs and usually don't do fossils, they sometimes do study bones, both animal and human, as well as soils and plant remains at archaeological sites. Many methods allow them to squeeze more information (though not blood) out of a bone, shell, seed, or grain of sand.

Animal remains: Zooarchaeology

Doing *zooarchaeology,* the study of animal remains from archaeological sites, means going beyond just identifying all the animal bone bits you have. (Remember, here I'm talking about ecofacts, the animal remains used by humans but not modified to become artifacts.)

Counting animal bones and shells

If you're lucky enough to have pieces that you can classify by species, you may also be lucky enough to tell which element (bone of the body) they all are and which side of the body they came from. So two deer leg bones may be from just one deer, but if they're both the same bone in the right front leg, that means you have at least two deer. This determination is called obtaining the *minimum number of individuals* (MNI) from each species in your assemblage.

MNI works for shells, too. For example, clams and other bivalves have a top and bottom or right and left shell, so you can count how many of each you have. After you determine how many of each kind of animal you have, you can know what animals your people got the most of.

Figuring diet from garbage

If the animals were food, how much food did the people really have of each kind? Another calculation is the amount of meat you can get from each kind of animal. Zooarchaeologists are always experimental archaeologists; they're always stopping the field vehicle to pick up fresh road kill (if it's native species past people would've used). They take sample animals, de-flesh the bones, and weigh the meat amounts each yields (a very smelly business). Based on the numbers, they can see the contribution of each kind of animal to the hypothetical past diet. This information is important because just the amount of stuff can be deceiving. A pile of 500 oyster shells is bigger than a deer leg bone, but it represents far less actual meat than one deer.

Another caution is that your animal bone assemblage may not tell you only or all of what your people ate. They may have thrown all fish bone back in the water because it was too smelly, so you never find it in their garbage. Or they may have hunted an animal for its fur but not eaten the meat; how many modern folks eat mink? Some bone may have been only for making artifacts, not from eating the animal. Though you can never be sure of the possibilities, you must at least mention them in your reports and interpretations.

Plant remains: Paleoethnobotany

Plant remains can tell a story similar to what you get from animal bones and shells — what people used for food, tools, homes, and other purposes. But plants are more fragile; they're usually not preserved unless they've been charred, waterlogged, or dried. The *paleoethnobotanist* (try saying that ten times quickly) is another specialized archaeologist who identifies plant remains from archaeological sites and figures out what they mean.

Macrobotanicals

Macrobotanical remains are bigger objects such as seeds, nuts, pieces of wood, charcoal from ancient fires, carbonized fruit rinds, rice grains, or corn-cobs. Even tiny fern spores (which can reveal that the site was in a wooded environment) can be identified under a magnifying glass. You need to compare all these with the kinds of plants found off the site area in the region. This way, you can see what would have been naturally occurring as compared with what the people at your site brought in or grew there.

Microbotanicals

Microbotanical remains are tiny things like pollen grains so small you need a microscope to see them. Pollen is interesting because each plant species has a different-shaped grain; if you know the characteristics of the species you identify, you can see what the landscape looked like (aquatic plants, trees, non-tree plants). You must be careful to know how much pollen different plants put out. If your sample contains more larch pollen than oak, that may be because one larch tree produces far more pollen than one oak, not because you have a predominantly larch forest. Comparing pollen on-site and off-site is also important so you can see what species people brought in.

Pollen was used in a modern archaeological-type study to determine the authenticity of an antique chair. Residue scraped off the underside of the seat of the old chair contained pollen from British trees, showing it to be a real antique rather than a later American copy.

Absolutely amazing tiny things discovered by botanists and other scientists can help archaeologists answer big questions. *Phytoliths* are tiny mineral deposits that form within plant cells as the groundwater runs through them, roughly like the mineral deposit left in your teapot from boiling water in it. Phytoliths (also called *silica bodies* or *plant opal*) have distinctive shapes based on the plant species they formed in. They're often preserved long after the plant decays, and they require fancy lab work to separate from the soil. Working with phytoliths of corn (maize) and banana, archaeologists have been able to see how early these plants became domesticated crops manipulated by ancient people.

Microscopic starch grains are a very new type of archaeological evidence just beginning to get attention. They're also preserved long after the original plant decays, so you may find them in residues on tool edges. New starch grain evidence in Borneo shows human foragers did complex processing of yams and other starchy plants some 40,000 years ago. They figured out how to leach out the natural poisons from these plants to make them edible.

Human bones, chemistry, and DNA

Human skeletal remains from archaeological sites are very special. They can reveal so much more about past people, including social and religious aspects of their societies. But bones are surrounded by more sensitive issues and subject to various laws, so you may need a permit or special permission to excavate them. You must also treat them according to the wishes of the descendants of the people they represent, if such descendants can be found.

If you do excavate and study (and sometimes even rebury) human bones (respectfully), you can obtain a wealth of information. Besides the kinds of burials and grave goods and the treatment of the dead in general, you can find out about the individual person's life.

Ancient Chinese noodles

Combining evidence and techniques of course improves the quality of your explanation. Another fascinating recent study followed the excavation of a perfectly preserved, upside-down bowl of 4,000-year-old noodles in Neolithic northwestern China. Both the phytoliths and the starch grains, still present despite noodle-making and noodle-cooking, were from an identifiable plant — no, not wheat, not rice, but millet. This grain (most often used in the U.S. as birdseed) may have been domesticated even earlier than rice in China.

What a skeleton can tell you

Bioarchaeologists (biological anthropologists who study human bones) can estimate age and sex of a person from skeletal markers (especially the pelvis). They determine how tall someone was by plugging in formulas based on length of one leg or arm bone. Some injuries and diseases leave marks on bone, as does the stress of hard labor and other factors (like obesity and childbirth — also hard labor). Cultural practices such as foot-binding or head-flattening from cradle-boards also show up in the skeleton. Dental cavities (or *caries*) show diet and hygiene practices.

When more of a body's soft tissue is preserved (such as in mummification) medical techniques such as x-rays and CAT scans are just as useful as they are for living people to see details — diseases, parasites, traumas, and even the cause of death (which may not show in just the bones).

You've seen all this stuff on crime-scene TV shows and maybe in autopsies. But such evidence can answer larger questions. For example, tuberculosis was once thought to be one of the many diseases Europeans first brought to the Americas in the 16th century. Now bone lesions and even dry lung tissue with the DNA of the tuberculosis germ has shown that this disease was already present in the prehistoric New World 1,000 years ago.

More clues from bone chemistry

You may be less familiar with studies based on the idea that you are what you eat and you are where you live. The chemical makeup of bones of all kinds (animals' too) may show what their owners were doing all their lives. Teeth may contain minerals from the water the individual drank as a child, when the teeth were forming. Later bone formation shows minerals according to the area where the person lived closer to the time of death. These can be compared with waters and soils in different regions to see where the person was raised, compared with where he or she lived at the time of death.

Bone chemicals also reflect types of foods eaten. *Stable carbon isotope analysis* of bone collagen (got that?) can show that people ate different types of plants that left traces in their bones. You can determine if they had domesticated grains yet or were still gathering wild foods. You can even help law enforcement agencies identify victims based on where their bones say they came from.

DNA: It's nice to have when you can find it

Deoxyribonucleic acid (DNA), the building block of life that controls genetic heritage, is hard for you not to leave everywhere you go. Modern archaeological detectives are solving more crimes with DNA evidence. But this molecule does decay with time, and the amounts left in ancient remains may be too small to study. Another complicating factor is that such study is easily contaminated with the DNA of the modern researcher in the lab. But look for DNA work to become more routine even in archaeology.

Coprolites: Fossilized feces

If you can identify *coprolites* (ancient, usually dried feces) as human, you have a whole new area of study that's not as sensitive as analyses of human skeletal remains. Coprolites give you information on what people ate, their health, where they got their food, whether they produced it or gathered it wild, and many other aspects of life. Human coprolites from archaeological sites can contain preserved intestinal parasites and other disease organisms, and even DNA that tells sex and genetic ancestry. They may also contain pollen or accidentally-ingested insect parts that give you clues about the past environment in which the people lived.

Getting a Date in Archaeology

How does an archaeologist get a date (professionally, not during free time)? The several different methods depend upon what kinds of remains you have, where you are in the world, and how old the materials may be.

What's datable and what's not

You can't get a radiocarbon date out of a stone because it doesn't contain any carbon. But you may be able to date the stone based on what it looks like and/or what it was found with. Stone tools of different types may have already been dated according to style and associated artifacts, so you can just look up your specimen in a guide to stone tools for your area. You may use similar methods with other materials, too. See what's already been done to get an age for your particular material and what datable materials you have at your site before you decide upon a dating method.

Indirect and direct dating

Direct methods date an artifact itself, and *indirect* methods date something it's associated with. Dating a stone tool or a clay potsherd directly is often impossible because radiocarbon dating requires something with carbon in it. But you may be able to date something made of carbon that's near the artifact, assuming they're the same age. You can date something directly if you have historic information about it. For example, a guide showing different china patterns may give the calendar date when they were first introduced and when they were discontinued.

Relative dating

Relative dating methods aren't the way you find out the real age of Aunt Ida. They're traditional archaeological methods that don't give an actual date, but an age in relationship to something else. For example:

- **The law of superposition:** Artifacts found deeper in the ground are older than those found nearer the surface (unless something has come along and churned things around).

- **Seriation:** Artifact types are arranged according to their stylistic similarities and/or frequencies of occurrence. You may not know the absolute dates, but you can arrange the styles that look most similar closest to each other on the chart. You can do this with any artifact that changes through time, from cars to ancient Egyptian pots (seriated by Sir Flinders Petrie in the 1890s). Some disadvantages of this method are that it assumes gradual change through time and that it wouldn't work with everything. Look at the radical shift from slide rule to pocket calculator or from paper notebook to hand-held computer — those artifacts don't look anything alike. Another disadvantage is that you can see change through time, but you often don't know which end of the series is the earliest and which the latest.

- **Fluorine dating:** This method is based on the principle that two bones buried together at the same time will take up the same amount of fluorine (and other elements) from the soil, so they must be the same age. Fluorine dating is famous because it exposed the hoax of the notorious "Piltdown man" fossil that was found in England in 1912. This "find" was an old human skull buried with a modern ape jaw that was filed to fit and dyed to match. It fooled famous anthropologists who wanted to find that the earliest ape-like-but-large-brained humans had emerged from England (rather than Africa).

Getting a calendar date

To get a date in actual calendar years, you can use absolute or chronometric dating. *Absolute dating* is only possible with objects that have dates *on* them, such as coins. *Chronometric dating* measures the time since something has elapsed.

Radiocarbon dating

The most common chronometric method, *radiocarbon dating,* is based on the radioactive decay of the carbon-14 isotope (written as 14C).

As the science-fiction shows say, Earth is full of carbon-based life forms. All living things take in carbon (through food, among other methods) and con-tain the same proportion of the carbon-12 isotope to carbon-14. When an organism dies, the 14C begins radioactive decay at a known rate, measured by the concept of the *half-life,* or how long it takes half of it to decay. Because 14C has a half-life of 5,730 years, archaeologists can measure how much of it is left in a piece of something that was once alive and calculate how much time has elapsed since its death.

The advantage of radiocarbon dating is that your site often has charcoal, bone, or other organic material that contains carbon. The disadvantages are as follows:

- ✔ You have to have something preserved that's *organic* (was once alive) — not stone, pottery, or metal — and you have to have enough of it to date (about a cup of charcoal or, for dating a large animal or human skeleton, an arm and a leg, or something as big as that).

- ✔ You have to have about $300 to pay for testing.

- ✔ The date comes out as a statistical approximation within two standard deviations; in lay terms, this means something like a 33 percent chance that your date is incorrect.

- ✔ The farthest back you can date organisms (because of that half-life) is about 50,000 years. So any human experience before that, up to 2 mil-lion years ago or more, is too old to date by this method. This is fine for North and South America, however, because they had no people that long ago.

An improvement in radiocarbon dating

AMS (accelerator mass spectrometry) radiocarbon dating is a wonderful refine-ment that allows the physicist to count the actual carbon atoms with a big parti-cle accelerator machine. This instrument needs far less material for dating, such as a piece of charcoal as big as a pencil point. This can be a great advantage if you don't have good organic preservation at your site. From my excavations of a shell midden in Florida, I obtained a sherd of fiber-tempered pottery that broke open to show a couple fibers of Spanish moss still unburned and undecayed in the clay. These were dated by the AMS method — one of the rare times that I *could* date a potsherd directly. The sherd turned out to be about 4,000 years old.

More improvement through tree rings

Another disadvantage of radiocarbon dating has now been corrected by using a totally independent chronometric method known as *dendrochronology,* or tree-ring dating. The previous assumption was that uniform amounts of radioactive carbon were present every year in the atmosphere to be absorbed by all living things. When someone decided to check this assumption by AMS-radiocarbon dating individual tree rings with known ages, it became clear that past levels of carbon-14 have fluctuated a lot. Dendochronology uses sequences of thick and thin rings from trees with overlapping lifetimes and works backward in time. You can even find living trees that are several thousand years old, such as the gnarly old bristlecone pine from the southwestern U.S.

Ring characteristics depend on annual weather patterns, so this method works best in areas with great variability, such as the desert. It also requires enough wood in your artifact to see the rings. Furthermore, the wood the artifact was made of may have been old already when used, or used for a long time, as in a house beam, but the date you get is for the year the tree was cut. On the whole, though, dendrochronology has changed radiocarbon dating by helping correct its errors; the story is a cautionary tale of science, and how you have to confirm your results by independent tests. Now whenever you get a radiocarbon date, it's corrected or calibrated along a curve produced by tree ring dates to give a more accurate calendrical age.

Other chronometric dating methods

Several other chronometric methods are based on measuring time elapsed since some physiochemical change.

- ✔ **Potassium-argon dating** measures the decay of a rare radioactive isotope of potassium that results in its becoming argon gas. Here the half-life is 1.31 billion years, so you can measure much older things. However, your object needs to have the required minerals. Luckily, the volcanic deposits that contain early human fossil forms in east Africa also contain potassium, so many of those finds have been dated by this method.

- ✔ **Archaeomagnetism** is another chronometric dating method (not a commentary on how attractive archaeologists are). It's based on the fact that earth's magnetic fields shift over time. When soil is heated, the iron particles in it align themselves with the poles. Because north moves over time at a known rate, archaeologists can measure the magnetic alignment in the ground and compare it with today's alignment.

Which dating method is best? Because each has favorable and unfavorable aspects, you should use more than one independent method if possible. Radiocarbon is the most important for the New World and later Old World prehistory, but if you can confirm your radiocarbon date in some other way, your results are much more reliable.

At a site in northwest Florida where I worked during 2002, we had already excavated typical prehistoric pottery that has often been dated to between A.D. 1200 and the time of European contact in the New World. Then we got a tiny glass bead from the fine screen of the flotation machine. We knew the Native Americans had no glass until the Spanish brought it in the 16th century. We had enough charcoal to get a radiocarbon date from a small pit feature that had the bead in it. The date returned as about A.D. 1500–1600, very early in historic times, confirming the estimation based on the bead. This part of Florida has no historic records that early, so I'm returning to dig a little more and see whether I can find more accurately datable evidence.

When You Need Help

Obviously, you can study and analyze all your artifacts and ecofacts at many different levels, beginning with the basics. You can classify artifacts using published typologies and estimate the relative ages of objects based on how deep you found them and whether they resemble already-dated types of artifacts.

Even the most accomplished archaeologist must send out for specialized analyses of animal bone, plant remains, human skeletons, dating, or other chemical and physical analyses. Finding specialists for these studies is easy on the Internet, where they list prices and time required.

Even after you've got all the analyses back, you as the archaeologist have to figure out what they all mean. For example, one specialist may tell you that fish and turtle remains constitute 90 percent of your *faunal* (animal) assemblage, and another may tell you that your human bone chemistry indicates a diet of seafood. To get the whole story, however, you must tie this information together with the remains of fishing gear and other artifacts you've excavated from the site settlement locations along waterways. Perhaps you also find that the occupation of the site ended when the water source moved or dried up. That, then, is the whole story.

Chapter 11

Reconstructing the Past: Piecing Together the Puzzles

In This Chapter

▶ Reporting what you've found and what it means

▶ Inferring past human behavior through analogy with known cultures

▶ Explaining your findings using various archaeological theories

---

*I*n this chapter, I show you how to prepare the results of your archaeological investigation. You use materials and information you've dug up to reconstruct human behavior in the past at your site and in your whole study region. You may interpret the same archaeological findings in many ways, and you have to watch for different kinds of biases. People may have done things very differently in the past than you've ever imagined!

The archaeological evidence relates to what you know of human activity in modern or historic times — so you're using analogy. You also may use several very different theoretical perspectives as you examine past human systems. Some of them are complicated philosophies, but they do make a difference in how you see the human past (trust me).

Reporting on Your Investigation

You have an ethical obligation to report your archaeological findings, or else you're no better than a looter. Besides, you can't just stick that lost ark up on the high storage shelf without describing what it means or what you went through to get it! Writing up your research, especially for *cultural resources management* (CRM) projects (archaeology done to comply with laws — see Chapter 3 for more), also means you must make recommendations about preservation.

Producing your report

An archaeological report describes everything you did in the field and laboratory, including all your background work and everything you found. You describe your results and what they show about human behavior in the past; you want to show what new information you have and where to go with the next research or the next actions at your site or project area.

The essentials

A good archaeological report should have the following sections:

- ✔ Introduction saying why you did the project and what the research goals were. List crew members and sources of support.

- ✔ Environmental background of the area of your site or survey, including resources available to past people.

- ✔ Cultural background — what's known of past cultures there.

- ✔ Archaeological background — what previous researchers found there, including local people and collections, and how your work fits in.

- ✔ Your fieldwork, including background research, where you dug, how (test unit, survey segment), how deep, and how you decided all this.

- ✔ Lists of all soils, strata, and features you excavated and what they show.

- ✔ Lists of all materials you recovered, usually by type (*lithic* [stone], ceramic, metal, bone, and so on), and discussions of what the *assemblage* (whole group) of each kind shows.

- ✔ Discussions of what all the evidence indicates about human behavior in the past and how it fulfills (or doesn't fulfill) your research goals.

- ✔ Maps of various scales showing where you worked and how your site(s) relates to other known sites and natural features in the region.

- ✔ Illustrations (photos or drawings) of interesting finds, photos of the ongoing dig and landscape.

- ✔ Information for any future researchers on where all your finds and information are stored.

- ✔ Ideas for future work in the area and on your same research questions.

Cultural Resources Management (CRM) reports

If your archaeological investigation was for CRM purposes, it was a survey or excavation done in the path of some proposed construction project. Therefore, you also need to include specific recommendations on how that project should proceed in regard to those cultural resources. Here are some possibilities:

- Your survey located several sites, and some look promising enough to conduct test excavation to see if they're significant. *Significance* usually means the site has undisturbed remains or materials from poorly known time periods, and the potential to produce valuable information. In the U.S., you often use the official federal criteria for significance defined by the National Register of Historic Places.

- Your test excavation demonstrated it's a significant site, so you ask that proposed construction be moved to go around it and preserve it. Or if it must be destroyed, recommend full-scale excavation to save what's left before construction.

- The site/sites you investigated didn't contain significant archaeological remains, so the builders can go ahead and destroy them. The work you did got as much information as possible from them before destruction.

Sharing your work

Usually, you submit your report to whoever initiated the work (such as a client of a contract archaeology company) and whoever paid for it (such as a granting agency). Others who should get copies:

- The agency that issued you a permit

- All who worked on the project

- Landowners and other interested parties

- Libraries in the area of the project and at universities or big cities

- State archaeological offices

- Anyone who provided background information for you, such as people you interviewed

Many archaeological reports are now available online, though sometimes this practice is a bad idea because it gives looters more information about exact locations of sites.

Besides simply submitting a professional report on your work, you should aim to write an article about it for publication in a journal or elsewhere to make your results more available to other researchers. You can also write a popular or less technical version to share your findings with a wider audience. (See Chapter 16 for suggestions on how to bring your results to the public.)

Telling the Story of What You've Found

I describe in Chapter 10 how to examine and analyze the archaeological materials and data you've obtained. In doing all that, you create additional information that you then piece together to explain what went on at your site or region. Here I show you how to put it together to tell the story of the past.

As an archaeologist, you may be stereotyped as someone intent upon digging up arrowheads, pottery, mounds, or pyramids. But you're really interested in the workings of whole cultures and in human culture as a whole.

Reconstructing human systems within past societies, you can see what worked and what didn't. You get a picture of how humans adapted to their environments through time, how culture change took place, what rose and fell, sometimes even why.

Your work may be a *synchronic* study, explaining what happened at a restricted slice of time at your site. Or you may reconstruct the *diachronic* picture, showing how things changed through time at your site or within a whole region. Either way, you're contributing to the knowledge of humanity.

The easiest human behaviors to reconstruct are how people made a living and obtained resources, and how long ago (technically categorized as subsistence, technology, and dating). More difficult is determining how past social and political systems worked. The most difficult thing to figure out from the archaeological evidence is *ideology* — what people believed, how religious or ritual activities took place, and why.

Describing what happened based on the evidence

The sections of your report describing the finds are easy compared to the parts where you try to figure out what they all mean. Go in an orderly fashion from what's known to your first level of inference — in other words, the safe suggestions about what the finds may mean. For example, if you find lots of deer bones, you can probably pretty safely assume the people from that site were hunting and eating a lot of venison.

You can then present more speculative and less certain interpretations — lots of deer statues may indicate the people worshipped deer, but they may just be toys or clan symbols. Remember, you're showing as much as possible of what past people did and experienced over space and time, that's all!

Detailing how people lived, got stuff, and settled the land

Artifacts (objects made and used by people), *ecofacts* (remains of plants and animals used by people), *features* (larger things people left in the ground), and soils show a lot about how people lived and got the stuff they needed. Environmental data, site distribution maps, and *artifact sourcing* (determining where artifacts came from) tell you where people settled and how they and their materials moved around.

Technology

Your artifact studies show what was used at your site, how these things were made, and sometimes what purposes they were used for. Besides finished artifacts, other items convey a wealth of information. *Lithic debitage* (stone chips) shows how stone implements were fashioned and with what raw material. Structural remains, whether standing ruins or postmold patterns in the soil, show how buildings were constructed. Pits full of fire-cracked rock or red clay soil may indicate cooking or heating techniques.

Technology is fairly easy to reconstruct because you have the material items that show it. But artifact function is tricky to establish sometimes, especially if the artifacts aren't for everyday utilitarian purposes. Remember also that the absence of those artifacts made of materials that rotted away (string, wood, and so on) may lead you to misinterpret or not understand some technological systems because vital pieces of the puzzle are missing.

Subsistence

Artifacts and features help you infer a people's *subsistence,* or how they got food and other necessities. Points and butchering tools may have been for hunting, and hoes for digging and planting. Fire pits with food remains and the occasional dropped kitchen implement give you ideas on how people processed foods. Human bone chemistry indicates what people were eating.

Animal and plant ecofacts tell you directly some of the species used and in what proportions. Be careful here. You may jump to a wrong conclusion if you assume

> ✔ That all these remains were for food. Many may have been for other purposes; shellfish may not have been for eating but rather for bait or for using shells to make tools. Others may be from species that got into the site after the people left (like animals that burrowed into the ground at your site and died there).

✔ That all the food remains represent the total diet. People may have discarded many remains elsewhere, such as fish bones thrown back into the lake because they were so smelly.

✔ That the remains show everything available to people in their past environments. They may have had resources available that they chose not to use. For example, most people today don't eat insects, even though the little critters are certainly abundant, nutritious, and easy to get.

Environment

Archaeological information showing human uses of and impacts on past environments (as well as the effects of environments upon human societies) is valuable knowledge for the modern world. You can see how people lived in and changed their ecosystems and how the changing environments affected the people.

In describing the ecological setting of your site, you indicate what natural resources would have been available for people to use. Where other sites are located — where other societies lived during the same time period — is also important because this forms part of the environmental setting. You want to show the *cultural ecology* of your site or region — how people's interactions with their natural and cultural surroundings shaped their ways of life.

Make sure the present natural environment of your site is what it would've been in the past. Landforms change, coastlines and rivers move, and later human activity messes up earlier ecosystems and sites. For example, the climate and landscape were significantly colder and dryer in most places on earth during the Pleistocene (Ice Age). Data you collected on soils, pollen, and other environmental indicators both at your site and away from it help you reconstruct past environments. For example, the pollen in the earlier levels of your site may be from plants that lived in a dryer, colder climate; shallower, later levels may have pollen from species that lived in warmer, wetter conditions.

In fact, archaeological information you recover may document important environmental change — and you may even be able to show how your past people coped with that change. (I describe in Chapter 13 the first human experience with global warming.) You can describe how people manipulated environments too, such as with canals, irrigation systems, deforestation, domestication of plants and animals, and so forth.

If you have no plant or animal remains preserved, you still get an idea of subsistence from the other artifacts and from the landscape. For example, I've dug up ceramic sherds impressed with corncobs at sites where no corn survived, so I can still know people were farming. Other ceramic sherds impressed with nets give more ambiguous information. People could have used nets for fishing or just as bags to carry things. Nets can also trap

1. Archaeological dig in northwest Florida: cross-sectioning the oldest (deepest) feature, a small garbage pit dating to A.D. 400, beneath the black shell midden soil.

2. Pile of large Archaic spear points (around 4,000 years old) in northeast Mississippi, possibly

3. Prehistoric pottery bowl from southwest Georgia (about 1,000 years old).

4. An archaeological field pack and contents, including trowels, field notebook, waterproof

5. Excavation in progress in 2003 of George Washington's distillery at Mount Vernon.

6. Archaeology lab work: numbering potsherds and measuring and examining projectile points under the microscope.

7. Moundville, Alabama, Temple Mound B: flat-topped, ramped pyramid that supported a sacred building (reconstructed) some 1,000 years ago.

10. Late Classic Maya Temple of the Cross in the jungle at Palenque, Chiapas

11. Pyramid of the Niches, El Tajín: Classic Veracruz Culture, Gulf Coast of Mexico.

13. Angkor Thom, Cambodia, South Gate, with guardian deities pulling a long mythical (now broken) snake (12th century A.D.).

14. Great Zimbabwe Hill Complex showing stone-brick human construction wrapping around natural rock; person standing at upper right shows scale.

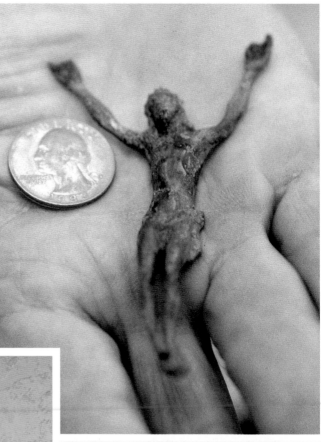

15. Metal Christ from a French colonial crucifix excavated at Fort Toulouse/Jackson Park, Alabama, dating to between 1717 and 1763.

16. The author with popular archaeology objects: inflatable plastic Egyptian mummy and replica of an ancient Olmec head at a Fort Lauderdale, Florida, Mexican restaurant.

animals, so they may indicate hunting as well as (or instead of) fishing. Similarly, small hooks can be for fishing and for many other kinds of tasks, such as hanging stuff up. So in my report I need to suggest these different alternative explanations, and which one I may favor and why.

Settlement systems

You may have dated your site directly through radiocarbon dating or other methods that I describe in Chapter 10. Or perhaps you know the general age based on the artifact types, which are well dated elsewhere. Combined with your information on landscape and resource use, your dates can help you reconstruct settlement patterns.

Within a region, the *inter-site settlement system* refers to the locations of and relationships among different sites at different times — people's spatial organization of the landscape, where they did what, and possibly why. Here's what inter-site settlement patterns can show:

✔ Sites of one kind may be in different sorts of places than sites of another kind. For example, economic centers may be on waterways for easier transportation, and religious shrines may be in mountains or other more isolated sacred spots.

✔ Locations of sites of different kinds at different time periods can indicate change through time. For example, sites of foraging people may have been in the uplands, but when they later started farming they may have moved to the river valley for fertile land and irrigation capabilities. Or earlier historic people may have lived along coastlines or rivers for easy travel but later moved to live along rail lines after the new railroads provided even easier transportation.

You also want to look at the *intra-site settlement pattern*, which reflects the differences within one site — different activity areas. For example, you may have a domestic area with houses, a public area with a plaza, and a religious area with a temple, perhaps at different times in the past.

Economic systems

Your maps showing the sources of artifacts and raw materials give you an idea of human interaction across the landscape. When you combine your data on subsistence and settlement with the information on how and from where people obtained materials, you can reconstruct past economic systems. If you compare what's available in the region with what's not, you may be able to see what people at your site were trading out and getting in return. You can even make a grand map with arrows showing what moved around where.

You want to notice where necessities or staple goods such as foods appear across your site or region. Then you can compare this information with where the wealth items appear. Did you excavate all the gold in the site from one big house? If so, your wealth items were concentrated in the hands of just a few. If you found a little gold in every house you dug, your society was a little more *egalitarian* (characterized by social equality).

When you reconstruct your past economic system, remember that artifacts at your site from far-away sources don't necessarily show trade with distant people. They may be from other kinds of exchange or even one-way movement — gifts, things owned by new people moving in, even materials obtained in raids or by theft. Raiding and pillaging is one kind of economic strategy, after all!

Describing social order, family, gender, and politics in the past

Using material remains to show how past social systems worked is more difficult than showing how people made a living, but it's still possible. You can look at gender, kinship and family organization, class or caste, labor specialization, and other ways people are structured into categories that make up whole social systems.

Social systems

You can classify social systems based on size, division of labor, prestige and social esteem, and differences in wealth or ability to get needed resources. The classifications are based on *ethnographic* (descriptions of cultures all over the world) and historical knowledge. Often categories go in order from simple to complex; the following is a list of these categories:

- ✔ **Egalitarian societies:** Everyone's pretty much equal and does the same things to make a living. Divisions of labor based on age or gender may exist, sometimes in the form of part-time specialists, such as religious practitioner or best hunter. Subsistence is usually simple, such as foraging or gardening. Sites are often seasonal because people move around to get different resources when they're ripe or ready. Groups tend to be small because the more people a society has, the more complex organization it requires. Indicators of egalitarian society in the archaeological record are small sites; similar houses, burial types, and skeletal health for everyone; and even sites with only seasonal plants and animals instead of species available year-round. I describe the archaeology of some early egalitarian societies in Chapter 12.

✔ **Ranked societies:** These societies feature real social differences —some people have greater importance or higher esteem. Rank is often based on family status, so the more important folks can be elders, chiefs, or other leaders. They may have authority to direct behavior but no real power or means to enforce their directives other than the group's respect for them. Though people may have different titles and ranks, they still all get the same resources and share them. Ranked societies may have non-farming craft specialists and leaders whose food comes from the labors of others. Subsistence may occur by obtaining wild foods, but ranked societies usually produce some of their own food. I describe some of the earliest societies showing such social differences in Chapter 13. You can recognize ranked societies archaeologically by markers such as special symbolic artifacts in a few houses or with some high-status graves but no real differences in wealth or health.

✔ **Stratified societies:** These groups have real economic inequality on top of the social differences — in other words, richer and poorer. Their leaders have power to make people do things and followers to enforce rules. Leadership roles may be inherited rather than achieved. Stratification often first appears along with the intensification of agriculture. Slave labor is a handy way to build irrigation systems, not to mention roads and big monuments. I describe early stratified societies in Chapter 13. Stratification is easier to recognize archaeologically because you can see concentrations of wealth in the ground, skeletal remains showing lives of hard labor or little hardship and better food, and images of power in art and architecture.

✔ **State-level societies:** These are the most highly stratified and complex forms ever developed, and all are based on large-scale agriculture and domestic animal production. Their powerful leaders can mandate behavior, punish disobedience, fight wars, and levy taxes. These early states are usually organized along hierarchical and bureaucratic lines in addition to the more traditional kinship ties. I describe the archaeology of early states in Chapter 14. You can recognize them archaeologically by their monuments, wealth, and cities, among other things.

In real cultures, social organization doesn't always fit perfectly into simple categories. (What a surprise — human behavior is complicated!) You may have intermediate and combined forms. For example, native peoples of the northwest coast of North America had hereditary chiefs and slaves and ranked everyone in between, which makes them seem like a stratified society. But they only fished and hunted — never grew any crops — and had seasonally moving camps and villages, characteristics more like egalitarian foragers. Prehistoric people of southern Florida were similar complex foragers. They had chiefs who demanded tribute, but they made a living only by fishing and hunting, with no agriculture.

Reconstruction of social organization

Going from descriptions of living people to your archaeological record is tricky. For example, if your site features no evidence of food production and lots of evidence of wild foods, you may infer simple egalitarian family groups. However, suppose the site has one larger building — you have to try to determine whether it was a home for one rich person (a scenario that doesn't exactly scream "egalitarian") or a dance hall and party space for everyone (which would support your egalitarian theory).

Your settlement patterns and economic data can show distributions of some social aspects in space and time. Perhaps you can determine where craft specialists were based if not all households have the same kinds of tools. For example, maybe only one house has all the chipping evidence from stone-tool production, and another one has the only shell bead-working debris at the site, indicating that these areas were the territories of these specific craftspeople.

Neighborhoods with different house sizes and numbers of wealth items in the houses can indicate social classes. Artifact distribution within a house or across a site can show where children gathered, where special people had ceremonies, and where sports players performed their special roles.

Human burials give lots of social information, but you may not be able to examine them depending upon the law and the wishes of their descendants and others. Skeletons can show better nutrition or a life of hard work. Richer graves indicate more important people or some other social distinction. But sometimes you can't tell if burials are just of higher social rank (a revered grandmother and clan elder) or if they were actually the leaders or wealthier people (the clan mother-chief with real power to tell everyone what to do).

Kinship and ethnicity

A fundamental organizing principle of human society is *kinship,* or family relatedness. Past societies were organized along kinship lines, so clusters of houses may show different clans or other family groupings. Different symbols or types of artifacts can also reflect family affiliation; you can see this today in plaid or tartan patterns for different Scottish clans.

Another basic principle around which people organize society is *ethnicity* (identity with the larger group beyond the family). Although ethnic identity is easy to determine by asking a living person, it's often very hard to see in the archaeological record. You may remember the Lone Ranger watching his faithful guide Tonto pick up an arrow and conclude it came from someone who was "Apache — Red Cloud's band." In reality, you seldom know whether the style of an arrowhead or any artifact is the result of purely utilitarian function, the maker's ideas of beauty, or markers specific to one ethnic group. What artifacts in your home show your nationality? Even knowing where an artifact comes from (through trace element analyses or other means I describe in Chapter 10) doesn't necessarily tell you the ethnicity of the users. Your home may have electronics made in Japan, clothes made in south Asia, and other imports. Even your small American flag may be made in China!

Bone and teeth chemistry can sometimes demonstrate whether people themselves came from the area in which they're found or grew up somewhere else. But remember that your ethnic group isn't only a matter of your biology but also of whom you belong to socially and culturally — as adopted people well know!

Gender

Another basic organizing principle of society is gender. Reconstructing the roles of men and women in the past is a popular area in archaeology. *Sex* is a biological designation, and *gender* is the social role (loosely) associated with it. Although some cultures have strict gender differences, others don't. Evidence for differences between male and female is extremely difficult to find in the archaeological record, yet interpretations abound. Most have been extremely biased, consisting of some version of the following:

- Men doing the interesting prehistoric and historic activities such as spearing big game, making neat tools, and ruling from the palace.
- Women (prehistoric and historic) just pounding away preparing food near the fireplace and holding the kids.

Interpreting gender is especially fraught with problems that archaeologists love to argue about. Modern Western standards creep in, but you can't assume that men made all the big sharp stone tools just because Dad carves the turkey in your society. Be careful not to impose your own society's models upon past cultures. They may have had very different divisions of labor by sex, or perhaps none at all. For example, women in many cultures hunt, and several cultures feature men who weave or make pots.

So how can you avoid this pitfall? You may find it helpful to compare known societies that are close in time, organization, or environmental setting to what you're digging up to get clues on gender systems.

Burials can give indications of male and female differences because you can tell the sex of a skeleton if it's well preserved. But burial objects can be misleading; do they actually represent a division of labor, or are they just male and female symbols? How do you tell whether the male or female tools or symbols are more important by the standards of the past society?

Seldom can you tell who actually made and used artifacts, especially in prehistoric times. Even if you find fingerprints or DNA on them, you won't necessarily know which sex made them or used them the most.

Although there are only two sexes, some cultures (including many Native American groups and cultures in India and Africa) really do have more than two genders! Even with only two genders, one sometimes tries to act like — and use the artifacts of — the other. (Think of the artifacts used by drag queens.)

Political systems

Politics means controlling and deciding for the group and keeping order. Every culture has some kind of political system, although not all of them center on one single person in charge. In simpler societies, the group may share decision-making, resources, and the sanction of unacceptable behavior. To discover more complex systems, you want to look for evidence that some individual or group has more power than others.

Archaeologists argue over whether construction of big mounds or other monuments means some central leader had power to command labor. Groups of people can perform many activities without coercion and without any one person in charge (like a potluck supper). Because kinship was the organizing principle of many traditional past societies, families could conduct activities (perhaps supervised by elders or those with experience). Again, you have to be careful that your interpretations don't impose the biases of your modern, hierarchical society.

When real centralized political power and hierarchy evolve, they go beyond the kinship structure. But signs of political hierarchy in the archaeological record are hard to separate from indications of social, economic, and religious power — and sometimes they all combine. Groups of larger, richer houses, for example, can indicate a real ruling class. But they may also just show a rich merchant class still subject to the power of the rulers.

Indications of organized warfare can show a society had the political might to mobilize armies and conquer. Even depictions of human sacrifice (not to mention graves of victims) show someone has power of life and death over someone else. In more complex societies, wealth, power, and inequality become more obvious. You certainly have less trouble interpreting a burial of one old guy in a pyramid with sacrificed servants and lots of gold!

Understanding past beliefs and values

A standing joke in archaeology says that any artifact or feature you can't explain must be ceremonial — in other words, for some religious or other ritual beyond everyday use. The stone point chipped so thin that it would break if used? Must be ceremonial! The pile of statues all buried in one spot? A ceremonial offering! You often see ceremonial functions in material items today. When the mayor offers a visiting dignitary a key to the city, it's not a real key but a huge cardboard key painted gold — a symbol that doesn't actually perform any real utilitarian function.

Not all evidence of ritual is religious; look at your graduation or birthday party artifacts. And not all your ideological system is magical or religious either. It can also include belief in the golden rule ("Do unto others. . ."), your country, political system, or home team. Art and other expressive things can be nonreligious as well — just for beauty, fun, decoration, or emotional response beyond the mundane.

So any artifacts, features, or other aspects of the archaeological record that seem to go beyond the practical aspects of making a living can relate to past shared belief systems. Even decorations on tools can show this. They may also indicate social status, political power, and other things besides ideology.

Here are some examples of how you can see belief systems in archaeology:

- ✔ *Caches* (hidden piles) or other deposits of artifacts that aren't just for everyday tasks can be offerings or evidence of some ritual behavior. An example is the pile of 3,000-year-old spear points in Color Figure 2, which look like they were in a bag, deliberately broken, and possibly too thin to be useful spears. At the upper right of the photo, under the north arrow and scale, is a round pile of red *ochre,* a powdery stone that may have been for pigment (red may have been an important symbolic color).

- ✔ Deliberate burial of fellow humans, which comes as early as Neanderthal times, may show some belief in an afterlife, especially if grave goods are left with the dead for use in that afterlife. But it may have just been sanitary disposal of the corpse and artifacts nobody needed anymore.

- ✔ Repeated use of images may show they were supernatural symbols or signs of something sacred. For example, the same bird image on pots, statues, and the engraved or painted sides of buildings may be a sacred figure.

- ✔ Arrangements of structures in *archaeoastronomical alignments* may show knowledge of the sun, moon, planets, and stars. Lining up your mounds or buildings so that the sun rises over them on the solstice or equinox takes expert knowledge of engineering and astronomy, and maybe expresses religious ideals too; why go to all that trouble to showcase objects that weren't sacred? The structures may have offered a means to worship the celestial bodies. After all, for most of human existence, they were the nightly show.

✔ Structures containing different kinds of artifacts from what you see everywhere else in the site can be evidence for the presence of religious practitioners such as *shamans* (part-time) and *priests* (full-time, supported by the rest of society). Certainly, burials of people with unusual items can indicate they were religious specialists.

✔ Anything unable to be explained in terms of simply making a living has the potential to be ideological in nature. But always be careful with your assumptions and biases; a common symbol found on a variety of artifacts could have meant something sacred but also could be just a pretty design or a brand advertisement!

Be careful to state alternative hypotheses in all your reconstructions of the human past, especially when you're dealing with belief systems. Explaining symbolism and ritual, especially in the distant past, may just be beyond the ability of most archaeology. If you have more recent historical records relating to your past peoples, you can do this more easily. But so much ideological behavior (like praying) just doesn't have material evidence.

You can't ignore ideology. What people believe is the basis for war and peace, ritual and art, monumental architecture, and so many other human accomplishments. So you explain it as well as you can, and expect to keep modifying the explanations in the light of new finds.

Using Analogy with Known Human Behavior

All archaeological interpretation is *analogy,* which means you compare the evidence of the past that you found with human behavior that you know in order to explain what happened. In this section, I give several different ways of using analogy and the cautions that go with them.

Ethnographic analogy: Using anthropological and historical data

Doing *ethnography* means living with and observing a particular society and writing down everything for scientific study. Cultural anthropologists and historians have collected knowledge of thousands of known societies all over the world. You can look up all this information to see the various ways people did things. You may get insights into the meanings of symbols on artifacts and beliefs about them that you'd never have otherwise.

The best strategy is to use ethnographies of cultures that have some histori-cal continuity with those you're digging up. Also, look at known cultures that are appropriate for your site or region, and use caution in projecting behavior back into the past. For example, decades of research on the hunter–gatherers of the Kalahari Desert in southern Africa give a great picture of how small groups of mobile foragers live, hunting elephants and giraffes. But you can't use this information well to reconstruct foraging behavior at your site in a temperate, wet, forested zone that had only deer and small game.

Here are some other examples of the disadvantages of ethnographic analogy:

✔ Research on modern hunter–gatherers and horticultural societies may be suspect because so few of them still exist and they inhabit the lands least desired by other people. Prehistoric foragers all over the world, especially in richer environments, may have lived very differently.

✔ Ethnographic data have been collected mostly in recent historic times, so the cultures described may have already been very changed by out-side influences — even by the people collecting information on them.

✔ Historic accounts of different cultures are usually biased in favor of those who wrote them, so they may be inaccurate.

✔ Ethnographic and historic accounts seldom say much about everyday life and especially material culture — the kinds of things archaeologists are seeing in the ground.

Ethnoarchaeology: Archaeologists doing ethnography

This (awkward) term means archaeologists studying living human societies to get insights into past cultures. Here you're doing your own ethnography and paying attention to the details of material culture. This technique works especially well with hunter–gatherers because you can follow them around to see how they catch and butcher animals, use tools, discard bones, and create garbage piles and other features. Archaeologists have studied other kinds of cultures besides foragers in this way too — even our own. (See my descriptions of archaeological study of our modern garbage in Chapter 2 and cellphones in Chapter 15.)

Some ethnoarchaeological studies:

✔ In an investigation of Arctic hunters, the archaeologist saw patterns of behavior that could have existed among prehistoric Ice Age folks in simi-lar frigid environments. The Eskimo did have modern artifacts, but used many traditional practices as well, like butchering game in ways that left distinctive patterns on the bone.

> ✔ A study of South American farmers making and using their own earthen-
> ware pottery showed archaeologists how broken pots were recycled in
> many ways, not just thrown away.

The same cautions noted in the preceding section for ethnographic archaeology hold true for ethnoarchaeology. You need some continuity between your
reference culture and the archaeological culture you're studying for the comparison to work well.

Experimental archaeology: Replicating ancient technologies

Experimental archaeology means you try to make the same kind of artifact,
mound, garden, or stone monument that you've excavated. Doing so can give
you great ideas about how past peoples did such things (and can be fun or
dangerous, too).

Examples of experimental archaeology:

- ✔ *Flintknapping* (chipping stone tools), making pottery in an outdoor kiln,
  and building *wattle and daub* houses (poles with woven branches and
  clay daubed on top) are all common archaeology activities. (Sometimes
  they can be hazardous if you cut yourself with sharp stone or let your
  kiln fire get out of hand!)

- ✔ Reenacting past ways of life or historic events gives you an idea of what
  it was like to wear the clothing, eat the food, use the tools, and even
  fight the battles or share the misery of the past.

- ✔ Filling up bags or baskets of dirt and piling them up to build a mound
  or earthen wall can give you an idea of how many laborers and how
  much time (and how many sore muscles) it took to construct such
  monuments.

- ✔ Cutting big stones out of a mountain and moving them on log rollers or
  barges helps you see how people created monumental constructions.

- ✔ Using chemical analysis of residues on ancient vessels as well as historical records, some enterprising investigators recreate ancient beer brew-
  ing and winemaking techniques (and get to drink the results).

- ✔ At least one person who donated his body to science after his death has
  been used to explore ancient mummification techniques (yes!) based on
  archaeological finds and Egyptian writings describing the processes.

Relating the archaeological story to the present

You want to see how people lived and behaved in the past. You can not only make a contribution to archaeological knowledge but also discover more about human nature and your own heritage. When you use analogy, you use present knowledge to understand the past.

The relationship can go the other way — making past information useful and appealing in the present world. The drama of what people endured or enjoyed, or how they lived on the land people inhabit today can be fascinating for modern folks and give practical insights for solving common human problems.

In Chapter 16, I give you a rundown of the practical uses of archaeological information. Here I simply emphasize the importance of telling the story well and relating it to human life everywhere. People dealt in very different ways with the basic necessities and more elaborate issues of life. They sometimes survived and recovered from natural disasters and political mistakes. Other times they didn't. But it always makes a great story!

When you relate the results of your archaeological reconstructions, be careful that the storytelling doesn't get in the way of the science! You should first state what you know is fairly certain, then what looks probable, and then other possible explanations. If you clearly label the things you know are fanciful speculations, then you don't look silly when someone's new finds shoot down your reconstruction later.

Using Archaeological Theories to Interpret Your Discoveries

As you interpret your discoveries and see what happened in the past, you're guided by different sorts of philosophical frameworks — whether you realize it or not. In this section, I describe theoretical terms and ideas you see floating around in archaeological circles. (I use all of them in this book.)

The *frameworks* or *theoretical perspectives* — in other words, how you see things — make a big difference in the story you tell and the science you do. They're a bit complicated, so stay with me here. Then you can throw around flashy theoretical jargon and impress your fellow diggers!

After you read through my description of the major theoretical perspectives, you may ask which ones to use. My answer is that modern archaeology uses all of them! As an archaeologist today you first establish your culture history to describe what happened, and then do science asking questions about cultural processes. You also heed the postprocessual criticisms of science (explained later in this section) and see the biases and weaknesses in your arguments.

Culture history: What, when, where

The *culture history* approach means you simply tell what, when, and where something happened. Culture history is description, setting up space-time frameworks. You describe material remains and what they show about how people lived and behaved in the past for each time period. You also try to get at the rules and standards used by your past people in their behavior. This approach has dominated most archaeology until recently, and is the first part of any project.

When you relate culture history, you give a list of succeeding cultures through time, with their characteristic artifacts and lifeways. The time chart in the appendix shows you a brief culture history for the world, from earliest prehistoric through modern times.

Processual archaeology: How, maybe why

The 1960s and 1970s marked the development of what folks called the "new archaeology" and, later, processual archaeology. Simply put, doing *processual archaeology* (also known as *culture process*) means doing science. It means you use the scientific method to study the processes through which culture works.

Within processual archaeology, one particular perspective is *middle-range theory,* meaning you find causal links between the material record in the ground and the behavior of living past people. Another specific perspective is *cultural materialism,* which means interpreting human culture as mostly structured by the limits of the material world. I discuss both of these in more detail later in this section.

Scientific archaeology

Processual archaeology developed when archaeologists became dissatisfied with just describing culture and not asking questions about how and why things happened. The following list shows you some of the goals of scientific, processual archaeology:

✔ See how cultural systems worked.

✔ Explain processes of culture change (or lack of change).

✔ Address big cultural questions like the origins of culture, food production, or civilization.

✔ Make general statements about human behavior.

Doing processual archaeology includes many strategies and techniques. Here are some of them:

✔ Using the scientific method, testing multiple alternative hypotheses.

✔ Using a *positivist* philosophy (thinking everything is knowable if you have the right tools, logic, and experience to find it out). This mindset is very characteristic of Western society — humans can definitely get to the moon (or cure cancer) if they develop the right technology.

✔ Studying artifact and site function, settlement pattern, and past landscapes.

✔ Analyzing quantitative data (numbers), including establishing huge databases that let you study your zillions of archaeological materials more easily.

✔ Computer modeling of everything from sites to past cultural systems.

✔ Using complex scientific technology and fancy instruments in the field and during laboratory analyses.

✔ Understanding past natural ecosystems in which cultures existed.

✔ Emphasizing the cultural ecology of past peoples — how they related to specific natural and social environments.

✔ Looking at the efficiency of ways prehistoric people made a living in their environments.

✔ Exploring how social class and religious ritual (like burial customs) can be analyzed and explained scientifically.

✔ Using the comparative method to interpret the evidence you've excavated in terms of human cultures worldwide.

Cultural materialism and middle range theory

Cultural materialism means you explain culture as primarily structured by the technology, environment, and economy — the material conditions of human existence. It's the philosophical perspective you often use when doing archaeology within a processual or scientific framework. These conditions are the systems that get you your basic necessities of life. Other cultural systems less directly related to those basic needs — like social organization, values and beliefs, and art — depend on that material infrastructure. When it changes, the rest changes.

Explaining culture in terms of the material conditions is useful because that's what archaeology has to work with. You don't get evidence that direct when you're trying to study social and religious organization. So you use cultural materialism because you can, though you know beliefs also cause behavior.

Middle range theory is a term meaning the causal links between the archaeological record in the ground and the long-gone human behavior and natural processes responsible for it. So middle range theory includes using all the types of analogy I describe earlier in this chapter. It also means you investigate site formation processes — not only the human cultural behavior of the past but also the geological and physical factors that left your site the way it is today. (I describe these site formation processes in Chapter 1.)

Postprocessual archaeology: Finding meaning and avoiding bias

Theoretical archaeologists came up with postprocessual archaeology in the 1980s and 1990s as a reaction against some of the weaknesses of processual archaeology (described a bit more in Chapter 1). *Postprocessual archaeology* means humanistic study — seeing culture through the arts, critique, and even speculation and philosophy (but not the hard empirical evidence of science).

Postprocessual theory is archaeology's version of *postmodernism,* a 20th-century philosophy that originated in (of all places) literary criticism. Postmodernists criticized the scientific view that everything was knowable. They "deconstructed" great books (and everything else) to see how they were put together and what the biases of the writers were. Social scientists and others began using postmodern viewpoints when they were useful.

Archaeology finally adopted postmodern ideas and gave them several names. Postprocessual archaeology includes all of them. I list the most prominent ones here, with explanations:

- **Critical theory:** Seeing the biases in your scientific assumptions about the past. They can be hidden or unnoticed racism, sexism, capitalist economic interpretations, and so on. Critical theory is probably the most valuable contribution of postprocessual archaeology.

- **Cognitive archaeology:** Finding out what had meaning to past people and what they thought and believed. You can do this better with historic archaeology because you have some written records showing what people thought. But you can't figure it out well for prehistoric times — those people are all dead, and they didn't write anything down!

✔ **Symbolic and structural archaeology:** Assuming that thought processes are similar in all humans, and that symbols express the structure of thought. So if you study how symbols are organized, you can figure out what people were thinking in the past. Again, this method only works well with historic archaeology.

✔ **Reflexive archaeology:** Recognizing that your interpretation of the past is just one among many possible explanations. This technique is useful to see your data in different ways. But after all, you're the archaeologist, so you probably have more expertise on the subject.

✔ **Marxist archaeology:** Seeing past behavior in terms of political power and control over resources and production. Marxist archaeologists existed long before postprocessual archaeology, but their ideas are more popular lately. Marxism sounds like a variety of materialism, but because it emphasizes more how people struggle not to be dominated by those in power, it's really a more ideological approach (and sometimes pretty pessimistic with all that struggling).

✔ **Feminist archaeology:** Looking for evidence of women in the archaeological past and correcting male bias in interpretation. This line of study also existed before postprocessualism. Many (especially women) saw how archaeological explanations always had men doing the neat things in the past. (See the section "Describing social order, family, gender, and politics in the past" earlier in this chapter for more on gender and social bias.)

✔ **Agency theory:** Looking for powerful individual leaders making choices and decisions in the past. Rather than talking about passive people at the mercy of their environmental or economic systems, agency theorists see active persons causing culture change. This theory goes well with gender and Marxist interpretations, but it's also easier to see when you have historical records to give you an idea of just who is out there grabbing power and how. It's nearly impossible to see in prehistory.

Doing postprocessual archaeology, you may reject a search for universal scientific laws about human behavior or cultural systems. You see cultures and individuals acting in different ways. You also may go beyond the data to tell many speculative, not-scientifically-testable stories interpreting the past. You're also interested in showing how all archaeology is political. You may demonstrate how inequality evolved and how people came to be subjected and controlled. You also see how the past and its interpretations and physical remains are used for political ends today as well. And you show how modern science isn't objective but is political in many ways. In Chapter 16, I give you more explanation of the politics of archaeology.

Explaining the past with multiple theoretical views

Archaeological theory is difficult; its complicated philosophical writing can be torture. But you need theoretical foundations before you dig. Here are examples of the different perspectives in studying Paleolithic (Old Stone Age) cave art of Western Europe. Ice-Age hunter–gatherers made the beautiful paintings and engravings on rock walls some 20,000 years for unknown reasons.

✔ Doing *culture history,* you describe and photograph the art and identify the animal species shown. You date associated artifacts or charcoal mixed in with the paints. You say what's there, where it all is, maybe how old it is, and how it's distributed across space. Using general analogy, you suggest the animals depicted are probably the ones often hunted; maybe the pictures were part of ritual magic to ensure a successful hunt.

✔ For *processual archaeology,* you analyze the paints and stone tools used to make the pictures. You look at the engravings and brush strokes or finger marks on the rock to see how they were created. You compare the animals shown on the rock with the food bones left at sites of this time period. Statistics you collect on what's portrayed can help, but you may have trouble classifying everything — is that partial outline a horse or a deer? For ethnographic analogy (part of middle-range theory), you read studies of people all over the world who do cave art to see why they do it and look for similarities between their other lifeways and your Paleolithic people. You also do experimental archaeology, mixing the minerals, plants, and animal fats you've discovered made up the pigments in the paint, and trying cave art yourself. Because most of the art is deep into caves, you realize Paleolithic people had to go quite a long way with unreliable torches and stone oil lamps in total darkness; you suspect the art had deep, probably sacred meaning. Maybe you hypothesize that these were places for special gatherings and then see if the artifacts and animal bones left in the caves show more unusual things than in the typical habitation sites. If they do, your hypothesis is supported.

✔ To do *postprocessual archaeology,* you start by assuming the art depicts symbols of beliefs. You note that animals portrayed aren't the same ones represented in the food debris, so they have much deeper meaning. You may look at where each picture is. Lions, bears, and other animals not typically hunted are far deeper in the caves, maybe signifying greater sacredness. One archaeologist interested in the structure of symbols thought bison represented females in the ancient mind, because bison were often portrayed over passage openings; horses, on long side walls, were male symbols. He interpreted all the pictures as portraying ancient myths about men and women. Many, many other explanations are possible here — just use your imagination!

Next time you read any archaeological reconstruction, see if you can determine the researcher's theoretical perspective. The approaches complement each other, so many archaeologists are now using them all. They also use even more tortured terms like "processual-plus" or "cognitive-processual" archaeology. Despite the jargon, remember to try to use description, science, and humanism too.

Part IV

Archaeology Reconstructs the Whole Human Past

The 5th Wave   By Rich Tennant

"Ooo – this inscription speaks of a time when Shu, the god of air and Tefenet, the goddess of moisture, were on a date down a dark lonely road. News comes of an escaped evil god who has a hook for a hand..."

In this part . . .

Most of human existence on this planet can only be known through archaeology, so in Part IV, I recount a little of what archaeologists have reconstructed about the prehistoric and historic human past from the material remains excavated and studied so meticulously. Chapter 12 begins with the earliest humans and their stone tools, which provide evidence for how they made a living hunting, gathering, or scavenging and spread around the world. In Chapter 13, you see how the first global warming affected populations everywhere, and what artifacts, remains of early domestic plants and animals, and settlement patterns tell about how people changed and adapted. Chapter 14 tells the story of the rise of the first ancient states (and some of the later ones) in all their glory. In Chapter 15, I detail some of the things you can discover by doing historic archaeology — uncovering things (or people) the written history never mentions.

Chapter 12

Early Humans: Original Cave Guys & Gals

● ●

In This Chapter

▶ Becoming human and developing culture

▶ Spreading from Africa to Asia and Europe

▶ Navigating the uncertainty surrounding the Neanderthals

▶ Developing more elaborate culture, including art, as modern humans

▶ Moving out to Australia and North and South America

● ●

*B*iological anthropologists examine the fossil bones of the earliest human ancestors in Africa to get an idea of what they were like 2 to 3 million years ago. Archaeologists look at the *cultural remains* these human ancestors left behind — the oldest *artifacts* (things made and used by people) and the ancient landscapes — to reconstruct how they lived. This chapter describes that archaeological record to give you the big picture about humanity's remote past. I take you through the ages from the earliest known artifacts — crude-looking stone tools of the Lower Paleolithic era — through the archaeology of Neanderthals and modern humans in the Middle Paleolithic.

By the time anatomically modern humans emerged some 100,000 years ago, people had spread all over Africa, Asia, and Europe. They made a living by hunting and gathering (mostly gathering — it's easier). By 35,000 years ago, the dawn of the Upper Paleolithic age, they had elaborate art and tools showing they were expert hunters of the Ice Age big game animals that roamed northern latitudes (and other big creatures in more southerly, warmer latitudes).

In the process of moving around all those latitudes, people first came to Australia around 50,000 years ago and to North and South America at least as early as 15,000 years ago. (The only continent left, Antarctica, wasn't too hospitable until the advent of modern technology.)

As you read through this chapter and see how archaeology documents the beginning of the human career, keep an eye on the chart in the appendix so you don't mix up your humans and time periods. The map in the appendix helps you see locations of the important sites I describe, and gives you an idea of how much land the earliest people had to cross to populate the world.

Our Family Tree

To set the stage for explaining the oldest cultural remains that archaeology investigates, first I'll describe a little of the biological background. Biological anthropologists called *paleoanthropologists* or human *paleontologists* have found fossil bones of many early *hominids* or *hominins* (creatures like us but maybe or maybe not directly ancestral to the modern human family) all over Africa. Everyone argues about how old each one is, which is our direct ancestor, or which branches of the family tree died out. And of course, they all have complicated species names (like *Australopithecus africanus*, one of the earliest in southern Africa). Some of the tiny bone and teeth fragments (you never get a whole skeleton) are as old as 5 million years. By 2 million years ago, they're close enough to modern humans to be in the actual human genus (*Homo*), and have species names like *Homo habilis* ("handyman" — the stone tool maker).We, of course, are *Homo sapiens*.

Scientific investigations of early human forms are not archaeology, though paleoanthropology uses many of archaeology's methods (picks, shovels, screens). Archaeology comes into play when you want to investigate how these human ancestral creatures lived, based on all the *other* material objects *besides* their bones.

Paleoanthropologists need archaeology to help interpret their own finds. You may be familiar with the famous work of Louis Leakey in Tanzania's Olduvai Gorge (see map in the appendix) in East Africa. He searched for early human ancestors there because he'd actually seen those rough, chipped stones he knew were early tools lying around.

Archaeologists also look at the entire landscape in which hominins lived, to see things like what resources were available and what dangers were out there. (*Not* dinosaurs, but certainly big African beasts.) They work with the other scientists to combine all this evidence with information from the fossil bones: Bigger teeth for eating plants? Smaller teeth for eating meat? Broken animal bones showing they did eat meat? Hands still adapted for climbing trees, as with their more ape-like ancestors? Hands with bone structure that could have gripped stone tools? The goal is to fill in the picture of how the earliest animals in the human family tree made a living in their environments.

Humans are set apart from the rest of the animal kingdom by our unique adaptation, *culture,* which includes everything from language to making artifacts, shaping environments, and planning. But chimps in the wild use and even make a few crude tools of stone and grass stems. In fact, even crows have been observed using rocks or wire as tools! So archaeology shows how humans became set apart as cultural beings as the evidence of more complex culture appears over the millennia.

The Lower Paleolithic Era: The Earliest People and Culture

As soon as you get artifacts — the remains of cultural behavior — you can do the archaeology of the earliest creatures who can be labeled people. To characterize this dawn of humanity, archaeologists use the term *Paleolithic,* meaning (from the Greek root words) "Old Stone Age." It's a cultural time period characterized by those well-preserved stone artifacts. The Paleolithic extended from over 2 million years ago to about 10,000 years ago. The *Lower Paleolithic* is the oldest division within this time period, beginning as soon as you have the oldest artifacts. New finds keep pushing this date back.

Oldest archaeological finds

The oldest known stone tools are some 2.5 million years old. The first actual artifacts were probably far older and made of softer materials like bark, wood, or bone. Chipping stone tools is hard — first you have to go find the right kind of stone, bash it in just the right way, and then quite possibly clean up the blood you just shed. But stone lasts, so the earliest artifacts still preserved are pebbles chipped to have sharp edges (see Figure 12-1).

Pebble tools may have been for digging out roots or chopping up vegetables or meat. They could have been for killing animals or hacking at scavenged carcasses. Some animal bones at hominin sites have teeth marks of other animals, overlapped by cut marks from stone tools. Some animal bones have been snapped and bashed open to get the nutritious marrow, something only humans would do (and would presumably need tools to accomplish).

The other very important and famous archaeological evidence of the earliest human ancestors is the hominin footprints excavated at the Laetoli site in Tanzania (see the map in the appendix) by Mary Leakey (Louis's wife, an archaeologist). They were made some 3 million years ago by at least two individuals, in the soft mud of a lake bed, where they were quickly covered by volcanic ash and preserved (along with footprints of other animals, possibly all running from the erupting volcano).

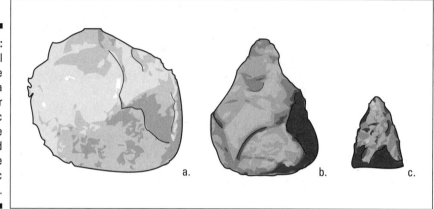

Figure 12-1:
A typical pebble tool (a), a later Lower Paleolithic hand axe (b), and a Middle Paleolithic point (c).

a.   b.   c.

The lives of early humans

Anthropological views of how our earliest ancestors made a living and became human have become more scientific. Combining the fossil evidence and archaeological reconstructions of material culture, interpretations have changed over the decades. Here's a sequence of these changing assumptions:

- ✔ Early humans came up with culture as they developed the skills to hunt and kill animals for a living.

- ✔ Our small (3-foot-tall), upright-walking ancestor probably did *not* hunt or kill much but mostly cooperated in gathering plants and other things that didn't run away or attack (eggs and small, slow animals).

- ✔ Scavenging for meat is an even easier way to get more nutritious food. So they probably waited for a better hunter such as a lion to kill some game, and then ate the leftovers (but weren't picky about cuts of meat from that chewed-up antelope).

Early society: Still a lot of mystery

Although archaeologists can reconstruct what early hominins ate and how they made some artifacts, they have no real evidence for what early society was like — not that that's stopped speculation. Here's another list of hypotheses on the earliest family values and how the interpretations have changed over the last several decades:

- ✔ Bigger skeletons were male, smaller ones female; men hunted and protected women and children, who foraged close to home.

✔ Bigger skeletons may just be separate species; each species lived somewhat differently in different environments.

✔ Men gathered and scavenged food and brought it back in return for sex from women, who stayed at camp to have and raise kids.

✔ Men maybe got some meat, but women gathered the plants that made up most of the diet and were used to make artifacts like baby-carrying nets.

✔ Everyone gathered, scavenged, and cared for each other and the kids; everyone had sex with lots of partners; families consisted of women and their children, with men hanging around the larger group. Meat came from scavenging, much easier than hunting.

You can imagine the arguments over these ideas! The material evidence is so slim that it can support many different and conflicting arguments. The most popular version is the "sex for meat" idea (probably because it looks good in the tabloids), but it reflects a modern bias of Western culture.

The Later Lower Paleolithic Era: Moving Out of Africa

Archaeologists recognize that big cultural changes took place sometime after 2 million years ago. Stone tools became more sophisticated, and other archaeological finds, like piles of tools and butchered bones, indicate human ancestors were doing more complex things like establishing base-camp living sites. Most important, the material evidence shows that some human ancestors were moving out of Africa to populate other parts of the world.

The *Pleistocene* or Ice Age is the *geological* time period stretching from 2 million to 10,000 years ago. Nearly all human development happens within this time. Note that the geological and archaeological ages end at about the same time (due to massive climate change). But the earliest human-like creatures and stone tools appear a bit before the Ice Age began.

Sometime after 2 million years ago, hominins spread from Africa into Asia and Europe (see the time chart in the appendix). New species were taller and more modern-looking. (One of these species is *Homo erectus,* but I won't worry about all the names here because they're not usually within the domain of archaeology). Archaeological evidence shows the use of fire (a good thing for staying warm, if they're moving north from the tropics) and many artifact types and remains of animal bones from meals.

Lower Paleolithic artifacts

The most typical stone tool of later Lower Paleolithic is the hand axe (refer to Figure 12-1). It's pear-shaped and chipped on both sides to get a sharp edge all around. The early people may have held it in their hands or used it with a handle to kill or butcher game, chop fruit, or dig up roots. Hand axes are the longest-used artifacts humans have ever had!

Early humans made chunky tools like hand axes by chipping away flakes from the stone pebble or cobble *core*. They then made other tools from those leftover sharp flakes. Their toolkits had artifacts called choppers, scrapers, chisels, and so on, based on what they may have been used for. Besides these new stone artifacts, by the later part of the Lower Paleolithic you see greater sophistication in the archaeological record, as I describe in the next section.

Lower Paleolithic sites

One famous Lower Paleolithic site is the 1.8-million-year-old Trinil site discovered in Java in the 1850s. Nobody believed at first that the stone tools and human-like skeletons (called "Java Man" and later *Homo erectus*) found there could be from so early, but modern dating methods (discussed in Chapter 10) confirmed their great age. Other famous Lower Paleolithic sites:

- ✔ 700,000-year-old Zhoukoudien Cave, near Beijing, China, had evidence of human-made fire, some 200,000 stone tools, and 40 *Homo erectus* skeletons. They were first named "Peking Man," but the bones were lost during World War II. (Luckily, someone had made plaster casts!)

- ✔ Olorgesailie in Kenya dates to 800,000 years ago and has thousands of hand axes and other stone artifacts as well as baboon bones.

- ✔ Atapuerca, in northern Spain, has earlier hominin remains dating to 800,000 years (with one tooth possibly well over a million years old), and in one cave, over 30 skeletons of people pushed into a 50-foot-deep pit around 350,000 years ago. Researchers argue over whether this find represents deliberate burial of the dead or just interesting corpse storage.

- ✔ Terra Amata, on the French Riviera, 350,000 years old, had hand axes, animal and fish remains, and rocks arranged in patterns suggesting they held up poles for huts, with fire hearths inside.

- ✔ Torralba and Ambrona sites in Spain had bones of butchered elephants and other extinct big game animals.

Lower Paleolithic ways of life

The animal remains at Zhoukoudien show that the inhabitants hunted and cooked over 90 different species of animals! Although a few archaeologists think scavenging was still the most important food-getting technique, most agree that the wide array of remains shows real hunting and cooking fires for the earliest barbecues.

Coprolites, or fossilized human feces (yes — prehistoric poop), at Terra Amata indicate people ate plants harvested in late spring and early fall. With the fish, shellfish, and animal bones also found there, the evidence suggests they were camping during specific seasons.

Lower Paleolithic people lived successfully in the early Ice Age, even though it was very cold. They organized hunts for those Ice Age *megafauna* (big game). But archaeologists have little evidence to figure out how they carried out other activities of daily life or organized their communities. Did they talk? Sing? Dance? Believe in the supernatural? Clearly, they shared food, help, and skills, but how did they think? Some scientists say they couldn't even talk yet, but I believe they did. How else can you teach someone to hunt rhinoceros, make a fire, dig up a ripe tuber, or build a shelter?

The Middle Paleolithic Era

Some time after 300,000 years ago (see the time chart in the appendix), the cultural evidence changed, so archaeologists give this time period a new name, the *Middle Paleolithic.* Complex planning and skills were necessary to produce the new Middle Paleolithic stone tools, such as triangular points (for spears or knives — refer to Figure 12-1). Butchered animal bones at sites show widely successful hunting. Neanderthals and other later hominin forms (very few skeletons are known, and scientists argue about what names to give them all) are associated with Middle Paleolithic tools.

Neanderthals

Of the many later fossil human forms living in Europe and western Asia, none is more of a puzzle than the *Neanderthal.* This hominin first appeared about 200,000 years ago. It had a rugged but modern-looking human skeleton, except for the head — Neanderthal skulls show a heavy brow ridge, flattened top, and elongated back. Their brain sizes averaged a little *bigger* than ours, and their muscles (which leave markings on the bone) were bigger, too. The robust bodies of Neanderthals appear to be a result of their cold Ice Age climate and rough environment.

Understanding Neanderthal skeletons is of course not directly part of archaeology. But because archaeologists excavate the cultural remains of these human ancestors, they need to coordinate them with the knowledge of their physical bodies.

In terms of time period of existence, the Neanderthals overlap with the anatomically modern humans, who first appeared by at least 100,000 years ago; they may or may not have lived with modern humans who moved into their lands. By around 30,000 years ago, all humans had modern skeletons like ours. Scientists argue about whether Neanderthals became extinct or mated with *Homo sapiens* immigrants from Africa to become part of our ancestral line. DNA analysis of bones from three or four Neanderthals shows that they indeed weren't as closely related to us as direct ancestors would be. But this is only a small sample size so far.

Neanderthal artifacts, food remains, and even burials show little about how their families and societies were organized. In fact, skeletal remains of early modern humans are in some cases associated with Middle Paleolithic tools. So the artifact types aren't necessarily specific to each hominin species.

Middle Paleolithic artifacts and sites

Middle Paleolithic people more frequently made their characteristic stone tools from large, thick flint flakes rather than the pebble cores of earlier eras. The more than 60 types of stone tools recognized include borers, scrapers, and serrated-edge implements, as well as several types of triangular points and knives. Cave and *rock shelter* (shallow cave) sites in Europe and the Middle East have produced piles of the chipping debris from the manufacture of these tools, as well as butchered bones of mammoth, wooly rhinos, and other Ice Age game, and even the occasional preserved wooden spear. A few sites have hearths or intentionally-constructed fire pits.

At Middle Paleolithic cave sites in South Africa, archaeologists have uncovered complex artifacts dating to 75,000 years ago, including polished bone tools, snail-shell beads, engraved bone, and pieces of red *ochre* (iron oxide, a red stone used for pigment) with engraved patterns in a cross-hatched design that could be the earliest art or symbolism.

The earliest intentional burials of the dead date from the Middle Paleolithic, so you can say this may indicate spiritual practices, though it may just be for sanitation and to prohibit scavenging by animals.

Neanderthal lifeways

At Shanidar Cave in Iraq (dug in the 1950s and '60s), Neanderthal burials 70,000 years old were excavated. One man's skeleton showed injuries that would have left him disabled. Yet he was over 40 when he died, a ripe old age (for the Stone Age, anyway), so somebody was obviously taking care of him. On top of another skeleton was pollen from many plants, a find that suggested different flowers were left on the body (though some argue the pollen was just a natural occurrence).

Other Middle Paleolithic sites have lots of red ochre with skeletons or artifacts. Red was clearly an important color. It can mean death (as in killing animals) and perhaps life too (women who menstruated could get pregnant). Neanderthals probably did have some kinds of spiritual beliefs, but reconstructing those beliefs from the evidence so far is difficult.

The Upper Paleolithic Era: Modern Humans Populate the World

Archaeologists originally designated the *Upper Paleolithic* era as the time in which completely modern humans took over and developed art and very complex, standardized tool types, beginning around 35,000 years ago (see the time chart in the appendix). The most accepted theory about human development is that anatomically-modern humans *(Homo sapiens —* sometimes known by the old-fashioned term *Cro-Magnons),* evolved in Africa over 100,000 years ago with superior brains and skills. They then spread out to Asia and Europe. An alternative theory is that all the hominins already existing across the continents shared enough genetic material to evolve slowly into *Homo sapiens* in many different regions.

Remember that much of this argument about Neanderthals and modern humans is in the domain of human biology. Archaeology can only offer evidence for the cultural abilities of these early human forms. The advances of the Upper Paleolithic may indeed be due to the superior brain power of modern humans (though it took them a while). Or maybe it was just the right time to do something new. But I must note that some Neanderthal remains have been found with Upper Paleolithic tools. The body type doesn't necessarily dictate how sophisticated the brain was!

Upper Paleolithic artifacts

Some of the stone-tool manufacturing processes went from banging and bashing to pressing during the Upper Paleolithic. With pressure-flaking, the craftworker used a stone, bone, or antler tool to press off tiny stone flakes. This process made the point or other tool very thin and fine; check out an example in Figure 12-2a.

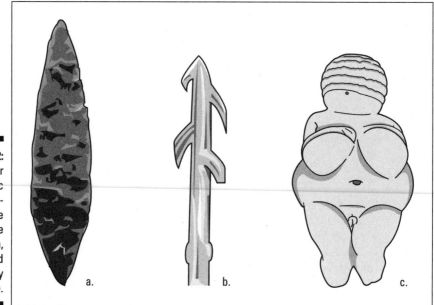

Figure 12-2: Upper Paleolithic pressure-flaked stone point, bone harpoon, and fired clay figurine.

a.   b.   c.

Blade tools were another Upper Paleolithic innovation. A blade is a flake that's twice as long as it is wide. If you prepare your flint core well, you can strike off many blades that are the same size and shape — and very sharp.

Other tools, such as barbed harpoons (refer to Figure 12-2b), were made of bone, antler, or ivory. Another characteristic of Upper Paleolithic artifacts is standardization. A whole pile may all be the same size and shape — prehistoric quality control!

Upper Paleolithic art

Art appeared on the scene in several forms during the Upper Paleolithic:

- ✔ Portable art, such as figurines carved of ivory or sculpted in fired clay (a new technology).

> ✔ Other portable objects, such as bone or antler pieces with engraved lines. These may have been art or perhaps maps, calendars, or tally sheets.
>
> ✔ Stationary art, such as paintings and engravings on rock walls of caves.

What this art means is constantly debated. Figurines of naked women (many very hefty) are commonly called symbols of fertility or sex (see Figure 12-2c) but could be prehistoric dolls, goddess figures, or portraits of mom. Other figurines are of men and animals, with equally mysterious symbolism.

Animals and occasionally human figures are depicted on Upper Paleolithic cave walls, too. The most famous cave, Lascaux, in southwest France (also discussed in Chapter 20), has colorful paintings of bison, horses, and deer, as well as other (nonhunted) animals such as lions and birds. The pictures also include enigmatic lines that may be spears, lightning, or something else entirely. Cosquer Cave, now underwater on the south French coast, has paintings of fish, penguins, and jellyfish.

Upper Paleolithic lifeways: People on the move

Maybe because they had better tools, Upper Paleolithic people were excellent hunters. Their art may have centered on hunting magic, to guarantee success. Or perhaps it was just shared symbols at places where annual gatherings took place and knowledge was passed on to the next generation. The people looked just like modern humans, yet the evidence is still not enough to tell whether they thought and acted like us.

Floating toward Australia (and leaving stuff behind)

During the Ice Age, ocean water was locked up in the ice that covered much of the Northern Hemisphere, so sea levels were lower than today. Islands in Southeast Asia were then connected land exposed on the continental shelf. Remains of modern humans dating as early as 46,000 years ago (the earliest human evidence in Southeast Asia) have been excavated in Niah Cave on Borneo (Malaysia — see the map in the appendix and Figure 12-3). With them were pig, monkey, and lizard bones with cut marks — probably from butchering — and fragments of nuts and yams that would be poisonous to eat without complicated processing. This evidence shows people developed complex skills early in the favorable environment of the tropical forest.

Figure 12-3:
Niah Cave in
Borneo.

It's no surprise that these sophisticated early modern Upper Paleolithic humans made it to Australia by as early as 50,000 years ago. They had to cross about 60 miles of open water; they probably used rafts of tied logs or even dugout canoes, but no watercraft are preserved.

After they got to Australia, they quickly adapted to its rugged mountains and deserts. On the coast, they left shell *middens* (garbage piles) full of fish bones and shells from the seafood they ate. Besides stone axes, the archaeology of Australia features rock art not that different from Paleolithic art in Europe. Engravings and paintings of animals, people, and geometric shapes on the walls of caves and rock faces are hard to date, however, so some of the sites may be later than the Paleolithic.

At archaeological sites around Lake Mungo in New South Wales, Australia, finds include fire hearths; shells; fish, mammal, and bird bones; eggshells; and bone and stone tools dating to between 32,000 and 20,000 years ago. Human bones have red ochre pigment with them, and one skeleton was cremated — the oldest known example of this treatment of the dead.

Heading to America by land or by sea

Both the date and the route of people's first entrance into the New World (North and South America) are hotly debated. Most evidence indicates that Upper Paleolithic people spread from northeast Asia into North America about 15,000 to 20,000 years ago. They hunted big game such as mammoths, mastodons, giant sloths, and a giant armadillo species as big as a compact car.

The lower sea level during the Ice Age exposed a land bridge where the Bering Strait is today between Siberia and Alaska (see the map in the appendix). Hunters following their hoofed food moved eastward from Asia. They probably had no idea they were walking into a new continent. Another idea is that fishers moving along the frigid coast cruised around the same way by water; this tactic would have been far easier because you can sit down in a boat.

Archaeologists evaluating these hypotheses face the problem that any ancient prehistoric sites on the coastline are now drowned, because sea level rose after the Ice Age when all that ice melted and ran into the ocean. Finding such submerged sites would be nearly impossible, especially in frigid northern waters.

Other theories that people sailed across the Pacific or Atlantic to get to America are far less likely. One older suggestion gaining new popularity is that Spanish and French Paleolithic folks cruised westward to North America. This idea is based on similarities between a few types of finely made stone spear points on both continents. But DNA studies show Native Americans are closer to Asians than to Europeans.

The first Americans probably did more than hunt big game for meat. Even modern cultures who hunt don't get meat that often; it's far easier to fish or gather plants, so mammoth burgers were probably a rare treat. The bias here comes because animal bones are better preserved than plant matter, so "kill" sites showing butchering of mammoths, mastodons, or extinct species of bison are more recoverable than early salad bars.

Paleo-Indian archaeological evidence

The earliest Americans are called Paleo-Indians. Until recently, their oldest characteristic artifacts were thought to be chipped-stone Clovis points (named after a site in New Mexico where they were first found) and other types of fluted spear points. A *flute* is a large flake up the center of each side of the point, possibly to make it easier to connect to the spear shaft. These long, thin points are the result of pressure-flaking (see Figure 12-4). They come from sites all over North and South America that date as early as about 11,200 B.C. (some 13,000 years ago).

A puzzle in Paleo-Indian archaeology is that, for some time, many of the very earliest known sites were in South America. Newcomers would have had to move through North America first (they may have just walked fast). Now archaeologists can see that, especially moving along the Pacific coastal route, the first Americans could easily have filled up the landscape in a few centuries of settling, prospering, and expanding. One factor may have been that the vast herds of game in the New World were easy to harvest because they weren't used to hunting pressure. Another factor may have been that these early hunter–gatherers were always on the move (following the herds throughout the year) and would have had no trouble spreading out in all the available attractive land. So far no evidence indicates any pressure they may have faced to move on except for their own expanding populations. And now some very old sites in North America have been verified.

Figure 12-4:
Fluted
Paleo-
Indian
points
of early
Americans.

A few archaeological sites older than Clovis (mentioned earlier in this section) have been discovered. One is Monte Verde, in Chile, on the west coast of South America, dated to at least 11,800 B.C. (see the map in the appendix). It's a wet site in a bog, so usually perishable remains were preserved, including wooden houses, vegetable foods, and a few animal bones of mastodon and extinct camels. I discuss it further in Chapter 18.

The Topper Site in South Carolina has produced the oldest dates yet in the New World. Digging below the Clovis layer, archaeologists found crude-looking flaked stone tools in a level dated to up to 50,000 years old. But the finds are controversial; some argue that the tools are really natural rocks chipped by some other process.

In Chapter 18, I detail more of the controversies on the first Americans and a cool new find from Oregon: human coprolites dated to older than 14,000 years ago. Watch for exciting new finds in Paleo-Indian archaeology as techniques improve and the search continues!

Combating stereotypes of cave guys

The cave man is a common stereotype, from Fred Flintstone to the misunderstood television characters. He's a hairy, hunched-over brute, dragging away his cave woman by the hair. This depiction is fun but scientifically all wrong. (For example, dinosaurs had been gone for 65 million years before early humans appeared on the planet — sorry, Dino!)

Most Paleolithic sites were probably in the open, easy to get to, and away from cave bears. But caves and *rock shelters* (shallow niches) are better preserved for archaeologists to dig. Yes, Paleolithic people had lots of stone tools, but most of their everyday artifacts were probably made of wood, fiber, and bone. These tools would have been easier to make but seldom are preserved.

The first complete Neanderthal skeleton discovered (in France in 1908) happened to be of a stooped, arthritic man. Unfortunately, it has served as the model for Neanderthals and other cave folks ever after. In reality, completely upright walking is the main characteristic defining all the hominin skeletons, going back over 2 million years. The crude, rude, and ignorant character for early humans may have originated as a racist view to help differentiate them from the superior moderns (especially the scientists doing the theorizing). But remember that Neanderthals were evidently stronger than modern humans and had bigger brains.

Archaeologists have absolutely no evidence that Paleolithic men did all the hunting and other interesting stuff. Women hunt and do other rough jobs in many cultures around the world, even while carrying the babies. (And who knows when the revolutionary concept of the babysitter was invented?) Artifact finds (so far) don't tell how families or the larger society may have been structured.

Archaeologists do now have evidence of Paleolithic nets and other fiber artifacts from preserved impressions in wet clay. This may mean that big game animals were actually hunted by setting traps and then throwing nets over the animals and clubbing them (less dangerous than running up to a mammoth or wild bull to spear it). So most reconstructions of Paleolithic life are educated guesses based on the evidence, but the evidence keeps increasing. But yes, they probably did wear fur outfits — the Ice Age was cold!

Chapter 13

The Last 10,000 Years: Climate Change and Early Food Production

*T*oday you may be worried about how global warming affects us, but never fear: This chapter shows how humanity already survived the same kind of massive climate change at the end of the Ice Age about 10,000 years ago, marking the end of the Paleolithic cultural period and beginning of what's called the *Mesolithic* era (Middle Stone Age) in the Old World (Europe, Asia, Africa) and the *Archaic* period in the New World (North and South America).

Ice Age big game became extinct, so people switched to hunting modern animals and continued gathering wild plants and fishing. They also began domesticating species and producing their food — a huge step, meaning far more work. Within a couple of millennia, the *Neolithic* (New Stone Age) began. Gardening intensified to become farming and herding. Significant social and economic divisions also appeared — the earliest rich folks.

Food-producing peoples all over the Earth changed their world. They managed and manipulated different plants and animals in large numbers. They cleared and burned forests for cultivating fields and raised herds of grazing animals that probably obliterated grasslands. They built mounds, earthworks, and huge stone monuments that stood out, and made villages and towns very human, in contrast to the natural landscape.

The later Neolithic era saw more specialization — metalworking, stone construction, and other crafts — so these times have more specific archaeological terms like "Bronze Age." The stage was being set for the emergence of the first civilizations, which I discuss in Chapter 14.

The Foraging Life: The First Global Warming, 10,000 B.C.

When the Pleistocene (Ice Age) ended, the climate warmed and environments changed enormously. But culture is conservative: People may resist change, but they often end up changing just by trying to do the same thing under different conditions. This is what happened during the Mesolithic period in the Old World and Archaic period in the New World. (Archaeologists give these time periods different names in different hemispheres because the changes supposedly took place slightly later in the New World.)

In the Holocene or current geological age, Ice Age ice melted and poured into the oceans. Rivers backed up and created estuaries and bays, productive environments full of aquatic species for people to harvest. Pleistocene *megafauna* (large animals) like mammoths and mastodons became extinct.

Archaeological finds of post-Ice Age foragers indicate they adapted well to massive change in their environments. Some groups probably did die out, but successful ones developed the following characteristics:

- Expertise in getting plants and animals from local regions
- Intricate craftwork in stone, bone, antler, fiber/fabrics, and ceramics
- More complex social organization and maybe even some societies with hereditary positions, though most probably remained pretty *egalitarian* (socially equal across the board)
- More settled life than earlier folks and larger settlements (camps and villages)
- Deliberate burial of the dead in cemeteries, perhaps to mark territories
- Good health; skeletons look fairly healthy (after all, they got fresh fruits, vegetables, meats and fish, and lots of exercise)

Postglacial foragers continued hunting the animals still out there; grinding stones show processing of more plants into soup, bread, or mush. Evidence for fishing and shellfish collecting becomes more widespread; shellfish beds would have spread all over those shallow estuaries and bays. *Shell middens* (garbage piles with these food remains) are common on coasts worldwide after the end of the Ice Age. They look like remains of giant clambakes. But among the shells they have bones of fish and other animals that would've produced more meat than shellfish.

No written records exist this far back in time. Everything known about the huge changes that took place in everyday human life comes from the archaeological record (although sometimes other sciences can help). Biologists and geologists can reconstruct natural environments, and linguists can trace origins of languages and their movements across the land. But for explaining the consequences of long-term changes in daily living, archaeologists are the best (even if they argue about causes and details).

Mesolithic and Archaic people didn't have to work too hard. Contrary to popular opinion, their lives weren't nasty and brutish. Studies of the few living hunter–gatherer–fishers around the world show that foraging isn't difficult, especially in rich environments. You have to work only three to four days a week getting wild foods; the rest of the time you can fool around or loaf. Growing crops or animals is much harder and takes more time.

Old World Mesolithic hunter–gatherers

The Mesolithic was the archaeological time period after the end of the Ice Age but before food production (see the time chart in the appendix). It begins sometime after 10,000 years ago, as world climates slowly warmed and rainfall increased. Forests replaced tundra in northern latitudes, and grasslands and lakes covered much of the Sahara. Human cultures developed new technologies and settled in favorable places.

Cave art and figurines apparently disappeared for a while, at least in Europe. People were probably making other arts and crafts of perishable materials like wood. But archaeologists have found evidence (house and village patterns in the soil) for more planned settlements. People became more sedentary, staying in one place year-round. Instead of following herds of game, they used more resources more intensively in one area (although this arrangement didn't necessarily mean less walking).

Mesolithic sites have evidence for early social ranking — in other words, some people look more important than others. Look for deliberate burial of the dead in cemeteries and especially for graves that may have more wealth items than the rest.

At Vedbaek in Denmark, burial offerings included red ochre coloring and animal-teeth jewelry from 4,800 B.C. onward. One grave had an adult female, with snail shells and deer teeth at her head and waist, next to a baby who had a flint blade and was lying on a swan's wing (the bones were preserved). This setup may have just been a soft bed, a social status marker, or a sign of some spiritual belief. Another skeleton in this cemetery, an adult male buried with a female and a child, had a bone point stuck through the neck. Was this evidence of early violence or warfare? Or just a bad hunting accident?

By 10,000 B.C., the Mesolithic Jomon culture in coastal Japan left typical shell midden sites full of fish bone. These folks also were the first to invent fired-clay pots to use for cooking and storing things. This was probably not a revolutionary idea at the time — they'd always had stone bowls, gourd bottles, and even waterproof baskets (covered in pitch). But archaeologists love pottery because it's usually preserved and provides more information about past people than just stone tools.

New World Archaic cultures

During the Archaic period (see the time chart in the appendix), North and South America experienced the same change as the Old World did during the Mesolithic, at about the same time or slightly later. Environments got warmer and wetter. As big game became extinct, hunters took deer and small game. Chipped stone projectile points changed from long lance-shaped forms of Paleo-Indian times to Archaic stemmed and notched shapes (shown in Figure 13-1). Foraging groups settled in forests and on coasts to collect fruit, nuts, and seafood. You can see the beginnings of social difference in burials with more or fewer grave goods. New World folks also invented pottery, a little later and independently from its invention in the Old World.

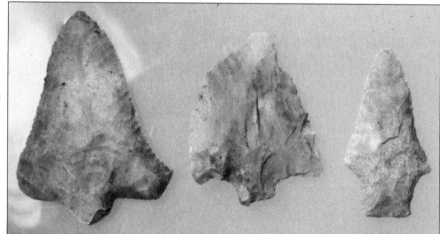

Figure 13-1: Stemmed and notched Archaic-period projectile points, 7,000 to 4,000 B.C.

Windover is a famous Archaic site in Florida dating to 5,000 to 6,000 B.C. It was a pond in which ancient Native Americans buried their dead; the wet conditions preserved usually perishable remains: wood, bone, and antler tools and many varieties of sophisticated woven fabrics. This discovery was already unusual and amazing when archaeologists made even more astounding finds: The brown slimy masses inside some of the skulls of the over 160 burials turned out to be preserved human brains! DNA and medical studies of these materials are producing information about health, genes, and diet. What archaeologists didn't find — more than a handful of stone tools — was also interesting. Nearly all artifacts were of organic materials that usually rot away. If the wet conditions hadn't preserved them, the site would've been considered insignificant and bulldozed away for a housing development.

Revolution in the New Stone Age: Growing Food

The hunter–gatherer way of life continued until modern times in many places worldwide (like Australia and California). But many cultures moved from just getting wild foods to growing their own. This shift was such a big deal that it's sometimes called the *Neolithic Revolution. Neolithic* means "New Stone Age," but *revolution* means fast change, and this transition was probably pretty gradual because it changed everything else about life too.

Producing your own reliable food sources sounds like it would be easier, but it wasn't. Tending crops or herds is much harder work than just getting stuff in the wild. Farming and herding require long hours of work every single day. You have to get up with the chickens, till the soil, plant the crops, feed the animals, water the crops, water the animals, weed and fertilize the crops, keep the animals from eating the crops, and so on — you get the picture.

Why would people want to change their lives to work so hard producing food instead of collecting it from the environment? Some possible reasons include the following:

- ✔ People gradually *domesticated* (genetically changed) wild species in their natural habitats by just helping them along with minimal cultivation (weeding, watering, and fertilizing).

- ✔ People domesticated species when they took them *away* from their original wild habitats to grow elsewhere.

- ✔ Gathering wild species increased people's knowledge and control of them over the centuries, so domestication came naturally.

- ✔ Populations may have naturally grown until people had to do something new to get more from the land and feed everyone.

- ✔ Climate changed enough to make many wild food sources unreliable, so people had to grow their own to be sure to eat.

- ✔ When climates warmed up in the Middle East, people and animals naturally gathered around *oases* (water sources) and became familiar with each other (and with local plants), leading to domestication.

✔ Some individuals were naturally greedy and wanted to build up surplus food wealth more efficiently, so they persuaded others to help them produce food.

✔ Some plants naturally responded better to a little care and became so productive that people picked them as staple crops.

Archaeologists keep arguing about whether domestication took place gradually or quickly, in times of abundance or stress, and at the hands of men or women. Different theories work better in different areas. The real reasons and conditions for early gardening and herding are probably different combinations of these factors in different regions of the world. Food production probably started out small, growing just a few foods in case of shortages in the wild. But after it began, few prehistoric societies went back to full-time foraging in the wild.

Believe it or not, genetic engineering is nothing new! For over 10,000 years people have been changing genes of plants and animals to produce desired characteristics. It works not through natural selection but rather *cultural selection,* breeding or planting only those individuals with characteristics closest to what you want. It takes a long time; you don't just bring in a wolf cub or wild calf and tame it — you have to breed many generations of gentle ones until you get a species that's always going to be that way. The only difference between early domestication and today's genetic engineering is that scientists today can go into the cell and change the DNA more quickly than waiting for many generations of breeding.

Archaeologists can see results of this selective breeding in Neolithic finds. The following list gives you some examples of genetically changed organisms:

✔ Bigger seeds, nuts, grains, and fruits (for more food).

✔ Wheat or other grains with seeds held securely to the plant. This development allows humans to collect and selectively redistribute the seed instead of letting the plant reseed itself.

✔ Larger, hairier sheep, goats, and cattle with smaller, less dangerous horns. This change provides more meat, wool, and hide and reduces the danger of injury to the herder.

✔ Dogs, cattle, and horses that are docile and ready to work for people.

✔ Plants and animals with other desirable characteristics of color, taste, and rapid growth.

Evidence of early domesticated species can be charred seeds or fruits, pollen grains, animal bone fragments, or even residues left when someone didn't wash the dishes! All give information on what gradually came under human production and where. Not everything was used for food; some animals were for working rather than eating, and some plants were for drugs or industrial uses such as making cloth.

Old World plants and animals (pasta, milk, wine)

Archaeological finds show many centers of domestication in the Old World (Africa, Asia, and Europe). Here's a list of some important species and where they were first deliberately grown:

- **Middle East (western Asia):** Wheat, barley, rye, lentil, pistachio, date, olive, grape, goat, sheep, and cattle

- **India/south Asia:** Millet, cucumber, cotton, cattle, melon, citrus, plants for dyes, flax for linen or seeds, mung bean, and black pepper

- **Southeast Asia:** Taro, citrus, sugarcane, banana, and mango

- **China:** Millet, rice, pigs, melon, ducks, chickens, tea, hemp, peach, and silkworms

- **Africa:** Sorghum, cattle, coffee, barley, wheat, melon, and bottle gourd

- **Widespread since the Paleolithic:** Dogs

Dogs were the earliest domesticated animal, for work (hunting, pulling, and carrying), protection, sometimes food (no kidding), and maybe friendship. Sheep and goats came next — making them follow you around is easy (as Mary and her lamb can attest). But imagine trying to breed wild cattle!

As new finds come in, archaeologists keep debating which plants were cultivated earliest and where. Wheat and barley were among the first crops; they contributed to early versions of staple foods like bread, pasta, and mushy cereal. Recent excavations in the Jordan valley uncovered remains of figs from around 9,400 B.C. that look like the edible kind, dried and stored with still-wild varieties of oats, barley, and acorns. The date may mean these fruits were domesticated much earlier than the grain crops.

Finds of the bones of older animals (rather than the tender young ones preferred for food) at later Neolithic sites in Europe suggest cattle came to be used more for milk than beef. Artifacts like clay strainers and baskets appear by 5,000 B.C.; they may have been for processing milk to make cheese (which lasts much longer). Pottery fragments from Iran and Turkey between 7,000 and 5,000 years old have residues of chemicals that can only be from wine. Though the wine was probably made from wild grapes, this plant soon became domesticated.

New World plants and animals (corn, chocolate, few animals)

The New World (North and South America) also had many centers of domestication. Think of where humanity would be without these important species that Native Americans gave to the world:

- ✔ **Mexico and Central America:** Corn (maize), squash, chocolate (cacao), and chili pepper
- ✔ **South America:** Potato, avocado, peanut, manioc (cassava), tomato, coca (leaf, for early drug use), llamas, guinea pigs, and quinoa
- ✔ **North and South America:** Bottle gourd, cotton, squashes, and beans
- ✔ **Midwestern U.S.:** Maygrass, little barley, knotweed, goosefoot, sunflowers, and tobacco
- ✔ **Widespread since Paleo-Indian times:** Dogs

Dogs probably came with the first people to America, but otherwise few other animals were around to domesticate. Prehistoric horses and cattle became extinct at the end of the Ice Age. These big animals didn't reappear until Europeans brought them in the 1500s, so they weren't around to be domesticated.

Is the lack of draft animals to pull them the reason that no wheeled vehicles were used in the Americas? Actually, the concept of the wheel was known; archaeologists have excavated tiny wheeled animal figurines along the Gulf Coast of Mexico. (They look like kids' pull-toys, but they were probably for ceremonial purposes.) Would history (not to mention prehistory) have been different if North and South America had had faster land-based travel methods than walking or taking a boat?

The changes brought on by food production

With food production came many changes in human ways of life that are visible in the archaeological record. Here are a few of them:

- ✔ Pottery-making (and breaking!) became widespread, which is why archaeologists find so many potsherds.
- ✔ People were less mobile and more settled, so houses and other buildings were more permanent and left evidence of repair and rebuilding in the ground. Because people moved around less often, populations were larger and denser, and people had more and bigger stuff, so archaeologists have more to excavate.

✔ Structures bigger and more important than houses appeared, indicating public buildings and group activities.

✔ Food production led to economic surpluses, so evidence of storage facilities such as animal pens and granaries appeared.

✔ Irrigation ditches may have been dug to water crops.

✔ Social differentiation became more evident, indicated by rich graves, larger houses, or other signs of wealth for a few people.

✔ Political organization shifted from the days of mostly egalitarian foragers. Leadership positions indicated by a few rich graves may have originally been socially determined, but later they became hereditary; you see this when you have rare wealth in graves of children who were too young to achieve such positions by the times of their deaths.

✔ People's health changed — often for the worse! A constant diet of grain can mean poorer nutrition; denser, larger populations make epidemic diseases more widespread.

Farming Takes Off in the Old World

The Neolithic archaeological picture is relatively similar throughout the Old World, as food production took hold. (See the preceding section for details on the Neolithic "Revolution.") The Old World archaeological record usually shows cultivated plants and animals being combined with wild ones obtained in the old ways. Each local region produced its own different domesticated species on its own timeline; the following sections give you information on the advent of farming and animal husbandry in some specific areas.

The Middle East: Early gardeners and herders

Food production began early in the eastern Mediterranean/western Asia region. Archaeological sites have produced bones of hunted gazelle and seeds of gathered wild grains from deeper levels as early as 10,000 B.C. Then in later levels (by 9,000 B.C.), finds include domesticated sheep and goat bones and cultivated grain crops. Some evidence is clear — goat toe bones with abrasive marks show goats were tied down all the time and not running wild.

A famous Neolithic site in Turkey is Çatalhöyük, a 30-acre settlement of mud-brick houses dating as early as 7,000 B.C (see the map in the appendix). Though the early levels show no pottery, the indigenous people obviously had the technology to make the bricks. The evidence also includes lots of figurines of women and images of bulls. What these items had to do with ceremony and ritual is unknown; some argue the women were goddesses.

The site of Jericho in Israel was settled by foragers camping near a spring as early as 10,500 B.C. Neolithic levels date as early as 7,000 B.C., with rich evidence of more complex lifestyles. Finds include trade items from long distances, such as salt, tar, and sulfur from the Dead Sea and turquoise, shell, obsidian, and greenstone from elsewhere in the region. A stone tower, wall, and ditch surrounded the site. This project was a major construction, requiring fancy planning and labor organization. Was it all for defense? If so, against whom? Some archaeologists think it was fortification against flooding and a tower for storage or community gatherings for social or ritual reasons. Jericho (famous for its later biblical battle and falling walls) also had Neolithic human burials with plastered skulls remodeled to look like heads — unusual ritual treatment. Some think it shows ancestor worship.

Africa

In northern Africa the annual flooding of the Nile fertilized the soil, so early gardeners planted barley and wheat in this area as long ago as 5,000 to 6,000 B.C. At about the same time, cattle herding was getting underway in the Sahara grasslands. Archaeological evidence and genetic studies suggest that distinct species of wheat and cattle were domesticated in Africa.

South Asia

Early farming peoples in India and Pakistan developed large villages and dense populations pretty quickly. In the Indus River valley, Pakistani and French archaeologists have excavated an interesting Neolithic settlement named Mehrgarh. Digging in several mounds, they found compartmental structures of clay bricks dating to earlier than 6,000 B.C. These constructions were probably houses or granaries. In the mud of the bricks were impressions of barley and other grains undergoing domestication. Animal bones showed a similar picture, a combination of wild gazelle, sheep, cattle, and goats, with what appear to be domesticated goats as well.

A cemetery had graves with items of turquoise, shell, *carnelian* (a red-orange stone), and *lapis lazuli* (a bright blue stone), indicators of possible social differences. Eleven human molar teeth had holes deliberately drilled, probably with the same flint drills that made the fancy stone beads. These teeth had the earliest signs of dentistry! Wear marks over the drill holes indicated the patients survived and kept chewing. No fillings were preserved, but this operation probably wasn't just for looks.

Later levels excavated at Mehrgarh, dating up to 4,000 B.C., had lots more bones of the local humped zebu cattle, now being raised rather than hunted. Finds also included more domesticated grains, dates, jujube fruits, and cotton seeds (preserved because they were charred). Food production was clearly intensifying (and the workload increasing), and pottery, figurines, and more luxury goods were now being made and increasing the wealth differentiation. This site shows the complicated social and economic systems that later developed into the Indus civilization (described in Chapter 14).

East Asia

Early cultivators in north China also settled along stream valleys, especially the Huang (Yellow) River, where the environment was much wetter than it is today. These people, called the Yangshao culture by archaeologists, used the following resources:

- ✔ Domesticated *millet,* a local a grain (you may be familiar with it as birdseed)

- ✔ Pigs and dogs, as well as some sheep and cattle

- ✔ Wild plants such as hazel, pine, and chestnuts

- ✔ Hemp and silkworms for fibers

- ✔ Many agricultural tools, like polished stone axes

- ✔ *Spindle whorls* (cylinders for spinning thread) and bone needles, which indicate a lot of textile weaving

- ✔ White-, red-, and black-painted pottery, including large jars in which they buried children

At about the same time in south China, the archaeological evidence shows domestication of rice, a more tropical crop. Before 6,500 B.C., rice farmers settled in the Yangtze River valley. At least one site has so many rice remains that it's thought to be a threshing floor. Both wild and domesticated varieties of this important plant show that it was brought under human control. Other early cultivated species were water chestnuts and water buffaloes; people still collected wild species like nuts and acorns, deer, elephant, rhino, and turtle. Other finds include stone tools and pottery impressed with twisted cords.

The farming of rice and domestication of pigs and cattle soon moved eastward toward Japan and southward into southeast Asia. Neolithic sites appear in Thailand at almost 4,000 B.C. Southeast Asian Neolithic artifacts include polished stone axes and various ceramics; the dead were often buried in large fancy clay pots. Though hunting, gathering, and fishing in the rich tropical rainforest continued (and continues today), migrating people apparently brought rice into southeast Asia's islands pretty early. Rice husks in the clay of pottery have been dated to before 2,000 B.C. in Borneo. This shows people were slowly combining gardening and then farming with foraging.

Europe

Excavations in southeastern Europe document how the growing of crops and herding of animals moved into the region from the Middle East by 7,000 B.C. Of course, archaeologists argue about whether the agricultural people themselves were moving westward, or just their ideas. Either way, the lifeways of local foraging peoples gradually changed. Farming made it to northwest Europe by 4,000 B.C. On the Mediterranean, the typical pottery is called cardial ware, decorated by impressing into the wet clay the scalloped edge of a cardium (cockle) shell. This pottery may indicate a specific ethnic group that brought and spread agricultural traditions.

Neolithic discoveries continue. Recently, archaeologists found fragments of the oldest known woven cloth, dating to 3,500 B.C., in a burial mound in the Czech Republic. Scientific analysis identified this textile as linen. Other material items are more controversial. One archaeological reconstruction of early Neolithic Europe is that it was a peaceful place full of goddess-worshipping, matriarchal cultures; this view is based on finds like the many figurines of women and symbols like *V* and *M* shapes thought to represent female bodies. The later appearance of graves of men with metal weapons and male symbols may mean that male-dominated warrior cultures from the east invaded to end this ideal society. As you can imagine, this scenario is much-debated by both men and women archaeologists!

Food Production in North and South America

Archaic foragers trekked seasonally between food sources in many places in the New World, and some continue to do so. Others would have kept on moving around if Europeans hadn't intruded and made them settle down. (In historic time, the horses that Europeans brought even helped make Native Americans on the Great Plains better hunters. But soon wild buffalo herds were replaced by stockyards.). But some Native Americans developed food production.

Finds of domesticated bottle gourd and squash date as early as 8,000 B.C. in both North and South America. Many grain and seed plants followed. Tiny cobs of early domesticated corn (maize) in dry caves of central Mexico show people were still moving around the landscape when they started cultivating. Thousands of years later, *sedentism* (staying in one place year-round) came after gardening in some places. Mound and pyramid construction also began as populations got larger and denser, often before farming took hold.

Prehistoric North American farmers

Some Late Archaic sites in the U.S. Southeast have the oldest monumental architecture, as early as 3,000 to 4,000 B.C. This date is 1,000 years older than any Mexican pyramids. Fired clay pottery appeared earlier (by 2,500 B.C.) in the Southeast as well, but not in Mexico and Central America until 1,000 to 2,000 years later. But central Mexican foragers were busy domesticating maize (corn) and other plants over 7,000 years ago. Over the millennia, maize would spread all over the continent to become the staple crop. Figure 13-2 shows you a typical early domesticated maize cob fragment, less than 2 centimeters long, preserved because it was charred.

Early gardeners in the eastern U.S.

The Poverty Point site in northeastern Louisiana (also discussed in Chapter 19) is a group of mounds and parallel concentric octagonal earthen ridges dating to 1,200 B.C. In the same region is Watson Brake, a site of 11 mounds and connecting earthworks dating earlier than 3,000 B.C. These sites are important because archaeologists once thought they were the earliest evidence of food producers — creating such monuments would have required the labor of settled farmers. New dating and analyses show that the ancient people at these sites were still foragers, obtaining the rich wild resources of the Mississippi Valley. But they were setting the stage for the widespread appearance of mound-building cultures all over the eastern U.S., who did begin gardening and domesticating local plants centuries later.

Figure 13-2: Tiny 1,000-year-old charred maize (corn) cob from the Southeastern U.S.

The reasons for the earliest constructions of earthen mounds and walls are unknown, but some ideas include the possibility that

- ✔ People came yearly to pile up dirt for some ceremonies, hauling baskets or bags of soil.
- ✔ People just wanted to live on high, dry ground on the floodplain.

Inhabitants of Poverty Point and Watson Brake didn't even have pottery yet, but they made tiny polished stone beads and animal shapes, fancy stone points and pendants, and fired-clay balls and other shapes that were probably for cooking.

By 2,000 years ago, finds of charred, preserved plant remains show that prehistoric gardeners in the eastern U.S. began domesticating homely little weeds like chenopods and amaranths, as well as squash and sunflowers. From the Mississippi Valley eastward, they settled in villages and began elaborating their earthen mounds for ritual purposes. Some mounds are shaped like animals, and others are conical burial mounds; Figure 13-3 shows Mississippi's Bynum Mounds, which date between 100 B.C. and A.D. 100. They also built huge earthworks in squares, circles, and other geometric shapes. These don't look like forts but instead probably enclosed some kind of ceremonial spaces.

Figure 13-3:
The Bynum Mounds in northeast Mississippi.

In early burial mounds, everyone seems to have at least a few grave goods. Later mounds show great differences among graves. Some have skeletons, others have cremated bone bits, and a few have elaborate wealth items.

Archaeologists are still arguing whether these discrepancies mean hereditary chiefs were emerging to run the show (or whether clan mothers were telling people what to do).

Archaeologists digging the Tremper mound in southwest Ohio found a pattern of postmolds in the soil at its base that turned out to be the remains of a large 200-x-100-foot wooden building. It was a charnel house, with basins for cremating the dead and the burned remains of some 375 people. The most spectacular deposits in the mound were *caches* (piles) of some 150 stone smoking pipes. Some were of the plain platform style, with the bowl on top of a curved or flat platform. But many had the bowls carved in the shapes of animals, including squirrels, bobcats, bears, wolves, cougars, beavers, otters, turtles, and birds such as herons, cranes, hawks, ducks, and owls.

An example of such a pipe appears in Figure 13-4; they're so realistic that you can distinguish different species within one animal type. The pipes and other offerings were all smashed before the mound was built over the building. It may have been a spiritual practice to free souls in death or consecrate a sacred place. Destroyed artifact offerings are common in burial mounds for a couple of thousand years.

Figure 13-4:
Animal (squirrel) effigy Hopewell pipe.

Tremper is one of hundreds of mounds of the Hopewell culture (named after one of the first such mounds excavated). And Hopewell is one of many local cultures within the Woodland period (see the time chart in the appendix) who built burial mounds of all sizes along river valleys in the eastern U.S. between about 200 B.C. and A.D. 600. Finds of fancy log tombs and elaborate offerings in the mounds show the rise of some kind of social and political leaders or special individuals. They also show that mound-builders had vast trade networks and exquisite craftwork.

Here are some examples of other artifact offerings in the thousands of Woodland mounds:

- Elaborate pottery with incised, stamped, and sometimes painted decoration; stone and clay figurines of people and animals
- Beads and cubes of *galena,* a shiny lead ore from Canada
- Hammered ornaments of copper from northern Michigan
- Other ornaments hammered from raw silver and meteoric iron
- Whole whelk shells from the Gulf Coast
- Piles of thousands of shell beads from jewelry or clothing
- Sharks' teeth from the coasts
- Cutout abstract and realistic shapes of shiny mica from the Appalachian Mountains
- *Celts* (axes and adzes) of polished greenstone from the Appalachians
- A few fancy points of chipped obsidian from the Rocky Mountains and other stone tools of multicolored Flint Ridge flint and other pretty stones
- Piles of large chipped stone blades too thin to use for tools
- Additional human skulls in graves, interpreted as either remains of honored ancestors or trophies from defeated enemies
- Cut animal jaws and teeth (from bears and wolves), perhaps to wear as costumes or symbols in rituals

You can imagine how excited archaeologists are to excavate such exotic burial offerings, especially because most of the mounds are now protected and specifically *not* available for digging.

Eastern U.S. farmers

The Woodland moundbuilders occasionally grew a little maize in their gardens. By around A.D. 1000, they'd recognized the amazing productivity of this grass. They became intensive farmers and transformed their society.

Maize agriculturalists were organized into complex societies, chiefdoms, of the Mississippian period (see the time chart in the appendix). They farmed, still hunted, and maybe domesticated turkeys. Each regional culture had different artifact styles, especially well-made pottery (see Color Figure 3). They still buried their important dead with pomp and ceremony (and riches) in burial mounds and cemeteries. They also built *platform mounds,* flat-topped pyramids with large temples or chiefs' houses on top. There were plazas for civic activities, and beyond that stood the large villages and surrounding fields.

Of course, archaeologists argue about how powerful the chiefs were, their competition and warfare, and whether they inherited their positions.

The largest Mississippian center is at Cahokia in East St. Louis, with over 100 temple mounds (see Chapter 19 for more details on this site). A walled compound surrounded Monk's mound, the largest (at 300 x 700 feet and 100 feet high). Circles of wooden posts left features named *woodhenges* that may have been for astronomical observations. In Mound 72 were successive burials of important individuals with lots of fancy, probably sacred offerings. Examples of these offerings include

- ✔ Caches of stone points and decorative pottery

- ✔ Hammered copper pieces

- ✔ Thousands of shell beads

- ✔ Shiny mica stone

- ✔ Piles of human skeletons (some mutilated) suggesting sacrificial victims, servants, or retainers of the important dead

Though Cahokia was apparently abandoned by A.D. 1300, other regional temple mound centers thrived at different times along the major river valleys. They may all have represented chiefdoms that cycled in and out of power. The intensification in production of maize, beans, and squash (the big three Native American crops) gave these centers a foundation for complex society.

Southwestern U.S. forager–farmers

By 3,500 years ago, foragers in the Southwest were growing maize as a staple crop, with squash and (later) beans, as well as domesticating turkeys. Some groups were only part-time farmers, and others developed sedentary villages.

Here are a few of the spectacular local cultures archaeologists have named:

- ✔ **Hohokam:** This culture developed large villages with platform mounds and irrigation systems to farm in the desert at sites like Snaketown in southern Arizona.

- ✔ **Anasazi or Ancestral Pueblo:** *Anasazi* (Navajo for "ancient stranger") sites such as at Chaco Canyon and Mesa Verde (see Color Figure 8) in the Four Corners region have large multi-roomed masonry dwellings *(pueblos),* and great road networks. (See Chapter 19 for more on these sites.) Later, the Anasazi shifted to more defensible cliff dwellings. (Check out Chapter 18 for details on the latest controversy concerning these ancient people.)

✔ **Mogollon:** These natives of the southern New Mexico and northern Mexico highlands were known for beautiful black and white-painted Mimbres pottery.

All these more complex farming cultures enjoyed several centuries of wetter climates and growing populations, but by around A.D. 1350 they disappeared, moved, or transformed into simpler societies. The reasons may be severe climate change, depletion of their environments, social and political factors like competition and conflict, or some combination thereof.

Mesoamerican farmers

Mesoamerica includes most of Mexico and Central America. Long before 5,000 B.C., squash, corn, chili peppers, cotton, and other plants were cultivated in central and Gulf Coastal Mexico by wandering Late Archaic foragers. The crops spread slowly but widely, and people eventually settled down permanently to become intensive farmers.

By as early as 2,000 B.C., the archaeological remains show complex societies with large villages, socially differentiated houses, shrines, fancy craftwork, and evidence of long-distance trade such as seashells far inland and jade and other stone far from quarries. For lack of a better term, archaeologists often call these societies chiefdoms (and continue arguing about whether they had permanent hereditary leaders, freedom or coercion, and other social aspects). By 1,000 B.C., these indigenous peoples were building earthen and stone pyramids as platforms for ceremonial buildings along the coast of the Gulf of Mexico. They were setting the stage for the development of true civilization with Olmec culture (described in Chapter 14).

Early South American farmers

South America's environmental extremes often result in extreme biases in the archaeological record because of what is and isn't preserved. Here are some examples:

✔ The desert Pacific coast is so dry that organic remains such as cloth, feathers, wood, and sometimes human mummies are preserved.

✔ The high mountains of the Andes featured plenty of rock for construction, so lots of structures are preserved.

✔ In the Amazon jungle and other low, wet environments, preservation of organic remains is seldom possible. It's also harder to see earthen and other monuments through the trees.

Fishing on the desert coast

Despite the desert on land, the Pacific Ocean is enormously rich in fish, especially tiny anchovies easily netted in huge quantities. Along with marine birds and other resources, this abundance permitted people to settle in large permanent villages without any agriculture and build major ceremonial centers on or near the west coast of South America.

El Paraíso, a site near Lima, Peru, boasts nine building complexes with rooms, courts, and corridors. Walls were made of cut, plastered stone painted in bright colors. The central complex has long parallel pyramids arranged in a U-shape with the arms surrounding a plaza. At 1800 B.C., it's the largest early masonry monument in the Western Hemisphere. Finds include grinding stones, wooden tools, lots of seafood remains, and net fragments, plus cotton, wool, needles, and feathers, all of which were probably for making woven textiles. Caral, another site 14 miles up the Supe River from the coast, has 25 platform mounds over 150 acres and dates to as early as 2,500 B.C. Finds include bird-bone flutes and preserved reed bags used to carry the stones to build the pyramids.

Many short rivers flow west from the Andes across the desert to the sea. Early gardeners used their valleys to cultivate industrial crops like cotton (for nets) and gourds (for bowls). They even dug irrigation canals and grew food crops like peppers and squash inland. Coastal people apparently traded for these plants and sent dried fish and shellfish up the rivers, so the people at Caral and other major centers inland got their protein from seafood. Later, maize, *manioc* (also known as *cassava,* a root crop made into bread and beer), and other foods were grown, but people still fished for those anchovies.

Herding in the mountains, gardening in the jungle

Sites of early farmers in the Andes are harder to distinguish because less is preserved. But some stone shrines and other monuments began to be built a little later here than on the coast. And highland hunters of animals like llamas and alpacas were transforming into herders and traders moving up and down the mountains according to the season.

Archaeologists once believed that complex society in the Amazon rainforest developed late and only through influence from other cultures to the west. After all, who wants to work hard farming and building monuments in the hot, steamy tropics? Plus, far less of the archaeological record is preserved there, and it's harder to do archaeology because, well, it's a jungle out there! However, recent finds in Brazil, Peru, and Bolivia show native people had early complex society and manipulated wetlands for crop production.

In these countries, some intrepid archaeologists have uncovered remains of well-developed farming cultures perhaps 2,000 years old that depended on manioc, maize, cacao (chocolate), and other cultivated plants. Densely populated early chiefdoms built elaborate systems of earthworks, causeways, and canals in the jungle. They dug ditches and piled the muck in raised areas that still have rich, black, fertile soil today. Their artifacts include beautiful painted pottery and other crafts. Scientists have only been able to find such sites with the aid of aerial photography and other tools of remote sensing (which I discuss in Chapter 6).

South Americans also traded widely in jungle products and ideas. Westward in the Andes and on the Pacific coast, you can find remains of rainforest coca leaves (chewed for the drug that relieves high-altitude stress) and images of jungle monkeys and lizards that may have had a spiritual importance.

Later Prehistory: Metal and Megaliths

Later Neolithic farming people were more settled in more densely populated towns and villages. They stayed in one place longer and so could accumulate more stuff (great for the archaeologist). They practiced deliberate burial of the dead, which provides more social and economic information like wealth and health differences too. They certainly were not egalitarian anymore but rather had rich and poor, oppressed and exalted.

When archaeologists began to use their finds to tell the story of the human past, they had to break it into manageable time periods. It's interesting (and very telling) that they picked technological criteria to divide up the human past. So the earliest tools (that we've recovered, anyway) are of stone, then humanity advances (supposedly) to metals. You could say the Western world is obsessed with technology, but you have to go with what you have — the hard materials of the artifacts that were preserved. So after the long, long Stone Age came the various ages of metals (Copper, Bronze, and Iron Ages) because the cool new artifacts left at archaeological sites were made of metal.

The beginnings of metalworking

The earliest metalworking was cold-hammering raw materials, during Neolithic times. Craftworkers heated raw copper (when they could find it) or even soft gold over the fire and pounded it into the shape they wanted. They could even rivet sections together or emboss pictures on it.

These specialists (probably pottery-makers already using kilns) figured out how to get hotter fires (usually by using bellows to increase oxygen flow into the furnace); with this technique, they could then extract metals from ores and develop metallurgy. They also discovered how to make *alloys,* or mixtures of metals. Bronze is an alloy of copper and tin (or rarely another metal). Iron came later because it needs an even hotter fire to produce.

Metals could be sharper and last longer than stone (for better plows and weapons). But they were produced many different ways in many different times in different areas of the world. So the terms Copper Age (or *Chalcolithic*), Bronze Age, and Iron Age are used most often to refer to Europe, Africa, and the Middle East. In some regions this is the time between developing intensive food production and developing true states. In other regions metals were developed within the first real state systems.

The health and wealth of food producers

Early farming cultures that depended upon starchy grains or root crops may have had more stable food sources. But they also often had more health problems. Starch on people's teeth turned to sugar, which meant decay and cavities. A diet full of carbohydrates but little protein means more risk of infection, the evidence of which is visible in the ancient bones.

Having to go get food wild meant unpredictability but lots of fresh air and exercise. Foragers may go through a time when they can't find anything, and their skeletons do sometimes show *acute* (one-time) stress. But farmers with more dependable but monotonous diets often had skeletons with *chronic* (continuing) stress from protein or other shortages. Their bones may also show new problems. For example, at the Neolithic site of Abu Hurerya in Syria, some skeletons showed stress on the neck bones from carrying heavy loads on people's heads. Skeletons of women had well developed muscle marks on the upper arms, arthritis in the knees and lower back, and marks or even degeneration on the toes typical of constantly tucking toes under when kneeling.

These clues show women knelt to grind grain on stone *querns* (hand mills), throwing the body weight into the grinding. The constant repetitive action left telltale indications on their bones.

You may think that producing their own food would give people more leisure time to develop other areas of culture — or just loaf around. But in reality, it takes *more* time to grow food than to gather it wild. So where did farming cultures get the time to build those monuments and develop those beautiful crafts and art?

The key is specialization and social differentiation. As soon as some people became more important, they didn't have to produce their own food. Craft specialists, political leaders (like chiefs), and religious specialists (like priests — sometimes the same as the political or economic leaders) could get others to produce their food and other necessities so they could devote their time to their specialized pursuits. So food production ends up meaning more work for the masses and time to engage (indulge?) in creativity for just a few of the special folks.

Metal becomes the next big thing

Because they're soft and easy to work with, copper and gold were the first metal artifacts to appear in most of the world. Usually they're just added into the regular Neolithic-type artifact inventory. At first, they were fancy wealth items because of their rarity, but later copper artifacts became so common that they were just everyday tools (much like computers today or, for a certain generation, televisions). Gold was always special because it was rarer and never tarnished or decayed.

One of my favorite Copper Age sites is Varna, on the Black Sea coast of Bulgaria. It dates to 4,500 B.C. and had some 190 graves. With the burials were red *ochre* (pigment) and artifacts of chipped flint and obsidian, clay human masks, shell beads, copper needles, marble cups, and fancy pottery decorated with graphite and gold. A major find was 14 pounds of golden items, including masks, axes, bull figures, bangle bracelets, and beads. A cylindrical container lying between the legs of an adult male skeleton could only have been a gold penis sheath!

Another famous Copper Age European is Ötzi, the Iceman. He's the famous 5,300-year-old frozen Italian guy who melted out of a glacier in 1992. He had a copper ax and other fascinating artifacts (described in Chapter 18).

The rise of megaliths

A great structure built with huge stones is a *megalithic monument;* in fact, the word *megalith* is from the Greek words for "huge" and "stone." Hundreds of thousands of monuments made of giant boulders occur in cultures around the world at different times. Most of them date to the Neolithic or later, when people were more settled and could organize the labor to build them (and grow enough food to feed all those laborers). You probably know about Stonehenge (shown in Figure 13-5) and Avebury in England, Newgrange in Ireland, or Carnac in France. They're famous among the thousands of megalithic structures all over Western Europe.

The following list gives you some of the kinds of megalithic structures:

- **Tombs** that may have once been (or still are) covered with sod or earth and used by the community or specific kin groups. Newgrange is a huge passage tomb with inner chambers reached by a long passage or hallway.

- **Stone circles** with earthen banks and ditches *(henges)* that served ceremonial purposes — perhaps for predicting or demonstrating the orientation of the stars and planets, or ritual healing. Stonehenge and Avebury are great examples; they even have ancient roads or causeways running long distances and linking them to the nearby rivers.

Figure 13-5:
The famous
Stonehenge
site in
England.

✔ **Individual standing stones** that may have marked sacred places. The stones may stand alone or in different arrangements (and sometimes on top of each other); Carnac is a mile of rows of standing stones.

Other archaeological evidence associated with the megaliths includes

✔ Carved designs on the rocks — often geometric circles or spirals.

✔ Surrounding ditches or other nearby mounds or earthworks.

✔ Fire pits or sacrificial deposits of pots and animal bone. These finds may be evidence of ceremonies and feasts carried out at such shrines.

✔ Houses or domestic middens (garbage piles) that indicate people lived nearby.

Megalithic monuments in Europe date to between 4,000 and 2,000 B.C. Some of them may have been built even in the late Mesolithic, but most date to the Neolithic, when people had begun food production, and later, into the Copper and Bronze Ages. The many different styles were built by many very different cultures, probably for quite different reasons.

An unusual example is the megalithic structures on the island of Malta, in the Mediterranean (see Color Figure 9 and discussion in Chapter 20). These tombs and monumental buildings began to be constructed during the Neolithic and lasted through the Bronze Age. They're associated with images of hefty women in both huge stone sculptures and tiny figurines (see Figure 13-6). Of course, archaeologists argue whether these are fertility goddess figures or something else. (Queens? Clan mothers? Rock stars?)

Figure 13-6:
Stone "Sleeping lady" statue from a megalithic tomb in Malta.

So how did they move those big rocks from quarries many miles away to build megalithic monuments? You may think this transportation was beyond ancient technology, but experimental archaeology projects have shown

various techniques that work, such as using log rollers, sledges, levers, counterweights, tough fiber ropes, and a whole lot of human muscles.

The real mystery of the megaliths isn't how societies built them but how they got people to build them. A few genius ancient engineers had to come up with the techniques, but then someone had to persuade people to sweat. What was the incentive? Archaeologists continue to argue about this, but suggestions include religious motivation or even promise of future gain in this world.

The origins of inequality

Most societies that learned to produce their own food, use metals, and build megalithic monuments remained organized as villages, towns, and chiefdoms for hundreds or thousands of years. Social and eventually economic inequalities developed; in other words, a few people went from being socially more important and respected to being economically more important too — richer and more powerful. Some Neolithic-level societies even eventually had slaves!

If you start out with a society in which everybody does his or her own chores, each family gets its own food, and everyone is treated equally, how do you get to a society with specialists, with inequality, with haves and have-nots?

Archaeologists ponder this question all the time, and the evidence is elusive. Some of the proposed ideas are as follows:

- People who excelled at certain tasks, perhaps hunting or religious ceremony, gained prestige and became leaders.

- Certain folks who could do particular jobs better than the rest became specialists (craftworkers, priests, engineers, organizers); they then didn't produce their own food but were supported by the rest of the population in return for their specialized products or skills.

- Individuals who were naturally *self-aggrandizing* (prone to promoting themselves) tried to get honors and extra supplies for themselves, and doled them out to followers who would support them. (Were these the first politicians?)

- However they attained power, these leaders originally *achieved* their status; however, their positions eventually became *ascribed* or inherited, and so hereditary rulers emerged.

- As more people tried to become leaders, and social positions became hereditary, real economic wealth began to go along with them. This setup is called *stratified society*.

The archaeological evidence can be inconclusive; does a burial with extraordinary wealth show a religious leader, a political leader, a rich merchant, the best athlete, the best storyteller, the family patriarch or matriarch, or just someone with inherited wealth who never accomplished anything ? Whatever the case, after millions of years of egalitarian life, humanity developed inequality.

Chapter 14

Ancient States

· ·

In This Chapter

▶ Defining civilization

▶ Using archaeology to study the first true states

▶ Exploring classical civilizations and some later complex civilizations

· ·

*I*n Chapter 12, I describe what archaeology has found out about our distant human ancestors of the Paleolithic, who foraged for food and resources for a couple of million years. In Chapter 13 you see the archaeological evidence for how people responded to the first global warming around 10,000 years ago. Some began producing their own food, changing society forever.

This chapter picks up the story later in prehistoric time. One of the biggest questions is "What led to the emergence of real civilizations?" Why did this most complex form of society ever seen begin to develop? In this chapter, I show you some of what archaeology has learned about the very first true states, and also some later ancient civilizations. It's more than written history can ever tell us — especially in some places, where writing was never used.

What Archaeologists Mean by Civilization

You may think that any past human culture is an ancient civilization. Or you may be hiking through the wilderness and think you've reached civilization when you get to a shower and a flush toilet. Or perhaps you consider civilization to mean proper behavior or elaborate arts. However, none of these is what archaeologists mean by civilization.

Anthropological archaeology reserves this term for the most complex societies that ever developed — true states. The independent development of the first states happened in only six places (as far as known today), beginning around 5,000 years ago. Many later states followed those first ones, sometimes right on top of them and sometimes far away.

Usually civilization is defined to include the following criteria, first noted long ago by famous archaeologist V. Gordon Childe (see Chapter 1):

- ✔ True cities with central government buildings, houses, public spaces, marketplaces, large living areas, and complex organization

- ✔ Rural agricultural space outside the cities

- ✔ Large, dense populations

- ✔ A formal, complex, and usually centralized government

- ✔ Full-time labor specialists in construction, arts, and crafts, as well as religious specialists (priests) — all fed and supported by the masses of food producers

- ✔ State bureaucracy and social organization that goes beyond family and kinship systems

- ✔ Real economic inequality, with social classes, gaps between rich and poor, and even slavery

- ✔ Economic surpluses — not only of food staples but also of wealth items — usually in the hands of the few elites and rulers

- ✔ Monumental public works like pyramids, palaces, plazas, reservoirs, and irrigation systems

- ✔ Extensive, long-distance economic trade and other exchange

- ✔ Engineering and mathematical systems

- ✔ Writing or record-keeping systems

- ✔ Organized state religions, often also under political control

- ✔ A standing military organization to defend all this

- ✔ Taxes or tribute to support all this

Some debate whether you need every one of these criteria to have a state. And many of these required characteristics are present in earlier, non-state societies too. But the coming together of so many of them is what makes this totally new form of society emerge.

Don't confuse the appearance of food production and settled society in the Neolithic (which I describe in Chapter 13) with the earliest state formation, which happened thousands of years later. Neolithic societies may have had big monuments or craft specialists or social and economic classes. They may even have conducted some organized warfare (probably not often). But they didn't have cities, or writing, or millions of government rules to obey and forms to fill out!

What Archaeology Brings to the Study of Ancient Civilization

The roots of all civilizations are in prehistoric times, when only archaeology can investigate them. Even later, when some of the earliest states developed writing, they usually wrote few texts, and most (especially on perishable fabrics) didn't survive over the millennia. Some early writing systems haven't yet been deciphered, and South American civilizations never did develop writing at all. So archaeology is the best way to explore ancient civilizations completely.

The most celebrated kinds of archaeology deal with fabulous ancient kingdoms and empires, and their art, monuments, and gold. These are the material evidence of past human greatness. Archaeologists continued to emphasize pyramids and palaces into the 20th century; however, they increasingly realize the importance of looking at what was going on down the city streets and out in the countryside. This way, you can reconstruct the workings of early states and get a fuller picture of how they developed.

The search for historic records

Most historic records of ancient states are lost. Even for Western civilization, most of the writing of antiquity was long gone a few centuries later — they don't call them the Dark Ages for nothing! Records from early civilizations that did get preserved tend to present some problems:

- Only a few actually exist.

- They're always biased. (For more on this, see the discussion of historic archaeology in Chapters 3 and 15.) They were written by the elites, so they say only what was important to rulers and upper classes.

- They don't even deal with much of the huge wealth of cultural behavior of those elites, such as what they did every day.

- They don't say anything about the lives of common people or how monuments were built, taxes collected, or crafts produced.

- The few records that have survived and been passed down (works from Greece and Rome, the Bible) were repeatedly copied (by hand until the printing press was invented in the 15th century). You can imagine how mistakes (or even someone's idea of jazzing up the story) crept in.

Texts can give a few clues, but archaeology is the key to understanding what was happening (and sometimes to digging up new texts). Archaeology brings these ancient people and their activities back to life. Its unique method means that you find the material evidence — from architecture to garbage dumps, from wealthy graves to the most humble, everyday artifact — to explain how people lived and how their social, political, economic, and even religious systems worked.

The problem of looting

Because of looting, very few tombs of ancient rulers or glorious prehistoric palaces anywhere are undisturbed. Most museum collections of ancient treasures were bought or otherwise obtained from looters. As I show you in Chapter 1, early archaeology itself centered around digging into monuments and bringing home treasures to exhibit.

Even today, you still see looting of all the ancient civilizations; head to Chapter 2 for a discussion of looting and the illegal antiquities trade. Sometimes it's subsistence looting — a poor farmer selling off a pot unearthed while plowing, for a few bucks to feed the family. But buyers and dealers then make lots of money smuggling and selling these items in international markets and art auctions. The artifacts' origins can often be concealed with the right faked paperwork. So archaeologists try to educate everyone about conserving the cultural heritage. Meanwhile they must interpret the past with much of the record missing.

Excavating the Earliest True States

The earliest states emerged independently in six places in the world: four in the Old World — Egypt, Mesopotamia, the Indus Valley, and China— and two in the New World — South America and Mesoamerica (Mexico and Central America). These six are sometimes called *pristine states* because each developed independently (though clear artifact evidence shows they communicated with each other within the Old and New Worlds).

In this section, I describe these early states and their famous archaeological evidence. The map and timeline in the appendix show you where they were located and when.

Mesopotamia (Iraq): Sumerian civilization

You probably learned in high-school history class about Mesopotamia, the "land between two rivers" (the Tigris and Euphrates) where the earliest states evolved. It's a desert, but near the rivers you have rich cropland, especially if you construct irrigation canals. Neolithic people had already started building large villages with religious centers. Excavations show dense settlements of rectangular houses and larger buildings of mud bricks, one built on top of the ruins of the next, until they all formed large mounds of mud and clay called *tells*. The thousands of tells across the southwest Asian landscape contain thousands of years of the garbage of everyday life. Archaeologists also find hundreds of miles of irrigation canals dug by the ancients to expand their crop yields to feed more and more people.

The ruins of larger, differently-shaped buildings may be non-residential structures — probably temples, because some have internal elements that look like altars and places for burnt offerings. As these temple buildings became larger and fancier through time, archaeologists hypothesize that religious leaders came to dominate politics and economic systems too, directing construction of even more monuments and irrigation systems. In this way real cities emerged and hierarchical leadership became entrenched.

First cities

The first city, Uruk, dates to around 3,500 B.C. Remains of its temple (built over ruins of earlier temples) sat on the *ziggurat*, or stepped pyramid, 40 feet above the ground. The elaborate architecture of whitewashed mud bricks shows leaders must have commanded a great labor force to build it. Its high walls suggest that temple elites (rulers, priests) separated themselves from the rest of the people. The largest, wealthiest houses sat closest to the temple. Other sections of the city had evidence of other types of people who wouldn't have produced their own food, but were supported by peasant farmers — the craft specialists. Finds at workshops for potters, coppersmiths, and carpenters include finished products and the debris from manufacture. These specialists developed the potter's wheel and made artifacts of fancy stone, shell, ivory, copper, and other raw materials obtained from great distances.

After Uruk, other major centers, such as Eridu and Ur, evolved into city-states, controlling large territories. This was Sumerian civilization, in which immensely powerful ruling dynasties were established. Several of these famous sites were excavated in the 19th and early 20th centuries, and continue to be studied (as the political situation in Iraq permits).

The temple at Eridu had 15 to 20 superimposed layers, each bigger and representing more elaborate construction, over 3,000 years (imagine excavating that!). British and American archaeologists of the 1920s dug up nearly 2,000 graves at Ur. Most were simple commoners' burials, with the bodies wrapped in mats or put into wood or clay coffins and accompanied by humble offerings. But royal tombs had elaborate stone or brick chambers and 16 graves with exquisite artifacts of gold, lapis lazuli (a blue gemstone), and other precious materials, like the famous bull-headed lyre, one of the world's oldest musical instruments. Other elite grave goods included rich clothing, games, jewelry, chariots, oxen, and even sacrificed people (servants, guards, and soldiers to work in the next world). You can easily see hierarchical society in grave archaeology in Mesopotamia.

The city-states show an archaeological settlement pattern of urban expansion through time — residential neighborhoods dating to later periods were farther from the center, and homes in the countryside were abandoned. From digs at both elite and commoners' houses, finds of bones and seeds indicate people were raising cattle, wheat, barley, and flax (for linen) and also fishing in the rivers and obtaining many other food resources. The wheel and the plow appeared by around 3,000 B.C., and metal artifacts became common.

What did they write when they started writing?

Writing systems developed in different parts of the world, and were used for different purposes. Mesopotamian cuneiform tablets (around 3,000 B.C.) were originally for accounting — lists of animals, grain, land records (think of the Internal Revenue Service). But when the value of written language became more widely known, people started writing poetry, stories, proverbs, letters, and even love songs!

Egyptians used hieroglyphic (picture) writing on tombs and temples for formal inscriptions like announcing who was ruling at the time. *Hieratic script*, a cursive writing that was faster to do than the elaborate pictures of the hieroglyphs, was for everyday stuff but also sacred ideas. Papyrus texts (the earliest paper artifacts — preserved in dry desert conditions) record everything from medical treatises to magical wisdom. Graffiti was also carved into stone buildings.

The earliest Chinese pictographs, written on oracle bones, were for *divination* — foretelling auspicious days and events and then describing those events (so, basically, fortune-telling). They evolved into the ideogram script (symbols for ideas, as opposed to an alphabet) used often for recording ceremonial rituals and sacred ideas.

The symbols of the Indus script (and many other ancient written languages) have yet to be understood. Ancient glyph systems from different Mesoamerican cultures remain mostly undeciphered, except for Maya writing. Its recently decoded glyphs represent words and syllables and record political history, lists of kings, conquests, and sacred stories.

Those who knew how to write *(scribes)* were important people. South American states had no writing but used the *quipu* (or *khipu*) system of knotted cords to record things. The Inca scribes who knew how to interpret the quipu were all killed off during the European invasion before anyone could write down how the system worked, so archaeologists and others are still trying to figure it out.

Early writing

Steps hypothesized in the development of Mesopotamian writing are very interesting. Originally economic goods were accompanied by clay tokens that probably served as a packing list. These then gave way to records made by impressing symbols onto wet clay tablets. Finally the impressions transformed into the stylized, standardized written language called cuneiform, made with a pointed tool on the clay tablets (shown in Figure 14-1).

After rulers and governments had writing, they had the power to control knowledge. Many cuneiform tablets have been excavated, and many wait to be translated. But some have already told details of how much wheat, barley, bread, sheep, and cattle people had — and how much beer they were making!

Technology, economics, and empire

Other Mesopotamian city-states appeared later and competed with one another. Metallurgy and bronze weapons (discussed in Chapter 13) gave a competitive advantage in combat, suggesting the early appearance of warfare, which archaeologists are still arguing about! But great defensive walls testify to the empire-building and the rise and fall of different centers over the next millennia. Native patterns of conflict in the region that seem to continue in descendant cultures today may have been established thousands of years ago.

Mesopotamian states were linked by economics (if not conquests). To get raw materials they needed but didn't have (like metals and precious stones), trade extended long distances. They went along those two rivers to northern Iraq and overland with the caravans to the Levant (eastern Mediterranean) and Iran. The artifact evidence shows interaction as far east as the Indus valley (Pakistan) and as far west as Egypt (see map in the appendix). That's a long way to go on a camel!

I've spent a little more time on Sumerian civilization, not only because it was the first but also because it expanded into empires. Consolidated city-states extended rule over farther territories to control those raw materials sources. Beginning around 2,500 B.C., the succession of kingdoms and dynasties such as at Ur, Babylon, and other archaeological sites of early history had begun.

Figure 14-1:
Cuneiform tablet in the British Museum, London.

Egypt: Pyramids and pharaohs

The Nile runs north to the Mediterranean and provides good cropland by flooding every year and leaving fertile soil on its banks. In Neolithic times, the surrounding area was wetter, but as it dried up people moved to large settlements on the big river. Excavations of farming villages have uncovered the foundations of mud-brick houses with thatched roofs, and remains of wheat, sheep, and goats (which would have come in from Mesopotamia) as well as cattle and other native African foods. Mummification of the dead slowly developed (wrapping corpses in resin-soaked linen), and the settlements become denser and more complex through time. Archaeologists interpret these changes as a transformation from chiefdoms into small kingdoms and, by 3,100 B.C., a consolidated civilization that lasted over 2,500 years.

Early Egyptian cities had wealthy homes and craft workshops where specialists made pottery, stone tablets, alabaster jars, copper pins, axes, and daggers, plus fancy jewelry and decorative items of gold, silver, ebony, ivory, and precious stones. The dry climate preserves normally perishable finds like wood, basketry, cloth, rope, feathers, and papyrus paper.

You can see through grave archaeology the evolution of hierarchy: The earliest tombs were small, wooden enclosures where the dead were buried with everyday items and food for the afterlife. By the fourth millennium B.C., a few tombs are more elaborate stone or brick constructions with fancy grave furniture, mummies of animals, and other wealth items showing how the new ruling class lived. Eventually, large cemetery-temple complexes with pyramids became funerary monuments to individual rulers, demonstrating not only their riches but also the power of the state. Portraits, animal images, and civic and religious symbols were carved into walls and statues.

In Chapter 2, I describe the common misconceptions about pyramids and prophesies in ancient Egypt (not to mention Hollywood's notion of extragalactic connections). But since Sir William Flinders Petrie developed careful digging methods in Egyptology in the late 19th century, systematic, scientific archaeology has been uncovering the real stories.

Consolidating power

The Egyptian state was much larger, more centralized, and more stable than Mesopotamian city-states. This may have been due to the concentration of people in the fertile valley (you couldn't do much in the desert) and so the concentration of wealth for the rulers. Written records on papyrus and carved stone monuments say that the first pharaoh unified the Upper (southern Nile) and Lower (northern Nile) segments of Egypt, and various dynasties followed, established through political alliances, warfare, and governing strategies. For example, pharaohs were god-kings, marrying their sisters to keep the power in the family! Excavations of their pyramids, huge tombs and palaces, and irrigation canals indicate that they had good engineers and lots of labor to carry millions of limestone blocks. Other archaeological sites such as outlying shrines and government outposts show how they established a complex, efficient bureaucracy to run everything.

Most of the rich tombs of Egyptian rulers were looted ages ago (some probably before the corpse was cold). The boy-king Tut ruled only ten years (beginning 1333 B.C.) and was not very important as pharaohs go. But he's famous now because his tomb was discovered mostly undisturbed. It contained amazing wealth: his solid gold coffin; his gold funerary mask inlaid with lapis, quartz, obsidian, turquoise, carnelian, and colored glass; statues of carved wood, gold, marble, and other stone; a big fan with ostrich plumes; and even clay jars with residues of both red and white wine. You can imagine what opulent offerings must have accompanied the divine personages of other, more important rulers.

In Egyptian archaeology today, you also excavate more humble graves and homes of scribes or common people. One investigation of the settlements of workers who built pyramids showed that these laborers were treated well. Numerous bones of cattle, sheep, and goats show that they got good quality meat every day —unlike the Hollywood image of slaves beaten while they hauled huge stone blocks around!

External connections

In ancient Egypt you see the influence of Mesopotamia in the written records and artifacts, but archaeology also shows you the independent development of native complex culture, with its own styles of art and crafts, architecture, religion, and political administration. Egypt had extensive trade networks to get valuable raw materials. The capital cities moved up and down the Nile depending on the ruler and who was overtaking whom. Farther upriver, archaeologists have investigated sites of the indigenous sub-Saharan African civilizations that emerged in Nubia (Sudan) by 1500 B.C., with their own pyramids and black-skinned people. Nubians were certainly in constant interaction with Egypt, but a few historians argue they were the originators of Egyptian civilization (and even later, of classical Greece). Archaeologists can't, of course, tell skin color from artifacts or even mummies, but Egyptian paintings do show Nubians with darker skin than the Egyptians themselves, who are usually anywhere from reddish-brown to paler yellowish-white.

By 1000 B.C. the centralization of Egypt was breaking down as regional leaders competed for power. You've probably read the history — Assyrians, Persians, and then Macedonians (led by Alexander the Great) later invaded to end Egypt's home glory. All these conflicts are visible in the archaeological record too, in everything from new artifact styles to changing religious symbols and settlement patterns.

Indus Valley: Peaceful civilization?

You may not have heard about the civilization that appeared in the Indus River valley. It was only discovered in the 1920s, and the British had already demolished some of the sites in the 19th century, using the ancient bricks to build their railroad lines! Because today the river forms the border between India and Pakistan, political difficulties (as well as looters and modern construction) continue to hinder comprehensive investigations. But intrepid archaeologists from these two countries, as well as other international teams, are now bringing many finds to public attention.

By the later Neolithic, larger farming settlements were developing in this area. (One example is Mehrgarh, which I describe in Chapter 13.) A true civilization then appeared around 2600 B.C. It lasted at least 800 years and controlled an area twice as big as ancient Egypt or Mesopotamia, stretching from the Arabian Sea to the foothills of the Himalayas. The sites of Harappa, Mohenjo-daro, and several other Indus cities and towns had clever engineers who tamed the unpredictable river with flood control systems. Great walls of mud brick protected people and stored water for crops like wheat and barley.

City planning

Extremely well-planned Indus cities were laid out along rectangular grids of streets — some paved with stone. Here are other aspects of exquisite planning:

- ✔ Houses had wells and indoor toilets, and the water and sewer systems were the most sophisticated in the world until Roman times. At Mohenjo-Daro citizens used a large public bath that had graceful columns and a pool with plastered bricks covered by natural tar.

- ✔ Craft specialists like potters, stone-workers, cloth-makers, bakers, or traders clustered in certain areas of the cities.

- ✔ Standard, precise systems of weights and measures are evident everywhere, from tiny artifacts like cubical stone weights to house sizes to the well-ordered streets.

- ✔ Large public buildings included granaries and other storage facilities.

Many mysteries

The symbols of the Indus writing system have yet to be deciphered, though archaeologists have excavated thousands of inscriptions on stone seals or pottery. Many images of cattle, which may have been sacred, provide a possible link to later Hinduism, though religious beliefs are not very discernible from the material remains. Cuneiform tablets and Indus artifacts in Mesopotamia indicate Indus merchants sailed the Arabian Sea and the Persian Gulf.

Interestingly, Indus civilization had no public art on a massive scale, no rich tombs or shrines, and no glorious palaces of supreme rulers. Archaeologists have discovered small statues (figurines of seated men or dancers), bone and ivory carvings, shell ornaments, precious stones and metals, and *faience* (fancy glazed pottery). But these wealth items are found in even modest homes, not lavishly displayed or concentrated in palaces or tombs. Little evidence so far indicates warfare or militarism. Some say it was a relatively *egalitarian* (socially equal), peaceful society that emphasized engineering for the benefit of all. But the newest finds do include just a few graves of individuals who were apparently richer than the rest, with a pile of pottery vessels or beads of gold, onyx, jasper, and turquoise.

Archaeologists of course argue about why the Indus civilization disappeared in 1700 B.C. Perhaps it was due to climate change and resulting collapse of trade, or maybe the river shifted and land fertility decreased. Some think that the deforestation (to get fuel to make all those baked mud bricks) made the environment unusable. But this civilization left a legacy of traditions that persist in the region, including depictions of yoga, ritual burning and bathing, and that sacred bull symbolism.

China: Vast empire

Written legends of the earliest Chinese ruling dynasties say that around 2200 B.C., one powerful warlord united several competing kingdoms in northern China. Secure archaeological evidence only dates to the later Shang dynasty, beginning around 1200 B.C.

Shang cities

The An-yang site is the oldest known of the ancient Chinese cities and the Shang capital. It centered on the royal household and had bronze foundries and other craftworkers' neighborhoods. Finds include thousands of oracle bones inscribed with questions about the future and outcomes of predicted events. Any writing about merchants' goods and sales must have been on something that didn't preserve, like cloth or wood. Other sacred inscriptions appear on pots of bronze. This precious mix of copper and tin wasn't for everyday tools but only for these ritual vessels and weapons.

Shang rulers had powerful armies with horse-drawn chariots. Royal burials included chariots and horses as sacrificial offerings (bones are preserved, as are marks in the soil from the decayed wood), as well as those huge bronze pots, jade, and other precious artifacts. Just like in Mesopotamia, rulers' graves also include sacrificed people — servants and even the chariot drivers — to help in the next life.

Zhou expansion

The Zhou dynasty took over in about 1100 B.C. Archaeological evidence shows power shifted to south China, and the state hierarchy expanded. Walled towns indicate military conquest, but also extension of economic systems. The famous Silk Road across central and southern Asia that connected China with the West became an important trade route. Settlements along this route showing the mix of peoples and goods that moved across the continent.

Qin dynasty and later: An empire emerges

The first imperial state emerged during the Qin dynasty in 221 B.C. and achieved some amazing accomplishments. The Qin emperor's administrators and builders finished the Great Wall, systematized the legal system, and built and expanded elaborate road and canal systems. The Chinese also standardized their writing system on newly invented paper. Archaeological finds include bamboo sheets bound into books.

Archaeologists have only partially excavated the Qin emperor's stunning tomb. It covers a 500-acre complex and contains thousands of life-sized terra-cotta statues of warriors (see Figure 14-2 and discussion in Chapter 20) and horses with wooden chariots. They're arrayed for battle, with swords and other weapons, and rich artifacts of gold, jade, silk, bone, pottery, and iron. Clearly, the guy had immense wealth and control!

Other dynasties came to power (and continued up to modern times). China was the biggest ancient state in the world, both in size and complexity.

Figure 14-2:
Replica of a terra-cotta warrior statue from Emperor Qin's tomb in China.

Mesoamerica: Olmec, Maya, and Aztec civilizations

Mesoamerica encompasses central and southern Mexico, Guatemala, and other parts of Central America. Here, in both highlands and low rainforest and scrubland, a rich archaeological record documents the earliest states.

Olmec culture: Perhaps the first Mesoamerican state

In the Mexican tropics along the Gulf Coast, the first monumental stone pyramids and other architecture and sculptures appear by 1000 B.C., marking the emergence of what archaeologists call Olmec culture. Major sites such as San Lorenzo and La Venta display famous stone monuments, especially the massive carved-stone heads like the one from La Venta (now displayed in Villahermosa, Mexico) shown in Figure 14-3. Other important finds are small beautiful jade figures with faces that have both jaguar and human characteristics.

The Olmec used symbols that may have been writing. They were the first to play team sports with a ball of rubber (tapped from the native trees), and a few preserved rubber balls and ball courts have been excavated. Figurines of both men and women players show them wearing arm and leg guards; the helmets on the giant stone heads may also have been for the ball game. It looks like rulers or important people were portrayed as ball players.

Olmec architecture and artifacts spread far and lasted a good 1,000 years. Archaeologists argue over whether this evidence is enough to indicate the earliest true Mesoamerican state, or just an art style, religious movement, or something else.

Teotihuacán and Maya city-states

In the highland valley center of Mexico was the home of the early great city-state Teotihuacán, beginning in the first centuries A.D. Irrigation systems fed abundant farmland, and obsidian sources provided raw material that could be traded widely. The great Pyramid of the Sun and Pyramid of the Moon, and many other constructions, highlight this huge religious and civil center. Archaeologists have mapped the city and located even neighborhoods of foreigners such as Zapotec and Maya natives. Although it lasted for many centuries, the site was abandoned after A.D. 750. It was an empty sacred place by the time the Aztecs came along.

In southern Mexico and Guatemala and Belize, ruins of Maya pyramids were long thought to be vacant ceremonial centers where slash-and-burn farmers came for ritual purposes, and peaceful native astronomers observed the skies. Later, archaeologists cleared trees and used remote sensing (discussed more in Chapter 6) to see the jungle better and discover these ruins were instead huge cities with raised-field intensive agriculture. Then the glyph system was decoded, so now you can read about how the Maya city-states were actually often at war with each other.

Figure 14-3:
Huge Olmec
head from
La Venta.

Classic Maya (A.D. 250 to 900) sites feature pyramids surrounding plazas, and rich burials with carved stone, fancy jewelry, and jade ornaments. In Guatemala, Tikal is a Classic-period major center with several huge pyramid complexes. Palenque (see Color Figure 10), in Chiapas state, Mexico, features the tomb of Lord Pacal. (*Pacal* means "shield" in native Maya language.)

Mesoamerican collapse (or transformation?)

You hear a lot in the popular media about the classic Maya "collapse" (though, curiously, little about why Teotihuacán and other cities were abandoned). But the people didn't go away (there are probably more Maya today than ever!); they just stopped building pyramids and living urban life. Some Maya pyramid centers in northern Yucatan did last longer than those in the south; later cultures build other towns with monumental architecture.

Whatever happened, it was a transformation not yet well understood. Some of the reasons may be climate change and drop in agricultural production, political over-reaching, social causes like peasant rebellion, or some combination of these and other factors.

Aztecs

Many other states flourished in Mesoamerica that I've not listed here, all known from archaeological evidence. But you know the latest and most famous, the Aztecs. Their capital, Tenochtitlán, (in today's downtown Mexico

City) was established in A.D. 1325 on a swampy island. You can see the excavated parts of this city today (as I explain in Chapter 20). The Aztecs built causeways to the island, as well as pyramids, aqueducts, raised farm fields, temples and palaces. Through conquest and alliance they created a large empire by the time the Spanish arrived in the early 1500s and defeated the native ruler Moctezuma. Archaeological data give a better picture of the Aztecs' downfall than do the historical documents, which emphasize European guns and bad choices by native leaders. Excavation of contact-period sites shows huge numbers of Aztecs quickly died from disease germs introduced by the Spanish, cancelling out their advantages — far greater numbers and seasoned warriors — over the very few conquistador invaders.

Aztecs and other Mesoamerican civilizations were very interested in bloody ritual sacrifice. Not all of these civilizations were necessarily militaristic, but the Aztecs certainly were fierce fighters who displayed racks of trophy skulls and apparently even practiced some cannibalism. However, for many thousands of years these cultures also had complex mathematics and engineering and developed elaborate calendars, writing systems, and incredible architecture and art. Who can say which civilizations are more bloody than others?

South American civilizations: Mountains, desert, and jungle

South American states arose in the Andes mountains and along the desert Pacific coast. These cultures never invented any writing, so everything known about them comes from archaeology. Their fascinating political systems were based on community organization, ancestor worship, and centralized state control, ownership, and distribution of all goods — an unusual kind of communism unknown to Western culture. You can see this both from the archaeological record and in the observations of the Spanish invaders recording indigenous society in the 16th century.

In Chapter 13, I describe how monumental architecture had already begun on the Peruvian coast and inland by 3000 to 2000 B.C.

Chavín culture: Arguably the earliest South American state

By 900 B.C., the emphasis shifted from coast to the high mountains with the site of Chavín de Huántar. Here's what you can see there:

- ✔ Massive architecture with stone block platforms, sunken plazas and courts, and mazes of passageways with ventilation shafts

- ✔ Depictions of humans and animals, in stone carvings and pottery designs, that show a peculiar art style with elements of serpents, jaguars, caymans (lizards), and humans combined in repeated geometric shapes

The dating of Chavín de Huántar and other Chavín culture sites, and the jaguars and other images suggest at least indirect connections with the Olmec in Mesoamerica. Chavín culture, especially artistic styles and religious symbols, spread westward to the Pacific coast, where it's called the Paracas culture. Here it's famous for its colorful textiles with the same designs, preserved in the desert conditions.

Chavín may represent the earliest true state formation, or perhaps some centralized religious movement or economic or military control (though evidence of militarism is so far nonexistent). Archaeologists are, of course, still arguing about this!

Regional states

Between 200 B.C. and A.D. 600, some clear state societies emerged. Here are two famous examples:

- **Moche,** on the north Peru coast. Its *huacas* (pyramids) were constructed with millions of adobe bricks with makers' marks (probably indicating those communal labor groups). Burials of lords were accompanied by gold, copper, feathers, textiles, and other riches. Moche pottery is famous for its depictions of everything from the spiritual to the humorous, and also of every conceivable area of daily life, including realistic sex scenes and jars shaped like vulvas and penises.

- **Nazca,** on the south Peru coast, with pyramid centers, elegant textiles, and colorful painted pottery. The famous Nazca lines are huge *geoglyphs* (shapes drawn by removing dark rocks to expose the lighter desert floor) over several hundred square miles. They're shapes of geometric figures and animals. You can see the lines more clearly from the air, but also pretty well from the ground or nearby hills. So you don't need ancient astronauts from another galaxy to explain how these shapes were created.

Moche and other regional states did practice ritual human sacrifice. You see not only artistic depictions of this custom but also skeletons of people who were cut up and killed. This evidence isn't necessarily proof of organized, large-scale warfare, though it's a bloody business (especially if you're one of the sacrificed prisoners).

South American empires

Between about A.D. 400 and 1200, the first South American empires arose. Wari (or Huari) was in southern Peru, and Tiwanaku (or Tiahuanaco) was in Bolivia and Chile. The Tiwanaku site, on the Bolivian *altiplano* (high plains) around Lake Titicaca, was a grand city with the famous stone-sculpted Gateway of the Sun. Distinctive artistic styles characterize this archaeological culture. Evidence indicates warfare and conquest, as well as diplomatic outposts for interaction between the two empires (and signs that they all drank lots of corn beer).

To support all this, llama herders moved up and down mountains each season, and Tiwanaku farmers engineered raised platforms to intensify agricultural production on low wetlands. (In Chapter 16, I show you how modern farmers are benefiting from these ancient practices discovered by archaeologists.) The archaeological record also shows how earthquakes and *El Niño* weather patterns (warm currents that killed off a lot of fish) affected the Pacific Coast and the highlands and sometimes interrupted the actions of states.

South American civilizations are the only ones that never developed writing. They recorded bureaucratic details with the *quipu* (or *khipu*), a system of knotted cords in different lengths and colors. Especially on the dry desert coast, many quipu are preserved. Archaeologists, mathematicians, and computer specialists are all working on decoding them.

The Inca

After the breakdown of the South American empires around A.D. 1000, smaller regional states again appeared. The Chimu are one of these states, known from both archaeology and the history that the Inca told to the Spanish. The Chimu capital at Chan Chan on the north coast of Peru was a huge city that controlled territory stretching from southern Ecuador to central Peru. The empire included great road and canal systems and craftworkers, especially goldsmiths, who made highly prized wealth items. The Chimu state lasted from A.D. 800 to 1470, when it was conquered by the Inca, who brought Chimu gold-smiths to their own capital.

The Inca were the last great native civilization of South America. They resembled the Aztecs in Mexico in gaining power by military conquest. They began creating an empire shortly before the Spanish arrived in 1532 and wrote about them, so investigating them is historic archaeology too.

The Inca empire was the largest in the world up to then. Along its road system connecting the coast and the Andes, relay runners brought messages (and fresh fish to the mountains). The capital was Cuzco, a highland city that still has prehistoric Inca stone-block foundations in modern buildings. Machu Picchu (see Figure 14-4 and Color Figure 12) is another famous site, an inaccessible highland estate. Inca construction techniques used trapezoidal doorways and huge pillow-shaped stones that fit together without mortar.

Other South American cultures: Not much to find in the jungle

Preservation conditions in South America create some bias in the archaeological record. On the dry desert coast you have feathers, leather, cloth, even natural and artificial mummies preserved. In the Andes, high-altitude Inca burials and frozen mummies of sacrificed kids (yes) ensure equally good preservation of organic remains. Also in the mountains, lots of stone was available to build lasting buildings.

The jungle isn't so friendly to archaeology. Ethnocentric views may be responsible for archaeologists' not seeing complex civilizations in the Amazon and other parts of eastern South America. In addition, the rainforest isn't good for preservation of most artifacts and also makes archaeology very difficult — after all, it's a jungle out there!

Hot, humid climates may seem unfavorable for human accomplishment. But this view (held by archaeologists from temperate climates) is now being challenged. Fascinating jungle finds indicate elaborate road systems and earthen mounds. Spanish records document complicated states in the "intermediate area" of northern South America not evident archaeologically because the construction and monuments were all of the abundant wood. Stay tuned for new discoveries.

Reasons for Civilization

Archaeologists exploring what causes true civilization to develop in the first place get to argue not only among themselves but also with historians! Different causes probably influenced different regions. Here are some of the hypothesized factors tied to the emergence of the most complicated societies humans have ever known:

- ✔ Irrigation to intensify food production was complicated enough to require large scale organization by some kind of leader. Hierarchical rulers and bureaucracy followed. This explanation is plausible, but different kinds of irrigation (from local to grand scale) appeared in different places.

- ✔ Population growth and resulting competition for resources led to the need for central organization. This explanation may work in some places. But in Egypt populations were pretty low; plenty of land was open, and no evidence exists for resource competition until after the complex state was formed.

- ✔ Long-distance trade networks led to economic control systems.

- ✔ Some characteristics of society — large populations, building irrigation systems — required more complex organization and bureaucratic administration.

- ✔ Warfare and conquest led to natural expansion of territories for rulers wanting to control resources and wealth.

Concerning the last point, everyone debates whether competition and warfare were necessary for the first true states to emerge. Even violent images depicted on pots or wall paintings can still mean small-scale feuds or human sacrifice. Real warfare is sanctioned, organized, paid for by the central government, and big enough to result in casualties of many people who aren't even fighting.

Before Maya history was known, archaeologists thought they were peaceful astronomers. Now that the glyph writing system has been decoded, it's clear that Maya city-states were beating each other up all the time! On the other hand, archaeologists excavating the Indus Valley civilization have so far unearthed little sign of violence — no defensive fortifications or weapons or mass burials of victims with battle wounds. Yet these people had amazingly engineered cities, beautiful crafts, great wealth, and widespread territory. This is also true (so far) for Olmec and Chavín.

Ancient warfare may seem like a fanciful question of no consequence, but it's really important. You may think that all societies have warfare, but anthropologists have collected enough information from enough cultures to show that some don't have any war at all! Furthermore, no scientific evidence supports the idea that humans are biologically prone to violence. Archaeologists can contribute a lot to this discussion about human nature.

Figure 14-4:
Inca site of Machu Picchu in the Andes mountains of Peru.

Reflections on New World civilizations

The Inca, Maya, and other native Mesoamerican and South American peoples aren't gone. But 500 years of colonial domination have radically transformed their cultures. Many Maya dialects, other Mesoamerican languages, and South American native languages such as Quechua, the language of the Inca, are still spoken. The native peoples also take great pride in the indigenous archaeological heritage of these lands (even though looting still occurs).

Later Ancient States and Early Historic Times

After the first civilizations appeared on the planet, many later ones followed. Most of this is the stuff of history, but archaeology adds lots more information. The following sections give a couple examples of what the archaeological record of later civilizations can contribute.

Greece

Civilizations you've heard a lot about, from both history and archaeology, are those classical places of legend that are the foundations of Western culture.

Bronze-Age Greece (1600 to 1100 B.C.) is where those heroic events of Homer's *Iliad* and other legends took place. Of course, he wrote them all down much later, so archaeology can help here. I mention the early work of Heinrich Schliemann's digs at Troy in Chapter 3, but he also dug at Mycenae, a fortified town on a Greek hilltop. Here he found rulers in tombs with immense riches — gold masks, cups, jewelry, crystal and glass, amber, ivory, silver, and other offerings. Mycenaean civilization disappeared for unknown reasons — no one has found evidence of climate change or conquest.

Archaeologically, the succeeding time periods each have their own distinctive styles of building ruins, pottery, and other artifacts. Between 700 and 600 B.C., coins appear, as well as the earliest monumental stone sculpture. With the emergence of the classic Greek city-states at this time came huge marble temples, large statues of heroic religious and political figures, and the rest of the vast record of material culture documenting the classical civilization that became the foundations for Western culture and democracy.

Rome

Rome expanded from a city on the Italian peninsula to become an empire stretching around the Mediterranean Sea. It began a few centuries B.C. and extended until the fifth century A.D. You know all this from history, gleaned from Roman documents, but of course archaeology makes great contributions to the reconstruction of Rome as well.

Material remains show the everyday lives of people, from the wealthy to the slaves, and from the early days of the republic to the fall of the empire Construction anywhere in Italy, and elsewhere throughout the extent of what Rome controlled, often hits buried ruins. Here are a few finds from 2008:

✔ Italian archaeologists digging 25 feet below the street near the Colosseum unearthed the ruins of a large temple dating to the eighth century B.C., the first real evidence of the time of Rome's second king. Near this temple were a paved street and two wells.

✔ Alerted by reports of grave robbing and looting, archaeologists found and excavated a necropolis (burial ground) near Rome's main airport that dated to the first century A.D. Most of the 300 male skeletons showed signs of carrying great loads on their backs. They were probably longshoremen and other working-class people who kept early imperial Rome running. The humble grave goods included simple jewelry and lanterns of clay and glass, probably to light the way into the next life.

✔ Excavation for a major subway station in Rome uncovered a ninth-century kitchen with pots, pans, and ovens. The finds are useful for showing daily life in medieval times, when there is little written record of such mundane aspects of culture.

Biblical sites

I discuss in Chapters 3 and 16 how a great deal of archaeology focuses on sites in Israel and the land considered holy by major modern religions. Many digs seek to prove the truth of the Bible, and others just want to find out what's really there. Much of the work is done by historians and others not anthropologically oriented, and frauds and sensational claims are common.

But scientific archaeology has uncovered Egyptian and Mesopotamian inscriptions with names mentioned in the Bible, as well as sites that are places named in the Bible. I describe a little of this archaeology for you in Chapter 13, discussing digs at the biblical city of Jericho. The Neolithic layers there were covered by deposits of later cultures, and archaeologists still aren't certain which is the time period of the written records amid the ruins of stone walls and towers.

The site of Megiddo in northern Israel shows the same kind of long occupation span that makes it difficult to tie into specific biblical times, but it's most likely the place named Armageddon in the Bible. It's a tell (mound) of 25 to 30 layers of succeeding settlements from the Pre-Pottery Neolithic village of 7,000 B.C. to the city dating to 500 B.C. Excavated remains include city walls, fortifications, palaces, water management systems, a temple with a mosaic floor and Roman altar, and even a storehouse that may have been a stable with stone mangers and pillars for tying up horses. One notable find was a carved jasper seal showing a lion and a Hebrew inscription with the name of Jeroboam, an early king mentioned in the Bible.

Some archaeological finds have included ancient texts, papyri, and Dead Sea scrolls that, under slow, patient examination, reveal ancient religious writings of Hebrews and early Christians.

Other prehistoric Asian and African states

All kinds of other ancient states command the attention of archaeologists (and historians and tourists). I've chosen just a couple more to describe, so you can get an idea of the greatness of past peoples all over the world, and also the archaeological contributions to the knowledge of great civilizations.

Angkor

Bronze and Iron Age technologies, religious influences from India and China, and extensive trade networks and maritime connections all influenced the development of the southeast Asian state of Angkor, in the Mekong River region of modern Cambodia. Around A.D. 800, a strong ruler united several smaller states into the great Khmer civilization that lasted some 600 years.

Different succeeding rulers each built new temples and monuments. (See Chapter 20 for another discussion on Angkor.) The individual artifacts from daily life and special ceremony that would have been in these grand ruins were removed centuries ago, but the architectural and artistic remains give many archaeological clues to past political and religious systems. Cambodian and international archaeological teams are also restoring some of the ruins.

The largest palace is Angkor Wat, shown in Figure 14-5, dating to around A.D. 1113. It's a huge complex of buildings and walled enclosures covered with carved reliefs of sacred stories, royal activities (processions and battles), and everyday scenes (merchants, cooks, people fishing and selling fish). Another major centers was Angkor Thom (see Color Figure 13), the last and biggest capital (8 miles long!), constructed in the late 12th century. It features long stone-carved pictures of animals and royal people, including one scene of elephants parading along a stone wall over 1,000 feet long.

With excavations, mapping, and remote sensing, archaeologists are exposing vast reservoirs and other constructions that show the Khmer civilization was founded on elaborate water management systems, apparently to control flooding and help enormous rice production. This indigenous Angkor civilization ended with invasions from Thailand in A.D. 1431. Archaeologists are only now realizing its tremendous extent and engineering technologies and are arguing over how and why they were created and possibly declined even before the palaces were all abandoned and left to the jungle.

Great Zimbabwe

Great civilizations based on iron technology and cattle herding arose in southern Africa from the 12th century A.D. onwards. Great Zimbabwe is one of the most famous and spectacular of these, originating around A.D. 1250 and lasting a couple centuries. (I describe this site also in Chapter 20.) Here archaeologists exposed and mapped terraces, walls, and great stone enclosures surrounding platforms with foundations of houses made of logs and mud.

Figure 14-5:
Palace
of Khmer
ruler at
Angkor Wat,
Cambodia.

The Hill Complex (see Color Figure 14) may have been for defense. It features stone walls beautifully connected to the natural rock formations. The Great Enclosure is a huge walled oval some 300 feet long, with distinctive chevron (V-shaped) patterns made in the stone bricks along the top. It surrounds other buildings, including a solid conical tower. Little is known about the functions of all these structures.

Artifacts from the site include native-made artifacts like iron tools; brass wire bracelets, pins, needles, and razors; gold jewelry; and stone spindle whorls that show cotton thread was spun and woven. A distinctive native artifact form is a bird figure on top a tall pillar, all carved of soapstone. Finds of Persian pottery, Chinese porcelain, cowrie shells from the Indian Ocean, Arabian coins, and European glass beads are evidence of extensive trade networks.

Archaeologists are still investigating the meanings and uses of the massive ruins at Great Zimbabwe and related sites, from which there are no written records. Decades ago, the racist colonial British rulers of the country (then known as Rhodesia) insisted that such a glorious civilization must have been built by Arabs or Portuguese traders — anyone but black Africans, who wouldn't be capable of such grand accomplishments. Thanks to good archaeology (and politics), it's now clear that Great Zimbabwe was indigenous. It was built by the ancestors of native Shona people who still live in the region. The site has become a national symbol, and the name was chosen for the country when it became independent in the late 20th century!

The demise of civilizations

Many of the elaborate cities and monuments of the civilizations described in this chapter were abandoned far back in ancient times. Different reasons and conditions (for archaeologists to argue about!) apply in each case, but "collapse" isn't as accurate a term for these events as "transformation" into something else.

Some ancient states did use up their resources and never recovered their former glory when unfortunate events (drought, earthquake, and invasion) hit them, so these civilizations can provide some cautionary tales for modern people and governments!

Chapter 15

Historic Archaeology: Reinterpreting the More Recent Past

*I*n Chapter 14, I explain how archaeology helps you understand the earliest civilizations, even those with written records. This chapter shows the importance of archaeology for more recent time periods, where it provides the kind of evidence you can't get from history. Some areas of life are just not described in what people wrote!

In this chapter, I describe the historic archaeology of classical and medieval folks, colonists, famous historic men, slaves, criminals, everyday people, and modern society. You may end up thinking twice about all the material evidence you yourself leave around!

What Historic Archaeology Shows That History Can't

History is the written record of what people did and thought. But it's very selective — it doesn't include everything or everyone. The everyday things people left behind tell you a lot about mundane life that history leaves out. Archaeology gives you a different perspective on the historic past. It may confirm what you thought based on the written information or expand the basic knowledge of history. But archaeology can also give a totally different view from what you expected.

Archaeology and the biases of history

Prehistoric people were either *non-literate* (never developed writing) or *pre-literate* (hadn't yet begun using a writing system they'd later develop). After cultures became literate, you can read about how they behaved and thought if you can decipher the writing. (Then of course you have the illiterate folks — who have writing and don't know how to use it — but they're not the subject of this book!)

Even in the early civilizations that developed writing starting over 3,000 years ago, few people could actually read and write. Most of the traditions and stories of culture were learned through oral history. People repeated the accumulated knowledge — legends, beliefs, everyday learning, and extraordinary events — often enough to pass it to succeeding generations. When the information was finally written down, it had usually changed a great deal from the original version. Beyond these compromised accounts, really very little about past human life has made it into written documents.

As I describe in Chapters 3 and 14, history is always biased for many reasons:

✔ It's written by those few who are literate and important.

✔ It favors the values, views, and stories of those writing it.

✔ It usually covers only high-status topics like politics and religion, not daily chores or people outside literate spheres.

Counteracting this bias is where archaeology comes in. Granted, bias certainly exists in archaeology too, but in very different ways. The major archaeological bias is that only certain material things are preserved, and only a portion of those get excavated, so you may miss major aspects of the past. But you can dig in splendid ruins of palaces and tombs or humble houses with the debris of everyday living, so unlike historical bias, you needn't discriminate in favor of those in power who knew how to write.

The people without history

Many people's history has been poorly written or never written at all. Maybe they weren't considered important by those invading, subjugating, or colonizing them. Perhaps they were slaves brought to other countries. Little knowledge of the past exists even for groups like women, children, the poor, or any folks who couldn't or didn't write down their own records. For those without a history, archaeology has the important job of helping us gain or improve knowledge of how these people lived.

People and objects with lots of history

You may think the archives and records document famous people and events well enough. Think again; plenty of information isn't written down. Archaeological excavation uncovers new data at important historic sites and even around standing structures. For example, much remains in the ground to investigate at battlefields, famous people's estates, even public monuments.

Historical Archaeology's Methods and Finds

Your historical archaeology research will probably be a lot easier if you're looking for something specific that you know actually existed. A lost cemetery or church, a famous building now gone, or even an early settlement long demolished usually leaves material evidence. You can use typical archaeological methods, supplemented by the written records, to find such sites. The following sections detail some of those methods and their uses.

Investigation methods and questions

The things you study in any archaeological investigation are important for historic archaeology. I include many of the procedures of historical archaeology in the explanations of field methods in Chapters 6 and 7 and laboratory analysis in Chapter 9; some of these standard methods are

- ✔ Looking at old maps of your site and any other documentary records.
- ✔ Interviewing elderly residents of the area and recording any other oral history available to discern what may have been there.
- ✔ Using remote sensing to locate buried structures and other features.
- ✔ Excavating with standard techniques, but possibly using historic units of measurement such as feet and yards.
- ✔ Showing artifact types and distributions in space and time and mapping activity areas.

Communities often support archaeological research and have historical questions they want you to address. Where were the first settlers located? Were our ancestors here? Maybe you wonder where something historic was actually built or who used it. Having legitimate questions to answer is imperative before you begin excavation, because you destroy the site as you dig.

Information from pipes and toothbrushes

The first Europeans coming to North America and seeing tobacco may have thought it was weird — smoke coming out of a person's nose and mouth! But they soon took up the nicotine habit themselves, and British colonists began growing tobacco on American plantations as the habit gained international popularity. White clay smoking pipes are ubiquitous at colonial sites — the pipes were cheap, mass-produced, and frequently discarded. Some pipes had makers' marks and shapes that changed through time, but most finds are fragments. From the thousands of pipes excavated at colonial sites, historic archaeologists have developed a neat dating method. They saw that the hole or bore in the pipe stem got smaller through time as the stem lengthened, so they developed a formula for dating a site based on the diameters of a large sample of pipe stem bores for pipes manufactured in England between about 1590 and 1800. Other studies are attempting to trace sources of the white clay in different parts of England and different makers' molds, to show how these simple artifacts were made and moved across land and sea.

Archaeological study of another small, every-day artifact from domestic sites examined the larger story. Toothbrushes began as hand-made items of bone and boar-hair bristles. In the late 19th century, industrialists developed technology to manufacture them, eventually from synthetic materials and with bristles in neat, machine-made rows. Toothbrushes increase in numbers through time at historic sites: Once only items in elite households, they became things everybody had by the mid-20th century. The new brushes reflected not only mechanized standardization of the artifact but also the idea of orderliness and individual hygiene spreading through society at the time. Though it was a humble item, this artifact was a symbol that people were becoming modern. The archaeology connected everyday life with intellectual currents and values. Another investigation defined different types of tooth-brushes well enough to use them to date archaeological sites where they were found.

The approach to historic artifacts

Often you can understand historic artifacts better than prehistoric ones because you're more familiar with them or because records describe them. Artifacts are nonverbal ways of seeing behavior in the past: Manufactured objects like bottles, dishes, or nails may sound boring or unremarkable, but where they're located and who used them can be fascinating. Plus, you can look them up and get a more exact idea of when and where they were made.

Mundane artifacts like crockery represent a larger social picture in some famous historic archaeology investigations. For example:

> ✔ Pottery in early colonial sites demonstrates how women mediated between the Spanish and Native Americans in early historic America. Native pots and dishes found in Spanish dwellings mean that Indian women worked and possibly lived there serving the Spanish men.

> ✔ Choosing to use worn, unmatched dishes, 19th-century African Americans in Maryland deliberately showed a separate identity from that of the dominant white culture, whose Victorian emphasis was on matched sets of tableware.

Underwater historic sites

Underwater archaeology is difficult and expensive (see Chapters 3 and 7 for more), but it can yield amazing finds. Shipwrecks represent one-time events, capturing a slice of life. Other underwater sites can be entire settlements that somehow slipped beneath the sea. They offer you a longer-term view of past life in many ways. The following sections give you some examples of information you can uncover at underwater sites.

Shipwrecks

The archaeology of shipwrecks presents fascinating pictures of local and international commerce or naval warfare. You get details of life at sea and the personal lives of individuals of different statuses who sailed together. From cargo, armaments, and the vessel itself you pick up information on trade, politics, economic systems, and techniques of historic ship-building that were never written down.

French explorer La Salle went down the Mississippi River in 1682, claimed all the land for France, and named it Louisiana. He then tried to go back through the Gulf of Mexico to establish a colony, missed the Mississippi, and lost his last ship, the *Belle,* on the Texas coast in 1686. Underwater archaeologists found the *Belle* and its whole cargo preserved under the mud; they knew they had the right ship because the cannon was inscribed with the ship's name. The ship's timbers still had numbers written on them for helping builders assemble it. Millions of artifacts were excavated: brass pots and candlesticks, Jesuit rings, glass beads and rosaries, weapons, the ship's ropes and rigging, and even the skeleton of one crew member with brain matter still in the skull! All this material filled in the little known story of what the French expected to do in their new colony.

Underwater cities

Human settlements can become submerged quickly or slowly by many natural forces, whether it be a tsunami or gradually rising sea levels. They're often port cities with lots of social and economic evidence; you just have to be willing to dive for it.

Here are a couple of the more famous underwater cities:

✔ The harbor of Alexandria, built on the Mediterranean coast of Egypt in 331 B.C., was inundated by earthquake, tsunami, and slower geological processes. Underwater finds from this ancient city complement the data from digs on land. Archaeologists have recovered some possible pieces of its lighthouse, one of the seven wonders of the ancient world. They're mapping buildings like wharves and the probable location of a palace (possibly Cleopatra's). Stone columns and engraved blocks, statues, and sphinxes show combinations of Egyptian and Greek architectural traditions and lively commerce connecting Europe, Africa, and Asia.

✔ Port Royal, Jamaica, a large, rich, colonial English city, partially sank in an earthquake in 1692. Underwater excavation uncovered details of architecture, craftwork, merchants' activities, and town planning. One building had a tavern, a cobbler shop, and a possible pipe shop. Skeletons of a few children lay in some buildings. The rich artifact assemblages include pottery, copper, brass, jewelry, and glass from many nations and items of native people. They all tell about the city's wealth and fabled wickedness, with all its grogshops, gaming houses, and brothels for pirates to spend their treasure. Pewter artifacts helped reconstruct Jamaica's previously unknown role in the pewter trade.

Classical Archaeology

In Chapters 3 and 14, I describe how classical archaeology studies ancient civilizations of the Mediterranean world — including Greece, Rome, and sometimes the surrounding states in Mesopotamia and Egypt — the cultural foundations of Western society. These civilizations existed from several centuries B.C. until about A.D. 500. Though classical archaeology traditionally emphasized monumental architecture and works of art like beautiful sculpture or vases, in recent decades anthropological archaeology — looking at how these past people lived — is becoming the norm.

Classical civilizations left historic records carved in stone, painted on pottery, stamped on coins, and written on animal-skin parchment scrolls. By the early Roman Empire there were bound books, and copyists kept important manuscripts available through medieval times. When you study classical antiquity, you're doing historic archaeology and adding to ancient history.

Here are some things you can do as a classical archaeologist:

✔ Excavate one famous place, such as the Agora (civic center) in Athens, and see how it changed through the centuries from the Greek heyday of the fifth to fourthth centuries B.C. through Roman times.

The problem of looting

Unfortunately, antiques and other historic artifacts command big prices at auctions. Looting of historic sites (even graves) is constant, even though it's usually illegal and always unethical and disrespectful. People are robbing the heritage of the human past and of someone's ancestors.

In a recent case, after a report of looting, archaeologists excavated a cemetery at a New Mexico Civil War fort. At least 20 graves had been robbed. One looter had displayed in his house various artifacts and a mummified soldier in a military uniform. Most of his finds were already sold off before government investigators arrived. The remains of the soldiers and others, including children, were reburied with dignity at other national cemeteries.

Underwater historic sites are constantly looted. Recently a treasure-hunting company, funded by investors hoping to get rich from a historic shipwreck, planned to dig a shaft through the ship to the place below decks where they think the gold is, thus destroying the ship itself and its artifacts.

✔ Examine tombs, houses, monuments, and paintings of the Etruscans (a pre-Roman people of Tuscany, Italy) to see how they held women in higher esteem than the Romans did, and taught Romans engineering.

✔ Investigate Roman soldiers' camps in Britain or other places that were far outposts of the empire.

✔ Uncover mosaics and architectural elements of Roman towns buried under medieval or modern cities.

✔ Trace commerce and other economic and social systems by studying certain artifact types such as *amphorae* (large ceramic jars for wine, oil, or other commodities) to see where they were made over the centuries and where they ended up around the Mediterranean.

Medieval Archaeology

Because the Middle Ages were often times of minimal literature and literacy, much of what historians know — outside of the workings of powerful leaders — comes from the archaeological record.

Medieval archaeology emphasizes post-Roman and later archaeological sites across Europe and elsewhere, up to about the 16th century. It gives you details of the lives of Celts, Saxons, Norse, and other poorly known cultures. The Middle Ages were a time of Germanic tribes, Muslim conquests around the Mediterranean, and persistence or loss of Roman systems. The many small kingdoms or chiefdoms that emerged over the centuries left only a few historic records, so archaeological knowledge is a welcome addition.

Under the volcano: Discovering Pompeii

Pompeii, near Naples, Italy, and its port town of Herculaneum are famous Roman sites. The volcanic eruption of Mount Vesuvius in A.D. 79 buried them under many tons of ash, leaving a wonderfully preserved archaeological record to compare with the few surviving written accounts of the city. The remains of people trapped as they tried to flee the volcano are heartbreaking. Some have gold and jewelry; others have no wealth items and have evidence of hard labor in their bones, showing they were slaves — but all died alike. You can visit there today and see houses, stores, paved streets, and theaters exposed by the excavation that has been continuous over centuries. My favorite spots are the public baths and public toilets — so civilized! Beautiful paintings on the walls show scenes of daily life and myths, legends, and religious ceremonies.

Even standing medieval structures like castles or abbeys have underground traces. At a typical dig, you uncover debris of daily life as well as evidence of political ceremony and religious ritual. You can go farther and explore the transformations of feudal villages into towns and the roots of modern nations.

Here are some things you can do in medieval archaeology:

- Excavate occasional buried hoards of treasure, caches of gold, silver, and jewels perhaps hidden from invaders.

- Relocate and map buildings like churches, convents, castles, and manor houses and see how early they were established.

- Find the quarry sites where medieval builders got the building stones and see how they went about stone construction.

- Investigate foundations in the ground of buildings whose stones were taken and reused long ago. You can establish how structure outlines changed over time with repair and expansion.

- Study change through time in artifact assemblages and architectural design at these places, many of which were occupied for centuries.

- Reconstruct what life was like for peasants, clergy, farmers, and nobles as social classes developed and changed.

- Compare your findings with architectural historians' studies of castles and cathedrals and historical studies of life at court and in the countryside.

- Do landscape archaeology incorporating the fortress or castle grounds, stables, outbuildings, and workers' quarters. You can investigate estate management, craft production, and other feudal systems.

- Explore change in land-use patterns showing clearing of forests and establishments of post-Roman farm and small-village systems.

> ✔ Investigate local and regional ritual and religion, for example as Roman villas became converted to Christian settlements or even monasteries.
>
> ✔ Document with material evidence larger historic trends such as the spread of Christianity or presence of Judaism throughout Europe or retention of various pagan practices.
>
> ✔ Discover cemeteries and investigate burials to see health, diet, and other physical aspects of these historic populations of different regions.

At a medieval dig, you may be unearthing traces of a knight's armor or a Viking ship. You gather knowledge of chiefs, battles, interactions across continents, and the historic foundations of the modern world. In the late Middle Ages, you can also see how traditions of long-distance exploration began. For example, the Norse or Vikings colonized many foreign lands, from Europe to Iceland and Greenland. They even made it to America nearly 500 years before Christopher Columbus!

Archaeology of Invasion and Colonization

Europeans and others who first came to North and South America began to write the history of the Native Americans. But they often gave distorted interpretations of native culture and customs, or didn't even see them at all. Archaeological work at *protohistoric* (contact-period) sites documents the routes the first explorers took through the Americas and the effects of first contact between indigenous peoples and invaders. Excavations of mission sites and early colonial settlements reveal how both groups interacted.

The same situation is true for European and other intruders into Africa, Asia, Australia, and the Pacific. Information from colonial sites demonstrates how natives were treated and how foreigners' lives changed as they became long-term residents and then creoles (the next generation, born there but of foreign origin). You can see this in the artifact assemblages when you compare distributions and uses of native-made items and imported goods or foods, or when you map the arrangement of natives' and foreigners' houses or religious and civic buildings across the town.

An abandoned Spanish town in the Americas

What early explorers experienced in making their way through the New World shows up in the archaeological record. One example is the site of the first European town in America, Christopher Columbus's 1493 La Isabella on the island of Hispaniola, in today's Dominican Republic. It's typically medieval, with walls and stone buildings for defense against the island's Taino Indians. The Spanish even established a stone quarry. But their town failed — they abandoned it in four years and went on to other, more lucrative places in the Americas. The records say the soldiers were starving and rebellious.

The Spaniards lived like they did at home: Excavated artifacts included pottery, carved and painted plaster fragments from walls, forged metal nails and decorative items, horseshoes, chain mail and armor, daggers and swords, crossbow bolt heads, gun parts, and Christian items. The lack of food remains suggests they wouldn't even eat local foods the Native Americans would have brought. They didn't accommodate to the material and social life of the people already there but tried forcefully to change the natives' religion, economy, and society. It was no surprise that the Indians resisted. Later Spanish colonies shifted towards adaptation, and their material remains show combinations of European, Native American, and African traditions.

Famous archaeological sites of Vikings

Vikings were Scandinavian farmers and warriors who sailed the seas, raiding and colonizing. They settled among Anglo-Saxons in northern England and established their capital at Jorvik, now in the city of York. Archaeological excavations there reveal amazing information on medieval life, far beyond what you read in the histories of kings. Digs uncovered houses and shops of leather-workers and bone carvers, and artifacts like wooden cups, iron tools, and cheap jewelry of lead or copper alloy, as well as gold, silver, glass, amber, and symbolic items of both Christian and pagan religions. Food and other remains in the dirt floors of houses included wheat, barley, wild plants, hemp and linseed oil, and herbs and spices like dill and celery seed. Human fleas and lice were also preserved, as well as a famous large human *coprolite* (dried feces) that contained parasitic intestinal worms. Other finds are trade items like silk and coins from distant places, showing that economic networks extended as far as western Asia. You can visit York today and see a complete reconstruction of what this settlement was like in the year 975.

Viking explorers also got to the New World by about A.D. 1000. The L'Anse aux Meadows National Historic Site of Canada is the earliest known European settlement in the Americas. Norse sagas tell of sailing from Greenland to a place that sounded like North America. The archaeological site, discovered in 1960 on the northernmost tip of Newfoundland, proves the legends to be true. They came for lumber and furs, but conflict with the local natives, whose archaeological remains show they'd already been there 5,000 years, soon drove the Norse away. The dig uncovered a small settlement with houses, workshops, and a forge that produced the first iron on the continent. Excavated buildings have sod walls and roofs over timber frames and central fireplaces, similar to 11th-century Norse buildings in Iceland and Greenland. Artifacts include a bronze cloak pin, an oil lamp, iron boat nails, even wood chips from trimming logs. A bone needle, whetstone, and soapstone spindle whorl for spinning thread show women's presence. A clay-lined pit framed with large stones was the furnace for smelting iron for the blacksmith shop and forge. Food remains included butternuts, which don't grow this far north. Neither do the grapes that were noted in the legends calling the place Vinland (place of vines). So archaeologists determined that this site was probably a base camp for people exploring farther south along the St. Lawrence River and New Brunswick areas.

Spanish missions in the U.S. Southeast

You may be familiar with the adobe or stone buildings of historic Spanish missions in the southwestern U.S. Missions were established earlier (in the 1600s) in the Southeast, but they left fewer traces — no standing structures, because the buildings were made of wood. Nonetheless, archaeologists have located many of them and excavated their churches, convents (where friars lived), and native houses and public buildings. Cemeteries are near the churches or within church floors. Spatial distributions of Native American artifacts and European goods such as glass and iron show the different activity areas of the sites.

In Chapter 19, I describe one of these missions — San Luis in Florida — where you can visit reconstructed Spanish and Apalachee Indian buildings. Continued study of these sites gives amazing insight into how both natives and newcomers changed to live with (or resist) each other. Native American skeletons show they labored harder under Spanish control than they had before the foreigners arrived. Yet historic documents indicate that these indigenous people invited the Spanish friars to their villages. Could it have been because they wanted the prestige goods like beads and metals that the intruders brought to trade?

A French fort in Alabama

The archaeology of Fort Toulouse/Jackson Park near Montgomery, Alabama, compares well with the historic records. Accounts indicate that French colonists, afraid of rival British advancement, built a fort there in 1717 and then rebuilt it in 1749. The Creek Indians were friendly, trading their deerskins for glass beads, guns, metal items and household goods. The French left in 1763, but in 1814 the Americans built another fort on top of the old ruins. This last settlement was abandoned in 1819.

Excavators went deep enough to uncover underlying prehistoric cultural deposits. The earliest inhabitants were Native American hunter–gatherers at about 5,000 B.C., and later natives had a farming village and earthen mounds. Archaeological features such as postmolds from the wooden palisades have shown the outlines of multiple French forts. The second fort was moved back from the bank of the river, which washed away part of the first one. The American fort is the biggest and latest. Artifacts include lots of Indian pottery, other indigenous craft items, and the European goods the natives traded for. A particularly striking find was the *corpus* (body of Christ) from a French crucifix, shown in Color Figure 15.

Investigating Famous Figures

Colonial archaeology is famous in the U.S. Homes and public buildings of historic figures always have archaeological remains that can become a big part of the story — or change the story.

Historic estates offer many clues into lesser-known areas of their owners' lives. Even the layout of their gardens and outbuildings reflects the orderly world views and high social status of their owners. Archaeologists compare the evidence in the ground with details from personal letters or other papers and information from architectural historians and other specialists. They can then see a broader picture of the lives of some famous personages and their social or political circumstances.

Thomas Jefferson's home at Monticello, Virginia, housed his family, free workers, and hundreds of slaves. Excavations at craft production areas (like buildings for blacksmiths and carpenters), as well as at artisans' and slaves' homes, show social and economic patterns of this complex society. Archaeology gives you great details of the labor and skills of those who conducted the agricultural and industrial production supporting Jefferson's political accomplishments. You can visit there today and see much of the estate accurately reconstructed.

I describe the excavation of George Washington's distillery in Chapter 3 (and see Color Figure 5) at his home in Mount Vernon (which you can also visit). Archaeologists combined information from his papers with what they dug up to reconstruct the techniques he used to produce and sell considerable quantities of whiskey! You may be surprised to see that archaeological excavation recently exposed another, less-known aspect of Washington's life: his slaves. (More on that in the next section.)

The Archaeology of Slavery

Much of the hidden lives of slaves comes alive through archaeology. You can see in the material evidence how they created distinctive cultures and customs within horrible systems of oppression. Archaeologists examine slavery especially in North and South America and the Caribbean.

In 2007, the U.S. National Park Service excavated the foundations of George Washington's 1790s house in Philadelphia. That city was then the nation's capital, so this presidential home was like the White House. Archaeologists uncovered a large basement not indicated in the historic records, as well as outlines of an early version of the Oval Office. They also exposed a hidden underground passage designed so that slaves could move in and out of the house unseen by important guests. Historians knew Washington kept nine of his 300+ slaves in Philadelphia, even though Pennsylvania was a free state;

they even knew the names of these nine. But you seldom see this part of the story in the history books!

Thousands of tourists and passers-by were amazed to watch what the dig uncovered and understand what it meant. At this spot (right next to the Liberty Bell and near Independence Hall), officials have to determine how to include this physical record of people in bondage in the planned exhibit. Archaeology forces a more balanced presentation of United States history.

Many other digs of slaves' quarters and work areas are producing fascinating finds. Here are some examples:

✔ In the eastern U.S., plantation record books show what foods slaves were given, but the quantities never seem like they would have been sufficient for survival. Excavations of pit features at slave quarters have uncovered bones of less desirable parts like heads and feet of cows and pigs, but also bones of wild animals. This material proves that slaves supplemented their inadequate rations by going out and hunting to get enough meat and then burying the bones to avoid discovery. Sometimes the bone assemblages show slaves had a more nutritious diet than that of the white master! Lead shot and gun parts also hidden under dirt floors show how they hunted.

✔ Plant remains indicate slaves often grew their own gardens and collected wild plants, not only for food but also for medicinal needs.

✔ Root cellars were originally sub-floor pits for storing root crops, but they're also filled with personal and domestic artifacts showing daily life, as are the dirt floors of houses and the areas outside house walls. The artifacts include handmade items like pottery and clay pipes; buttons of metal, bone, and shell; and African cowrie-shell charms and glass beads.

✔ Pits in slave-house floors from the 17th century to the Civil War may also have been West African-style shrines. Groupings of seemingly unrelated artifacts (nails, unusual bone pieces, shells, crystals, pierced coins, and symbols similar to African ritual markings) reflect traditional spiritual practices.

✔ Digs in Brazil have unearthed details of communities of runaway African slaves or *maroons*. Called *quilombos,* these 17th-century settlements escaped Portuguese and Dutch control. They developed their own distinctive language and culture based on African standards. Excavated native, European, African, and African-style artifacts such as pottery support historic accounts of their heroic resistance and show how they forged a new ethnic identity.

For another story of how slavery's material record is expanding history, see the sidebar in Chapter 16 about the African burial ground site in New York.

Excavating Daily Life, Historic Industry, and the Military

The archaeology of pioneer settlements, railroad workers, miners, tenant farmers, other minority groups, and ordinary folks gives life to these often-undocumented people who built nations. Much of what we know about them comes from the material record, not written history. The same is true for historic industrial sites and military sites from forts to battlefields — what's in the ground helps reconstruct the big picture.

Daily life in society

Much historic archaeology is digging up the remains of past households to see details of domestic life at different times in the past. Some examples of what archaeologists are investigating:

✔ How newcomers settled and interacted with people who were already there.

✔ Trends in architectural styles that left evidence in the ground.

✔ Artifacts from distant places that show how much local residents participated in national or international economic systems.

✔ How neighborhoods developed, including the origins of social inequalities or poverty as opposed to wealthier sections of town.

✔ Evidence of gender-specific activities. Gender studies are increasingly important in historic archaeology. You can sometimes identify tangible signs of male- and female-related sites or areas in sites where each did different tasks. Typical female activity locations are boarding houses, religious communities, missions, orphanages, hospitals, and even houses of prostitution. Common tasks such as washing clothes or feeding boarders leave many distinctive artifacts like laundry tubs and bleach bottles or kitchen utensils and tableware.

✔ Artifacts pointing to the ethnicity of a site's inhabitants. Ethnicity is a little harder to see archaeologically, as I describe in Chapter 11. Historic sites tend to show more when you know a little about who was there. The smallest artifact may indicate how traditional practices were kept or changed as various groups moved in and changed.

✔ Particular kinds of sites or remains that give information on illegal and other questionable activities. Archaeologists have excavated 19th-century opium dens in the western U.S. and houses of prostitution in New Orleans. I've even documented a 1930s moonshine still hidden in the Florida swamps.

Here are a couple examples of archaeological work that has shed some light on the daily life of the recent past:

✔ Studies of historic human skeletal remains indicate changing health patterns. *Rickets* (a bone-deforming vitamin D deficiency caused by lack of sunlight) was common among the rich in 17th- and 18th-century England. Wealthy folks who could lounge around indoors all day were more susceptible, and the poor who worked outside on farms were fine. But as England industrialized, this pattern changed. Skeletons from the 19th century show rickets was widespread among the urban poor because they worked indoors all day and walked where sunlight was cut off by tall buildings and narrow streets (not to mention the growing air pollution in manufacturing towns).

✔ Archaeologists knew from historic records that a mid 19th-century California neighborhood was occupied by Chinese miners. Excavations at a boarding house site unearthed Chinese artifacts but also British ceramics and food remains showing standard Euro-American diets. Sites of merchants' homes produced more typical Chinese porcelain and bones of pork, chicken, and Asian fishes. The interpretation was that wealthier merchants and boarding house owners lived more traditionally but bought cheaper stuff like California fish and British dishes from American agents to use even for their Chinese lodgers and staff at the boarding house.

Industrial archaeology

Industry and technology leave lots of complex archaeological remains. Whether standing ruins or features in the ground, the physical evidence of old mills, mines, bridges, and other structures tells you the history of technology and engineering; it's the heritage of the early Industrial Revolution. Here are some examples of what archaeologists can find:

✔ Machinery once powered by water or steam.

✔ Slag and other waste from ore processing.

✔ Waste from brick-making kilns or potteries.

✔ Ruins of railway constructions.

✔ Remnants of aqueducts, water towers, and other systems.

✔ Artifact assemblages that show social and economic processes like how the working classes were treated or how individual enterprise succeeded from small beginnings.

✔ Past industrial processes that may even reveal less wasteful technologies worth reexamination for their energy-saving virtues.

Industrial sites in the American East and South include many locations for obtaining *naval stores,* which were timber and other supplies for shipbuilding. These sites are sawmills, turpentine stills (where resin from pine trees was processed), and camps for workers, whose lives of labor are poorly known outside the archaeology of their houses.

Industrial archaeology explores the roots of the modern world. You can see change from traditional family-oriented, agriculturally-based communities in which everyone knew everyone else to a larger society based on market economics, industry efficiency, specialization, and material progress.

Military and battlefield archaeology

You'd think that the precise recorded detail required by military institutions would leave nothing unknown. But excavations of military sites from forts to battlefields fill in lots of details about strategies, events, lives and deaths.

Military sites

Archaeological investigations at military *installations* (any kind of camp, base, or support post) are growing in popularity. Such studies demonstrate previously unknown historic details, many of which can be valuable data for military historians and planners today.

Here are some examples of what archaeologists are doing at military sites:

- ✔ Determining whether a fort was actually constructed according to the historic plan in the original documents (if they were even preserved).

- ✔ Digging up finds at forts and other installations that show details of *procurement* (how they got supplies), construction techniques, locational strategies, weapons, storage, hospitals, and camp layout. Personal things soldiers used most of the time, when they weren't fighting (like parts of clothing, musical instruments, and leisure items), are often in the ground as well.

- ✔ Seeing differences between the material conditions experienced by ordinary soldiers and by officers and others.

- ✔ Digging at prisoner-of-war camps to get insights into captivity conditions and daily lives of prisoners.

Battlefield survey and excavation

Battlefield archaeology is a growing field that uses metal detectors and forensic techniques to locate and interpret evidence. (See the following section for more on forensic archaeology.) You can discover information about tactics and movements of units and individuals from the distributions of artifacts. Even across a vast landscape where conflict took place, material culture is patterned in particular ways. You see what happened from the viewpoint of the individuals fighting.

Battlefield sites from the U.S. Civil War, World War II, and even older conflicts in Europe back to the Roman Empire are all giving up archaeological secrets.

You may have heard the story of General Custer and his 7th Cavalry at the Battle of the Little Bighorn in Montana in 1876. The Lakota and Cheyenne Indians won overwhelmingly, but now archaeology has corrected some details. Finds uncovered include army equipment, different bullets from army and Native American guns, metal arrowheads, spent cartridges, clothing and personal items, and even skeletons of the horses that died in the fight. Ballistics and other firearms and weapons studies show that the Native Americans actually outnumbered, outgunned, and outstrategized Custer. Human bones provided information on individual victims and indicated that the lives of soldiers in general were pretty rough — they had bad teeth and used lots of coffee and tobacco. One victim was identified as a mixed white-Sioux civilian scout for Custer who had warned the general not to fight.

Understanding Modern Society and Behavior from Artifacts

The *archaeological method* — examining human behavior from the starting point of the artifact itself — gives you lots of otherwise unknown knowledge about your own society. Looking at the stuff people have and how and where they use it is a way of finding out information about consumer choices and other behavior you just can't get from sociology studies or market surveys. In Chapter 2, I describe how *garbology,* the archaeology of modern household garbage and landfills, provides previously unimagined knowledge of economic systems, waste, and spending.

In the following sections, I give you some other examples of how archaeological research is useful today to solve crimes, market products, and understand what people really do with their material possessions.

Forensic archaeology

Forensic archaeology studies material evidence at crime scenes for legal investigation. As I detail in Chapter 3, it involves the meticulous archaeological methods of mapping, excavating, and analyzing the distributions of objects to figure out what happened. You discover hidden stories and details of the nastier side of society. With forensic biological anthropologists (who analyze human bones) and other specialists, you study everything from individual victims' burials or sites of violence to mass graves resulting from genocide. Even mapping blood spatters is archaeology! So is using luminol on the artifacts. *Luminol* is a chemical that shows traces of blood invisible to the naked eye (you've seen this on crime-scene shows); it makes them glow in the dark, even years later and after burial. (Just for fun, I've tested it with my own blood!)

Radios and cars as artifacts

Two famous studies of everyday items establish archaeology as a different method for understanding consumer behavior and business strategies of Western culture. Economic historians say Japanese manufacturing and marketing genius overtook America's in consumer electronics by the mid-20th century. But examination of the types of old radios, as well as original company documents, tells a contradictory story through historic archaeology.

The portable radio was actually invented and first made in America. But sophisticated adults weren't enthusiastic about its tinny sound or appearance as a toy or novelty item. The Japanese, also interested in miniaturization, then took up production of them and succeeded enormously — not due to their creativity, but to an accident of timing. The late 1950s saw the emergence of rock-and-roll and a sudden emphasis on youth and mobility. The cheap, shirt-pocket transistor radio became crucial for teen culture and was a hit. The sudden popularity of the artifact shows the picture of culture change and social transformation.

Another archaeological study documents the interaction of people and artifacts in the case of the electric car. Traditional economic history says that many types of self-propelled vehicles emerged in about 1900, but gasoline power was clearly superior to steam or electricity. Examination of the cars themselves gives you other perspectives — the story becomes one of the archaeology of gender and class. Early electric cars were clean, quiet, simple, and convenient for short hops around town. They were perfect for doctors, salesmen, and especially women (who were typically the errand-runners). Gasoline-powered vehicles were expensive, unreliable, noisy, and stinky, and you had to get out in the mud to crank them up. But they were fast and went a lot farther before refueling — just what farmers far from town, wealthy tourists, and men in general wanted. Gasoline prevailed, but now that electric cars are returning for reasons of energy conservation, saving the planet, and gas prices, electricity may have the last laugh.

Archaeology of cellphones and communication

A 2007 study used archaeological methods to get information on cellphone distribution and use (by culture, gender, and other social categories) previously unknown to the industry's engineering and marketing folks. More men carry phones in pockets, and more women have them in purses (resulting in more missed calls for women). Belt pouches for men are popular in China but not as popular in Japan or Italy. In general, people in Asia seem to love phone covers, decorative straps, and hanging charms.

Much of the patterning was tied with communications strategies. Most cellphones are used for talking with just a few people and for last-minute planning and meetings; land lines are more frequently used for formal business and organizational functions. People tend to use text messaging more for intimate communications, e-mail for more official reasons and sending files, and instant-messaging for having the communication channel open while doing other things. The most frequent and advanced users of fancy communications technology were immigrants talking or sending webcam imagery to folks back home.

Archaeology of everyday items and technologies

Many other recent technologies can be explained very differently when you look at what the artifact can tell you about society. New work on the history of the pencil, for example, is really archaeology, demonstrating how this simple item reflects social transformations and economic change. Items that once were common in your home or workplace — floppy disks, film for cameras, videotapes, cassette tapes (not to mention vinyl records, typewriters, or carbon paper!) — are rapidly becoming artifacts of the past that will need good archaeological interpretation!

No matter how you live or what behavior is included in your day, you interact with material culture at every moment. So think about what the archaeology of your stuff says about you.

Public drinking in the historic American West

You never know when you may find cool indicators of ethnicity, class, gender, or other social categories. A recent study compared results of excavations at different saloons operating in Virginia City, Nevada, during the gold- and silver-mining boom of the late 1800s. The poorly known lives of miners were illuminated by finds like musical instruments, decanters, and Tabasco sauce bottles. A German-owned opera house saloon and an African-American establishment produced more elaborate furnishings and food remains than two other contemporaneous saloons. All of these places were typically considered to be hangouts for men, but DNA on a white clay pipe stem from the African-American saloon proved to be from a woman. Buttons and beads also confirmed a female presence.

Part V

Archaeology Is for Everyone

By Rich Tennant

"Never ask a retired archaeologist to go find something in the basement."

In this part . . .

All archaeology these days is public archaeology, so in Part V, I explain what all that designation includes. Chapter 16 defines public archaeology, heritage, and preservation of the past and shows you practical applications of archaeological knowledge in today's world. Chapter 17 lists the many ways you can get involved in learning, visiting, and doing archaeology. Chapter 18 describes the latest hot archaeological controversies and why you should care about them.

Chapter 16

The Uses of Archaeological Findings

*Y*ou may have the impression that archaeologists are researchers confined to their digs or laboratories and publishing their findings in obscure academic journals. But nowadays, archaeology is everywhere, and archaeologists have to be aware! In this chapter, I show you how everything you do in archaeology relates to public concerns and how different kinds of people and groups are interested in what you do as an archaeologist. Different uses of your archaeological findings can be for many, sometimes opposing purposes!

All Archaeology Is Public Archaeology

Archaeology has a duty to publicize its knowledge of the entire human past. You can't just get into your trench and dig, or sequester yourself in the lab to piece together potsherds. Your findings have meaning in the wider world, and people know that!

What public archaeology is

Public archaeology includes all of the following:

✔ Any digging or investigation done with public money or support.

✔ Any archaeological investigation done in a public place, with onlookers and maybe even participants who are members of the public.

✔ Archaeology done with descendant communities, people related biologically or culturally to the past people you're investigating.

✔ Your archaeological findings written up not only in fancy academic journals but also in publicly available, popular forms (books, articles, brochures, Web sites, pamphlets, videos, and so on).

✔ Media presentations of archaeology, from books to TV to films.

✔ *Cultural resources management* (CRM) archaeology, which is survey to locate sites, sometimes excavate them, and save the information before they're destroyed by construction or other land disturbance.

✔ *Community heritage* archaeology, tying past people and their activities to present groups in the same community, related or not.

✔ *Amateur* or *avocational* archaeology, which involves people doing it for fun or hobby (usually with the help and supervision of professionals).

✔ Museum displays and other interpretations of the human past in general or at a particular place and time.

✔ Educational archaeology for schoolkids, adults, or any other groups.

✔ Heritage conservation and historic preservation, whether in lawmaking, lobbying, or other advocacy for preserving archaeological and historic sites and structures.

✔ *Archaeo-tourism* and community economic development — earning money from visitors interested in viewing local evidence of the past.

✔ Application of archaeological knowledge to modern human issues and problems — in other words, applied anthropology. (See Chapter 3 for more on applied anthropology.)

How public archaeology is funded and publicized

Most archaeology is funded by public money, government grants or contracts. Some private foundations offer grants, and other times it's paid for by private firms who need to do cultural resources management investigations to conform with public laws before they build something. (For more on cultural resources management, check out Chapter 3.) In all cases, you report on your work and findings to the funding agency and also to any other interested parties.

Funding agencies

Because archaeology is labor- and equipment-intensive, most archaeologists write proposals to request support for their work. Lists of places to go for funding are in libraries and university research offices and also online. Potential funding sources are national and state government granting agencies, public and private entities that need contract archaeology done to comply with laws, and private foundations. Reading the agency's mission statement and proposal guidelines gives you an idea of whether it's appropriate for the kind of project you want to do. The key to writing a good proposal is tying your archaeological research to the philosophy and aims of the granting agency.

Bringing the work to the public

Always consider involving the public in your archaeological research somehow. Your dig volunteers and knowledgeable local residents can be enormously useful in excavation, lab work, and even supporting and publicizing your project. After the dig, it's only fair to let everyone know how the analyses are proceeding and what knowledge the project produced.

No matter who helps you or funds you, you have the obligation to finish your archaeological work and make it available. Writing and other publicity for the general audience is just as important as your professional report. Here are some tips for public presentation of your archaeological research:

- ✔ Compose a press release to describe (properly) the details of the archaeological investigations and send it to local news media.

- ✔ Write a popular report on the project along with the professional report you submit to the funding agency. Some U.S. federal agencies actually require a popular report for big projects.

- ✔ Give talks at the community library, civic association, or local school on the archaeological work and finds.

- ✔ Produce a newsletter or regular bulletin showing how the laboratory analyses are going and what new revelations have occurred as bags of artifacts are processed in the lab.

- ✔ Create (and update) a Web site to show what's new in the research.

- ✔ Include photos of volunteers, other supporters, and community people in all this publicity.

Recognizing Different Stakeholders in the Past

Many different people and groups have an interest in archaeological work. Here's a partial list of who these *stakeholders* may be:

- ✔ Other archaeologists — professionals, students, and amateurs.
- ✔ The general public.
- ✔ Owners, managers, and users of the land.

- ✔ Descendants of the past people being studied by the archaeological work, including supposed or claimed descendants, even those with religious or mystical connections.

- ✔ Local residents of the area where you are doing the archaeology.

- ✔ People who don't even care about archaeology but have some interest in the land. (See Chapter 8 for my tale of a forgotten stakeholder — the officials pointing out unauthorized parking for the crew's vehicles on our campus dig.)

- ✔ People wanting to use the archaeology for other purposes, such as preventing construction in their neighborhood, bringing tourists and commerce, or identifying with the heritage of the past for traditional, sentimental, or political reasons.

- ✔ Artifact collectors, both ethical ones and unethical looters and treasure hunters interested in selling artifacts for private gain.

Digging up someone's ancestors and traditions

Every archaeological project investigates someone's ancestors' stuff. You're obliged to find out who this someone is, if at all possible. Many laws concern the exposure and excavation of human skeletons, but whether obliged by law or not, you should consult with descendant communities to make sure you're doing nothing disrespectful to their human burials, sacred sites, or artifacts. You want to bring the knowledge of the community or ethnic group's past to those there today, not trample all over it.

All archaeologists know this ethical requirement, but a few ignore it. Others genuinely want to do it but can't because the remains are so ancient or decayed that no specific descendants are known.

Identifying people's heritage

Archaeology is useful in identifying the heritage of a particular people. Sometimes the archaeological interpretation fuels ethnic pride and identity very nobly. Other times it can cause controversy in contested regions. Still other times the heritage is commercialized for profit.

Here are examples of archaeological documentation of a people's heritage:

- ✔ In 2007, archaeologists uncovered a 2,000-year-old mansion under a parking lot right outside the walls of Jerusalem's Old City. The location is now an Arab neighborhood in the place known as the City of David, where the poor once lived. Jewish texts mention one wealthy family there: that of Queen

Helene of Adiabene. The family had ruled a region in Iraq (Adiabene) before they came to Jerusalem, converted to Judaism, and helped the poor. Their home was destroyed, along with the rest of the city, when the Romans put down a Jewish revolt in A.D. 70. The size and luxury of the house suggest it was Helene's; artifacts included pottery, stone items, and coins. The dig is controversial: Israel captured East Jerusalem from Jordan in the 1967 Mideast War; some Jewish groups want control of Palestinian property in this neighborhood, but Palestinians want this area of the city for the capital of a future state.

✔ A religious congregation got archaeologists to examine the site of the first Anglican church in northern Virginia. The 1740 Elk Run Church, which was abandoned in 1806 and had its construction materials carried off for use elsewhere. Over several years, volunteers including Boy Scouts and 4-H club members excavated the building's cross-shaped foundations and discovered an adjacent cemetery as well. Finds included window glass, nails, ceramics, plaster, and brick fragments. The community wants to preserve the place as a historic park to show its illustrious past; after all, the first rector of the church was a grandfather of a U.S. Supreme Court justice.

✔ Any construction in Rome exposes archaeological remains in the ground. In 2008, digging for a much-needed subway line encountered important ruins all along the way. Finds from the imperial period included a palace and homes with kitchens containing pots and pans. Archaeologists also uncovered Roman tombs, a 6th-century copper factory, 8th-century pavements, and a bit of a famous medieval road. Conservation laws ended up delaying the subway project, but what's saved (or uncovered, documented, and then either destroyed or reburied) is far more than ever before. Most construction in Rome has destroyed its past evidence. Medieval folks mined Roman ruins for blocks to make their own houses. Building the first subway in 1937, Mussolini's workers obliterated many famous ruins and carted away untold amounts of relics to dumps.

Finding the excluded past

Sometimes community heritage has been deliberately lost, excluded, or stifled. Archaeology can recover this heritage by unearthing the tangible evidence of ethnic and national traditions. Material culture can document a people who've been discriminated against or stuck in a category based on their physical appearance or ethnic or religious background.

A recent dig in Warsaw, Poland, uncovered the remains of the famous Saxon Palace. Originally the 17th-century home of a court official, it was expanded by a Polish king in the 18th century and enlarged again in the 1830s by a Russian merchant. The palace became a Nazi headquarters when the Germans took over Poland before World War II, and it was then blown up in 1944 by the retreating German army (who'd also destroyed most of the rest of the city

Slaves in New York: The African burial ground

The site of a planned 34-story federal office building in New York City became the center of a public archaeology controversy in the 1990s. Old city maps showed a mid-18th-century "Negro Burial Ground" at this location outside the boundaries of New Amsterdam, the Dutch town that later became New York. The first archaeologists hired to investigate thought there'd be nothing left of this cemetery after two centuries of development and land filling, but problems arose when more digging exposed many burials, and a backhoe even destroyed some skeletons. People criticized the original inadequate research design and the lack of communication with the African-American community descended from the people buried there. Many thought it was disrespectful to dig up graves, and black communities, the first African-American mayor of New York, and other politicians pressured for changes in strategy. Eventually, over 400 burials were excavated (and an estimated 200 graves probably remain in the area around Broadway all the way down to City Hall). The whole cemetery was estimated to stretch over six city blocks and contains about 20,000 people (both slaves and free blacks) buried from the 1690s to 1790s. (New York didn't abolish slavery until 1827.) Construction of the building was halted in order to dig and preserve the remains and redesign the planned building to include a memorial center.

No tombstones or other records exist for the dead, but the skeletons and other evidence show all were Africans. Artifacts include beads of glass, amber, and cowrie shells, as well as a few decorated coffins, one with an African symbol. The bones show signs that these people performed very hard labor. One skeleton had a musket ball lodged in the ribs.

The National Park Service declared the area a historic landmark, and the visitor center has displays for the public to learn about this hidden dimension of history. These remains of New York's ancestral African community were reburied with solemn rites to commemorate their sad stories, as many dignitaries and thousands of people attended the ceremonies. Some artifacts around the burials were replicated for the display, with the originals reburied in the coffins. Archaeologists learned an important lesson — you need dialogue with everyone affected by the past! The public got other lessons. You never learn in your school history books that New York had the second-largest enslaved population (after South Carolina) in the early 1800s, and that early New York was built by those slaves.

without regard for the historic record lost in the process). Now it's producing amazing archaeological finds from all these time periods. Artifacts include everyday items like tiles and pottery and valuables like sculptures and even a 19th-century diamond ring dug out of a toilet! Nazi-era discoveries included helmets and even dangerous unexploded artillery, as well as a surprising secret tunnel connecting the building's wings. A basement casino had artifacts like wine corks, bar receipts, and even betting slips.

Once a center from which invaders had crushed Polish independence, the palace is now an important national symbol. It will be rebuilt to house the city government and archaeological displays, restoring pride in Polish tradition and identity. Emotional attachment to the site is so great that prominent people of opposing political views all want to protect it and benefit from the archaeology.

Archaeology reconstructs hundreds of thousands of years of prehistory and historic times for everyone. Most archaeologists understand and comply with laws protecting skeletal remains and graves. A few cases have garnered huge publicity because something went wrong in the process of trying to respect the multiple views and often opposing political uses of the past.

Archaeology's Political Nature

The different stakeholders listed in the preceding sections may have conflicting aims. Different groups may claim they should control the excavation and interpretation of the archaeological record, not to mention the artifacts and other finds.

Finding out who's interested

Most archaeologists understand the political nature of the past and make efforts to locate anyone with an interest in what's being dug up. Sometimes you forget or don't know about particular groups, or you just don't realize the full implications of the research. Some arguments can be resolved by just sitting down for a conversation with everyone involved. Other controversies remain for decades or centuries, such as the dispute over who should have the Elgin marbles from Greece, now in the British Museum. (See Chapter 2 for the story on these artifacts.)

Taking authenticity and value into account

Sometimes just preserving something gives it value and makes it useful in various arguments; it can even generate economic gain. But standards of authenticity aren't valid for all times and cultures. Restoring ruins may damage the original traces, and reconstruction may destroy authenticity.

The arguments over who owns the past, what is the reality of the past, and who controls archaeological remains are constant, whether the subject is a standing building or a custom of your ancestors. (I've seen fights over whose cookie recipe is closest to grandma's original family tradition.) So when you do archaeology, you have to anticipate these disagreements.

Changing meanings of the past

Just like history keeps getting revised with new, sometimes contradictory analyses, archaeology and its finds continually change in meaning. You see deliberate attempts to manipulate the past, retell the story differently, and invent new traditions or claims to power by association with powerful sites, graves, and artifacts, regardless of whether they have any real connection.

You often get destruction right along with preservation. An Italian restaurant whose main counter is a piece of a 2,000-year-old Roman column is both paying homage to the past and aiding in its destruction by making it desirable to use pieces of the ancient artifacts in the present.

Interpretations of Stonehenge (shown back in Figure 13-5) have changed dramatically over the years, because of new archaeology but also because of people wanting to be part of its mystery and symbolism. It was a gathering place and monument aligned with the summer sun, built between 3,000 and 1,500 B.C., but it changed in function and meaning over time. Peoples of later centuries had the existing circle of standing stones as an already-ancient monument and made their own physical additions and added meanings. Today New-Agers, hippies, pyramid-power folks, drug dealers, neo-Druids, and families on holiday all gather there at the summer solstice, each finding some connection with the powerful, visible past (and leaving new material remains of garbage). One archaeologist (jokingly) suggested that Stonehenge's configuration could even make it a space ship landing pad as well!

Archaeology provides details not found in the photos, written records, or oral traditions of a community or ethnic group. Whether archaeological information contradicts these other sources or supports them, it gives additional voice to the people of the past, which can serve many purposes.

Collecting, Looting, and Selling Artifacts

Some types of stakeholders in the past are those who collect artifacts, sometimes for fun and with ethical concerns, and sometimes for the profit in selling to the highest bidder.

Ethical collectors

Avocational or amateur archaeologists usually collect on their land or in their own region to identify with the past there. Many are hunters and fishers who use the landscape as past people may have. Some even make their own stone tools and other craft items. Good collectors keep track of the *provenience* (location and other information) of their finds and work with professionals to document sites. They show you where their artifacts came from and allow you to take photographs. Like amateur astronomers discovering a new planet or comet, avocational archaeologists help advance archaeological knowledge.

Treasure hunting and looting

Pothunters or *looters* are undesirable types of collectors after artifacts for personal gain; they don't really care where anything came from or what it can reveal about past societies. They just want the relics to have or to sell for profit. This includes everyone from arrowhead hunters to underwater archaeology companies searching for treasure and wealth. They ignore (or worse, destroy) the scientifically priceless archaeological context to get some monetarily valuable objects. Chapter 2 discusses the differences between these folks and actual archaeologists.

Real archaeologists don't buy or sell artifacts. They consider this behavior highly unethical, just like a good surgeon wouldn't buy and sell kidneys or livers for profit. Archaeological resources belong to everyone.

A few archaeologists think that laws against looting (described in "Antiquities markets and laws" later in the chapter) are about as effective as drug laws or the prohibition of alcohol: People are going to do it anyway, so why not legalize it and then regulate and tax it? But artifacts are not drugs — they're *non-renewable resources*. After you damage or destroy an archaeological site, the record of the past there is lost forever.

Using reproductions to prevent looting

Many collectors are happy with reproductions of ancient and beautiful artifacts. I love buying these items at museum shops — they're useful for teaching but also lovely to display. And because they're copies, you don't have to worry if they get chipped or broken! You can also get archaeological replicas in fun formats like toys, postcards, and games; little kits let you excavate tiny buried pyramids or artifacts.

A few archaeologists say the market should be flooded with fakes to help conserve the real items. Others say copies can never replace the feelings of authenticity provided by the real things. But views of authenticity and value change. Many artifacts (like all those crystal skulls I mention in Chapter 2) have garnered huge prices only to be proven as modern frauds. And many artists' best works were completely unappreciated until they suddenly became fashionable and only then sold for record high amounts at auction.

Educating the public about looting

Many souvenir-hunters don't realize they're irreparably damaging the past. My own brother went on a Caribbean diving vacation and brought back a plate he'd grabbed from a shipwreck. As he proudly showed it to me, my

The disputed bones of Kennewick Man

Need more proof that you're better off to consult with all interested parties in advance? The following incident is a pretty good example of how *not* to do archaeology:

A human skeleton discovered near Kennewick, Washington, in 1996 became the subject of controversy and a legal challenge to the Native American Graves Protection and Repatriation Act (NAGPRA). Under this law, jurisdiction over ancient remains not clearly related to living native groups is hard to determine. The so-called Kennewick Man skeleton was thought to be of a Native American; a bone fragment was radiocarbon-dated to over 9,000 years of age, and a stone spear point was stuck in a hip bone. One anthropologist claimed the skeleton looked "Caucasian," which was interpreted to mean "white"; other experts said the bones appeared closest to those of ancient people in northern Japan. Five different Indian tribal groups claimed descent from the skeleton, as did a group of California white people claiming to follow an old Viking religion. The Indians wanted the skeleton for reburial, but archaeologists wanted to study it first because so far they know little about people of such ancient times in North America. Some Native Americans said their religious beliefs both prevented study of the bones and proved that they'd always lived in that region. Scientists and one tribe went to court to gain control over the bones; a U.S. Appeals court finally ruled that these Indians didn't have a clear relationship with remains that old. The controversy became so heated that the federal government agency controlling the land buried the site in loads of dirt to prevent further investigation. Some scientific studies of the bones continued, but DNA recovery is proving difficult. The controversy and legal actions continue, and the skeleton sits locked in a museum.

Many books, articles, and Web sites on the Kennewick case show the continuing dispute boils down to a few clear arguments: Scientists say that study of the bones has benefits for all, and that the skeleton may show little biological relationship with modern Native Americans, but it can help determine the process of colonization of the New World from Asia. Native American groups say that their oral histories document how they've been in North America for thousands of years and that the skeleton is their ancestor because it's from their land. Scientific study is disrespectful and a violation of their religious beliefs, and they want immediate reburial. Watch for new legislative action or scientific information related to the Kennewick case in the near future.

horrified look made him say, "What's wrong? I only took one thing, and it's just a plain dish. You're an archaeologist — you should love this!" I had to explain that what he did was plundering and get him to think about what would happen if everyone did it. Many people are just not aware (or aren't willing to see) the consequences of their actions. Fortunately, archaeological and historic sites, parks and monuments, museums and kids' camps are all beginning to teach the public to be enlightened stewards of their own human heritage and not damage the material remains of the past.

I like the slogan used to protect endangered species of flowers or other things in parks because it's equally applicable to visiting archaeological sites: "Take nothing but photos; leave nothing but footprints."

Antiquities markets and laws

Most countries have national laws and international agreements that prevent importing or exporting *antiquities* (archaeological artifacts). The strongest international document, signed by over 90 countries (including the U.S. and Britain), is the "Means of Prohibiting the Illicit Import, Export and Transfer of Ownership of Cultural Property" from the 1970 United Nations Environmental, Scientific and Cultural Organization (UNESCO) Convention. This agreement allows member nations to recover stolen or illegally exported antiquities from other member nations. Many states and smaller government entities also have antiquities regulations, as well as laws against disturbing human skeletal remains and graves.

The UNESCO Convention agreement and other such declarations have helped curb some of the trade in artifacts, but these rules are very hard to enforce and have different interpretations in different places. Most are later 20th-century rules and do permit traffic in specimens obtained over 50 or 100 years ago (which covers most of the looted artifacts in most of the world's museums). Luckily, well-meaning collectors, museum staff, and archaeologists are realizing that selling the material items from the past means destroying the sites and the human story, of which very little is left.

Combating the desire to collect and own unique ancient treasures is difficult. Art dealers, auction houses, and wealthy collectors lobby against historic preservationists and archaeologists (and those groups' lobbyists) to influence legislation.

Relating the Archaeological Story to the Present

You want to see how people lived in the past, not only to contribute to archaeological knowledge but also to preserve what's been discovered and discover more about human nature — your own heritage! Scientific and humanistic knowledge is valuable for its own sake, of course, in expanding intellectual frontiers. But you can also derive very practical lessons from archaeology's finds: ideas to help deal with issues in the modern world.

Israeli–Palestinian peace through archaeology?

In April 2008, a team of Israeli, Palestinian, and American archaeologists announced a landmark agreement concerning archaeological sites and remains; they hoped this document could be part of a Middle East peace process. They'd worked in secret for five years to try to protect some 6,000 archaeological sites and thousands of artifacts in the area of the West Bank and East Jerusalem.

Amid all the enormous conflict and political disputes existing since long before Israel occupied those territories in 1967, they wanted to cooperate to protect the past that's so important to all parties today, as well as to the rest of the world. The sites (and collections already excavated from them) contain evidence of many different archaeological cultures over thousands of years. But claims of ownership or control of physical space and objects have seriously hampered scientific study. For Jews, the material remains establish Jewish claims and history; for the Palestinians, they are stolen property.

Some thoughtful critics say a better accord would change the ideological foundations of nationalist archaeology. But perhaps *any* compromise will help recognize a shared archaeological heritage in this region and make a contribution in the wider political arena.

Saving the past for the future

A huge part of public archaeology is conservation of sites, artifacts and other materials, and records. This process is laborious, time-consuming, expensive, and difficult (for some details, see my discussion of curation and collections management in Chapter 9). But it's necessary work if you're going to have the resources to study! Archaeologists may team up with heritage specialists, legal experts in cultural properties, legislators, and preservationists to try to save threatened sites.

Why save or dig more when so much is excavated and known already? Actually, most of the human past is a big mystery. And science develops new questions as it answers others. Think of how much more you know now that radiocarbon dating, trace element and DNA analyses are possible. Much of the lost human record can be recovered.

Telling the human drama of the past

Your archaeological reconstructions telling the drama of how earlier people dealt with various problems faced by any human group is often very moving. Readers can identify with both great tragedies (such as a natural disaster like the volcanic eruptions at Pompeii) and everyday issues (such as how to get food, water, love, and devotion).

Enjoying the connection with the past

In many countries you can't go anywhere without seeing a reference to the glorious past known through archaeology. Though an obvious one, Italy isn't the only example (although of course Roman stuff is everywhere). But many nations feature ruins and artifacts on their currency, stamps, flags, and designs of public buildings. They often take a fierce pride in these relics. For example, the ancient temple at Angkor Wat is a national symbol of Cambodia. Its picture has been on the country's flag for nearly 150 years, and it's also on the currency. In 2003, riots erupted in response to a false rumor that a Thai celebrity had claimed Angkor once belonged to Thailand! (See Chapters 14 and 20 for more on Angkor Wat.)

In the U.S., regional establishments sometimes feature connections with the Native American past, and government buildings or banks may hearken back to classical Roman or Greek styles. Immigrant groups may bring some of their heritage for entertainment and education too. And museums exhibit the glories of many ancient cultures.

In Color Figure 16, I show you a fun combination of artifact replicas that serve public archaeology well. After seeing the traveling exhibit of King Tut's treasures when it came to Florida, I had to buy an inflatable Egyptian mummy doll in the gift shop. Then I carried it with me as our group went into a Mexican restaurant in Fort Lauderdale that celebrated its heritage with reproductions of Olmec heads on the walls. The combination of plastic Egypt and plaster Mexico of the past was too colorful a celebration of different ancient traditions not to photograph!

Practical Applications of Archaeology

In all the knowledge archaeology produces about everything from daily life to the regimes of kings, you can find useful tidbits everywhere. Findings about what past human systems worked (or didn't work) have valuable practical uses today. Details of ethnic, community, or national heritage and tradition are useful in expanding identity and pride in the past, as well as gaining political power and support. Forensic archaeology gives real knowledge of crime scenes and of mass graves from war and genocide and scenes of natural and human disasters.

Past technologies can be valuable too: If you happen to survive a nuclear holocaust, you'll be much better off if you know some archaeology and can make a few stone tools and net bags!

Archaeology and warfare

Warfare is one of the hardest situations for protecting archaeological resources; you're thinking of human lives, not ancient sites and artifacts. But the heritage of war-torn countries takes a real beating, especially when looting goes unchecked.

Operation Iraqi Freedom resulted in thefts of tens of thousands of artifacts from both the display galleries and the storerooms in the National Museum of Antiquities in Baghdad. Huge stone sculptures, clay tablets, and many famous pieces pictured in archaeology books for decades were gone. Even databases were taken or damaged, so nobody could fully document the extent of the losses. The world reaction was outrage; not only were these artifacts the cultural heritage of the Iraqi people, but they were also the Mesopotamian foundations of Western civilization. Public media attention and Internet stories, including photos of the items taken, resulted in thwarting antiquities smugglers in many countries. About half the artifacts have been returned.

In early 2008, for example, Syria returned over 700 specimens, from pots to gold necklaces, to the Baghdad Museum, with great ceremony. Other artifacts were actually still in Iraq, where they'd been secretly hidden away to prevent just such treasure hunting. The loss is still great, but it's actually minimal compared to the destruction still being perpetrated by looters with pickaxes around the Iraqi countryside at archaeological sites, including many that are unexcavated or not even documented.

Human-environment interaction

Probably the biggest contribution of archaeology to modern society is the information on how humans affected their environments and were affected by them over the long and very long term.

Getting along in different regions

Archaeological remains show you daily details of how people used available natural resources in different regions and learned to live in deserts, mountains, wetlands, and even the frozen north. You see how they perfected techniques for obtaining plants and animals and in many places came to produce their own food. You also see failures. For example, according to their archaeological remains, medieval Vikings who settled Greenland continued to live as Europeans, keeping their traditional foods (grains, cattle, goats, sheep) and clothes (wool) rather than adapting Arctic native ways (eating the abundant seafood and wearing warmer furs). They did well while the climate was favorable, but the colony died out when it got colder.

Climate change and natural disasters

A valuable process that's very visible in the archaeological record is the ability of humans to adapt (or not) to changing natural environments. In Chapter 13, I describe how the first massive global warming at the end of the

Pleistocene (Ice Age) led to changes in human hunting, probable increase in fishing, and eventually domestication and control of plants and animals.

How people got along in different ecosystems also includes how they reacted to earthquakes, storms, volcanoes, or other disasters that destroyed both the natural and built environment. Some societies failed completely or abandoned the region after a disaster. Others survived, rebuilt, and carried on in the old and sometimes new ways. Volcanic-ash-covered Pompeii (discussed in Chapter 15) is one example, but archaeology provides countless others. Archaeologists in Arkansas are now researching large soil features that indicate big earthquakes at different prehistoric times, and linear sand-filled cracks from smaller quakes. Combining this geological evidence with the artifact finds and cultural features, they can reconstruct how human settlement changed over centuries in response to these disasters.

Human-made environmental damage

Archaeology demonstrates human impacts on environments, both destruction of ecosystems and how long it took for the natural resources to recover. You also see how people manipulated environmental resources, or harvested them in a sustainable fashion over the long term. Sometimes exploitation of different abundant materials allowed a culture to prosper for a time but perhaps led to a crash later. In Chapter 14, I describe the Indus Valley civilization, which thrived for centuries before disappearing around 1800 B.C. One suspected cause of its demise is the massive deforestation needed to fuel the ovens baking the millions of bricks required to build its cities. Sustainability studies, "green" construction design, and alternative energy research (all now the rage worldwide) draw from archaeological knowledge of how past people did things efficiently or wastefully.

The development and use of past technologies

Ancient and more recent historic technologies usable and desirable in the modern world are rediscovered in the archaeological evidence. These include ways of producing renewable energy through wind and water power, or making cool houses out of mud or adobe in hot climates. Also important are techniques of artifact manufacture in stone, bone, fiber, and other natural materials. Scientists are even investigating the lost, complex processes of producing medieval iron, steel, and other artifacts from archaeological digs. A recent materials study of the building blocks used to construct great pyramids of Egypt indicates that not all were carved limestone, which required great labor with only copper tools. Some appear to be of cast concrete that was easily transportable and poured on-site. The recipe of limestone particles mixed with silica-rich binder indicates Egyptians may have invented a cheap and non-polluting process for making long-lasting concrete.

Archaeology provides rich information on how a society's waste is disposed of and what it does to the landscape over the long term. In Chapter 2, I describe the archaeological digs into modern garbage dumps that show what's really disposable and degradable. In the ancient Mediterranean, archaeologists and other scientists have shown that Roman lead mining and metals industries produced a large amount of pollution 2,000 years before the Industrial Revolution. Lead was important for medicines, pots and pans, water pipes, even cosmetics, but it left its harmful traces both in soils and in human skeletons.

Prehistoric South American agriculture today

Prehistoric Peruvians had greater agricultural production than their modern descendants. They built canals and irrigation systems that brought water from mountain rivers far into the western desert coast. The systems lasted for centuries but were defeated not only by earthquakes, but also by slow tectonic movements of the ground that continually damaged the canals, even made them run uphill. Such damage apparently caused agricultural collapse that helped bring down prehistoric political regimes. While modern governments take pride in reusing ancient canals, they should heed the archaeological lesson that the Andes, young, continually rising mountains, may defeat these systems again.

On the other side of the Andes in northeastern Bolivia, archaeological discoveries are helping to promote sustainable agriculture. The tropical lowlands are either covered in water during the rainy season or parched in the dry season, seemingly not good for farming. But aerial photos showed a pattern of raised rectangular fields, now mostly filled in over the centuries. Archaeological excavation uncovered a system of canals and elevated plots where native people grew crops for over a thousand years, from 100 B.C. to A.D. 1100. Using experimental archaeology (discussed in Chapter 11), researchers dug out canals, piling nutrient-rich muck on the elevated plots. They worked with local farmers to grow corn, beans, manioc, and other crops. Archaeologists found similar long-abandoned raised fields in the highland plateau of Bolivia and Peru, around Lake Titicaca. These vast water-management systems once produced large agricultural yields to support great pre-Columbian civilizations. Excavation of the platforms and canals was accompanied by experimental archaeology here too. Scientists demonstrated that the canals next to the raised plots stored solar heat, kept the planted plots warmer, and prevented potato crops from destruction during a hard freeze.

Farmers today are now using these forgotten systems of indigenous knowledge in both areas. They require only simple tools and a modest investment in rural development, providing good economic support in these very poor regions.

Chapter 17

How You Can Explore Archaeology

*I*n this chapter, I show you many ways you can get involved in archaeology. One option is to become a real archaeologist yourself (which requires years of really hard work). But you can also get an informal archaeology education, volunteer for digs, and more. After you dive in, you may find even more archaeology out there than you'll be able to absorb.

Taking Archaeology Courses

Learning in person from a professional archaeologist is fun because you can get first-hand real-world information, ask questions, and even challenge interpretations. The following sections describe a few of the different routes you can take depending on your level of interest or amount of free time.

Lectures and short classes

You can hear professional archaeology lectures at museums and universities, local libraries, and even community centers that emphasize lifelong learning. Checking out these institutions and their scheduled programs is as easy as looking around your community, online, or in the phone book.

For a lengthier (but still short-term) option, consider week-long workshops or seasonal training programs in archaeology; these offerings usually include lectures in the classroom as well as digging. The following list gives you some examples of these programs:

- ✔ **Week-long archaeology camps** for kids or adults may be offered at museums in the summer.

- ✔ **Scouting groups** have some archaeology programs, like the Boy Scouts' merit badge in archaeology.

- ✔ **Elderhostel** programs for older folks usually include background lectures and field trips to see archaeology.

- ✔ **Universities** may have short-course offerings (right in there with piano lessons and conversational Spanish) for anyone who isn't a regular student enrolled for a degree.

- ✔ **Land management agencies or your State Historic Preservation Office** may have courses on cultural resources like archaeological and historic sites or short volunteer digs.

College archaeology courses

You can find full-fledged courses in archaeology at universities, colleges, some community and junior colleges, extended learning programs for adults, and various other places. You don't have to be a degree-seeking student to take a course — universities may even allow older people over a certain age to *audit* courses (attend classes without receiving credits) for free.

I enjoy having lots of different kinds of people in my classes — the diversity makes discussion more interesting because more kinds of opinions are involved. I sometimes let people sit in if I have room, even if they aren't registered through the university (don't tell my deans). And these folks often take more courses for credit later. I've even had retired folks who took a course for fun and then came back to enroll and earn bachelor's and even master's degrees.

College courses in archaeological method and theory, prehistory and historic archaeology, and historic preservation are valuable background for professionals in so many other fields. Here's why:

- ✔ You can discover something about your human heritage.

- ✔ You can get some practical information possibly directly applicable in your profession or everyday life.

Joining Archaeological Associations

Archaeological associations, societies, and clubs are everywhere. Some are national and international, but many are regional or based in a particular state and have smaller local chapters. Members are students, professionals, amateur archaeologists — really, anyone who's interested. Most require only the membership fee, which typically gets you a regular publication like a magazine along with information on new discoveries, activities you can participate in, and opportunities to join digs. Look for these online.

Be wary of looter or pothunter groups interested only in digging, collecting, buying, and selling rather than in preserving or carefully investigating the past. Most reputable organizations will have a code of ethics.

From international to local groups

Here are some good groups you can join (check their Web sites):

- ✔ **Archaeological Institute of America (AIA),** which sends you *Archaeology* magazine with your membership. You can also join local AIA chapters, which sponsor lecture programs and other events.

- ✔ **World Archaeological Congress,** which covers the globe and emphasizes professional and public archaeology and indigenous peoples' rights. It has an online newsletter and discussion forum that often highlights ethical dilemmas.

- ✔ **Society for American Archaeology (SAA),** which is for professionals but allows anyone to join, attend meetings, and receive the journal.

- ✔ **National archaeological societies,** in many countries and languages.

- ✔ **Regional societies** such as the Southeastern Archaeological Conference and Plains Anthropological Society, which all have annual meetings you can attend and regular journals for members.

- ✔ **State societies,** which also offer annual meetings, journals, and sometimes booths at the state fair! More amateurs and lay people are usually members of these groups, but also professionals and students.

- ✔ **Local clubs** or chapters of the state society, which (like the others) usually have a mix of members, a newsletter, and often monthly meetings and various activities (lectures, digs).

Professional groups

Some archaeological groups are only for professionals. You usually have to fill out an application, meet training qualifications, and pay a fee to be a member. Most of the time you need at least a master's degree. But these groups often have Web sites anyone can access, explaining great archaeology and new discoveries. The best-known of these societies:

- Register of Professional Archaeologists
- State-based professional societies such as the Arizona Archaeological Council and the Council of Virginia Archaeologists

Public Programs and Teacher Training

Many states, associations, and museums have public "archaeology day" or "archaeology month" programs for the general public, and often specific workshops for teachers, as well as traveling programs or speakers for schools. Teachers can get lesson plans for bringing archaeology into their classrooms in many published sources and online too. A good resource is the Society for American Archaeology Web site's link to their "Archaeology and Public Education" section. Museum shops offer artifact replicas and kids' archaeology books, as well.

Volunteering or Joining Archaeological Digs and Laboratories

You'll probably have a ball if you sign up for an archaeological project. Whether you're in the field digging or in the lab, you see first-hand how archaeology operates and what level of precision is necessary to interpret finds. Many opportunities are volunteer, and sometimes you pay a fee for the experience and training. Also keep in mind that most digs that take volunteers require participants to be of high-school age.

Joining a local dig

You can get involved in digging in a lot of ways; joining the local archaeology association (see the preceding section) is usually the easiest and cheapest method. One of the best programs is that of the Arkansas Archeological Society. For two and a half weeks every June, these folks train people in excavation, survey, and laboratory techniques. They work with state parks and Native

American groups to provide a comprehensive experience. Then these members are available for other digs, such as emergency excavations to salvage a site being destroyed.

It's getting harder to find volunteer opportunities where you don't have to pay (whether because of insurance concerns, because archaeological training is so specialized, because training and digs require lots of supervision, or because supplies cost so much). Sometimes you pay living costs only, or those costs on top of training fees.

Volunteer archaeology with no cost to the participants does occur — even in some of the societies noted above. Archaeology is labor-intensive, and professionals really need a workforce to get things done. Many welcome serious volunteers with the right attitude and ethics.

If you go to hear a speaker who's working on a project, ask afterwards about joining the project. Also, you can call universities and museums to ask if they have such opportunities (often labs in winter, digs in summer — for obvious reasons). I've had volunteer high school students and retired folks on digs during some field seasons and in the laboratory during the school year.

Joining digs across the country or abroad

Many organizations sponsor excavations that draw people from everywhere. This is a great way to plan a vacation! Here's a list of some of the best (along with some of their Web sites):

- ✔ **The Passport in Time Program** of the U.S. Department of Agriculture, Forest Service (USDA FS in federal lingo) takes volunteers for all kinds of archaeological projects. Head to www.passportintime.com to get started.

- ✔ **The Archaeological Institute of America (AIA)** lists fieldwork opportunities, both formal field schools and volunteer projects all over the world that you can sign up for. Costs vary widely.

- ✔ **The Center for American Archaeology** in Kampsville, Illinois, offers everything from single-day opportunities to workshops for adults to digs open to kids, adults, and families with children as young as 7. Costs vary from low to high; you can find more info at www.caa-archeology.org.

- ✔ **Crow Canyon Archaeological Center** in southwestern Colorado offers short and long programs for high-schoolers, adults, families, and teachers. Costs here also vary; check out the official Web site at www.crowcanyon.org.

- ✔ **Earthwatch Institute** offers opportunities to join scientific expeditions of all kinds, including archaeology. Participants volunteer their time and pay living expenses and fees (which can be steep if you're traveling to a faraway place). For information, go to www.earthwatch.org.

Becoming a Professional Archaeologist

You can spend many years joining digs and archaeology labs, really doing archaeology, and making contributions to the profession. But doing archaeology for a living requires much greater dedication!

You don't do archaeology to get rich and/or famous or to experience constant adventure, so if those are your goals, stop right here! You have to be ready for the tedium, endless paperwork, and even the prospect of redoing things in a different way after you've already finished them.

Education requirements

The lowest-level archaeology jobs require at least a bachelor's degree, usually in anthropology or classics, with an archaeological specialty. Courses required for the BA usually include all the sub-fields of anthropology, a formal archaeological field school, a lab course, and other science classes such as geology, biology, or geography. Supervisory positions usually require a master's degree. Additional courses in everything from historic preservation law to GIS (geographic information systems) and mapping techniques also enhance employment possibilities.

The most common skills archaeological employers require are these:

- ✔ The ability to put together a good archaeological research design.
- ✔ The ability to write very well.

Fancier jobs, from college professors to directors of archaeological companies or government programs, require a PhD with an archaeological specialty. They also require you to have experience so you can teach, organize research, direct projects and employees or students, write up research results, meet deadlines, and be cheerful about it all!

Job opportunities and realities

In Chapter 3, I describe all the many different kinds of archaeology you can do (and sometimes many kinds at the same time). In this section, I discuss the types of jobs you can get doing those different kinds of archaeology.

Most archaeology jobs don't pay well compared with other professions. Even geographers, geologists, biologists, and other specialists you'd think would be roughly equivalent usually earn far more than archaeologists. Pay, benefits, and working conditions also vary by location and employer, of course.

The good news is that archaeologists get that aura of romance about them that makes everyone else say, "Oh, I always wanted to do that!" You also get those rare thrills of discovery and, as a field archaeologist, good physical conditioning doing excavation.

Most of the archaeology jobs out there are contract archaeology work with private firms. Work in cultural resources management for national, state, or local government agencies is the next most common kind of archaeological occupation. Museum and academic jobs are rarer, as are jobs with private foundations and other non-profits.

Contract archaeology fieldworker

This job specialization is pretty well summed up by the term *shovel bum*. Requirements: usually a bachelor's degree or sometimes an associate's degree in anthropology, including field school and lab training.

Disadvantages:

- Lowest paying archaeological job; few or no benefits.
- Possibility of layoffs when work is scarce.
- Lots of travel to various survey and excavation projects around the state or country (although some think of this as an advantage).

Advantages:

- Usually the first to unearth exciting discoveries.
- (Almost) constantly doing something new and different.
- Experts in motel amenities.
- Get to do fieldwork and engage in healthy physical activity most of the time (unless you're assigned to the lab or report writing).
- Get experience while you're in school for an advanced archaeology degree, or move up to long-term employment with the company.

Contract archaeology supervisor or principal investigator

In this job, you organize and run the archaeological projects. Requirements: usually a master's degree or PhD and lots of archaeological experience.

Disadvantages:

- Have to write proposals to bring in survey and excavation jobs.
- Have to write reports on finished projects and meet strict deadlines.
- Get to do less fieldwork because of all the writing you have to do.

Advantages:

- ✔ Better pay, often salary and benefits.

- ✔ Potential to make neat discoveries in the laboratory while processing the field finds (see Chapter 10 for more on lab analysis and discovery).

- ✔ Can organize research and extract articles from your reports to publish or present at professional meetings.

- ✔ Possibility of promotion resulting in a (rare) higher-than-average archaeological salary.

Government archaeologist

Jobs with federal, state, and local government entities are available in every state of the U.S. and in most countries (though usually you must be a citizen of that country). Requirements: range from bachelor's degree to PhD, depending upon the position.

Disadvantages:

- ✔ Usually involves less fieldwork and more paperwork and regulatory activity (unless you like that kind of thing).

- ✔ Bewildering number of acronyms, official government spellings and procedures.

- ✔ May have to travel often or shift to new position or town without much choice.

Advantages:

- ✔ Usually good salary, benefits, and work hours.

- ✔ Get to review and participate in a great deal of archaeological research.

- ✔ Get to write *scopes of work* (directions and requirements) telling other archaeologists what to do on projects.

Museum or other non-profit foundation archaeologist

These jobs are rarer and often more varied. They include curator, collections manager, conservation specialist (who stabilizes fragile artifacts), and lab worker and may overlap with government jobs. Requirements: usually at least a bachelor's degree and specialized training.

Disadvantages:

- ✔ Usually low pay and average benefits.

- ✔ May never get to do fieldwork (though this may be an advantage if you're happy in the lab).

- ✔ May have to spend lots of time fund-raising.
- ✔ May have to do other work unrelated to archaeology. (I once had to take care of a hurt baby bird brought in by a museum visitor because I was the only museum scientist at work on a Saturday.)

Advantages:

- ✔ Can make neat discoveries from museum collections in the laboratory or use the collections for your own interesting research (which is usually encouraged by your employer).
- ✔ May get to work with artifacts and neat historic documents every day.
- ✔ Can work with specialists in other fields (biology, geology) who are right there in your museum.

Academic archaeologist

You can be a professor or instructor at a university, college, or community college. Requirements: usually a PhD

Disadvantages:

- ✔ Usually pretty low pay, average benefits.
- ✔ Long years of study — perhaps five to eight years past bachelor's degree.
- ✔ Fierce job competition.
- ✔ Whining students to teach (just kidding).
- ✔ Teaching and university committee requirements may leave little time for actual archaeological research and fieldwork.
- ✔ Requirements to do research and get it published to show you're worthy of being *tenured* (guaranteed a position based on fulfillment of requirements and length of service).
- ✔ Have to write grant and contract proposals to get funding for said fieldwork.
- ✔ No job security for about five years because you're not tenured (and none at all in newer universities that don't offer tenure).

Advantages:

- ✔ Non-academic peers think it's a more prestigious job. (They don't know about the low pay and whining students!)
- ✔ Flexible work schedule.
- ✔ Job security if you do get tenured.

✔ Summers off to do research and digs if you can get funding and good students who don't whine as much.

✔ The opportunity to teach others about the excitement of archaeology and mentor and train the next generation of archaeologists.

Other qualities needed to be a professional archaeologist

As you can see from the list of job requirements and conditions in the preceding section, being an archaeologist isn't easy. I've seen some professionals and even students in graduate school burn out and quit; I even know of an archaeology professor who left his perfectly fine university job to find a simpler life, and he became a bus driver!

Most professionals don't mind the stiff requirements, however, and this attitude is the key.

The thrill of the find is worth it, even if it's just the uncovering of a tiny, mundane artifact made centuries ago or the discovery of a great bar in your motel with free snacks during happy hour while you're writing your daily field notes. Mostly, you're honored that you get to be part of the continuing quest by humanity to understand itself — in the case of archaeology, over the very long term!

Chapter 18

Controversies and Sensational Findings

In This Chapter

▶ Exploring some famous archaeological discoveries

▶ Examining the mysteries of early peoples and migrations

▶ Understanding the controversial nature of many finds

*A*rchaeologists argue over both the tiny details and the wider meanings of many of their finds. You can document the material evidence pretty clearly, but then you may have many different explanations for it.

In this chapter, I describe some of my favorite recent archaeological controversies, with opposing interpretations by different archaeologists. You may even see some of the controversies on the news. I also describe some disputes between archaeologists and others (often groups with very different claims on the evidence of the past).

But many other sites, artifacts, and archaeological interpretations not discussed in this chapter are the subject of constant argument, at least in professional circles, if not in the popular press. The debate is part of the continual self-correction of science with each new finding. It's also part of the fun of archaeology — never knowing what you're going to learn next — even when it changes what you already thought! Such controversies show that archaeologists don't have a monopoly on their own finds. Public archaeology means the past is for everyone!

The Ice Man Cometh (and Other Archaeological Wonders)

Many archaeological investigations produce results of huge significance. Religious objects, traces of a lost heritage, or even an ancient human body itself trigger emotional responses, enormous publicity, and always controversy! The following sections show you some well-known cases and the hubbub that surrounded them.

The Ice Man

The frozen, 5,300-year-old Italian guy who melted out of a glacier in 1991 is a famous European celebrity. He was discovered by hikers in the high Alps; they thought he was just another recent lost climber because such corpsicles thaw out often. But his artifacts and radiocarbon dates proved he was from the late Neolithic-Copper Age. He'd died in a small depression at 10,500 feet elevation, and he'd been quickly covered in snow and ice and freeze-dried!

Unaware of the Ice Man's importance, authorities crudely hacked him out of the ice with ice axes — not the best archaeological technique! Both Italy and Austria claimed him until surveyors determined he was about 100 yards inside Italy. He was studied in Austria first then put in a special exhibition freezer in the South Tyrolean Archaeological Museum in Bolzano, Italy.

The man

Ötzi, as he was named (after the glacier where he was found), has been continuously tested and scrutinized. Here's what scientists have learned:

- ✔ He was between about 40 and 50 years old (pretty old for his time!) and about 5 feet, 5 inches tall.

- ✔ DNA and mineral studies of his teeth and bones show he grew up in a nearby valley and later lived in another one slightly farther north, inside today's Italy. He apparently spent most of his life within about a 40-mile area of his birthplace.

- ✔ Stomach contents show his last meal was 8 hours before death and consisted of bread, greens, and red deer meat. A wheat grain was even on his clothes. Before that he'd eaten *ibex* (wild goat). Pollen grains showed it was spring, and he'd just walked in a valley to the south.

- ✔ His lungs are black from smoke that would have filled ancient houses from the central hearth. He had intestinal parasites and possibly fleas.

- ✔ He had arthritis in his neck, back, and hip. His bones indicated he'd done lots of climbing.

✔ Tattoos on his back and legs were in hidden places, probably not for display but possibly for medical or healing reasons — they roughly corresponded with areas that may have hurt.

✔ He had deep cuts on his hand and wrist and a stone arrowhead stuck in his back that was probably the cause of his death.

The artifacts

Ötzi's gear gives archaeologists a stunning opportunity to study late Neolithic material culture because it includes a wealth of normally perishable artifacts:

✔ An unfinished bow of yew, a quiver of 14 arrows (12 unfinished), and bowstrings.

✔ Bone points, a needle, and two birch-bark containers.

✔ A wooden frame, also of yew, probably of a backpack. (One of its sticks was unwittingly used to help dig him out of the ice!)

✔ A flint knife with a wooden handle and woven sheath; other chipped-stone tools like a scraper, an awl, and a flake; and a bone and antler tool for fine chipping and sharpening tools.

✔ A nearly pure copper ax hafted into a yew-wood handle with leather binding and birch tar (sap heated for glue).

✔ A net, perhaps for hunting.

✔ A charcoal ember and probable fire-starting kit.

✔ A piece of ibex horn and a marble pendant.

✔ Pieces of antibacterial fungus possibly used as medicine.

✔ Seven articles of clothing, including a leather loincloth, vest, and leggings; a belt with a pouch (that held the small tools and fungus); a deerskin coat; a woven-grass cape (or possibly mat); a conical skin cap with chin strap and fur on the inside; and skin shoes filled with grass for warmth.

Reconstruction of what happened

Every new discovery about Ötzi fueled different arguments and popular news stories unfolded like in a modern-day scandal investigation. He had no food on him, and many of his artifacts were unfinished or needing repair, but they were neatly laid aside. The original guess was that he was perhaps a hunter or lost shepherd. Then researchers discovered his wounds, so they thought maybe he was running from warfare in the valley below. Or he'd stolen the newfangled copper ax and was being pursued. Or he was a robbery victim killed by someone wanting the valuable ax. Or he just fell down and hit his head and died. Distinguishing actual wounds suffered while he was alive from damage inflicted on the body by poor handling during excavation is difficult.

The arrow point in his shoulder wasn't seen until a new x-ray revealed it a decade after he was found, and scientists then located a matching cut in his clothes. Was it a murder or a hunting accident? Then DNA analysis showed blood of four other people on his clothes and tools. The depth of the arrow into his body indicates he probably bled to death, but the arrow shaft may have been pulled out before he died. Was he a powerful shaman with a fancy tool kit who was ritually murdered? Some say his remains demonstrate the level of constant violence in the Neolithic. Others say his bloodied companions may have left him sadly but peacefully to die in his (not so) final resting place. Still others argue over whether he was a leader or an outcast, or even if he was heterosexual or homosexual!

While scientists debated the various scenarios, experimental archaeologists duplicated Ötzi's equipment, and a famous shoemaker even replicated his shoes and tried them out in the cold. Archers have tried shooting scenarios at different angles and distances. A few people are even arguing over who should be recognized as the Ice Man's discoverer!

Meanwhile, reconstructions of what he looked like (complete with long stringy hair) and did (always with violence and blood) appear regularly in magazines and television specials. Looking for something you can take home? You can buy Ötzi merchandise at the Bolzano museum, or you can make like actor Brad Pitt and get a tattoo of the Ice Man on your arm!

More famous frozen finds

Freezing is the best way for organic remains to be preserved, so frozen finds are usually more spectacular. They provide rare opportunities to study human bodies and normally perishable artifacts, and more finds to argue about!

Ice mummies in the Andes

Inca ritual in the Peruvian Andes involved high-altitude burial of sacrificed children; climbers and archaeologists have discovered several of these burials over the years. These frozen mummies were given *chicha* (corn beer) and hit in the head to knock them out. They were wrapped in layers of elaborate woven textiles with artifacts of feathers, shell, silver, gold and other rich materials, as well as food offerings of llama meat and corn.

Although some see the poor children as hapless victims, others note that they were honored, pure offerings to the sacred mountains. Displaying and studying the frozen bodies has also generated controversy. Even a U.S. president viewing the exhibition of a frozen girl made a comment about how good she looked, offending some Native Americans and others. But continuing study of the mummies and their artifacts brings fascinating data on health, genetics, and everyday life of these 500-year-old kids.

Other frozen bodies

Extinct *Pleistocene* (Ice Age) bison and other big mammals have been found melting out of glaciers and ice fields too, as have a few humans in the Arctic. A frozen man recently found in British Columbia was dated to about 550 years. He was clearly ancestral to living Canadian First Nations (native) people. They named him "Long-Ago Person Found" and asked for respectful study of his body. He wore a squirrel- or gopher-fur coat and a hat woven of cedar and spruce roots, and had a leather bag with plants and dried fish in it, a bone and metal knife, and a spear. He was about 20 years old. His DNA continues to be studied, but has already tied him to North and South American Indians.

Thawed artifacts and reindeer manure

Global warming usually has negative effects, but melting Arctic ice can reveal amazing archaeological evidence. Finds currently thawing out include stinky reindeer manure and artifacts from the last 8,000 years. Spear and arrow shafts, an *atlatl* (hooked stick for spear throwing), stone, antler, and ivory points, and sinew, feathers, and red ochre were all hunting equipment. Scientists recently identified the glue holding an antler point from the Canadian Yukon to its spear shaft as spruce resin. The finds also help determine how early the bow and arrow were introduced (recently, perhaps in the last 1,000 years). Even the animal dung is valuable — showing what critters were eating, clues to past environments. It also indicates that the natives knew where to wait for the game to pass by so that they could get dinner.

Cannibalism in the U.S. Southwest

Ancestral Pueblo farmers (also called the Anasazi) in the southwestern U.S. are famous for their glorious ruins. (See Chapters 13 and 19 and Color Figure 8 for more on these sites). But these late prehistoric people are also embroiled in a controversy over cannibalism.

The finds

Archaeologists have interpreted human bones with signs of cutting, breaking, smashing, and boiling as evidence of butchery and cannibalism at many sites dating between A.D. 900 and 1250. They were found amid other signs of violence such as destroyed houses and artifacts, all dating to the time the settlements were abandoned. According to one archaeological interpretation, the violence may have been triggered by drought and hard times.

Alternative explanations

But other archaeologists say that cutting up bodies may have been a treatment for witches, not wholesale violence or cannibalism (or perhaps the witches themselves were the only cannibals). They cite folklore of modern Pueblo Indians, who have many witch stories. These folks resent the term

Anasazi because it's a Navajo word meaning "enemy" or "stranger." They're horrified at the portrayal of their ancestors as warlike cannibals. But then, some scientists argue, most people in the modern world are repulsed by cannibalism anyway. However, some cultures actually practice cannibalism out of respect for the honored dead (though that's clearly not what was happening here), so to some extent repulsion is in the eye of the beholder.

One decisive find

When I read about all this controversy in the 1990s, I knew just what it would take to prove that some people ate other people in the ancient past: a human *coprolite* (preserved feces) with human tissue in it. Lo and behold, in 2000, a report surfaced documenting such a coprolite from southwestern Colorado. At a small site occupied for about a generation and abandoned in A.D. 1150, the butchered bones of seven people were found. Human myoglobin (from muscle tissue) was in a coprolite deposited in a hearth (what a strange place to defecate) and also on a cooking pot, and human blood was on stone tools.

Archaeologists found no evidence of foods, suggesting that these were indeed starvation times. People's possessions were lying around the site, indicating that the residents had no time to gather their things and flee before dying. Reconstructions of the scene portrayed savage massacre and gruesome ritual. Of course, the news media sensationalized all the findings and kicked up the level of outrage on all sides!

More thoughtful explanations

But wait! Things are never as simple as they seem in archaeology. Ancestral Pueblo people (a better name for the Anasazi) weren't either violent savages or peaceful, noble natives — those are silly Western stereotypes. These groups clearly had some warfare, but it wasn't their standard way of life most of the time, according to the majority of the archaeological evidence.

As the debaters realize that the situation is ambiguous, a new opinion by a coprolite specialist was published in 2006. He pointed out that researchers still only have this one coprolite with human tissue and no plant remains in it. He studied hundreds of other fecal samples to reconstruct the Ancestral Pueblo diet: They were about 70 percent vegetarian. They grew corn, beans, and squash but mostly ate some 50 wild plant species, as well as bighorn sheep, antelope, dogs, and rodents. The single coprolite from someone who ate another person was so unusual that it probably wasn't from an Ancestral Pueblo native but a weird stranger. I like this explanation best, though archaeologists will probably never know exactly what happened.

Who Are They, and Where Did They Come From: Disputed Ancient Peoples and Processes

Some of the biggest anthropological questions are how and when people first spread across oceans and continents, and many mysteries of these human cultural processes can only be explored through archaeology. Even in early historic times, most of the knowledge of movements and clashes of different peoples comes from archaeology. The following sections discuss the uncertainty surrounding the first inhabitants of many regions (and how they got there in the first place).

Ancient Southeast Asian "hobbits"

In 2003, excavations in an Indonesian cave on the island of Flores (east of Java) uncovered skeletons of unusual human forms. The bones were from an adult female and portions of up to eight other individuals who were very small — 3 feet tall — and dated to about 18,000 years ago. Archaeologists and other anthropologists continue to argue whether these unusual bones are from a previously unknown species of human, a creature who became extinct, or people with genetic conditions of dwarfism. Though the biological name given them was *Homo floresiensis,* they were labeled "hobbits" (after the famous Tolkien characters) in the popular press. Artists even drew pictures of them as tiny, very hairy creatures, though of course no hair was preserved!

The earliest *Homo erectus* forms got to Java over a million years ago (see Chapter 12), and modern humans probably arrived around 50,000 years ago, according to their excavated bones. They were smaller than modern humans, though not that small. But size is reduced in many species as they adapt to islands. Other animals on Flores include dwarf elephants that were clearly hunted by these little people. So these people may have descended from the original human forms who made it across the sea to the island, and just gotten smaller as they stayed so isolated. Or they may have had a pathology that made them *microcephalic* (tiny-headed) or otherwise dwarfed.

As specialists in human biology and evolution continue debating all the different explanations, the archaeology gives good clues to the behavior of these little people. Hundreds of mostly small, even delicate, flaked-stone tools were uncovered in the cave excavations, as were animal remains. The finds include

- ✔ Points from spears or darts and lots of waste flakes from chipping.

- ✔ Perforators, blades, and microblades that the excavators thought were hafted as barbs.

- ✔ Burned, reddened, and cracked stones, including some arranged in a circle, that suggest a hearth.

- ✔ Bones of those dwarf elephants (especially the young ones), sometimes with cut marks showing the little people were hunting (or scavenging) and butchering them.

- ✔ Bones of other animals like rat, bat, fish, frog, snake, birds, large rodents, and Komodo dragon — all of which could have been part of the diet (though in a tropical rainforest they probably ate mostly the abundant plants).

Some of the stone tools are similar to others excavated in deposits dated as old as 95,000 years ago, so perhaps human forms got to Flores and carried on their traditional ways despite slowly evolving smaller bodies. Stay tuned for new findings as the "hobbits" and their artifacts are carefully scrutinized with new scientific studies.

Identity of the Celts

The ancestral people of northern and western Europe before the Roman Empire took over are called the Celts. Greek and Roman historians described them as Keltoi, Gauls, Galatians, and other related names for the many groups who sacked Rome and Greece in the fourth and third centuries B.C. and even made it to Turkey. Romans interacted with them for several centuries — in trading, fighting, or other kinds of relationships. They described Celtic warriors, priests, and slaves.

The Celts themselves never wrote their own history, so they're often better known through archaeology. But Celts may actually be a composite group invented by generations of historians seeking ancestors of today's deep cultural heritage of Ireland, Scotland, Wales, and Brittany (a region across the English Channel in northwest France).

Archaeologically, the time of the Celtic peoples was the Iron Age, from about 800 B.C. to 50 B.C. and later, when Julius Caesar and succeeding emperors were busy conquering them all for Rome. However, Celtic cultural traditions continued around the edges of the Roman Empire, for at least another 1,000 years (until Christianity and its ways took over).

Celtic artifacts

Digs in tombs of important political leaders and other sites have produced sensational evidence of what Celtic society must have been like. Here are some of the important finds in Celtic archaeology:

- *Hillforts,* which are major political and economic centers with ditches, embankments, palisades, and often stone walls.

- Features in the ground indicating round houses with *wattle* (woven branches) and *daub* (clay covering) walls (or stone walls where stone was available), and a central hearth in the dirt floor. Houses were inside hillforts or in smaller settlements.

- Artifacts such as grinding stones for the wheat and barley they grew, and bones of the sheep, goats, cattle, and pigs they raised.

- Rich burials of elite individuals, with wagons, huge bronze jars and drinking vessels for alcoholic beverages, and other rich grave offerings. These goods demonstrate the presence of kings, war leaders, and nobles.

- Distinctive types of pottery; glass cone beakers for drinking at feasts; beads of bone, stone, glass, and amber; and everyday objects like wooden bowls, combs, spindles, furniture, and fancy carvings.

- Lots of iron artifacts — swords, knives, axes, harness fittings, ornamental stuff.

- Elaborate jewelry — brooches and pins of gold and other precious metals.

- Imported artifacts showing trade with the Mediterranean, eastern Europe, and even more distant lands.

Interpreting the Celtic past

Popular reconstructions are made from all these finds. Picture a bunch of big, pale guys with big mustaches wearing armor, feasting, and raising toasts as they boast about their battles. Or imagine druids chanting magic around the bonfire. These people certainly had skills in metalworking, and their exquisite gold jewelry and lots of other finery suggests they liked to show off their stuff. They also made lots of carved stone monuments with symbols whose meanings are still unclear.

The latest Celts remained in northwestern Europe, carrying on their pre-Roman traditions. The few Celtic inscriptions (mostly on coins) are in languages related to modern Welsh, Gaelic (Irish), and Breton. Pagan religious festivals and legends of gods in later historic times also may be related to Iron Age symbols on artifacts. Celtic art — long a favorite subject of art historians — is quite distinctive, with complex patterns of spirals and circles and fantastic figures of birds, horses, other animals, and humans.

Relating history, archaeology, and heritage

Problems in understanding who the Celts were come when you try to relate the few (and biased) historic texts to archaeological finds. Ethnicity is hard to see in artifacts. (For more on ethnicity and archaeology, check out Chapters 15 and 16). Many different tribal groups fell under the heading of the barbaric Celts whom others were writing about. And cultures always change over time, though they can of course maintain some continuity. Celts may have been just a term ancient classical writers used for assorted groups of foreigners, and later historians made them into some kind of unified people with a group identity they never really had.

But identifying with noble warriors and resistance against empire stirs a lot of passion and fascination with the archaeology of the supposed Celtic people. Ethnic heritage is often squeezed out of the artifacts by the public wanting a past to call their own. Some critics argue that this emotion is tied with British pride and nationalistic identity in the face of today's multicultural society and that archaeologists may be serving racist ideals if they classify materials as ethnically Celtic instead of by time period or other designation. Similarly, the early medieval archaeology of Ireland is tied to a search for Celtic origins of Irish culture.

However you interpret the debate, archaeology contributes to the study of post-Roman northwestern Europe with good scientific goals. The material record is producing evidence for change and continuity over time. Pagan traditions were maintained in some areas, but Christian artifacts show patterns of how the church penetrated into other areas by medieval times and radically changed everyday life and politics. The goal of research isn't just to revel in hoards of golden artifacts but to reconstruct social organization and economic systems that interacted with the historically documented world.

How the Americas were first discovered

A huge and long-lasting controversy in American archaeology concerns the first people coming to the *New World* (North and South America). Passionate arguments continue over how and when they got there. (See my discussion of Paleo-Indian culture in Chapter 12.)

Age and culture of the first Americans

For a long time scientists thought humans had only been in the Americas for a couple thousand years. Then in 1908, an African American cowboy-naturalist found a human-made spear point stuck into the skeleton of a Pleistocene (Ice Age) bison near Folsom, New Mexico. This species was known to be extinct for the last 10,000 years! In the 1930s, archaeologists excavated at Clovis, New Mexico, and found other spear points with mammoth bones. The Clovis and Folsom archaeological cultures were later radiocarbon dated (after that dating method was invented in 1950) and other distinctive types of spear points were named. *Paleo-Indian* culture was the term encompassing all of these groups who inhabited the Americas during the Pleistocene.

Here are the typical Paleo-Indian site characteristics in North America:

✔ Distinctive types of long, thin, beautifully made chipped-stone spear points, often with *flutes* (a big flake removed to make a channel up the middle on each side). I show you one of these points in Figure 12-5 in Chapter 12.

✔ Other associated stone tools and flaking debris *(lithic debitage)*.

✔ Clovis points associated with mammoths and radiocarbon dates as early as 12,000 years ago.

✔ Folsom points found with bison and slightly later radiocarbon dates, between 10,900 and 10,200 years ago.

✔ Other lance-shaped points associated with Ice Age animals and slightly later dates in both North and South America.

From all the evidence, archaeologists reconstructed an ancient way of life emphasizing big-game hunting in the cold Pleistocene environment (before the animals became extinct with climate change at the end of the Ice Age — see Chapter 13 for more). At many Paleo-Indian campsites, excavations uncovered butchered bones of hundreds of the large herd animals. Some theorists did argue that the first Americans certainly ate lots of plants, too, as do modern big-game hunting cultures, but seldom are those remains preserved. Another important argument was that early coastal fishing sites are unknown because they would have drowned after sea level rose at the close of the Ice Age.

How people got to America

A huge debate also rages over how these first people arrived in the New World. Here are the three most commonly proposed routes and their suggested means of travel:

✔ **Walking over the Bering Strait when it was actually a land bridge between Siberia and Alaska:** Ice Age glaciers took up lots of water, so sea level was far lower and the land was exposed.

✔ **Boating along the shore from Siberia to Alaska and down the Pacific coast:** This is the most likely method (and probably easier); people may have branched off and moved inland as they went south.

✔ **Walking on land and ice and maybe some boating from Europe:** This hypothesis is less reasonable; the distance was too far, and only a vague similarity exists between French Paleolithic and American spear points. Plus, Native American DNA is more closely linked to northeast Asian roots.

So this was the scenario of the "peopling of the Americas": Mighty hunters following their game moved eastward and "discovered" the New World about 12,000 years ago, not realizing they'd come to a new continent.

Newer finds of older artifacts down south

A few sites in the Americas do actually date before 12,000 B.P. (before the present). Some sites in South America have produced radiocarbon dates a couple centuries earlier than those in North America, a bit curious because it would take more time for the first settlers to move south and fill up a second continent. Excavators thought some other controversial sites in North America were as old as 17,000 years B.P., but most of the archaeological establishment questioned the integrity of these finds, the accuracy of the radiocarbon dating (which is, after all, a statistical approximation) and even whether the crude-looking chipped stones were human-made artifacts at all. (See Chapter 10 for more on radiocarbon dating.)

In the 1980s, a few sites with good, uncontaminated dates began challenging the notion that the so-called Clovis people were the first on the continent. One breakthrough came at Monte Verde, Chile, on South America's far southern coast. Because this ancient camp was a wet site, things that usually decay were excavated from the boggy creek bank. The radiocarbon dates showed people living there 14,200 years ago or earlier.

Here are some of the remains from the Monte Verde site:

✔ Wooden foundations of rectangular row-houses with clay-basin fire hearths and (apparently) animal hide covers on the walls.

✔ Foundations of another, more oval-shaped structure off to the side that contained unusual remains like mastodon bone, salt, and several bits of uncommon plants, including some that may have been medicinal. This building was interpreted as the home of a shaman (religious practitioner or healer).

✔ Bones of other animals, like llamas, birds, reptiles, and amphibians. Other indicators of diet are shells (from shellfish) and even a piece of mastodon meat.

✔ Some 42 species of plant remains, like wild potato, berries, seeds, nuts, fruits, and even chewed bits of seaweed and leaves. Nine species of marine algae and seaweed remains on a sharp stone tool edge show use of coastal resources and support the idea that people spread through the Americas along the Pacific coast.

✔ Wooden digging sticks and spear shafts, twine, and cordage.

✔ Stone tools (especially grinding stones) but no chipped-stone points.

It took many years for Monte Verde to be accepted as a pre-Clovis ancient American settlement, and archaeologists are actually still arguing about it. Meanwhile, another dig at a cave in the Brazilian Amazon uncovered quartz stemmed points very unlike Clovis points but securely dated from 11,200 to 10,000 years old. They were associated with 30,000 stone flakes and the remains of thousands of fruits, seeds, nuts, shellfish, small and large fish, and animals. This evidence indicated the earliest people were foraging widely in the tropical forest and river, not hunting big mammals.

Newest discoveries

More really early sites have come to light recently, though archaeologists thoroughly debate the authenticity of each one. A Virginia dig produced stone tools dated to 16,000 years ago, and the Topper site in South Carolina is supposedly well over 40,000 years old. Another new development is the recalculation of all the original radiocarbon dates for early Paleo-Indian sites with Clovis points. They cluster within a very small time range, from about 13,000 to 12,800 years ago, suggesting not a particular people spreading out and filling up the land but rather a new technology spreading quickly to the people who'd already filled up the land.

The most fascinating news comes from Paisley Caves in south-central Oregon. For decades, digs there had unearthed unusual materials preserved in the dry soil: wooden artifacts, twine, basket fragments, and bones of birds, fish, and large animals like extinct camels and horses. New dates showed some of these finds were as old as 14,000 B.P. Even more amazing are the coprolites (dried feces) that contain recently identified human DNA and even a human hair, dated to about 14,300.

You can imagine the joking about the coprolites! But they do allow study of ancient humans without disturbing any bones (no bones this old have ever been found anyhow). Their great age adds more support to the idea that people came to the New World as early as 15,000 years ago. Several centuries must have passed before they developed the distinctive technology to produce Clovis and other Paleo-Indian points. Their lifeways clearly included hunting big game but more often were far broader, focusing on lots of local plant resources, smaller animals, and fish as well.

The later "discovery" of America

Millions of prehistoric people came to inhabit North and South America, foraging, settling, farming, and developing civilizations (which I discuss in detail in Chapters 13 and 14). They spread throughout both continents with thousands of languages and cultures before some weird strangers arrived from Europe. The first of those were the Vikings or Norse, who sailed from Scandinavia via Iceland and Greenland in the 11th century. They got to the Canadian coast but didn't stay long, leaving only the smallest archaeological traces in the ground. (For more on the Vikings, head to Chapter 15.)

But a few hundred years later, Spanish, Portuguese, and British explorers (along with others of many Old World nations) invaded and began the process of major colonization and change that's visible in the archaeological record.

Spanish invasions and the effects of the conquistadores

Columbus arrived in the New World in 1492; in Chapter 15, I describe the archaeology of one of his early settlements in the Caribbean. Lots of Spaniards followed him across the Atlantic seeking adventure and fortune, and (later) souls for the Church. The conquistadores' early invasions of Mexico, Peru, and the southeastern U.S. have been documented by chroniclers and analyzed by historians ever since. But archaeology now contributes an enormous amount of information not found in the writings.

The paths of the conquistadores across the continents are reconstructed from their artifacts and even the bones of their horses and pigs (animals new to America), but the exact routes they took are controversial. Native Americans would use and trade the artifacts they got (or took) from Europeans, so these items often moved across the landscape independently from the journeys described in the Spanish records.

Early contact-period sites have Native American pottery, corn, and stone tools combined with bits of Spanish armor, chain mail, crossbow *quarrels* (dart tips) and other weapons, coins, and glass beads. Beads may have been given as cheap trinkets, but they became important ceremonial items and markers of status for Native Americans, included as burial goods with the important dead. Meanwhile the gold and silver statues, jewelry, and sacred items the Spaniards did find among the civilizations of Mexico and South America were melted down and sent to Spain to make money to fuel the conquest.

Some archaeologists have worked with medical researchers to trace the evidence of the introduction of European germs into New World populations. Cemeteries and burial mounds document massive numbers of native deaths in the early 16th century from epidemics. Occasionally, sword cuts on the skeletons show the violence that took place, but more often the signs point to deaths from Old World diseases. Smallpox, influenza, and even common colds that didn't bother Spaniards could wipe out entire towns because natives had no resistance to these imported illnesses. Debate arises over whether Native Americans died out fast or whether the impact of the foreigners wasn't so bad. Skeletal remains and the abandonment of native towns give clues to what was apparently a demographic disaster in some areas, but not in others.

Colonization

Early Spanish missions were devoted to converting natives and making them labor in the fields. Although controversy rages over how badly Europeans treated Native Americans, studies of native skeletons show they worked much harder farming during the colonial period than they did in prehistoric times. Other fascinating archaeological investigations concern how much of Native American culture the Europeans took on, and how much like Europeans the natives became. This exchange is visible in the kinds of artifacts and house patterns in the ground. For example, Native American pottery began to conform to European shapes, such as pitchers or dishes with ring stands on the bottom. They used certain European artifacts as wealth goods, although other foreign trinkets became commonplace.

European powers had different strategies and goals for colonization as they fought wars on their own continent that spread to the New World. Sites such as forts and homesteads (and their accompanying artifacts) show the nature of interaction among Europeans and indigenous peoples. Key players in the game of exploration and colonization took different approaches:

✔ The Spanish were medieval — dominated by crown and church — and kept natives in servitude on missions and haciendas. They brought European plants, indicated by excavated peach pits and other things, and also their domestic animals. But wild animal bones show Indian hunting traditions remained. Spaniards traveled in big ships and armored on horseback, so artifacts from these activities are common.

✔ The French explored rivers in the continental interior by canoe and traded beads and metal goods for deerskins. Excavation of their colonial settlements often turns up deer bones and typical European crockery and metal implements, as well as religious items (see Color Figure 15).

✔ The British were budding capitalists interested in profit; they also brought metal tools, cauldrons, and glass beads to the Native Americans in return for deerskins. They changed native hunting from a means of subsistence to a profit-making enterprise (which decimated deer populations too).

Heritage issues

Some archaeological finds support the historical records of struggling colonists, but others show these Europeans had lots of luxuries. Still other excavations fill out the picture of natives who didn't get a chance to tell their own story. Hundreds of indigenous groups became extinct after being barely mentioned in the early histories; archaeology is the only way to know them. Archaeologists work with Native Americans to locate the historic towns, missions, plantations, or other places their ancestors fled or were chased from in the 16th through 18th centuries and give them back the evidence of their former homes.

Further, as English-speaking America celebrates its historic heritage with monuments at colonial British sites such as Williamsburg, Virginia, archaeologists document the struggle between the European powers to control the continent through 18th century. How European countries routed each other's colonies and soldiers is visible in the ground. Re-enactors of historic events, from the War of 1812 to the conquistadores' battles, call upon archaeologists for details of costumes, weapons, food, and forts. Long before the *Mayflower,* the Spanish began the process that could have ended up with everyone in the U.S. eating tortillas and chili peppers! Details from the ground show the duration and success or failure of colonial settlements, and the superior strategies and trade goods the English used to prevail in the end.

How the far Pacific was discovered

Islands of the vast Pacific Ocean were among the last places humans came to inhabit. Polynesian ancestors sailed canoes around millions of miles of sea over the last three millennia with no real navigation instruments. The ancient people archaeologists call *Lapita,* after their distinctive pottery, colonized hundreds of remote islands — Hawaii, Fiji, Samoa, Tahiti, and New Zealand, just to name a few. Archaeological evidence shows they may have set out deliberately to colonize — bringing objects not originally available on these islands, like livestock, taro plants, and stone tools. But controversies arise over where they came from and when and how they did it.

Ancient origins and sailors

On an island in the nation of Vanuatu, a recent investigation of a 3,000-year-old burial ground uncovered 62 graves. Chemical analysis of the teeth of some skeletons indicated they were of people who hadn't grown up on the island but came from elsewhere. DNA studies are still underway. Offerings in the graves included rare whole Lapita pots, with their stamped decorations, and stone tools like knives and scrapers. The chemical makeup of the obsidian raw material for these tools was characteristic of a source in New Guinea, thousands of miles to the west.

Linguistic anthropologists see the origins of the languages of western Polynesians in Taiwan, and DNA study of teeth from prehistoric and modern varieties of pigs shows the Pacific species are closest to those of Southeast Asia. Regardless of whether they had more northerly or southerly Asian origins, the people who colonized the Pacific developed their sailing skills over centuries as they hopped eastward from one island to the next one that they could see. The real test of their skills came when they began to go farther on pioneering voyages thousands of miles into the empty central Pacific.

Presumably, they had outrigger sailing canoes, but no ancient vessels or rigging have survived so far for archaeologists to dig up. The native canoes first described by 18th-century British visitors were fast but small; some argue they were too small and useless in a contrary wind to be able to go deliberately to faraway new islands. The Polynesians must have had knowledge of currents, waves, swells, winds, and other natural phenomena. Aside from that, the explanations for how they did it vary wildly; the following list presents a few ideas being floated (pun intended):

- They knew how to *tack* into the wind (change direction by turning the sail).
- They sailed toward volcanic plumes in the sky because they knew it meant land.
- They followed migrating birds (or brought birds who would know the way to land).
- They weren't skilled sailors at all; they just landed in all these remote islands by chance, through the action of winds, currents, or special *El Niño* (climate-shifting) events in unplanned voyages.

Regardless of how the Polynesians got to these islands, their colonization shows up in the material record, and not just in the things they brought and made. On many islands they settled, the largest species (whether tall, flightless birds or big shellfish) are present in the deepest, earliest archaeological levels, only to be absent in later levels and extinct today. Human occupation and overuse of new foods may have been a disaster for some of the islands' plants and animals.

Easter Island

Easter Island (also known as Rapa Nui) is a small volcanic island in the southeastern Pacific. I discuss it in Chapter 20 as a fabulous archaeological place to visit. Over 2,200 miles west of South America, it was the most remote place humans ever inhabited (until today, when humans have figured out how to live at the South Pole or in space). Yet Polynesian seafarers made it here by about A.D. 500. They had tools of obsidian, animal teeth, and wood. They cut the palm forest, established settlements of stone houses and shrines, and began raising chickens and yams that they'd brought. Most famous are their hundreds of huge carved stone statues called *moai,* which apparently represented sacred chiefs or gods.

Within 1,000 years of the first human arrival, the limited resources were mostly gone: no trees for canoes, for rollers or sledges to move statues, or for fiber to make rope to pull them. People were trapped in a seriously damaged environment. The ensuing conflict between villages led to desecration and toppling of the statues and great hardship. Europeans arriving there in 1722 found it a barren environment. Some modern popular accounts call it a sad tale of human-made ecological destruction. But the earliest Europeans failed to mention how they contributed to the destruction of both the people and the natural resources, not to mention the archaeological sites.

In addition, archaeologists studying ancient nut remains and animal bones now find it may not have been people but rather the rats they inadvertently brought with them that caused deforestation. Rats multiplied quickly and ate so many palm nuts that the trees became extinct. This unintended natural disaster, not the continuing competition among chiefs wanting ever more palm forests cut to move statues, may have been the reason for ecological disaster. Meanwhile, today tourism and international commerce is severely threatening the prehistoric sites on Easter Island.

Chicken in Chile

As the disputes over Easter Island continue, it's clear that ancient Polynesian navigators continued to explore eastward. Archaeologists recently discovered bones of chicken in prehistoric Chile, securely dated to a century before Spaniards arrived. This bird is native to the Old World and was thought to have been brought to South America by the Spanish. But DNA studies show the bones are most closely related to chickens from Easter Island, as well as elsewhere in Polynesia. So far, no other remains showing the Polynesian presence have been found in South America, but South American bottle gourds and sweet potatoes have been found on some Pacific islands. Some even argue that prehistoric California's complex fishhooks and sewn-plank canoes look like Polynesian ones. The Pacific explorers who got to South (and maybe North) America may have found too many people there, left a few things and ideas, and gone back west to their island homes, bringing a few souvenirs. But look for more debate on this in years to come!

Controversies among Archaeologists and Others

Often, the significance of archaeological finds derives from their political implications and importance to different interested parties, many of whom aren't archaeologists. I describe many of these cases in Chapter 16, and in Chapter 2 you see the dispute between Greece and England over the Elgin Marbles, relics looted from the Parthenon in Athens in the 19th century and now displayed in the British Museum. Disagreements over artifacts typically occur between countries of their origin and countries who've been taking care of them for a long time. Disagreements over sites happen when different people want the land for different reasons, from profit to preservation.

Machu Picchu remains claimed by Peru

UNESCO (the United Nations Educational, Scientific, and Cultural Organization) declared Machu Picchu one of its World Heritage sites, and with good reason: the Spanish never discovered (and therefore didn't destroy) this prehistoric Inca estate as they conquered Peru. (See Machu Picchu in Figure 14-4 in Chapter 14 and color Figure 12). It's an amazing monumental structure of cut and fitted stones in the highlands beyond the Inca capital of Cuzco. I describe for you how worthwhile it is to visit in Chapter 20.

Hiram Bingham, a Yale University explorer, discovered Machu Picchu (okay, made the ruins public to the outside world) in 1911. He was an adventurer and potential model for fictional characters like Indiana Jones. He got permission from Peru to take some 5,000 artifacts back for study. Archaeology takes a long time, but 95 years is pushing it. In 2006, Peruvian officials demanded that Yale return these materials in a highly publicized claim. The original agreement was a loan, but it wasn't well designed or understood. Protests by archaeologists and politicians escalated. Yale finally agreed to give some artifacts back and sponsor a traveling exhibition, but the dispute continues.

Meanwhile, tourism is increasing so much that it's endangering the site. In 2000, a crane hired to help film a beer commercial accidentally chipped an important stone monument. Uproar continues over helicopters landing on the site, and now archaeologists and the public are protesting the government's plans to construct a cable car to the Machu Picchu and a tourist complex with luxury hotel, boutique stores, and restaurants. Watch for new developments to come, and try to see the site before it changes forever from a remote, astounding outpost to a tourist trap!

Miami Circle site

A huge controversy followed discovery of the Miami Circle. This unusual prehistoric site is a circle of postmolds cut into the limestone bedrock, measuring 38 feet in diameter and outlining what must have been a big building on Brickell Point in downtown Miami, Florida. Over these postmolds was black *midden* (garbage) soil containing artifacts like pottery and tools of bone, shell, and stone. Radiocarbon dates indicated the site was built and used from 750 B.C. to A.D. 550, and then later occupied between 1330 and 1680.

The site was found when a developer tore down an old apartment building to build a luxury condominium. Laws required him to have an archaeological survey first, and when this spectacular site was found, several results ensued. The developer worried about losing income and offered to cut out the site and move it so he could continue building on this prime real estate at the mouth of the Miami River. The city worried about losing tax revenues if the planned commercial endeavor was halted. Popular support for preserving the site grew among archaeologists, Native Americans, and other protesters, and threats of legal action and disputes over the value of the land followed. In a stunning move, the state of Florida, using its own money and various donations, purchased the site in 1999 to preserve it.

Archaeological controversy

Because the septic tank for the old building was still there in the ground within the circle, some archaeologists thought the site was disturbed and not worth saving. They argued it may be too damaged to produce useful information. And it doesn't end there:

- ✔ Some (including archaeologists and a paranormal investigator) thought the circle wasn't a real prehistoric site but a result of cutting into the bedrock to install the septic tank.

- ✔ Others thought the ground-stone axes looked Mexican and hypothesized a prehistoric Mayan colony (or people from Stonehenge, or extraterrestrials).

- ✔ Finally, some archaeologists were angry that $27 million in state funds and many more millions in donations were spent to buy and preserve the site when plenty of more important sites all over Florida were being bulldozed daily in the path of unbridled construction.

Scientific investigation

Continued excavation and mapping of the site demonstrated that it really is the remains of a prehistoric structure, with intentionally marked cardinal direction points and possible alignment with astronomical calculations.

Similar circular buildings are known from other sites of this time period in the eastern U.S., though most have postmolds dug into the soil. But other prehistoric sites with cut-rock postmolds occur in south Florida.

Miami Circle was probably a ceremonial center inhabited by local Florida natives but with wide-ranging connections. You can see this in the finds:

- ✔ The *chert* (flint) raw material of the stone tools is from hundreds of miles away. (Little natural stone occurs in south Florida).

- ✔ Two *galena* (shiny, silvery stone) artifacts are made of raw material traced to Missouri.

- ✔ The (so-called Mexican) ax is made of stone traced to north Georgia.

- ✔ A complete shark skeleton, dolphin skull, and sea-turtle shell were uncovered in the ground within the structure; they were probably some kind of ancient offerings.

- ✔ The holes cut for the ancient posts are much older than the septic tank hole, according to geological studies.

- ✔ 19th-century artifacts from Seminole Indians and from the trading post that once sat here as late as 1900 are in the upper levels of the site.

- ✔ Food remains include shark teeth and bones of many other marine and freshwater fish, turtles, squirrel, rabbit, deer, dog, birds, amphibians, and the (now-extinct) Caribbean monk seal. These remains all show high-intensity use of the *brackish* (not salty but not fresh) water habitat around the site.

Though the site is still controversial, the majority consensus now is that it was built by ancestors of the historic Tequesta Indians that the Spanish encountered in the 16th and 17th centuries. These people were quickly wiped out, but their site remains preserved for the public to understand at least a little about how they lived and what they may have thought was sacred.

Part VI
The Part of Tens

The 5th Wave   By Rich Tennant

CAT

"Theory has it the island was once part of Manhattan."

In this part . . .

1 list ways you can get involved with archaeology your self, whether from your armchair, as a tourist, or as a participant in a dig. If you're planning a vacation or other trip around the U.S., Chapter 19 lists ten of the many exciting places you can see exceptional U.S. archaeological sites, museums, and reconstructions of past lifeways. For those wanting to visit archaeology outside the U.S., Chapter 20 gives you some of the most spectacular archaeological places to tour worldwide. In Chapter 21, I show you some of the many ways to get more into archaeology, from reading to digging.

Chapter 19

Ten-Plus Archaeological Places to Visit in the U.S.

In This Chapter

▶ Exploring great archaeological sites across the United States

▶ Checking out the country's best natural history museums

*E*very state in the U.S. has great archaeological sites and museums. You can find listings in state travel guides or with a quick online search. Look for Web sites of the state historic preservation offices (SHPOs), archaeological societies, or tribal historic preservation offices of different Native American groups.

In this chapter I list some of the most fascinating archaeological places you can visit. All have museums or interpretive centers. You may even find volunteer programs that feature digging, reenacting, or otherwise learning about the past. Not looking for a hands-on experience? Another great option is shopping in gift stores for those really unusual items, like artifact replicas. If nothing else, this chapter can help you plan your vacation!

Alabama: Moundville Archaeological Park

Not far from Tuscaloosa on the Black Warrior River, Moundville had 26 flat-topped earthen mounds (see Color Figure 7) inside a wooden palisade. Though the wood decayed, the mounds remain. It was a major town and religious center from A.D. 1000–1450, with chiefs residing in special buildings on top these temple mounds. The wealth of high-status people included exotic luxury items of copper, mica, and marine shell. Starting as a major town, it became a ceremonial place for burying the important dead.

While you're in Alabama, catch Russell Cave National Monument up in the northeastern corner of the state. This huge cave has archaeological remains from native people who lived in it over 8,000 years of prehistory!

Arkansas: Toltec Mounds Archaeological State Park

At this site near Little Rock, prehistoric people of the Late Woodland culture built a major settlement and ceremonial center between A.D. 600 and 1050. They hadn't yet begun intensive farming but had gardens of domesticated crops. The site features at least 15 mounds, many aligned to correspond with the solstices and equinoxes (the heavenly bodies were the best nighttime show during prehistory), and a surrounding earthen embankment. The state of Arkansas even funds a research station here, and a lovely museum.

Colorado: Mesa Verde National Park

In the high plateau country of southwestern Colorado, Mesa Verde's 4,000 archaeological sites bring alive the ancestral Pueblo (or Anasazi) culture, which lasted from A.D. 600 to 1300. Distinctive architecture styles feature adobe, stone, and layered masonry, with houses joined in compact clusters. Trails link excavated and stabilized sites. You can see mesa-top settlements, pithouses, towers, *kivas* (religious areas), terraces, and check dams built by these early farmers. Or check out the spectacular Cliff Palace (or one of the other 600 cliff dwellings) built later in prehistoric time. (See Color Figure 8).

Georgia: Etowah Indian Mounds Historic Site

Etowah was a center of late prehistoric Mississippian-culture chiefdoms in northwest Georgia inhabited from A.D. 1000 to 1550. It features six earthen mounds, a plaza, a large village, and what may be a defensive ditch surrounding it all. Mound C is a 63-foot-high, flat-topped pyramid that would have supported a priest-chief's home or important ceremonial building. Other mounds are the burial sites of important people, complete with shell beads, feathers, copper ornaments, paint, and fancy pottery. The museum interprets it all for you very nicely.

Florida: Mission San Luis de Apalachee

The Spanish invaded Florida in the 1500s, then set up colonies with missions in the 1600s, *long* before the more famous missions in the Southwest. But the Florida buildings of wood decayed rapidly. San Luis, in Tallahassee, was excavated well enough that archaeologists now know exactly where the Spanish church, convent, and native buildings stood. They've reconstructed them all with awesome results. You can contrast how a Spaniard lived with how an Apalachee Indian lived and see an exhibit that includes the story of how the descendants of the last known original Florida Indians were located in Louisiana, of all places.

While you're in Tallahassee, also check out the late prehistoric Lake Jackson Mounds State Park, with towering flat-topped temple mounds and plaza. Also, the Museum of Florida History has prehistoric pottery, stone, wooden canoes, and historic Spanish gold excavated from shipwrecks.

Illinois: Cahokia Mounds State Historic Site

In East St. Louis (across the Mississippi River from Missouri), Cahokia flourished from A.D. 700 to 1400. It was the largest major center of the most sophisticated North American culture that ever evolved north of Mexico. It features more than 100 mounds; the largest (which you can climb) is Monk's mound, named after a monastery that was once there. It measures 100 feet high, over 1,000 feet long, and over 700 feet wide — the largest earthen pyramid on the continent.

In Mound 72, archaeologists excavated the burial of what was probably a chief: an old guy lying on a bed of 20,000 shell beads with offerings of arrowheads, other fancy artifacts, and also skeletons of people who were apparently sacrificed. The site was mysteriously abandoned over a century before Europeans arrived in the New World. The museum is beautiful, and the walk to the top of Monk's mound is awe-inspiring.

Louisiana: Poverty Point State Historic Site

The early hunter–gatherers who built this huge site in northeast Louisiana hadn't even started farming yet when they brought in exotic stone from afar to fashion fancy tools and beads. Dating from 1800 to 1300 B.C., Poverty Point boasts several mounds and many huge concentric earthen rings. This site has some of the very oldest monumental architecture on the continent. Other fascinating and mysterious artifacts include figurines and unusual fired clay balls of various shapes that may have been for cooking. In the 1950s, aerial photography made the previously unrecognizable earthworks visible.

Maryland: St. Mary's City

Less than two hours from Washington, D.C., near where the Potomac River reaches Chesapeake Bay in southern Maryland, St. Mary's City was one of the few early permanent British settlements in North America. It's the most intact 17th-century English town in the U.S., and it was Maryland's first capital. You'll see costumed interpreters telling stories about daily life in such a young colony and how Native Americans and colonists got along, changing each others' worlds forever. You may even be able to watch excavations in progress.

New Mexico: Chaco Culture National Historic Park

Chaco Canyon was a major settlement area for prehistoric Puebloan peoples (ancestors of today's Hopi and other Native Americans) between A.D. 800 and 1250. The park has scores of sites and a road system engineered by the ancients. You can see famous and distinctive Pueblo architecture that includes monumental public and ceremonial buildings. The largest great house is Pueblo Bonito, but the park has tons of other ruins as well. They feature clusters of houses in a fascinating community pattern.

Many other famous and exciting archaeological sites cluster around the Four Corners region where the states of Utah, Colorado, New Mexico, and Arizona come together. Consider visiting Mesa Verde on the same trip! (See the section on Mesa Verde earlier in this chapter.)

Ohio: Hopewell Culture National Historical Park

Formerly known as Mound City, this complex of burial mound and earthwork sites dates from 200 B.C. to A.D. 500. The Ohio River valley was a rich environment, but these people weren't yet intensively farming (though they may have had small gardens). The geometric earthen walls and enclosures form circles and squares. The honored dead were buried with grave goods like fancy clay pots, mica, copper, and clay or stone smoking pipes in the shapes of animals. Many of these beautiful artifacts are displayed in the museum.

While you're in southern Ohio, check out other mound sites, especially Serpent Mound, a 1,330-foot-long earthwork in the shape of a partially coiled snake. Archaeologists are still arguing whether it's 2,000 or 1,000 years old.

Virginia: Historic Jamestown

Located within colonial 18th-century Williamsburg in coastal Virginia, Jamestown is the first permanent English settlement in America (though it kind of failed at first, until they moved to higher ground away from bugs and swamps). You can see the 1607 James Fort excavation and original and reconstructed 17th-century buildings. The settlement contains a lot of history, including costumed reenactors, but a lot of archaeology as well — determining where objects and buildings were and exhibiting artifacts of this early colonial period.

Wisconsin: Aztalan State Park

Aztalan is an important late prehistoric settlement and ceremonial center within the drainage of the upper Mississippi River (yes, the Mississippi goes up that far) that features several mounds and a village with a reconstructed stockade and interior fences. Dating to between A.D. 1000 and 1300, this settlement is a very northerly expression of late prehistoric Mississippian chiefdoms. Because the flat-topped earthen temple mounds resemble Mexican pyramids, long ago this site was mistakenly given the name of the mythical homeland of the Aztecs, who said they came from the north. (But in reality, Aztecs didn't originate *that* far north!) It's surrounded by other historic areas and towns worth visiting.

A Few Museums You Should Visit

Though not always on archaeological sites, museums feature all kinds of archaeological finds and stories about the prehistoric and historic past. The U.S. boasts thousands of museums; here are three important ones.

Connecticut: Mashantucket Pequot Museum

This small Indian tribe has put together one of the most elegant and impressive museums in the world. It features Native American culture (the local Pequot and many others, including Ohio Valley mound builders) and tells the story of the New England indigenous peoples from the earliest Americans to colonial days to modern times. Artifact finds and scenes of daily life help reconstruct past native lifeways, and you can contrast scientific interpretations with the native peoples' own sacred stories of their origins and other traditions. And you can see beautiful art as well!

New York: American Museum of Natural History

This huge museum has exhibits of archaeological finds and cultural reconstructions from all regions of the world, as well as other natural history emphases. It's one of the oldest and most impressive museums in the country and full of glorious ancient art and architecture and lots of classic stuff.

Washington, D.C.: Smithsonian Institution

Situated on the National Mall in Washington, D.C., the Smithsonian sponsored some of the earliest and most famous archaeological expeditions in the U.S. and worldwide. Its exhibits also have artifacts and cultural reconstructions from all regions of the world. It consists of many different museums in separate buildings, but the National Museum of Natural History is the main place for archaeology. However, the new and beautiful Museum of the American Indian is full of Native American artifacts and art and has traditional reconstructions of the past that sometimes contrast with scientific interpretations.

Chapter 20

More Than Ten Archaeological Sites to Visit Outside the United States

....

In This Chapter

▶ Exploring ancient tombs, temples, pyramids, statues, and rock art

▶ Checking out famous cities and empires

....

*Y*ou can see archaeology at thousands of places all over the world, in every country. If you're really interested, go beyond thinking of just typical stuff like ancient Egypt (though that's neat too — see pyramids on a cruise down the Nile) or Pompeii (spend days there and at nearby related sites once covered by the volcano). To plan travel, look up archaeological sites and museums in guidebooks available in libraries or bookstores, and online in tourism and government Web sites. You can go on organized tours with guides or make your own way with printed directions.

If you have the time, funds, or opportunity to choose only a few special places to visit archaeology, begin by looking at the United Nations World Heritage Sites list (available online at whc.unesco.org/en/list/en/list, with lots of links). At many sites you may even find conservation/reconstruction projects or excavations in progress, often by teams from different countries. You can also see the results of damage to famous ruins, not only from natural processes such as erosion but also from centuries of looting!

In this chapter, I list some spectacular and famous sites outside the U.S. that I know are exciting to visit. Check the map in the Appendix for their locations.

Cambodia: Angkor Archaeological Park

In the Southeast Asian tropics, Angkor consists of many sets of stunning ruins near the modern city of Siem Reap. As various rulers of the Khmer Empire came to power, they established several different capital centers from the 9th through the 15th centuries. (See Chapter 14 for a discussion of this history). The galleried passages and beautiful stone carvings of Angkor temples depict battles, dancing people and animals, both Hindu and Buddhist sacred stories and ideals, and much elaborate decoration.

The most famous ruin, Angkor Wat (see Figure 14-5 in Chapter 14) is the world's largest religious monument. Among the dozens of other temples (from massive constructions to tiny rubble piles) is Angkor Thom (see Color Figure 13), with its spiritual center, the Bayon Temple. It was the latest city built in this civilization, with towers that feature huge half-smiling faces on all sides. Another magnificent ruin is Ta Prohm, famous for being left to the large jungle trees trying to reclaim it — huge trunks sprawling over the stone ruins and cracking them apart. Yes, this site was also featured in the movie *Lara Croft: Tomb Raider* — though she certainly didn't go there to do scientific excavation!

Archaeologists interpret Angkor today with remote sensing methods such as satellite imagery. Many think it was the largest pre-industrial city in the world. The rise of this civilization depended upon engineering and managing water resources. As you fly in you see the large lake, Tonle Sap, which normally flows southward to the Mekong River delta but flows northward in monsoon times. You can also see the humongous *barays* or reservoirs upon which this complex civilization depended. Some of these large, walled areas still have water, but many are covered by rice fields.

Canada: Head-Smashed-In Buffalo Jump

This site is in the foothills of the Rockies in Alberta, Canada. It was used continuously from as early as 6,000 years ago into the 19th century. For Blackfoot Indians of the Great Plains (in both Canada and the U.S.) and their ancient ancestors, it was a way to get dinner — stampeding American buffalo (or bison) off the 35-foot-high cliff to their deaths below. Lines of stone piles funneled herds to the cliff edge. Below the cliff are some 35 feet of stratified deposits — piles of animal bones with stone tools used to butcher them over the millennia. Bone remains at the nearby camp show how the hunters processed the animals: They dried the meat, boiled the bones for grease, and then pounded the dried meat with the fat and other foods to make long-lasting *pemmican* cakes.

The site also contains stone *tipi rings* (circles of stones that would have anchored these tents). The surrounding area includes a natural gathering basin with a water source where herds grazed. The interpretive center (museum) built into the rock cliff features Blackfoot culture, myths, and ecology, giving viewpoints of both scientific investigators and the native people themselves.

Polynesia (Chile): Easter Island

Easter Island is in the far Pacific Ocean, over 2,200 miles west of the South American west coast. Polynesian sailors got here by about A.D. 500 and settled down to grow crops and chickens that they'd brought. (See the discussion on peopling the Pacific in Chapter 18.) They carved hundreds of *moai* — huge, famous stone statues of important personages. Less than a millennium after people arrived, the environment was depleted. The first Europeans to reach the area (in the early 18th century) reported that the forest was nearly gone, the moai statues mostly toppled, and groups of inhabitants were in conflict. Popular descriptions ignore the European contributions to this destruction. But the spectacular statues and ruins are certainly part of a romantic tale of historic loss.

You can go to Easter Island by plane from Santiago, Chile, the country that has jurisdiction over it. Besides the moai, the island also features carved petroglyphs and paintings on the rock faces. You can visit house sites and earth ovens, and the quarry site where statues were made and unfinished ones remain. The museum features maps and artifacts, including a coral eye once inlaid in one of the statues. Tourism is escalating, so get there fast before things degenerate!

China: Mausoleum of the First Qin Emperor

The first ruler to unify China under the Qin dynasty was Qin Shih Huang Ti. He used military might to conquer other states and become the first Chinese emperor in 221 B.C. (For more on the Qin dynasty, check out Chapter 14.) Joining existing walls, he built the Great Wall along the northern boundary (another good site to see, albeit a 1,500-mile-long one).

He had his own huge tomb built to mirror the universe and his empire. It was called Mount Li, in Lintong County, just east of Xian, Shaanxi Province. Though his actual grave remains undisturbed, archaeologists have excavated the outer areas of the tomb over the last few decades and found amazing evidence of wealth and power. Most famous are the galleries of over 8,000 *terra-cotta* (fired clay) statues of larger-than-life warriors and horses ready for battle (see Figure 14-2 in Chapter 14). Each is a portrait of a real person, and they all have wooden chariots, real weapons, and rich artifacts of gold, jade, bronze, pottery, and even silk.

France: Lascaux Cave II and Paleolithic Art

The famous cave paintings of Lascaux were discovered in southwest France in 1940. These sophisticated artworks were produced nearly 20,000 years ago during the Upper Paleolithic. For a while, over a thousand people a day visited the site, but their breath and other effects caused deterioration, so the site was closed by the French Ministry of Culture in 1963. An amazing replica was built close to the original cave, using the same pigments (magnesium dioxide for black, iron oxides for reds and yellows). It's a stunning archaeological site recreating the most renowned and beautiful segments of the original Lascaux, the Hall of the Bulls and the Axial Gallery.

Aside from the Lascaux, this famous region in the Dordogne Valley is a center for Paleolithic archaeology. You can see the town of Les Eyzies, where the beautiful new National Museum has everything Paleolithic but the kitchen sink (which they hadn't invented during the Ice Age anyway). You can still visit many other real cave art sites. At Rouffignac, a tiny railway takes you through miles of long passages painted and engraved with over 100 mammoths and other animals. Another cave, La-Roque-Saint-Christophe, has a 1-kilometer-long cliff face with Paleolithic remains at the bottom and medieval structures on the ledges above.

Jordan: Petra

This famous site is built at (even carved into) rugged rock canyons; it's easy to get to if you've already scheduled a visit to the Holy Land or elsewhere in the Middle East. Petra (like Great Zimbabwe) has a great combination of human-made and natural stone landscapes. Its architecture incorporates natural undulating rose-pink rock surfaces and towering cliffs — you may even do some climbing! The ancients engineered an amazing system of canals, dams, and cisterns to control the little water they had.

Petra was inhabited as early as Neolithic times. By 200 B.C. it became a religious and trade center for the Nabataean people, who were Bedouin merchants. It was an important crossroads city for caravans traveling between the Red Sea and the Dead Sea and Arabia, Egypt, and Phoenicia (Syria). The architecture and artifacts blend Eastern and Hellenistic (Greek) traditions. The site contains rock-cut tombs, sculptures, and major public buildings (some of which may be temples). Some fragments of painted murals still cover walls. Finds such as ancient coins from many places show the international commerce that took place here in silks, spices, and many other valuable commodities. Parts of *Indiana Jones and the Last Crusade* were filmed here; Petra portrayed the temple of the Holy Grail!

Malaysia (Borneo): Niah Cave

In the exotic jungle of East Malaysia (northern Borneo), Niah Cave (on the Niah River) is one the most spectacular archaeological site in Southeast Asia (see Figure 12-4 in Chapter 12). When you cross the river, you can see the museum before making the long trek through the rainforest (don't forget your canteen!) to the caves. Archaeologists excavated the earliest skeletal remains of modern humans in Southeast Asia here, up to 46,000 years old (See the discussion of Upper Paleolithic people moving toward Borneo and Australia in Chapter 12).

In later levels, archaeologists discovered Neolithic artifacts and even later metal jewelry, cloths, fancy Chinese jars, and glass beads. One cave has wall paintings of red boats, apparently signifying the journey to the afterlife. Excavators found wooden, boat-shaped coffins holding the dead nearby, dating to between 2,000 and 1,200 years ago. Walking up and down the long cave passages is a real adventure — you need to go through complete darkness (so bring a flashlight).

Malta: Megalithic Monuments

In the Mediterranean Sea just between Sicily and North Africa lie the island of Malta and its neighbor island of Gozo. Farming and herding people constructed the oldest known stone buildings in the world here from Neolithic times through the Copper Age. They built these *megalithic* (giant stone) tombs and other monuments (see Color Figure 9) with precision architecture and beautiful carved decorative motifs. The monuments show interesting alignments with the sun and other heavenly bodies and may actually have been for sun worship. (See Chapter 13 for a discussion of megalithic sites.)

Other fascinating archaeological remains on the islands are colossal stone statues and smaller clay figurines of very chubby women (see Figure 13-6 in Chapter 13). They may have been goddess figures worshiped by a peaceful, happy culture, Or perhaps they were images of real political or religious leaders, or something else entirely — archaeologists are still debating their significance. The islands' museums display pottery, ornaments, and other fascinating artifacts.

Mexico: Teotihuacan, Maya, and El Tajín

Mexico is so packed full of towering pyramids and romantic ruins that choosing what to visit can be hard. Luckily, Mexico is a pretty inexpensive trip, so you may not have to choose. (Can you tell I love this country?) Many native cultures erected civilizations that flourished and interacted with one another, which gives you a lot of options.

You'd most likely fly into Mexico City, which has one of the best museums in the world (National Museum of Anthropology). While you're in the nation's capital, check out the ruins of the Aztec city of Tenochtitlán, only recently excavated downtown, with its pyramids and bright new museum. This was the capital where the native emperor Moctezuma met the Spanish in 1519 (and continues to get his revenge).

The following are some of the best sites to visit outside Mexico City:

Teotihuacan

A short ride from Mexico City, Teotihuacan was the largest city in the Americas in its time. It was first occupied in about 200 B.C. and grew to be a center of trade, politics, and religion. At the south end is the Ciudadela ("citadel") with its distinctive Pyramid of the Feathered Serpent. Running north from here is the Avenue of the Dead, with many smaller pyramids, palaces, and residential compounds on both sides. At the north end is the massive Pyramid of the Moon, and to the east is the even more humongous Pyramid of the Sun, built over a cave (probably for ritual purposes). Over the centuries, the native people enlarged it until it reached 740 feet square and 200 feet high — a great climb with a stunning view from the top!

The pyramids supported various temples and contained burials and exotic artifact offerings. With extensive mapping projects over the decades, archaeologists have shown the great extent of this city and the skills of ancient urban planners. But by A.D. 700, it was mostly abandoned; the reasons for its collapse are still mysterious, as is the identity of its people.

Maya Ruins: Palenque and Chichén Itzá

Among the many Maya ruins you can visit, Palenque and Chichén Itzá are two of the best and most famous. Maya city-states began to emerge around the 2nd century B.C., and they competed for power and built remarkable pyramids, palaces, and compounds with rich artifact offerings and elaborate stone carvings. The whole civilization began its mysterious "collapse" around A.D. 800. But archaeologists have now deciphered Maya writing and found some clues.

✔ **Palenque:** This awesome site sits in the jungle of the state of Chiapas. It has many temple-pyramids, some still waiting for excavation (see Color Figure 10). At the magnificent Pyramid of the Inscriptions, you can not only climb up the pyramid but also go down into the interior. (This gives a workout to both your acrophobia and your claustrophobia!). Way at the bottom is the tomb of a famous ruler, Pacal, rich with offerings and stone carvings.

✔ **Chichén Itzá:** This Maya site is in the northern Yucatan peninsula, easy to reach from the coastal resort of Cancun. The city center rose to power around A.D. 600, as the southern centers declined, and lasted some 400 years. It features many amazing pyramids and palaces, as well as ball courts for the ritual game. Archaeologists have recovered many rich sacrificial objects from its sacred *cenote,* or water-filled sinkhole.

El Tajín

Less famous but really spectacular, El Tajín sits on the Gulf Coast in the state of Veracruz. It was occupied from at least A.D. 100 through the 13th century, built by ancestors of Mexico's Totonac Indians. The inhabitants abandoned it (mysteriously, of course) by the time the Spanish arrived in the 16th century. A very distinctive architecture characterizes this Classic Veracruz culture. The site features pyramids, palaces, and ball courts for playing the widespread sacred ball game that may have originated here. Stone relief carvings and even a few painted wall surfaces are preserved. The most famous monument is the Pyramid of the Niches, 60 feet high, with stepped stone levels into which 365 square niches were cut (see Color Figure 11).

For extra fun, see the Indian *voladores* (flyers) perform their ancient ritual in front of the beautiful museum. They jump off a 150-foot pole attached by ropes on their feet that slowly unwind as they descend, flying around the pole, to the music of a native flute played by a guy sitting on top of the pole.

Peru: Machu Picchu

After (or before) you catch ruins of the Inca and earlier civilizations in Peru, not to mention the wonderful museums, in Lima and other towns, you'll probably want to go to Cuzco, the Incan capital high up in the Andes. (And, yes, they do give you tea made from coca leaves to adjust to the altitude.) From there you can easily reach Machu Picchu, the most famous Inca site (see Figure 14-4 in Chapter 14 and Color Figure 12). For more information on the Inca and their ancestors, check out Chapter 14.

Machu Picchu is perched a mile and a half high on a mountain top often shrouded in mist, with an astounding view of the countryside and the Urubamba River 2,000 feet below. It's a masterpiece of the Incas' classic architecture, using distinctive trapezoidal doorways and big cut stones fit together so well that they didn't need mortar. You can see imposing temples, water control facilities, houses, steps, and the great ancient road system. The mountainsides are all terraced to allow for growing crops to support the empire. It was built in about A.D. 1450 and lasted only a century before the native empire collapsed under the Spanish invasion. But the new regime simply forgot about the site instead of destroying it. The ride up the mountain itself is full of excitement (especially if you're afraid of heights) with its many *switchbacks* (in Spanish: zigzags).

Zimbabwe: Great Zimbabwe

This site is a national shrine for this southern African country. It was built by a great civilization that thrived from the 11th through the 15th centuries. (See Chapter 14 for more on the history of Great Zimbabwe.) The large Hill Complex (see Color Figure 14) has stone blocks built into the outcropping rock in a wonderful combination of human-made structure and natural surfaces. South of this complex is the Great Enclosure, a circular wall within which at least 300 other structures were built, including a mysterious conical stone tower. The architectural elements include stone blocks fitted together without mortar into curving walls, with distinctive decorative elements in *chevron* (V-shaped) patterns. The most famous artifact finds here are the enigmatic bird figures carved on top of tall soapstone columns. Other finds are Persian and Chinese pottery, Arabian coins, and European glass beads that show trading connections with far-flung places.

Consider visiting other sites of this fascinating lost civilization, such as the Khami ruins near the city of Bulawayo.

All the magnificent ruins were originally interpreted by the racist colonial powers in southern Africa as being the result of ancient Arabs or European traders — anyone who wasn't considered black! But archaeologists demonstrated this site was an indigenous civilization of the local Shona people, a Bantu-speaking group who still live in the region today. Why they abandoned this and other ancient cities and transformed their culture into something else remains a proper archaeological mystery.

Chapter 21

Ten Fun Archaeological Experiences

*I*n this chapter I list some of my favorite examples of ways to experience the pleasure of archaeology with more or less effort or cost (or discomfort). Some are free and easy (your local library); others require planning and layout of funds (archaeology guided tour or cruise).

Reading Archaeology in Fiction

In mystery novels, detectives solve crimes with archaeological methods, and lots of murder mysteries have archaeological settings. The well-crafted books of Agatha Christie, especially *Murder in Mesopotamia* (1936) and *Death on the Nile* (1937), are great. She was married to archaeologist Max Mallowan and helped on his digs in Iraq; she said an archaeologist was the best kind of husband because the older she got, the more interested in her he became!

Some mysteries feature the archaeologist as the actual sleuth. Elizabeth Peters (a real Egyptologist) has Victorian archaeologist Amelia Peabody (beginning with *Crocodile on the Sandbank,* 1975).

Archaeological adventure thrillers may have science fiction settings. A recent one is *Xibalba Gate: A Novel of the Ancient Maya* (2005), by Rob Swigert, taking place within a computer simulation of the Maya world.

You can find online various lists and bibliographies of archaeology in fiction, including mystery and science fiction novels.

Reading Archaeology in Nonfiction

Delving into nonfictional archaeology is often more exciting than reading novels because it's about real discovery. Here are some of my favorites:

- ✔ C.W. Ceram's popular books, especially *Gods, Graves, and Scholars: The Story of Archaeology* (1949, but still in print in new editions) have inspired generations of readers to go into the field.

- ✔ Egyptologist Barbara Mertz's *Temples, Tombs and Hieroglyphs: A Popular History of Ancient Egypt* (new edition, 2007) is a lively presentation of stories reconstructed by archaeological work.

- ✔ Some fun archaeology guides are *Dug to Death* (2003) and *Death by Theory* (2001), mystery novels/textbooks by Adrian Praetzellis, and *Archaeology: The Comic* (2003) by Johannes Loubser.

- ✔ Colin Renfrew's thoughtful *Figuring It Out* is a philosophical treatise and stunning comparison of ancient artifacts and modern art.

Watching Movies about Archaeology

Movies featuring archaeology can be really bad, and archaeologists alternately identify with Indiana Jones or Lara Croft and wring their hands over the awful stereotypes. But these do offer opportunities to learn, laugh, and show off your knowledge of good archaeology. Plus you have great dialog lines to quote (trust me!). So get friends and popcorn together and find a copy of the original 1932 horror classic *The Mummy*, starring Boris Karloff in the title role, back to life after thousands of years. This film set the pattern for the character of the archaeologist for ever after. One archaeology textbook had a photo from the scene where the mummy, arms outstretched, approaches the young archaeologist bent over work in the lab. The caption said that the archaeologist was about to be attacked by what should be his data.

Watching Movies about Prehistoric People

Many classic films show Ice-Age cave people in horribly inaccurate circumstances — like *One Million Years B.C.* (1966), which features humans with dinosaurs, or *10,000 BC* (2008), in which humans with mastodons build pyramids. Some movies about prehistory try to be archaeologically more accurate (though they're not without scientific problems). Two favorites:

✔ *Quest for Fire* (1981): Paleolithic hunters learn how to make fire, use rudimentary language, and practice some interesting customs.

✔ *Iceman* (1984): An Arctic expedition discovers a frozen Neanderthal guy, expectably dark and wild (though Neanderthals were probably very pale). Thawed out, he hunts and makes fires in captivity, and of course grabs the female scientist. Don't confuse this film with documentaries on Ötzi, a real 5,300-year-old Ice Man discovered melting out of an Alpine glacier. (See Chapter 18 for more on this Ice Man.)

So pop that corn and watch for each scientific mistake you see in how past people are portrayed, but also think about what our distant ancestors went through and survived!

Attending a Lecture and Exhibit

Museums may exhibit archaeological materials, and often the archaeologist who dug the stuff up or organized the exhibit will appear to give a lecture on it. This is a great way to see the results of an archaeological project and hear its background. You can chat with the specialist(s) afterwards, ask questions, and sometimes even sign up to work on the project. Most such programs are free, and sometimes you can even get free refreshments after a lecture.

While you're munching cheese and crackers and sipping punch, sign up to be a member of the sponsoring organization to receive information on future events. You can even meet others interested in archaeology who are also standing around drinking punch (or at really good exhibits, wine).

Planning Your Vacation to See Archaeology

Planning a vacation to visit archaeological sites and museums? First look online or in state guidebooks and maps (usually under "points of interest" or "historical places"). The U.S. National Park Service's "Visit Archaeology" Web site (www.nps.gov/history/archeology/visit/index.htm) lists archaeological parks and travel itineraries. Online information changes so fast that I won't list more-specific Web sites here.

A great book (also online) listing sites by state is *America's Ancient Treasures*, by F. and M. Folsom; similar sources are available for different countries. Also see my lists of cool U.S. and foreign sites to visit in Chapters 19 and 20, respectively.

For a fancier trip, find (or have a travel agent find) tour companies that specialize in archaeological itineraries. Professional archaeologists lead many of these trips. For real luxury, you can find cruise ships specializing in art and archaeology of many regions, with archaeologists onboard.

Planning Your Vacation to Do Archaeology

In Chapter 17, I listed some ways you can sign up to participate in digs all over the country and the world. If you're really gung-ho about this idea, you can plan your vacation around it for the whole family, even the kids.

Being a Museum Volunteer

If you love how artifacts let you touch the past, consider volunteering at your local museum (history, science, or art). You can be a *docent* (leading gallery tours) or lab worker, and get involved with helping professionals.

Trying Out Archaeological Field School

Courses in archaeological field methods — field schools — can be in exotic places or close to home. See the Archaeological Institute of America's listings (www.archaeological.org/webinfo.php?page=10016) or call your local college. Courses certified by the Register of Professional Archaeologists (RPA; www.rpanet.org/displaycommon.cfm?an=1&subarticlenbr=10) give high-quality training in case you want to become a professional. The RPA now also offers scholarships for participants.

Being an Archaeological Donor

If you can afford it, consider donating funds or other support toward an archaeological project, university research program, museum, or foundation such as the Archaeological Conservancy that buys and protects sites. Most archaeology is chronically under-funded. Donation means doing more than most to unearth the human past and bring it to the present!

Appendix

Timeline of Human History and Sites Map

· ·

Timeline

This timeline, which starts in the recent past and moves to the ancient past, shows past human activities, cultures, material remains, and examples of archaeological sites mentioned throughout the book.

Beginning Date	Cultural Adaptation	Material Evidence	Africa	West Asia	East Asia	Europe	North America	South America	Pacific
A.D. 1000			Great Zimbabwe		Angkor states, Cambodia, and other historic archaeology	Medieval and more recent historic archaeology	Cahokia, Illinois; Moundville, Alabama, other Mississippian sites in southeastern U.S.; Chaco and Mesa Verde in Southwest; late Mesoamerican civilizations like Aztec in Mexico	Chimu state, Inca empire, Peru	Pacific islanders with chickens get to South America
A.D. 100	Later civilizations, (but some cultures continue simpler foraging life)	Historic and prehistoric settlements, material remains of everyday life not recorded in history		Succeeding states	Qin empire, China, succeeding dynasties' empires	Roman Empire	Hopewell and other mound-builders with only gardening and villages in eastern U.S; Maya, Teotihuacan, other city-states in Mesoamerica	Moche, Nazca states, then Tiwanaku and Wari empires, Peru and Bolivia	Easter Island colonized by A.D. 500

Beginning Date	Cultural Adaptation	Material Evidence	Africa	West Asia	East Asia	Europe	North America	South America	Pacific
1500 B.C.	True civilizations in New World, continuing in Old World	Cities, great monuments, sculptures, writing systems seen on artifacts, finds showing extreme long-distance trade	Egypt, Nubia, regional kingdoms			Bronze Age Greek civilization	Ancestral Pueblo, Hohokam farming in southwestern U.S.; mound building in East, Olmec civilization in Mexico	Chavin civilization, Peru	Western Polynesia colonized
3500 B.C.	True civilizations in Old World		Egyptian kingdoms, pyramids	Uruk, Ur, other Mesopotamian states	Indus Valley civilization, Pakistan and India; An-yang, China	Stonehenge, England; Malta megalithic monuments	Poverty Point, Louisiana and other early mounds (but no agriculture yet north of Mesoamerica); early farming settlements in Mexico and Central America	Aspero and Caral, Peru and other early farming sites with pyramids	
5500 B.C.	Copper and Bronze Ages in Old World, large villages, towns	Metal artifacts common, a few signs of warfare	Many sites			Varna, Bulgaria; Ötzi the Ice Man, Italy		Coastal shell midden sites	
7000 B.C.	Neolithic-earliest food production in Old World, large villages	Remains of earliest domesticated plants and animals, farming and herding tools, houses, village sites	Sites along the Nile, Egypt	Çatalhöyük, Turkey; Abu Hureyra, Syria; Jericho, Israel	Mehrgarh, Pakistan; sites on Yellow and Yangtze rivers, China	Many sites	Windover, Florida, Watson Brake, Louisiana; shell midden sites	large villages	

Beginning Date	Cultural Adaptation	Material Evidence	Africa	West Asia	East Asia	Europe	North America	South America	Pacific
8000 B.C.	Mesolithic/Archaic-hunting modern animals, gathering plants, fishing and shellfishing, larger social groups	Stone tools, pottery, utilitarian and decorative artifacts; small campsites and structures, some large settlements and rare earthworks	Many sites	Many sites	Jomon culture, Japan	Vedbaek, Denmark		Foragers' camp sites	
35,000 B.C.	Upper Paleolithic-hunting Ice Age game, gathering, fishing, small social groups	Fine points, other tools of stone, bone, wood, antler, ivory; figurines; cave art; all humans = Homo sapiens; small sites	Many sites	Many sites	Many sites	Lascaux cave, many other sites	Clovis, New Mexico, and many other Paleo-Indian sites	Monte Verde, Chile, and many other Paleo-Indian sites	Earliest Australian sites ca. 50,000 years
250,000 B.C.	Middle Paleolithic-hunting, gathering, small social groups	Spear points, other stone, bone, and wood artifacts, animal bones, bones of Neanderthals, and Homo sapiens by 100,000 years ago, caves and other small sites	Many sites	Shanidar Cave, Iraq	Niah Cave, Borneo	Many sites			

Beginning Date	Cultural Adaptation	Material Evidence	Africa	West Asia	East Asia	Europe	North America	South America	Pacific
2 million B.C.	Later Lower Paleolithic- scavenging, foraging, possibly hunting	Handaxes, other stone tools, animal bones, bones of many early human forms, cave sites preserved	Olorgesailie, Kenya	Many sites	Zhoukoudian	Atapuerca and Torralba, Spain, Terra Amata, France			
2.5–3 million B.C.	Earliest archaeological evidence, Lower Paleolithic age begins	Pebble tools, bones of *Australopithecus,* and *Homo* forms, footprints, some possible living sites	Olduvai Gorge, many other sites						
3–5 million B.C.	Earliest hominids (human ancestral forms)	Fossil bones	Many sites						

Sites Map

This map shows the locations of important archaeological sites mentioned throughout the book.

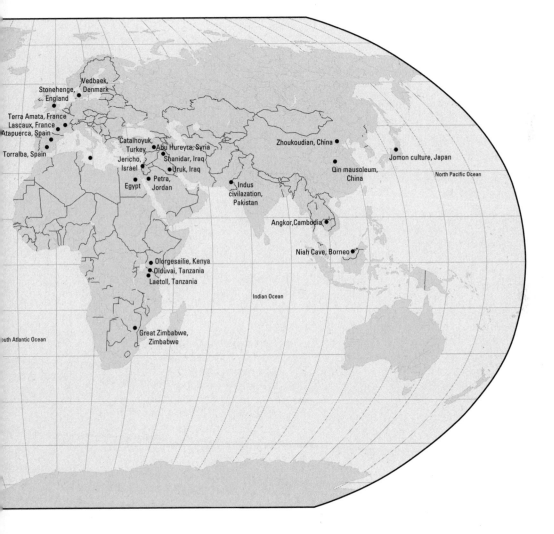

Index

• B •

● *T* ●